W9-BXN-071

# WRITING THE CIVIL WAR

# WRITING
## THE
# CIVIL WAR
### The Quest to Understand

EDITED BY

## James M. McPherson

## William J. Cooper, Jr.

University of South Carolina Press

Published in Columbia, South Carolina, by the
University of South Carolina Press

Manufactured in the United States of America

02 01 00 99 98    5 4 3 2 1

Library of Congress Cataloging-in-Publication Data

 Writing the Civil War : the quest to understand / edited by James
M. McPherson and William J. Cooper, Jr..
   p. cm.
 Includes index.

 ISBN 1-57003-259-9
 1. United States—History—Civil War, 1861–1865—Historiography.
I. McPherson, James M. II. Cooper, William J. (William James),
1940–
 E468.5 .W75 1998
 973.7'072—ddc21                                      98-19681

For All Participants in the Quest

# CONTENTS

# WRITING THE CIVIL WAR

# INTRODUCTION

## JAMES M. MCPHERSON

## WILLIAM J. COOPER, JR.

*Writing the Civil War* is unique. Although there have been lengthy annotated bibliographies, never before has a book attempted what *Writing the Civil War* sets out to do: present a wide-ranging discussion of the history of writing the history of the Civil War.

The Civil War was the most momentous event in American history. Because of the war, the United States underwent fundamental changes that transformed the country. Before 1861, Americans grappled with the permanence or impermanence of the Union as a major political and constitutional question, with respected public figures and constitutional interpreters taking opposing sides. In addition, the racial slavery that kept four million black Americans in bondage claimed the protection of the Constitution and was legal in fifteen states as well as in the District of Columbia. This institution based on human property shaped the economy, society, politics, and ideology of a substantial portion of the Union and influenced all of it. In 1857, the United States Supreme Court even ruled that black Americans—whether slave or free—could not be citizens under the Constitution.

The Civil War profoundly altered that landscape. Although arguments about state rights did not end in 1865, continuing, in fact, until today, discussion about the permanence of the Union halted abruptly. After 1865, only fringe groups talked about the legitimacy of breaking up the Union. Likewise, racial slavery was obliterated. While race remains a divisive and even explosive issue, no one advocates returning to an unfree labor system. The conversation about race occurs on a vastly different level because of three crucial Constitutional amendments made possible by the war—the thirteenth, fourteenth, and fifteenth, which prohibited slavery, defined and nationalized citizenship, and banned race as a reason for disfranchisement. Repealing any of these amendments is unthinkable today.

Constructing this new United States exacted an extraordinarily high price: the fighting of a great war that convulsed the country for four years. In material terms, the war cost some $20 billion, more than eleven times the total expenditures of the federal government between 1789 and 1861. One part of the Union was wrecked. The South, or the Confederate States of America, experienced massive physical devastation as farms, homes, railroads, factories, towns all felt the hard hand of war. The value of property in the Confederate States declined from over $4 billion in 1860 to approximately $1.6 billion at the end of the conflict.

Most important of all, more than 620,000 Americans died in the ferocious struggle. That figure far outdistances the number of dead in any other war; even in the global World War II, American dead reached only 407,000. In all other American wars, from the Revolution through the Gulf War, the sum of those who gave their lives barely eclipses the total of those who made the supreme sacrifice in the Civil War. At least another 500,000 suffered wounds, carrying the complete casualty count to an incredible 1 million out of a population of 32 million.

From that time to this, Americans have been engaged in studying and interpreting what has been called the American Iliad. Union and Confederate participants, the initial chroniclers, had a common purpose. They generally strove to justify their causes while they celebrated the bravery and courage of their comrades. As 1865 receded, celebration began to outweigh justification in publications such as *Battles and Leaders of the Civil War* (1887–1888), in which both sides praised their flags between the same covers. With the waning of the nineteenth century, the dwindling battalion of survivors found a shared identity as a band of brothers who had experienced the glories and horrors of an epic event. Joint reunions on the bloody fields of 1861–1865 underscored the replacing of *Union* and *Confederate* by *American*.

Just about the time that the veterans were hearing their final roll calls, serious scholarly studies of the Civil War got under way. From those beginnings, historians of the war have investigated an enormous variety of subjects. From the outset bugles and guns commanded great attention, and for many decades the battles and the generals were the central topics, though never the only ones. Their popularity has not declined, for publishers still pour out books on battles, units, and generals, along with officers of lesser rank.

Military history clearly still dominates the popular interest and in recent years has received renewed scholarly attention, but with a different dimension. Many historians no longer look at military history as a hermetically sealed commodity existing completely apart from the larger world. Study of the war and society has become paramount. Historians probe connections between the men on the battlefield and the civilians at home. Armies are looked upon as microcosms of the societies that produced them. Attitudes toward the war and its fighting are studied as part of the entire social and intellectual milieu. The soldiers themselves have become prominent subjects. Who were they? Why did they fight? Did their views of the war and their roles in it change during its course?

In the last generation Civil War scholarship has exploded. Military history remains a major area of investigation, but it has by no means shouldered aside other subjects. In fact, never before have scholars of the war ranged so widely over so many fields. Civilians are scrutinized as never before. Historians recognize that they were also caught up in the maelstrom of the conflict, especially in the South, but in the North as well. The war affected them, and they, in turn, affected the war. Among civilians, women and slaves have received considerable attention. Historians focus on the roles women and blacks had in supporting the war, in buttressing morale, and in creating the circumstances that led to emancipation. The nature of both societies, Union and Confederate, and the character of each government have become important research topics. Financial, economic, business, and constitutional issues have come under the scholarly microscope, as has politics. Scholars consider the role of political parties; they explore the mechanisms for opposition to the administrations of both Jefferson Davis and Abraham Lincoln; they examine more fully and critically the relationship between the battlefield and political decision making. The crucial place of leadership on the presidential level and within the military establishments has undergone new inspection. Did those in leadership positions really lead, or are they better understood as persons moved about by larger, impersonal forces?

This scholarship in all its vastness and variety makes up the subject of *Writing the Civil War*. In this book recognized specialists provide authoritative, interpretive guides to the historical literature in their respective fields. Four essays focus on military history: Gary W. Gallagher on Union strategy, Emory M. Thomas on Confederate strategy, Joseph T. Glatthaar on battlefield tactics, and Reid Mitchell on the soldiers. Although each centers on a military topic, all relate their subjects to broader issues. Mark E. Neely, Jr.'s consideration of presidential leadership makes the direct link between military and political considerations. Then Michael F. Holt on Union politics and George C. Rable on Confederate politics concentrate on the political dimension. With his discussion of constitutional questions, Michael Les Benedict also bridges political and societal concerns. Phillip Shaw Paludan on northern society and economics and James

L. Roark on southern society and economics confront directly those broad themes. Focusing sharply, Drew Gilpin Faust on gender and Peter Kolchin on slavery and race relations underscore those critical components.

Despite the extraordinary breadth of topics discussed in *Writing the Civil War,* the editors make no claim for total coverage or absolute inclusivity. There are simply too many specialized subjects for every one to have a place in a single volume of reasonable length. At the same time, we believe that *Writing the Civil War* deals with the most significant topics. Although our authors do a superb job of analyzing and interpreting what has been written, perhaps these essays make an even more important contribution: pointing out the gaps yet remaining in our understanding of the Civil War and suggesting directions for future scholarship on the war.

The discovery of significant lacunae in the huge literature on the Civil War may come as something of a shock to many readers. Even the most dedicated scholar finds it impossible to keep up with existing works in the field. New books as well as reprints of older studies keep pouring from the presses to join the tens of thousands of titles that have appeared since 1865. Nevertheless, the authors of the four essays in this volume dealing with the literature on military operations—the area in which the number of books is the most overwhelming—find important omissions and shortcomings. One striking example is the prisoner-of-war issue. Although good books and articles on individual prisons (especially Andersonville) have appeared in recent years, only one general study of this important matter has been published since 1930.[1] It does not fully meet the need for a modern reexamination of an experience that affected more than 400,000 soldiers and left 56,000 of them dead.

The essays by Gary Gallagher and Emory Thomas on military strategy note several fine studies of *army* strategies. Gallagher points out that the Union navy played a crucial role in ultimate northern victory. But while we have several narratives of the naval war, no historian has undertaken a systematic study of *naval* strategy in the context of the overall war effort—an omission all the more ironic because Secretary of the Navy Gideon Welles appointed a naval strategy board in June 1861, something the Union army never did.

Historians of Confederate military operations have examined the East *vs.* West debate among Confederate leaders, but there are no counterparts in analyses of Union strategy. And while the roles of Presidents Davis and Lincoln as commanders-in-chief have been thoroughly examined, the impact of their respective Congresses and of public opinion—which was considerable, especially in the North—has been neglected. Emory Tho-

that have received a great deal of attention in discussions of twentieth-century wars but very little in the writing about the Civil War. Victorian reticence may have shrouded these subjects in the 1860s, but historians skilled at teasing out meaning from medical and court-martial records, newspapers, and personal letters should be able to penetrate the shroud.

The disruption, weakening, and finally destruction of slavery by the war and the various wartime experiments in free or quasi-free labor have been much studied. But as James Roark notes, the actual operation of slavery in areas remote from the fighting fronts has received a great deal less attention. Since the majority of slaves continued to live in these areas until virtually the end of the war, efforts to recover that experience would make important contributions to the history of slavery as well as of the war.

Finally, there is the $64,000 question in a field perhaps best described as political economy, a question at least as old as Charles and Mary Beard's *The Rise of American Civilization*, published in 1927. Was the Civil War a Second American Revolution that launched the U.S. economy into the industrial age by destroying the plantation economy and entrenching the robber barons in control? Or did the war, as Thomas Cochran maintained in a seminal article in 1961,[6] actually retard economic growth and development? Although many historians have tried to answer these questions since 1961, their responses seem to have left us farther from a consensus than ever, as Phillip Paludan's essay makes clear. One is reminded of the story of the several blind men who tried to describe an elephant—each historian seems to have run his hands over a different part of the evidence for the economic changes in the Civil War era, so each one has described a different animal. And part of the elephant has remained unexamined; as James Roark writes, the impact of the Confederate economic experience on national economic developments during this period has been largely ignored.

The twelve essays that follow demonstrate the richness and variety of Civil War scholarship in the twentieth century, especially the final third of it. This volume is therefore an indispensable guide through the labyrinth of literature for expert and neophyte alike. Of even greater value, perhaps, the essays point the way for historians coming of age in the twenty-first century to take up the tasks of Civil War scholarship their elders have left undone.

# Blueprint for Victory

## Northern Strategy and Military Policy

### GARY W. GALLAGHER

The United States government and its loyal citizens confronted an imposing task in suppressing the Confederate rebellion. The fledgling southern republic spread over 750,000 square miles, and it quickly demonstrated the ability to field armies numbering in the hundreds of thousands and commanded by a cadre of professional soldiers. Only a gigantic effort would yield success on so vast a landscape against so numerous an enemy. Yet many historians, seemingly entranced by the image of Confederate surrender at Appomattox, have explored the military side of the Civil War with the assumption that the southern effort was a quixotic struggle against impossible odds. Northern manpower and industrial might, goes a common argument, represented obstacles too great for the Confederates to overcome. Shelby Foote, whose impressive trilogy on the conflict has reached a huge audience, typified this approach. "I think that the North fought that war with one hand behind its back," Foote observed in 1990. "I think that if there had been more southern victories, and a lot more, the North simply would have brought that other arm out from behind its back. I don't think the South ever had a chance to win that war."[1]

Had northern advantages predestined Confederate defeat, the Union's search for a suitable strategy would not have been critical. Lincoln's government simply could have raised more regiments whenever necessary and waited for the inevitable southern collapse. But observers in 1861, well aware that material factors favored the North, understood that the side with the strongest battalions does not always prevail. They had to look no further than the American Revolution to find evidence of that fact. A perceptive Confederate typified the degree to which people at the time appreciated the magnitude of the North's challenge. George Wythe Randolph, who served the Confederacy as both a brigadier general and secretary of war, commented in the autumn of 1861 that northern forces "may overrun our frontier States and plunder our coast but, as for conquering us, the thing is an impossibility." Randolph believed that history offered no instance of "a people as numerous as we are inhabiting a country so extensive as ours being subjected if true to themselves."[2]

The North developed strategic plans on two levels to meet the challenge of defeating the Confederacy. The first and higher level, usually termed national or grand strategy, consisted of deciding just what political goals the United States hoped to achieve from the war. Would the majority of northerners settle for restoration of the status quo ante bellum, or would they use the conflict to redefine the nature of the Union? Debates in this arena were shaped by the president and his cabinet, the Congress, public opinion, and the actions of thousands of people, both black and white, who lived in the seceded states. The second level of strategic planning, typically termed operational or military strategy, involved deciding how best to employ the North's martial resources to achieve national political goals. Here the principal actors included the president and a group of senior generals, but Congress, public opinion, and the press also played noteworthy roles. Planning at both levels proceeded concurrently, and decisions about political goals dramatically shaped the ways in which the North applied its military power against the Confederacy.[3]

Because literally thousands of books have addressed northern strategy and military policy, coverage in this essay must be highly selective. For example, Abraham Lincoln, Ulysses S. Grant, William Tecumseh Sherman, Winfield Scott, George B. McClellan, and Henry W. Halleck stood out among leaders who influenced northern strategy, but a survey of the biographical literature on these figures is impossible (virtually every biography of Lincoln devotes some attention to his role as Union strategist). A review of the myriad general works on the Civil War that inevitably accord some attention to strategy is equally infeasible. The focus will be on twentieth-century works specifically addressing issues relating to national or operational strategy and to the individuals who shaped and directed them.

The most important questions examined in this historiography may be summarized quickly. Did the North win because of sound strategic planning and execution, or would the Confederacy have lost in any event because it struggled against impossible odds? The latter view, propounded by southern Lost Cause writers in the late-nineteenth and early-twentieth centuries, has proved remarkably tenacious (as suggested by Shelby Foote's image of a North using just of half its energy and resources). It depends in large measure on interpreting Grant's contribution to victory as simply committing without limit Union manpower and material resources. This conception conceded minimal skill to northern military planners and held sway in much of the literature until the third and fourth decades of the twentieth century. In the 1920s and 1930s, scholars increasingly argued that only good strategic decisions brought Union success, a formulation that pushed other questions to the fore. Who framed that northern strategy? What impact did political imperatives affecting national strategy, including the debate over emancipation, have in the operational sphere? Did this political dimension trigger a shift from limited war to a more modern form of total war? Once freed from the restrictive Lost Cause framework within which "Grant the butcher" acted as the agent of inevitable northern triumph, the literature touching on northern strategy and military policy assumed greater interpretive depth and complexity. The best work demonstrated that neither the North's national nor its operational strategy could be understood in isolation; they intersected and influenced one another at myriad points.[4]

The North's national strategy evolved during the course of the war. Initially framed to bring the wayward states back into an unchanged Union quickly and with minimal bloodshed, it eventually became a strategy designed not only to destroy the Confederate political state but also, through the eradication of slavery, to transform the southern social system. Lincoln articulated the early Union strategy in a message to Congress in December 1861. "I have . . . thought it proper to keep the integrity of the Union prominent as the primary object of the contest on our part," stated the president, who hoped the conflict would not "degenerate into a violent and remorseless revolutionary struggle."[5] Over the next two and a half years, emancipation joined union as a strategic political goal for the North. In Lincoln's terminology, the struggle became far more revolutionary, as Union armies targeted Confederate slaves and all other civilian property that might bolster the southern resistance.

Emancipation too often has been cast exclusively as a political element of the war when in fact it figured prominently in both the North's national and military strategies. Virtually all scholars now agree that the addition of emancipation to union as a northern goal altered the strategic configuration of the war, but they part company in allocating credit for the shift in policy. More than sixty years ago, W. E. B. DuBois argued that, after an initial period of waiting to see where their interests lay, slaves decided that northern armies held out an excellent opportunity to seize freedom. "[A]s it became clear that the Union armies would not or could not return fugitive slaves," wrote DuBois, ". . . the slave entered upon a general strike against slavery by the same methods that he had used during the period of the fugitive slave. He ran away to the first place of safety and offered his services to the Federal Army." With what DuBois termed "perplexed and laggard steps," the United States government "followed the footsteps of the black slave." By the time of Lincoln's proclamation, hundreds of thousands of slaves had reached Union lines and were "free by their own action and that of the invading armies, and in their cases, Lincoln's proclamation only added possible legal sanction to an accomplished fact." Most Confederate slaves still lay beyond Federal reach, however, and could cast off their bondage only if they emulated those who already had left their masters. Stressing Lincoln's vision of emancipation as a military measure intended to harm the Confederate war effort—as opposed to a revision of the North's national strategy—DuBois argued that the president sought to inspire an exodus of slaves from Confederate plantations that would "break the back of the rebellion by depriving the South of its principal labor force."[6]

Recent work has expanded on DuBois's points, insisting that the slaves themselves, rather than Lincoln or Congress or Union armies, played the central role in placing emancipation alongside union as a national strategic goal. In *Been in the Storm So Long: The Aftermath of Slavery,* Leon F. Litwack cautioned readers that the "various dimensions of slavery's collapse—the political machinations, the government edicts, the military occupation—should not be permitted to obscure the principal actors in this drama: the four million black men and women for whom slavery composed their entire memory." The editors of the Freedmen and Southern Society Project's massive *Freedom: A Documentary History of Emancipation, 1861–1867* joined Litwack in suggesting that slaves took the lead in the "varying, uneven, and frequently tenuous" process that destroyed slavery. "Once the evolution of emancipation replaces the absolutism of the Emancipation Proclamation and the Thirteenth Amendment as the focus of study," they commented, "the story of slavery's demise shifts from the presidential mansion and the halls of Congress to the farms and plantations that became wartime battlefields. And slaves—whose persistence forced federal soldiers, Union and Confederate policy makers, and even their own masters onto terrain they never intended to occupy—become the prime movers in securing their own liberty."[7]

No one has taken this argument further than Barbara J. Fields, who maintained that the United States "government discovered that it could not accomplish its narrow goal—union—without adopting the slaves' nobler one—universal emancipation." Fields declared that preservation of the Union, "a goal too shallow to be worth the sacrifice of a single life," had become impossible to achieve by January 1863. Emancipation would have to be added to the northern national strategy if victory were to follow. Fortunately, slaves had flocked to Union lines, forcing first the military and then Congress to address the issue of emancipation: "By touching the government at its most vulnerable point, the point at which its military forces were fighting for its life, the slaves were able to turn their will to be free into a political problem that politicians had to deal with politically." A recalcitrant Lincoln lagged far behind Congress but finally got on board with his proclamation. "The slaves decided at the time of Lincoln's election that their hour had come," concluded Fields (in a statement that begs an obvious series of questions). "By the time Lincoln issued his Emancipation Proclamation, no human being alive could have held back the tide that swept toward freedom."[8]

Mark E. Neely, Jr., challenged Fields and others who posited what he called the theory of self-emancipation. He acknowledged that writers who cast Lincoln as the "Great Emancipator" ignored the "quietly heroic roles" of tens of thousands of African Americans who actively seized freedom. "But, to say we should not ignore the small acts of individual heroism of nameless slaves who turned a proclamation into an actual emancipation," he stated, "—to say that is *not* to say that Abraham Lincoln was *not* a great emancipator." Neely observed that advocates of the idea of self-emancipation were vague about how many slaves took an active role and suggested, quoting Lincoln and Frederick Douglass from late summer 1864, that most slaves remained unaware of the possibility of emancipation until they came into contact with the Union military. By mid-July 1862, Lincoln had decided that the "formidable power and dimensions of the insurrection" demanded "extraordinary measures to preserve the national existence." He cited military necessity as he pushed his cabinet to support emancipation, counted on northern arms to carry the promise of freedom ever deeper into the Confederacy, and hoped thousands of slaves would avail themselves of the opportunity to cast off their shackles. In the end, argued Neely, Lincoln's proclamation brought freedom to a great many slaves.[9]

James M. McPherson and Joseph T. Glatthaar both noted that Lincoln's proclamation initially served as part of the North's military rather than its national strategy. The president expected it to subtract laborers from the Confederate work force and add black soldiers to northern armies, thereby, as Lincoln put it, striking "at the heart of the rebellion." "But if it remained merely a *means* it would not be a part of national strategy—that is, of the *purpose* for which the war was being fought," wrote McPherson. Lincoln's reconstruction policy, which required acceptance of emancipation and other Union measures relating to slavery before seceded states could rejoin the Union, revealed the president's intention to make emancipation part of the national strategy. McPherson believed Lincoln's "sense of timing and his sensitivity to the pulse of the Northern people were superb" in this instance. Navigating deftly among the demands of constituencies ranging from conservative Democrats to Radical Republicans, the president forged a coalition among War Democrats and Republicans that eventually accepted emancipation as part of the national strategy.[10]

Glatthaar discussed Lincoln's ability to adapt his strategic vision to meet changing circumstances. Early in the war, the president used "razor-like acuteness" to discard "all extraneous concerns until only a single, core issue remained: the reunion of the states." Juggling military commanders and sometimes promulgating revolutionary policies in pursuit of this national strategy, Lincoln eventually admitted that "slavery was the root cause of the sectional crisis and by seeking its destruction, he elevated emancipation from a military policy to a political objective as well." For him and for the North "restoration of the Union and emancipation became *sine qua non,* the indispensable demands for cessation of hostilities. They were the goals of Lincoln's national strategy."[11]

However much credit may be apportioned to Lincoln and the slaves for advancing the cause of emancipation, there can be no doubt that the radical wing of the Republican Party consistently demanded that black freedom be made a national strategic goal.[12] T. Harry Williams highlighted this point in *Lincoln and the Radicals,* which has stood for more than fifty-five years as the fullest—if scarcely the most temperate—treatment of its subject. "Almost from the day when armed conflict began," noted Williams, "the radical and conservative factions clashed over the purposes of the war." Lincoln considered emancipation "incidental to the larger issue" of union and worked to build a coalition of Democrats and moderate and conservative Republicans. But the radicals "felt no enthusiasm for a war that did not include as one of its inevitable results the destruction of slavery." In language that revealed his dislike for the radicals (if not for their stance on emancipation), Williams wrote that "the Jacobins inveighed, ranted, and sneered" against Lincoln's mild program and eventually "forced the adoption of emancipation as one of the objectives of the war."[13]

Writing nearly three decades after Williams, Hans L. Trefousse adopted a far more positive tone in underscoring that radicals wanted emancipation to be the focal point of the North's national strategy. Aware that the war presented a unique opportunity to strike a decisive blow for freedom, they consistently badgered Lincoln to move more quickly. The fall of 1862 marked a watershed: "Lincoln's promulgation of the Preliminary Emancipation Proclamation and his dismissal, little more than six weeks later, of General McClellan, emphasized more clearly than anything up to that time the similarity between his and the radicals' war aims. Like them, he was determined to carry on the conflict as rigorously as necessary." Whereas Williams had claimed that the radicals frequently dominated Lincoln, Trefousse argued that the president cooperated with them in "a voluntary relationship in which he always retained the upper hand."[14]

One important variable too often has been absent from the equation of emancipation. In one of the war's many ironies, the Confederate people almost certainly influenced northern policy to a far greater degree than did slaves who fled to northern lines. They joined the army by hundreds of thousands, accepted a national draft before the conflict was a year old, died in huge numbers, and otherwise displayed a willingness to wage a costly war for independence. In the absence of such impressive resistance, the war might have ended before it took a revolutionary turn toward emancipation. Confederate actions mocked the idea, embraced by Lincoln and many other northerners during the war's first year, that a majority of the white South really opposed secession and had been seduced or duped by evil secessionists. Radical Republicans and abolitionists never doubted that most white southerners supported the Confederacy. They also understood that Confederate resolve abetted their hopes to convert the national strategy to one of union *and* freedom. Every enemy victory lengthened the conflict and increased the odds that the northern populace would have to strike at slavery to bring down the Confederacy.[15]

Democrats fought bitterly against expanding the North's national strategy to embrace emancipation. Although thousands of Democrats stepped forward to fight for the old Union, they almost universally loathed the prospect of risking white lives for black freedom. For them, the perfect end to the conflict would be a return to the Union as they had known it before Lincoln's election. As Joel H. Silbey observed in his perceptive survey of the North's opposition party, Democrats "forcefully challenged the government's policies, particularly the administration's determination to use whatever means necessary to destroy the South and inflict blows against its social system in the name of winning the war." In a study of the Democrats most supportive of making war against the Confederacy, Christopher Dell admired Lincoln's political skill in creating a "mighty force—the so-called 'War Democracy'—which agreed to fight against its own instincts and prejudice, at the expense of men and theories and principles it had been worshipping for many years." Yet Dell demonstrated that even most of the War Democrats balked at emancipation as a part of the national strategy.[16]

The transformation of the North's national strategy heralded a change of policy toward Confederate civilians and their property that many historians writing since World War II have described as "total war." Definitions of what constitutes total war vary, but Civil War scholars who apply the term generally agree that it represents a conflict in which the enemy's entire war-making capacity is targeted. A limited war strategy seeks to conquer places and occupy territory; total war seeks to destroy armies, lay waste to economic infrastructure, and erode civilian will.

T. Harry Williams spoke of the conflict as "the first of the modern total wars." A clash of ideas in which neither party "could compromise its political purposes, it was a war of unlimited objectives." Bruce Catton similarly wrote that northern generals fought "a total war, and in a total war the enemy's economy is to be undermined in any way possible. Slavery was the Southern economy's most vulnerable spot, and a Northern general could not be neutral in respect to it. . . . Slavery, indeed, was the one institution which could not possibly survive an all-out war." James M. McPherson averred that "Lincoln's policy toward slavery became a touchstone of the evolution of this conflict from a limited war to restore the old Union to a total war to destroy the Southern social as well as political system." Most recently, the authors of *The American Civil War: The Emergence of Total Warfare* stated that the Emancipation Proclamation "signaled the demise of conciliation, and by early 1863 Union policy makers increasingly realized that more destructive measures were necessary." The war's final year, concluded these scholars, "witnessed the full bloom of total war," a key component of which was the North's decision to target for destruction "Southern crops and resources."[17]

Despite their use of the phrase *total war,* the authors of this last work noted that Union armies never resorted to "wholesale killing of Southern civilians." This fact alone, argued Mark E. Neely, Jr., proved that the Civil War never met the savage standard that has become all-too-common in the twentieth century. "[N]o Northerner at any time in the nineteenth century embraced as his own the cold-blooded ideas now associated with total war," wrote Neely. "The *essential* aspect of any definition of total war asserts that it breaks down the distinction between soldiers and civilians, combatants and noncombatants," he maintained, "and this no one in the Civil War did systematically, including William T. Sherman." Nor did the northern war effort meet the modern test of national mobilization. Lincoln's government never sought to control the economy or to muster resources for anything like World War II's Manhattan Project. Neely conceded that the Civil War "*approached* total war in some ways" but quickly restated his main point: "By no definition of the term can it be said to *be* a total war."[18]

Neither Charles Royster nor Mark Grimsley, who produced the most extensive works on this theme, accepted the idea of a northern total war. In *The Destructive War: William Tecumseh Sherman, Stonewall Jackson, and the Americans,* Royster specifically rejected it because there were no mass killings of civilians. He pointed out, however, that some northerners, especially Republicans, were prepared to attack the Confederacy's economy and social structure from the outset. Lowering his analytical lens from civilian and military leaders to Union soldiers in the ranks, Royster found growing sentiment that the entire South must suffer for the sins of the slaveholders: "In order to overthrow the principle 'that capital ought to own labor' and to show the hollowness of 'rebel cavaliers who claim to be better stuff than Puritan mud-sills,' it finally seemed necessary to ruin the Confederacy, not just defeat its armies and government." Sherman stood first among generals known for their skill at "drastic war-making"—a function of both his actions during the last eighteen months of the conflict and his brilliantly inflammatory rhetoric. Many northerners equated his name with "war that punished all rebels," even as thousands of Union soldiers, "making their vision of the country an extension of their pride in their own success, . . . vindicated free labor through combat and devastation." Curiously, Royster devoted little attention to the ways in which emancipation fit into his portrait of the North's waging "destructive" or "drastic" war.[19]

Grimsley borrowed Sherman's phrase "hard war" to describe the North's ultimate military policy regarding Confederate civilians.[20] He situated hard war third in a progression of northern policies. At first hoping to attract support from southern unionists with a conciliatory approach, Lincoln and the North shifted gears after military reverses in the summer of 1862. The Emancipation Proclamation "firmly repudiated the conciliatory policy" and ushered in a "pragmatic interlude" that preceded the appearance of hard war. During this interlude, which lasted about eighteen months, Union generals "sought victory exclusively on the battlefield; their stance toward civilians tended to be whatever seemed best calculated to produce operational results." The dividing line between pragmatism and hard war tended to blur, acknowledged Grimsley, with commanders in the western theater moving more rapidly than eastern counterparts "who clung to a conservative style of warfare much longer." By the spring of 1864, with Grant in control as general-in-chief, the North's hard war program witnessed major military operations that sought "to demoralize Southern civilians and ruin the Confederate economy, particularly its industries and transportation infrastructure."[21]

Yet even at its most destructive hard war differentiated among overt secessionists, neutral or passive people, and unionists. In contrast to

Royster, who described a pervasive wish among Federal soldiers to punish Confederates of all classes, Grimsley found that wealthy secessionists suffered most harshly from the new policy. "The three-way division among Southern civilians remained to the end of the conflict," he suggested: "So did orders that forbade wanton acts of destruction. And although needless destruction occurred, it is remarkable that generally the policy held up." Generals and politicians wanted this discriminating policy to work, but "[i]t also survived because tens of thousands of soldiers—toughened by war, hungry for creature comforts, and often angry at the civilians in their midst—nevertheless understood the logic and abided by it." Only by examining "the interplay between formal directives issued at the top; informal attitudes held by Northern generals, private soldiers, and civilians; and the actions of Union forces in the field," asserted Grimsley, is it possible to grasp the evolution of Union policy toward Confederate civilians.[22]

In a pioneering social history of the army that marched with Sherman through Georgia and the Carolinas, Joseph T. Glatthaar reached conclusions about attitudes among Union soldiers that anticipated both Royster and Grimsley. Glatthaar described, as would Royster, Union soldiers eager to execute "a strategy to make southerners feel the iron hand of destruction derived from prolonged years of hardship and sacrifice and an unfaltering commitment to the cause of reunification." Sherman's soldiers, virtually all of whom were veterans, "adopted the total-war concept as retaliation for the deaths and tragedies that their ranks had endured and also because they saw it as the most effective means of winning the war." Yet Glatthaar's Federals, like Grimsley's, differentiated among groups of Confederates—in this instance wreaking greater havoc on civilians in South Carolina, which had led the way toward secession, than on those in Georgia and, especially, in North Carolina, where there had been greater unionist sentiment in 1860 and 1861.[23]

Archer Jones reminded readers of a historical context within which the North's strategy of taking the war to Confederate civilians appeared almost benign. Sherman knew the history of England's wars to control Ireland, wrote Jones, and would have understood that his campaign through Georgia and the Carolinas "was a humanitarian venture compared to Irish warfare, which traditionally depended on raids to cow opponents, burning barns and villages and taking cattle being routine military operations." The English responded to Irish resistance by deliberately starving thousands of noncombatants and attempting to replace them with English settlers. Several hundred years earlier, William the Conqueror initially pursued a conciliatory policy but later resorted to brutality when English opposition persisted, devastating a portion of "the country so thoroughly that many died and for years afterwards it remained uninhabited wasteland." Although Jones appreciated the destruction wrought by Sherman's raids and comparable Union operations, as well as "the malevolence and viciousness" of the some of the conflict's guerrilla warfare, he concluded that the "Civil War was hardly more a total war than many others in the past in which invaders encountered or provoked popular resistance."[24]

Whether described as total war, hard war, drastic war, destructive war, modern war, or in some other way, the ultimate northern military strategy met the test of saving the Union and killing slavery. By the spring of 1865, northern arms had persuaded the Confederate people that further resistance was futile. A Georgia woman grimly catalogued the decisive impact of Union military operations. "We never yielded in the struggle until we were bound hand & foot & the heel of the despot was on our throats," wrote Sarah Hine: "Bankrupt in men, in money, & in provisions, the wail of the bereaved & the cry of hunger rising all over the land, Our cities burned with fire and our pleasant things laid waste, the best & bravest of our sons in captivity, and the entire resources of our country exhausted—what else could we do but give up."[25]

Who deserved credit for formulating and implementing the successful northern military strategy? T. Harry Williams addressed this question in the 1950s and 1960s in a series of works that made his reputation as an immensely influential interpreter of northern military leadership. Notable for their attention to the conjunction of politics and military affairs, Williams's writings prompted other scholars to take a similarly broad approach to questions of northern strategy (regrettably, many historians persist in divorcing the political and military spheres).

In *Lincoln and His Generals*—the best-known of his Civil War books—as well as in shorter studies, Williams celebrated Lincoln's genius, praised Grant and Sherman, and dismissed the rest of the Union high command as utterly unable to comprehend the nature of the massive war that engulfed them. Williams considered Lincoln "a great natural strategist, a better one than any of his generals. He was in actuality as well as in title the commander in chief who, by his larger strategy, did more than Grant or any other general to win the war for the Union." Lincoln rapidly grasped the advantage inherent in superior northern manpower and material resources "and urged his generals to keep up a constant pressure on the whole strategic line of the Confederacy until a weak spot was found—and a breakthrough could be made." Equally important, according to Williams, was Lincoln's early insight that "the proper objective of his armies was the destruction of the Confederate armies and not the occupation of

Southern territory." The North must ceaselessly press the offensive, believed the president, who conveyed this message to Union generals with his famous order for simultaneous advances to begin on Washington's birthday in 1862 (Williams argued that Lincoln knew this was impractical but wanted to jar his generals out of lethargic postures).[26]

Williams described most of Lincoln's generals as disciples of the Swiss military thinker Antoine Henri Jomini. In Williams's view, Jomini's strategic thinking ignored the profound connections between war and politics. Jomini "disliked the destructiveness of warfare," emphasized cities and territory rather than enemy armies as targets, and taught concentration of force for action at one point. Lincoln's generals had learned Jominian theory at West Point from Professor Dennis Hart Mahan, and they proposed to fight the Confederacy "in accordance with the standards and strategy of an earlier and easier military age. . . . They hoped to accomplish their objectives by maneuvering rather than fighting." This was impossible in a contest between two democratic societies, each of which refused to compromise on its major political objectives—independence for the Confederacy and reunion for the North. Officers such as George B. McClellan, Don Carlos Buell, and George G. Meade failed to see that the American conflict "was bound to be a rough, no-holds-barred affair, a bloody and brutal struggle."[27]

One by one, Williams classified Union generals-in-chief as strategically naive or inept. Winfield Scott's Anaconda Plan amounted to "more a diplomatic policy than a plan of strategic action"; the old hero further entertained the illusion that "the war could be won by a single effort of some kind." Scott's successor McClellan lacked a talent for grand strategy, preferring to focus on the Virginia theater and his beloved Army of the Potomac. Although McClellan devised in August 1861 an ambitious blueprint for Union action against many points in the Confederacy, the document left Williams notably unimpressed: "It was a pretty paper exercise, and it had no relevance at all to anything in the existing condition of affairs." Henry W. Halleck fared marginally better than McClellan, emerging as a doctrinaire Jominian whose western victories in 1862 had been won by Grant and others but who belatedly realized that only "techniques of total war" would vanquish the rebels. As the general-in-chief who served between the tenures of McClellan and Grant, however, Halleck "exercised little control over military operations. . . . because he disliked responsibility and did not want to direct."[28]

Williams considered Grant "the greatest general of the Civil War," an officer who towered "head and shoulders above any general on either side as an over-all strategist, as a master of what in later wars would be called global strategy." Unlike the narrow Jominians, Grant possessed a "modern mind" most evident "in his grasp of the concept that war was becoming total and that the destruction of the enemy's economic resources was as effective and legitimate a form of warfare as the destruction of his armies." He shared Lincoln's vision of simultaneous Union offensives and knew "the great truth that the ultimate objective in war is the destruction of the enemy's principal army." (Williams claimed elsewhere that Lincoln had to school his new general-in-chief about the need to make Lee's army rather than Richmond the goal of northern arms in the East—an instance of the historian's clearly misreading Grant's original intention for the spring 1864 offensives.) Grant also accepted the political nature of the conflict "for what it was, an inevitable and perhaps even desirable concomitant of modern war."[29]

Sherman completed Williams's triumvirate of successful northern strategists. A "typical Jominian at the beginning of the war," the Ohioan grew into the conflict's "greatest exponent of economic and psychological warfare" and thereby moved "the art of warfare significantly forward." Sherman excelled Grant in understanding "that the will of a nation to fight rests on the economic and psychological security of its people and that if these supporting elements are destroyed all resistance may collapse." Sherman's kind of war inflicted deep wounds on the enemy, but only the death of Lee's army could topple the Confederacy. That fatal blow would come from Grant—a general "who made his best preparations and then went in without reserve or hesitation and with a simple faith in success."[30]

Williams invoked the name of German military theorist Karl von Clausewitz to add a comparative dimension to his analysis of Union strategists. In Grant and Sherman, the "North was fortunate in finding two generals who between them executed Clausewitz's three objectives of war: to conquer and destroy the enemy's armed forces, to get possession of the material elements of aggression and other sources of existence of the enemy, and to gain public opinion by winning victories that depress the enemy's morale." Here were *modern* warriors who, together with their brilliant commander-in-chief, developed a strategy that took note of the enemy's entire society and willingly attacked it root and branch. They anticipated the future of warfare while the backward-looking Jominians fumbled along, defined the enemy and the war in outmoded terms, and became anachronisms long before Appomattox sealed the North's military triumph.[31]

Historians writing about northern strategy before and after Williams also typically focused on Lincoln, Grant, and Sherman, giving different emphases to the relative strategic abilities and contributions of each. Winfield Scott, George B. McClellan, and Henry W. Halleck, the other major strategic players on the northern roster, also inspired considerable analysis but usually fared poorly at the hands of historians. Grant's reputation underwent the most dramatic change. Frequently characterized through the mid-twentieth century as an unimaginative, straight-ahead basher whose only strategic insight lay in knowing the North's resources should be committed unsparingly, he has, over the past several decades, more often been labeled a surpassingly gifted soldier whose strategy as general-in-chief brought Union victory.

A trio of British historians who also were professional soldiers contributed to the historiographical shift in the 1920s and 1930s away from Lost Cause explanations for Union victory. Two of the three also helped rehabilitate Grant's reputation as a strategist. Major General J. F. C. Fuller, the more influential of this pair, published *The Generalship of Ulysses S. Grant* in 1929 and *Grant & Lee: A Study in Personality and Generalship* four years later. A self-styled admirer of Lee who accepted much of the "Grant the butcher" interpretation when he commenced his study of Civil War military leadership, Fuller soon found himself unabashedly enthusiastic about Grant. The Union commander understood the meaning of grand strategy, stated Fuller, which he defined as "the correlation of the operations of war and the policy of the Government supported by the resources of the country." For Fuller, Grant's "central idea was concentration of force from which he intended to develop a ceaseless offensive against the enemy's armies, and the resources and *moral* of the Confederacy." Grant possessed "something cosmic" that permitted him to grasp features of a new type of warfare that involved civilians and their property as well as soldiers. Grant also knew how large Lee's army loomed in both the northern and Confederate popular minds: "Thus we see that whilst Grant's outlook was general, embracing the whole theatre of war, his leading idea was single, namely, the destruction of the enemy's main army."[32]

Lieutenant Colonel Alfred H. Burne joined Fuller in praising Grant's strategic "broadness of conception and singleness of aim." He argued that Grant took in the whole strategic picture but made his overriding goal in 1864 and 1865 the destruction of Lee's army, "to which all resources direct and indirect were to be devoted." Burne anticipated Williams's use of Clausewitz to categorize Grant: "Clausewitz placed as the principal object in war 'to conquer and destroy the enemy's armed forces.' Clausewitz was right, and Grant knew it." (It is unclear whether Burne thought that Grant had read Clausewitz—he had not—or that he simply reached the same strategic conclusions on his own.) Sherman, whose style of warfare in 1864 and 1865 Burne incorrectly described as place-oriented, "might help to prepare the ground" for final Union victory, "but it was Grant who struck the blow." In one sense, Sherman's destructive marches contravened Grant's efforts to achieve the North's national strategic goals. "[W]hatever military claims may be made for such a policy," wrote Burne in apparent belief that Grant had not urged Sherman to do just what he did in Georgia and the Carolinas, "it had in the long run unfortunate effects, causing such an intensity of animosity in the South as to delay by at least a decade the true unification of the country—the object for which the Northerners went to war."[33]

Colin R. Ballard's aptly titled *The Military Genius of Abraham Lincoln*, which appeared in a British edition in 1926, looked to the Executive Mansion rather than to Grant's headquarters for northern strategic direction. A general in the British army, Ballard wrote that Lincoln proved an exception to the rule that civilians should leave military strategy to their officers, asserting hyperbolically that "Lincoln was solely responsible for the strategy of the North." Anticipating many of T. Harry Williams's points in *Lincoln and His Generals* (the first American edition of Ballard's book appeared the same year Williams's book was published), Ballard listed five crucial areas in which the president displayed his strategic talents: he saw the importance of sea power in helping to isolate the Confederacy; understood the profound connections between politics and military strategy; called for northern pressure across an extensive geographical line; specified the best rebel army (Lee's) as his primary target; and never settled for half measures. Ballard described the Emancipation Proclamation as a move with both national and operational implications. It placed the North on record in favor of freedom, thus barring the way to foreign intervention—"perhaps a decisive factor in the war." It also brought manpower to northern armies and weakened the economic infrastructure supporting their Confederate opponent.[34]

Kenneth P. Williams, Bruce Catton, Russell F. Weigley, and John Keegan, whose work spanned the period from the late 1940s through the 1980s, added to scholarship crediting Grant with essential contributions to northern victory. In his preface to the first volume of *Lincoln Finds a General: A Military Study of the Civil War*, Williams defined the North's strategic dilemma: "Lincoln's chief military problem was to find a general equal to the hard task the North faced in the Civil War. . . . Great superiority in man power and munitions was needed; but it was not sufficient. It was a case of Napoleon's maxim of the necessity of *the man*." That man, affirmed Williams, was Grant, "a soldier's soldier, a general's general" who combined offensive spirit, strategic grasp, and respect for the problems his superiors faced. Of all generals in the conflict, only Grant demonstrated the ability "to plan and direct the operations of several armies." Williams completed four volumes and part of a fifth that brought the war nearly to the point at which Grant assumed command of all Union forces. Although death cut short his plan to carry the series through Appomattox, there can be no doubt that Williams would have laid out in great detail the reasons he saw Grant as the irreplaceable part of the Union's war machine.[35]

Catton seconded the observation, made by Kenneth P. Williams and many others, that Grant utilized resources previously available to all of his predecessors. "[W]hat the Northern war effort had always needed was a soldier who, assuming the top command, would see to it that they were applied steadily, remorselessly and without a break, all across the board." Grant was for Catton, as he was for Williams, *the man*: "He used the means at hand to discharge the obligation which had been put upon him. The war was won thereby, and it is not easy to see how it would have been done without Grant." In language reminiscent of T. Harry Williams, Catton also noted Grant's coming to terms with "an all-out war in the modern manner," his sensitivity to political imperatives in a democracy at war, and his ability to coax simultaneous action out of far-flung elements of the Union military.[36]

In his widely influential *The American Way of War*, Russell F. Weigley discerned in Grant's strategic planning as general-in-chief a combination of Clausewitzian and Jominian elements. Rejecting Napoleon's "infatuation with the battle as the supreme means in war," Grant nonetheless knew heavy losses would be necessary to defeat the Confederacy because he "accepted a Napoleonic strategy of annihilation as the prescription for victory in a war of popular nationalism." In the spring of 1864, he hoped to obliterate the Confederacy's major field armies but "could not ignore the Jominian territorial objectives" because it "was threats against the political and logistical centers of Richmond and Atlanta that compelled Lee's and Johnston's armies to fight." Grant envisioned annihilation of the enemy's military forces through attrition along an extensive front rather than through climactic battles. The high cost of crushing Confederate armies via direct confrontation, however, led him to add another element to his strategy. While he fought and bled Lee's army in Virginia, other Union armies would savage the South's logistical capacity: "To strike against war resources suggested an indirect means of accomplishing the destruction of the enemy armies."

Sherman further refined this prescription for victory by adding a psychological dimension to what Grant initially had envisioned as campaigns against Confederate logistics. Sherman declared that the North fought "not only hostile armies, but a hostile people." He therefore "not only carried on war against the enemy's resources more extensively and systematically than anyone else had done, but he developed also a deliberate strategy of terror directed against the enemy people's minds." The team of Grant and Sherman ensured that the North would pursue total military victory. Grant concentrated Union power to ruin Confederate armies and logistics and also encouraged Sherman's strategy of terror. Of the pair, Sherman better understood "the war as a contest between peoples beyond the contest of armies." Weigley concluded, much as T. Harry Williams and Burne had earlier, that Sherman's indirect pressure applied during the March to the Sea and in the Carolinas could not have been decisive by itself. Indeed, those campaigns were possible only "because the main Confederate armies either had already been destroyed by a direct strategy of annihilation or were otherwise occupied." Sherman's campaigning after the fall of Atlanta probably prompted some desertion from Lee's army, but "there is no good reason to believe that the Army of Northern Virginia could have been destroyed within an acceptable time by any other means than the hammer blows of Grant's army."[37]

British historian John Keegan harkened back to T. Harry Williams in emphasizing Grant's non-Jominian approach to a total war. Unlike Union generals hamstrung by Jomini's "narrow geometrical strictures," Grant, whom Keegan labeled an "anti-Jominian," "knew, or was quickly to discover, that in a war of people against people, dispersed in a vast, rich but almost empty land, an army need have no permanent base at all." Union forces could use rivers and railroads to the greatest extent possible and procure food and fodder from the areas through which they campaigned. In May 1863, Grant reached the "momentous decision" to cut loose from his bases during the Vicksburg campaign: "And to this strategy of making the enemy give him what he wanted he added the twist of denying the Confederates what they wanted for themselves." As an old Jominian, Sherman at first opposed this "strategy of 'baseless' campaigning" but "a year later would take it to extremes that Grant had not yet contemplated." Above all, Keegan pointed to Grant's willingness to slug it out with the rebels if necessary. While others "dabbled in remembered classroom theory, aped their European counterparts, or even sought to reincarnate Napoleon, he confined himself to practicalities." Grant took the war to the rebels, made Confederate civilians experience the burden of conflict, and constructed a strategy that supplied enough victories to maintain northern morale.

In his enthusiasm for Grant, Keegan failed to note that the general's decision "of immense daring" in May 1863 almost certainly owed a good deal to the example of Winfield Scott's brilliant campaign from Vera Cruz to Mexico City in 1847. Keegan also incorrectly claimed that Grant did not defer to Lincoln on strategy—only on "non-strategic matters" such as emancipation and recruiting black troops.[38]

In fact, Grant understood perfectly that he lacked ultimate authority to determine either national or military strategy. For example, he preferred an indirect raiding strategy in North Carolina to a major effort against Lee in the spring of 1864, but Lincoln, supported by Secretary of War Edwin M. Stanton and Henry W. Halleck, insisted that the focus in the eastern theater be on the Army of Northern Virginia. Sensitive to the political pressure that helped explain Lincoln's stance, Grant quickly acquiesced. John Y. Simon, whose editorship of the Grant papers project has given him unequaled knowledge of the general, neatly summarized both Grant's challenge as general-in-chief and his relationship with Lincoln: "Charged with vast responsibilities, General-in-Chief Grant had to act vigorously within the military sphere, tread softly in the political sphere, and understand as well the politics of command. Under Lincoln's guidance, sometimes oblique, sometimes imperious, Grant succeeded." The key to the two men's association was that Lincoln "held the reins and taught Grant what was permitted and what was not."[39]

Grant stood out among top Union commanders in his ready deference to civilian control of northern strategy. "Because he had plain sense," wrote T. Harry Williams, "Grant was capable of grasping the political nature of the war. This was the aspect of the conflict that McClellan raged at and Sherman sneered at." The addition of emancipation to the North's national strategy set in especially stark relief a difference between Grant and Sherman. Michael Fellman has explored the ways in which Sherman actively worked against his government's policies on emancipation. "Of all the leading Union generals," observed Fellman, "Sherman was by far the most outspoken in his resistance to this revolution . . . and the most openly insubordinate to civilian dictates, from those issued by the president on down." The terms of surrender Sherman offered Joseph E. Johnston at Durham Station in April 1865, which amounted to a lenient policy of reconstruction, showed the general's contempt for parts of the national strategy.[40]

Sherman's terms surprised Grant. Brooks D. Simpson, author of the best analysis of Grant the soldier and politics, remarked that the "general-in-chief could not believe that Sherman, far from avoiding issues of civil policy . . . , had plunged right into the maelstrom of the peace process." Throughout the conflict, added Simpson, Grant "embodied Clausewitz's most important maxim: 'War is merely the continuation of policy by other means.' . . . Grant understood Clausewitz's argument that 'the first, the supreme, the most far-reaching act of judgment that a statesman and commander have to make' is that 'the kind of war on which they are embarking' is shaped by the goals of policy."[41] Lincoln allowed Grant great freedom in the realm of operational strategy not only because the latter was a proven winner, but also because he knew that Grant respected the North's national strategy and would bend every effort to make it a success through his military decisions.

Joseph T. Glatthaar reminded readers how important Lincoln considered this trait in a general-in-chief. "The president had struggled to find a commanding general who could utilize the Union's resources efficiently, campaign actively, and serve dutifully within the political parameters that the government established," a combination of strengths lacking in both McClellan (who opposed emancipation and refused to fight aggressively) and Halleck (who adopted a passive stance during his time as general-in-chief). By late winter 1864, Lincoln knew Grant was his man: "His military exploits, sensitivity to political necessities, and wholehearted implementation of government policies distinguished Grant from all other Union generals in Lincoln's mind."

Although Lincoln had found his ideal general-in-chief, he did not abdicate his role in helping to formulate operational strategy. Glatthaar suggested that Lincoln was slow to comprehend Grant's strategy of exhausting the Confederacy through logistical raids. Lincoln believed victory lay in defeating rebel armies (especially Lee's); Grant and Sherman had decided that gutting the Confederacy's interior would bring the same result. In 1864, northern forces made great strides toward accomplishing both goals, demonstrating that "the raiding strategy operated well in conjunction with a more traditional strategy that sought the destruction of Confederate armies." Pleased from the outset with General-in-Chief Grant's simultaneous advances, Lincoln did not appreciate fully the potential value of raids against logistics until Sherman captured Savannah. "Piecing together Confederate newspaper reports and snippets from Sherman," wrote Glatthaar, "Lincoln finally visualized just how disruptive to Confederates and productive to Federals these raiding campaigns could be." Although lacking Grant's skills at operational strategy and sometimes vetoing good ideas, Lincoln proved his greatness as a war leader by generally giving Grant and Sherman freedom to achieve national strategic goals.[42]

Grant's three predecessors as general-in-chief never worked out a comparable arrangement with Lincoln, and their strategic thinking has garnered few encomiums from historians. Winfield Scott almost certainly possessed the analytical and administrative skills to succeed but, at age seventy-five, lacked the physical stamina to oversee the northern war effort. Scholars such as T. Harry Williams and John Keegan have argued that Scott hoped merely to sit back and allow the blockade and northern seizure of the Mississippi River to precipitate a Confederate collapse. Many other historians, after an obligatory mention of the Anaconda Plan, have simply ignored the old general in assessing northern strategy. In fact, Scott foresaw large-scale invasions of the South as a possible feature of northern operational strategy. In March 1861, long before the Confederacy exhibited its ability to mount an impressive military effort, he advised William H. Seward that the North might have to "[c]onquer the seceding States by invading armies." "The destruction of life and property on the other side would be frightful—however perfect the moral discipline of the invaders," noted Scott presciently, and would entail a toll of "enormous waste of human life to the North and Northwest" and bitter postwar feelings that would frustrate the northern national goal of speedy reunion. A modern study of Scott as a soldier, which should give full attention to the early period of the Civil War, is long overdue.[43]

George B. McClellan's strategic planning as general-in-chief has attracted far less attention than his actions as a field commander in Virginia. Many scholars have emulated T. Harry Williams in labeling him an inveterate Jominian who became seriously engaged with strategic questions only when they pertained to Virginia. None of "Little Mac's" critics has been more blistering than Kenneth P. Williams, who stated that "McClellan was not a real general. McClellan was not even a disciplined, truthful soldier. McClellan was merely an attractive but vain and unstable man, with considerable military knowledge, who sat a horse well and wanted to be president."[44] Although T. Harry Williams dismissed as foolish McClellan's comprehensive strategic plan in August 1861, Bruce Catton and Stephen Sears credited the general with trying in 1861 and 1862 to apply the type of simultaneous pressure that Grant would achieve in 1864. "[T]he difference was," wrote Catton, "that he could not make anything happen the way he wanted it to happen." Sears lauded McClellan's "activist interpretation" of the position of general-in-chief and his "formulation of a grand strategy for prosecuting the war" that was not matched "until another general with the same vision, U. S. Grant, took over the post." But McClellan's obdurate refusal to bow to civilian direction "virtually nullified his accomplishments."[45]

A few scholars have offered a more sympathetic reading of McClellan's strategic failures. Edward Hagerman mentioned the general's political squabbles with the Republican administration but argued that the main limiting factor was a logistical framework that made it difficult to maneuver large bodies of men over distance and time. Grant and Sherman succeeded later, stated Hagerman, in considerable measure because they benefited from improved Union "field transportation and supply organization." Warren W. Hassler rendered an even more favorable verdict. McClellan's early attempts at simultaneous advances ran afoul of weather, logistics, and balky lieutenants. By 1862, the Radical Republicans bombarded him with "intense and unrelenting attacks" that eventually triggered his removal. Hassler considered McClellan a fine soldier whose "achievements had been substantial—some masterful," but whose hope to fight the war free of political entanglements had proved impossible.[46]

The scholarly consensus portrays Henry W. Halleck as a general-in-chief unwilling to exercise the power proffered by a chief executive anxious to have a controlling hand at the strategic helm. Refusing to accept authority equal to that Grant later would wield, wrote Bruce Catton, Halleck "reduced himself to a sort of high-level adviser, a paper-shuffler who neither laid down nor enforced a comprehensive strategy for the war as a whole." Joseph T. Glatthaar similarly observed that Halleck "never seized the reins of the Union war effort," and Stephen E. Ambrose, in the most detailed (but perhaps not the most satisfying) examination of Halleck's Civil War career, judged that he "made no outstanding contribution to either tactics or strategy." John Keegan pronounced Halleck "a pedant of the worst sort"; of all the generals-in-chief, this rigid Jominian "comprehended the war's nature least of all." Keegan went too far in charging Halleck with unwavering allegiance to Jomini. As T. Harry Williams, Ambrose, and others pointed out, Halleck modified his initial Jominian attitude to embrace a much tougher operational strategy that punished Confederate civilians—though he never took the lead in pushing for this type of war.[47]

The best broad treatment of northern military strategy is Herman Hattaway and Archer Jones's *How the North Won: A Military History of the Civil War*. Exhaustive, perceptive, and often revisionist, it might have come first among the books discussed in this essay. Because it plays off much earlier literature, however, it seems a good candidate for a position closer to the end. Hattaway and Jones dedicated their book to T. Harry Williams, adding that they sometimes disagreed with him but sought to continue "the same tradition of Civil War military history that he did much to establish." Departing from Williams's Jominian/Clausewitzian classifications, they assessed the roles of Lincoln and all of his principal generals in harnessing northern resources to crush the Confederacy. The authors gave well-deserved credit to Winfield Scott, who "focused his powerful intellect and vast experience on the North's infinitely complex strategic problem." Analyzing both the Anaconda Plan and Scott's ideas about what else might be needed to achieve victory, Hattaway and Jones observed that "[e]xcept for underestimating by one-half the number of men and the time needed, the old general had provided a fairly accurate forecast of most of the . . . elements of the strategy ultimately used."[48]

Lincoln's generals understood that the rifled musket gave defenders the tactical advantage and rendered decisive battlefield victories unlikely. "Avoiding a futile pursuit of the strategy of annihilation," wrote the authors in opposition to some of Russell F. Weigley's points, "Union generals sought to conquer the Confederacy to deprive its armies of their source of supplies, weapons, and recruits." This strategy of exhaustion initially worked well in the West, where Henry W. Halleck coordinated brilliant offensives along the Mississippi, Tennessee, and Cumberland rivers. When the North ran out of these vital logistical lifelines, however, progress stalled and a restive northern public and its political leaders (most notably the Radical Republicans) "grew impatient for decisive victories that would end the rebellion quickly." This tension bedeviled Lincoln throughout the war as he searched for a means to satisfy the popular clamor for Napoleonic victories even as he understood that "military realities" militated against such triumphs.[49]

By the summer of 1863, the strategy of exhaustion predicated on seizing territory "began to seem quite dubious when the Union armies confronted the task of conquering and holding the large, populous, and thoroughly rebellious state of Georgia." (It had taken the North two years to conquer East Tennessee, with its large unionist population.) In response, Lincoln and Grant each devised a variant strain of the strategy of exhaustion. The president's "was political and psychological in that he sought to draw states from the Confederacy by amnesty and a liberal reconstruction policy while demoralizing the enemy through wholesale employment against them of their former slaves enlisted as soldiers." If successful, this plan would deprive the Confederate economy of crucial workers. Grant proposed a series of huge raids into the Confederacy by Union forces that would "occupy no territory" but "would destroy the logistical base of the Confederate war machine." Grant's friend Sherman later used the raiding strategy to bring "the war home to all rebel states, thus exhibiting the inability of the Confederacy to protect its territorial integrity."[50]

Lincoln determined by early 1862 that simultaneous pressure against the Confederates at several points held the key to victory. Scott had understood this, as did McClellan and Halleck; so acknowledged Hattaway and Jones. They aligned with many earlier scholars in stressing that not until Grant assumed command of all United States forces in March 1864 did the North find a general-in-chief capable of orchestrating the requisite pressure. During the war's final year, Grant, bowing to public and political demands, confronted Lee directly in Virginia. Meanwhile, Sherman captured Atlanta, which slaked northern thirst for dramatic victories, and then cut his destructive swath through Georgia and South Carolina. Other northern forces inflicted significant damage to the Confederate logistical base in the Shenandoah Valley and elsewhere. By April 1865, "Grant's systematic application of the strategy of exhaustion through raids had been truly successful in carrying out his objective to 'leave nothing for the rebellion to stand upon.'"[51]

Having underscored how effectively northern arms gutted the Confederacy's material resources (by April 1865 the Confederacy also had lost half of its military-age white men killed or maimed), the authors reached the somewhat puzzling conclusion that "Union victory was not exclusively, nor perhaps even predominantly, military." The war ended, they insisted, because the Confederate people, who had only a weakly developed sense of nationalism, lost their will to resist.[52]

Hattaway and Jones bestowed primary credit for northern military achievements on Lincoln and Grant. "Lincoln's military performance supports his acknowledged greatness"; his preeminent gift "lay in his intelligence, which enabled him to learn the elements of the art of war of the mid-nineteenth century and grasp quickly the realistic and sophisticated ideas of the country's capable military leadership." The president kept his eye on the big strategic picture, consistently called for broad pressure against the enemy, and evinced "a superior ability to integrate military and political factors." His use of black troops, for example, strengthened the Union army, heartened the Radical Republicans, and weakened the Confederacy. Among Lincoln's generals, Grant "made the major military contribution to victory." The strategy of exhausting the Confederacy through raiding was his brainchild—though Sherman, who executed the most famous such operation, often gets the credit. To an unerring grasp of the right course of action "Grant added his unobtrusive but firm dominance of his subordinates, his talent for delegation, and his good management."[53]

Hattaway and Jones affirmed that they worked in the tradition of T. Harry Williams. They represented that tradition at its analytical and descriptive best, often disagreeing with Williams's conclusions and imposing a stiff standard for subsequent scholars who adopted a similar approach. Anyone undertaking an evaluation of Lincoln, Grant, Sherman, or other top Union leaders as strategists must take into account their interpretation.[54]

Neither the size of the existing literature nor the excellence of such studies as *How the North Won* should obscure numerous aspects of northern strategy that beckon future scholars. Several examples will illustrate this point. Since publication of T. Harry Williams's *Lincoln and the Radicals*, only one scholar has examined in depth the influential Joint Committee on the Conduct of the War as it related to northern strategy. In *Over Lincoln's Shoulder: The Committee on the Conduct of the War*, Bruce Tap agreed that Williams was "probably correct in his negative assessment of the committee's overall effect on the Union war effort." Among other things the committee "contributed to the unhealthy practice of basing military appointments on political considerations," pursued "blatantly political and partisan ends" in investigating the operations of the Army of the Potomac, and too often drew simplistic conclusions because as a group its members lacked military knowledge. More analysis of the ways in which Benjamin F. Wade, Zachariah Chandler, George W. Julian, and their allies on the committee, through hearings and other means, sought to sway Lincoln and the northern public on a variety of strategic issues would be useful. On a larger canvas, the role of Congress as a whole concerning the North's military strategy and policy deserves additional attention. Scholars studying the Civil War Congress too often have avoided delving into the ways in which its members influenced operational and, to a lesser degree, national strategy.[55]

Historians interested in military campaigns similarly have given minimal attention to how northern armies reacted to congressional policies affecting the strategic shaping of the war. In an essay on the Army of the Potomac during early 1864, John J. Hennessy suggested why this weakness in the literature must be rectified. Many of the army's officers, wrote Hennessy, "fiercely resisted radicalization and spent much of their energy in 1862 and early 1863 trying to define northern war aims." Letters from generals and commanders of lower rank reached "newspaper editors, senators, congressmen, and governors" as well as uncounted family members. "Theirs was not an organized effort," continued Hennessy, "but it attained considerable volume and hence influence. It simultaneously reflected and contributed to social divisions afflicting a nation caught up in a transforming conflict."[56]

Emancipation ranked among the divisive issues that prompted these letters. Quite remarkably, there has yet to be a comprehensive examination of the impact on northern soldiers of the Emancipation Proclamation, the recruitment of African Americans for military service, and the addition of freedom to Union goals of the national strategy. John J. Hennessy has noted that Lincoln's proclamation "stimulated an avalanche of commentary" in the Army of the Potomac during the winter of 1863, but a detailed study of responses across time that includes a geographical comparison would be enlightening. Did soldiers from the Midwest react differently than their Middle Atlantic and northeastern comrades? Did soldiers in the Army of the Potomac, many of whom retained a fondness for McClellan throughout the war, differ from western counterparts who fought under Grant and Sherman? Estimates of support among white veterans for emancipation as part of the North's national strategy thus far have been impressionistic. It would be helpful to have a better sense of the proportion of men who were or became genuinely committed to emancipation as a major strategic goal.[57]

A pair of recent historians probed largely unexplored connections between the northern press and Union strategy. Eric T. Dean, Jr., wrote that numerous historians who have characterized "the Civil War as the 'first modern war' . . . have seemingly overlooked the communications revolution and the effect it might have exerted on perceptions, expectations, and the course and outcome of the war." Dean argued that the press created "extravagant expectations" regarding McClellan's 1862 Peninsula campaign that resulted in a public belief that the general had failed strategically. Later in the war the media exercised "a modicum of self-restraint and the government began to employ methods of news management and censorship," which together muted the "excesses of the expectations game." In an essay on Grant's overland campaign, Brooks D. Simpson took issue with Dean's conclusions, maintaining that by May 1864 "[t]hree years of war apparently had taught the northern public little about the patterns of war." Northerners still craved decisive battlefield triumphs and pushed their generals to achieve them. Editors encouraged such thinking prior to Grant's commencing operations against Lee and continued to do so even after two weeks of bloody and indecisive combat. Democratic editors proved especially strident in calling for quick victory, but their Republican counterparts also "gave in to the notion of swift triumph." A detailed study of how the press dealt with strategic questions would constitute a worthy addition to the literature.[58]

The role of the navy languishes among the most neglected aspects of northern strategic planning. Beyond perfunctory consideration of how the blockade figured in Winfield Scott's Anaconda Plan, most discussions of northern strategy virtually ignore its naval component. In light of the absence of a modern, manuscript-based study of the United States Navy during the Civil War, it should not be surprising, though it is lamentable, that no historian has written a specialized study about Union strategists and the navy.[59]

Rowena Reed took a step toward remedying this problem in *Combined Operations in the Civil War*. In a narrative flecked with analysis that went against the prevailing interpretive grain, Reed praised McClellan for attempting to employ the full array of Union military might in his planning as general-in-chief and especially in devising his 1862 Peninsula campaign. Having "built his grand strategic design around interservice cooperation," he failed when Lincoln's government reduced his authority over the North's armed forces. No other northern general ever matched McClellan's grasp of the potential inherent in combined operations, argued Reed, and his peers as Union army commanders "agreed with the Lincoln administration that wars were only won by slugging it out on the battlefield." McClellan's retreat from the Peninsula "signalled both the demise of Federal grand strategy and the breakdown of combined operations planning." Subsequent Union success along the western rivers and the Gulf of Mexico, which included an obvious naval component, did not impress Reed. "The Federal offensive on the Mississippi and the Gulf after the collapse of McClellan's plan, taken as a whole," she wrote, "is probably one of the worst examples of combined operations strategy in the history of war." The North succeeded only because of "the enemy's tremendous relative weakness."[60]

The advent of Henry W. Halleck as general-in-chief "practically ensured that, except for the capture of Vicksburg, all subsequent major offensives were conducted by the land forces." This short-sightedness, in Reed's opinion, might have lengthened the conflict. For example, Sherman's famous march to Savannah represented a spectacular but ultimately empty campaign that, "leaving aside Sherman's personal ambition . . . accomplished nothing that could not have been more quickly and cheaply attained by other means." Had Sherman's army been shifted to Baltimore after the fall of Atlanta to cooperate with naval forces in a massive expedition against Wilmington, "Lee would have been maneuvered out of Richmond in December 1864."[61]

A pair of historians challenged Reed's conclusions about the quality of combined strategic planning and execution in the western theater. Writing thirteen years before Reed's book appeared, John D. Milligan attributed to Grant and naval squadron commander David Dixon Porter a working relationship that permitted the North to achieve its strategic goal of seizing control of the Mississippi River. Porter sought always to defer to Grant: "This fact alone made it possible for Grant to lay his plans with the navy always included as an equal partner, and only because he was able to do this could the final Vicksburg campaign take the form he gave it." Joseph T. Glatthaar took a similar view in *Partners in Command*, which devoted a chapter to the successful collaboration among Grant, Sherman, and Porter. Highlighting the ways in which the navy contributed to the Vicksburg campaign, Glatthaar emphasized the respect for one another and confidence in joint operations that developed among the three men. As Grant put it after capturing the Confederate stronghold, "Without this prompt and cordial support [from Porter and his naval squadron], my movements would have been much embarrassed, if not wholly defeated." Porter subsequently fell out with Grant over the 1864–1865 campaign to capture Wilmington, North Carolina, a venture for which the naval officer believed Grant took credit despite having done little to help ensure its success.[62]

One last naval title deserves mention. In *From Cape Charles to Cape Fear: The North Atlantic Blockading Squadron during the Civil War,* Robert M. Browning, Jr., lamented the fact that American historians have treated "the United States Navy as a minor player." His study of one component of the Union naval effort serves as a case study of how seaborne power bolstered the North's strategic agenda. Operating along the coasts and rivers of Virginia and North Carolina, the North Atlantic Blockading Squadron intercepted blockade-runners, which harmed the southern economy and by extension its armies; disrupted Confederate transportation in coastal areas, thereby exacerbating Robert E. Lee's logistical problems; and tied down thousands of troops who otherwise could have reinforced rebel field armies. Like Rowena Reed, Browning criticized the North's neglect of naval power as a potentially decisive weapon in Virginia after the Peninsula campaign (unlike Reed, he labeled McClellan unable fully "to understand the advantages that the navy provided him"). "The successive Union commanders attempted to outmaneuver the Confederate army to capture Richmond," averred Browning, while failing to exploit "the advantages that control of the water could give them." The situation changed during 1864 and 1865, when Grant made full use of the squadron to guard communications and bases of supply, transport soldiers, and support vulnerable positions along the James River. At Wilmington, the army and navy eventually mounted "a model operation" that "dealt a severe blow to the Confederacy." Browning quoted Confederate Secretary of the Navy Stephen A. Mallory's observation in April 1865 that Confederates were "weary of the war and desire peace." "The United States Navy," he concluded, "was a key factor in making this happen."[63]

Scholarly interest in the development and application of northern strategy undoubtedly will continue. Compelling figures such as Lincoln, Grant, Sherman, and McClellan invite constant re-examination.[64] The seismic impact of emancipation on Union policy makers and on armies in the field virtually guarantees that this dimension of the North's strategic debate will be explored repeatedly. Some historians undoubtedly will follow familiar analytical paths in responding to and revising the conclusions of T. Harry Williams, Herman Hattaway and Archer Jones, and other influential writers. Just as surely, future scholars will come up with new questions and approaches that illuminate heretofore obscure facets of the subject. The navy should receive a larger share of scholarly attention, which will illuminate the nautical dimension of Union strategic planning. The result will be a more nuanced understanding of how the North traversed its difficult course from Fort Sumter, which signaled the need to confront a monumental military challenge, to Appomattox, which placed the stamp of victory on national and operational strategies that had experienced a fascinating evolution.

# Rebellion and Conventional Warfare

## Confederate Strategy and Military Policy

### EMORY M. THOMAS

The armed forces of the Confederate States lost the American Civil War. Such was and is the ultimate reality of Confederate military policy and strategy. And this fundamental fact of failure has driven subsequent discussions of the Confederate military. The central question, once wailed by those who survived the war and even now debated over breakfast by otherwise postmodern people, has been, What went wrong? Why did Southern arms suffer defeat?

At the most defining moment of Confederate defeat, at Appomattox Court House on April 9, 1865, Robert E. Lee answered this question quite simply. "After four years of arduous service, marked by unsurpassed courage and fortitude," Lee said in his farewell statement to his army, "the Army of Northern Virginia has been compelled to yield to overwhelming numbers and resources." For Lee, the contest that had been uneven from the beginning had resisted his efforts to alter the odds. In the words of the historian Richard N. Current almost a century later, "in view of the disparity of resources, it would have taken a miracle . . . to enable the South to win. As usual God was on the side of the heaviest battalions."[1]

Lee's simple assertion that his army had been "compelled to yield to overwhelming numbers and resources" has persisted in the historical literature and continued at the core of numerous analyses of Confederate failure. However, the "overwhelming numbers and resources" answer to the question of why the South lost a war for independence has been only one answer among many. Lee in his time was aware of what later historians have also known: that nothing in human experience is inevitable simply because it happened once. And human experience contains ample examples of military policies and strategies that have triumphed over "overwhelming numbers and resources."

Framed as answers to the quandary of southern defeat more than several dissections and critiques of Confederate military policy and strategy have emerged. This context is important. Analyses of southern policy and strategy thus far either directly or indirectly begin with fundamental assumptions about why the Confederacy lost the war. As often happens, the questions historians ask and the presuppositions upon which those questions rest determine the answers.[2]

The first challenge to Lee's explanation, "overwhelming numbers and resources," came very soon after Appomattox. Edward A. Pollard was an acerbic journalist who spent the war period writing for the *Richmond Examiner*. He also attempted to write instant history in a series of books that chronicled the war in a volume for each year. In 1866 Pollard published *The Lost Cause*, with the subtitle *A New Southern History of the War of the Confederates*. In his conclusion Pollard observed:

> There has been a very superficial, and, to some people, a very pleasant way of accounting for the downfall of the Southern Confederacy, by simply ascribing it to the great superiority of the North in numbers and resources. . . . This explanation of failure is of course agreeable to the Southern people. But the historical judgement rejects it, discovers the fallacy, and will not refuse to point it out. It is simply to be observed that the disparity of military force, as between North and South . . . , is not the natural one; and that the fact of only 174,223 Confederates being under arms in the last period of the war was the result of mal-administration, the defective execution of the Conscription law, the decay of the volunteer spirit, the unpopularity of the war, and that these are the causes which lie beyond this arithmetical inequality, which, in fact, produced the greater part of it.
>
> . . . The fallacy consists in taking the very results of Confederate mal-administration, and putting them in comparison against a full exhibition of Northern power in the war.

Pollard believed that the southern government, and especially President Jefferson Davis, was to blame for defeat. Davis failed to mobilize his armed forces effectively or to use the forces he did mobilize intelligently and so undermined Confederate morale everywhere. "[T]he great and melancholy fact remains," Pollard wrote, "that the Confederates, with an abler Government and more resolute spirit, might have accomplished their independence."[3]

Historians since Pollard have tended either toward some variation of Lee's explanation or toward some analysis emphasizing Confederate deficiency in leadership, as Pollard did, or deficiency in a variety of other factors from social structure, to gender, to ethnicity. What follows is an overview of this literature, with emphasis upon more recent themes.[4]

Within the classic works on the Confederacy is a rich variety of interpretations that speak to the sources of southern defeat and thus to military policy and strategy. Frank Lawrence Owsley in *State Rights in the Confederacy* (1925) contended that state rights, the political principle which lay at the base of secession and the would-be southern republic, doomed Confederate hopes for independence. State governors, Owsley pointed out, were seldom willing to give over troops to the larger cause and less willing to share supplies with troops from other states. Governor Zebulon Vance of North Carolina seemed to embody Owsley's thesis, and Owsley calculated: "at the same time Lee's men in Virginia were barefooted, almost without blankets, tents, and clothing, Vance had enough uniforms to give every man in Lee's army two apiece."[5]

When Owsley reached his conclusion that the very nature of the Confederacy doomed the southern cause in an industrial war with the North, he was the only academic historian among a school of southern poets (in the broadest sense of the term) who soon published their manifesto, *I'll Take My Stand* (1930). Convinced that the antebellum South had been an agrarian "best of all possible worlds," these intellectuals, loosely clustered about Vanderbilt University, called Fugitives because they seemed in flight from the present into the past, had firm ideas about what had gone wrong between 1861 and 1865.

Andrew Lytle and Allen Tate, especially, became convinced that "the West [trans-Appalachian] was the main theater of the war . . . and that Confederate failure there meant total failure." Lytle wrote *Bedford Forrest and His Critter Company* (1931); Tate produced biographies of Jefferson Davis (1929) and Stonewall Jackson (1928). They perceived Forrest and Robert E. Lee at opposite poles of Confederate strategy and endorsed Forrest's guerrilla-style warfare. "Lee was a European to the last and Forrest was a Southern American. [Lee] valued his own honor more than the independence of the South. If he had taken matters into his own hands, he might have saved the situation; he was not willing to do this. It would have violated his Sunday School morality."

Tate and Lytle were often bitter and desperately sought some way in which their homeland might have won its independence. They were better poets than strategists, though, spinning dreams about Forrest and the Confederate heartland and characterizing the legacy of those who died in vain. In Tate's words from "Ode to the Confederate Dead":"The hound bitch / Toothless and dying in a musty cellar / Hears the wind only."[6]

Bell Irvin Wiley's considerable reputation as a southern historian rests in large measure upon his ground-breaking research in works such as *Southern Negroes, 1861–1865* (1938), *The Life of Johnny Reb* (1943), and *The Life of Billy Yank* (1952). Wiley's most thoughtful attempt at synthesis and interpretation is *The Road to Appomattox* (1956), in which he emphasizes dissent and contention within the Confederate government and military command and harkens back to Pollard in his criticism of Jefferson Davis. At the very end of this extended essay, however, Wiley makes a telling observation that most readers overlook. Among "failures that were fatal" Wiley lists as "most serious" southern failure to appreciate the depth of the North's devotion to the Union. He concludes: "Even if Lee had won at Gettysburg and captured Washington, New York, and Philadelphia, it seems extremely doubtful . . . that the outcome of the war would have been other than what it was."[7]

Douglas Southall Freeman wrote four volumes (1934–1935) of biography on Robert E. Lee and three volumes (1942–1944) about command in the Army of Northern Virginia. Freeman's extended association with Lee and his army rendered the historian much in thrall to the campaigns in Virginia and to Lee's perceptions of policy and strategy. It should be no surprise that Freeman, like Lee, believed that the Confederacy yielded to "overwhelming numbers and resources." But Freeman added much of substance to this judgment. Careful study convinced him, to cite one example, that a nation possesses only a finite number of potentially good general officers and that by May of 1863 the Confederacy had exhausted its supply. Freeman concluded: "It perhaps is a mistake to assume that when a small nation wages a long war it trains in the exacting but instructive school of battle an inexhaustible supply of general officers." So does Freeman add "talent" to numbers and resources in his analysis of the long odds that confronted Confederates.[8]

Other classic works in Confederate history connect one or more flaws or failures to military defeat. Charles W. Ramsdell in *Behind the Lines in the Southern Confederacy* (1944) identified financial policy as the "greatest single weakness" because the irredeemable paper currency crippled the government at the same time that it destroyed the security and morale of the citizens. The titles used by other historians indicate the focuses of their studies: Albert B. Moore, *Conscription and Conflict in the Confederacy* (1924). Ella Lonn, *Desertion during the Civil War* (1928); and

Georgia L. Tatum, *Disloyalty in the Confederacy* (1934).[9] The list could continue; the books cited above are but a sample of a large corpus.

Few of the historians who wrote important books during the first century after the war believed that they were writing military history. But they did. They posed solutions to the riddle of Confederate defeat, solutions to problems that directly or indirectly conditioned military policy and strategy. In so doing they expanded the definition of military history to encompass the total experience of a people engaged in war—an important and enlightened revision for the most part. More recently, during the last three or four decades, the best scholarship on the Confederacy has followed this pattern and attempted to explain military events by examining an expanded context both on and off the battlefield.

Please notice the care taken above to say that "the best scholarship" about the Confederacy took an expansive view of the South and the war. Much too much that has passed as Confederate military history has constricted, and so contorted, the field. Scholars obsessed with a zeal to discover with precision what happened, when, and to whom have filled library shelves with tomes about narrow topics possessed of neither context nor conclusion. Such writing all but screams, So what? Why should anyone care? Too often, what has passed for military history, and this is especially true of the military history of the American Civil War, has been antiquarian chronicle—perhaps the product of prodigious research, sometimes artfully written, a tale well told—but not history because the authors seem neither to know nor to care what their facts mean.

Perhaps Italian historian Raimondo Luraghi has said it best. In the preface of his *Rise and Fall of the Plantation South* (1978), Luraghi states the case for an expansive understanding of military history. "Military problems, if studied in a vacuum, do not make much sense. War is the hardest test to which a given society is subjected. Every society meets this challenging strain in a way that is directly linked to its social, moral, ethical—in other words, its cultural—scale of values. Consequently, we could say that any people are led, both politically and militarily, in the way they deserve to be; or, less drastically, that any society wages its own peculiar kind of warfare. It was not by chance that the Romans, during the Punic wars, used a wide levée en masse, whereas the Carthaginians had to rely mainly on mercenary troops, or even that modern, industrial countries make use of technological warfare, which was pushed by Hitler to the very point of industrializing death."[10]

By the time that Luraghi wrote this, he had already established himself as an innovative scholar of the American experience. *The Rise and Fall of the Plantation South* is a distillation of ideas he had developed in his *Gli Stati Uniti* (1974) and *Storia della Guerra Civile Americana* (1966).

Luraghi understands the American Civil War as the triumph of industrial capitalism in the North over the seignorial, agrarian South. Nevertheless, Luraghi credits the Confederacy with creating an industrial wartime economy *ex nihilo* and for generating this industrial base without raising up a "powerful industrial bourgeoisie." "Instead they chose the way of 'state socialism,' a solution that is as far from capitalism as the earth is from the moon." Luraghi continues, "It is amazing to see how clear-mindedly, how creatively Southern leaders discovered this direction, previously unknown, and followed it. The man who, more than any other, embodied this stroke of genius was President Jefferson Davis. Be it only for this, he should rank among the major statesmen in history."

Here is Jefferson Davis the soul-mate of Mao-tse Tung. But, however heroic its effort, the agrarian Confederacy succumbed in the war against industrial capitalists. Southerners built twenty-eight ironclad warships; the Union built fifty-three and even sold two more to the Italian Royal Navy. "This fact, far more than a million books and a billion statistics," Luraghi concludes, "helps to explain why the South lost the Civil War."[11]

Frank E. Vandiver and Raimondo Luraghi are friends. Yet, they are quite unlike—the former president of Texas A & M and an Italian Marxist. Nevertheless, Vandiver and Luraghi share some fundamental understandings of the Confederacy. Vandiver's *Ploughshares into Swords: Josiah Gorgas and Confederate Ordnance* (1952) informs Luraghi's and everyone else's admiration of the wonders wrought in southern war industry. In *Rebel Brass: The Confederate Command System* (1956) Vandiver offers a thorough critique of the failings of southern military policy—the rigidity of the "departmental" system of command, rancor within the high command, brief enlistments for initial volunteers, and insufficient planning for the logistics of an extended war. Vandiver, however, also recognizes the creative efforts of the Davis government to overcome these failings— institution of "theater command" in the Confederate West, conscription of southern troops, central control of war industry, and, eventually, acceptance of African American soldiers within the southern armies.[12]

These latter themes Vandiver emphasizes in his later works, the most significant of which is *Their Tattered Flags: The Epic of the Confederacy* (1970). In this epic, the hero is Jefferson Davis, and Vandiver (no less than Luraghi) gives the Confederate president credit for creative statecraft and Confederate nationalism. Like Lee, Luraghi, and others, Vandiver contends that the southern nation succumbed to superior numbers and resources. As he phrased it in his *Basic History of the Confederacy* (1962). "For four terrible years the South sustained a total war, mobilized and managed a modern industrial effort, and lost utterly. The very totality of defeat is evidence of maximum effort. . . . The Confederate States was first exhausted, then defeated."[13]

Vandiver also shifts the emphasis of his analysis away from factors political, social, and economic toward the military circumstance. At issue is a chicken/egg, cause/effect relationship between southern armies and the other elements of the Confederate nation. Vandiver points to the truth, so obvious as to have been overlooked, that the Confederacy always existed in the midst of a war for its national survival. As he writes with regard to southern diplomacy, "the best Southern chance rested always with Confederate soldiers. When they gained victories, independence came close; when they lost, nothing else mattered."[14]

Not the least of Jefferson Davis's claims to greatness as a wartime president in Vandiver's view was his capacity as commander-in-chief. Although Davis possessed all the limitations Vandiver catalogues in *Rebel Brass,* the Confederate president also developed the strategy of the offensive-defense—allow enemy armies to penetrate, and then, when circumstances are most favorable, strike these armies decisively—a strategy that Vandiver pronounces "seemed the only true course for the inferior side."[15]

The most recent biography of Davis, *Jefferson Davis: The Man and His Hour* (1991) by William C. Davis, echoes Vandiver's judgment. Davis is especially acute in his account of the Confederate president as commander-in-chief. Biographer Davis concludes about "overall military strategy" that "it would be difficult to conceive of another better calculated to postpone the inevitable." The "defensive-offensive" as Jefferson Davis practiced it, "allowed an underdog to stay alive as long as possible, in the hope of wearing down the opponent's will to continue, as with the colonists during the Revolution."[16]

My own variation of the Lee-Freeman-Luraghi-Vandiver strain of thought regarding Confederate policy and strategy begins with an extended essay, *The Confederacy as a Revolutionary Experience* (1971). The focus of this book is on the radical nature of the movement for secession and then upon creative ways in which Confederate southerners transformed the very way of life they had seceded to protect. In keeping with the revolutionary theme, I stress the unconventional aspects of Confederate warfare—blockade-running, commerce-raiding on the high seas, the partisan activities of John S. Mosby and John Hunt Morgan, and the unconventional campaigns and raids of Nathan Bedford Forrest, J. E. B. Stuart, and Stonewall Jackson. I suggest that the Confederates attempted to emulate those other American revolutionaries and win independence in the same way that George Washington and the Continental Army had done. And I contend that some Confederates, including Davis, "rose above traditional military wisdom and waged revolution."[17]

In *The Confederate Nation, 1861–1865* (1979), a subsequent work in the New American Nation Series intended to expand and elaborate upon ideas expressed in *The Confederacy as a Revolutionary Experience,* I revise this unconventional emphasis significantly. I argue that "as long as partisan activity threatened Southerners' commitment to people and place, invited reprisals from the enemy, and precluded the maintenance of racial subordination in slavery, the Confederates eschewed guerrilla warfare." And in the conclusion I use the rejection of guerrilla warfare as evidence that southerners "affirmed that culture of the folk—the primacy of people and place—that perhaps best defined them as a people."[18]

The larger focus of *The Confederate Nation, 1861–1865* is upon the transformation wrought by Confederates of the crucial tenets of their antebellum way of life. In the quest for independence, "the Confederacy became characterized by tendencies toward political nationalism, industrialism, urbanization, realism, an aristocracy of merit, national culture, and liberated womanhood." And ultimately white southerners showed themselves willing to emancipate their slaves in the vain hope of victory. Of course, none of these sacrifices and transformations was sufficient to save the southern nation. Nevertheless, I contend, that nation existed, and the creative energies of Confederate southerners were impressive indeed.[19]

Emphasis upon Confederate nationalism and achievement in a war that Confederate southerners lost is, of course, tenuous. At best, such emphasis is analogous to four ounces of liquid in an eight-ounce container; the container is half-full. But the container is also half-empty, and numerous historians emphasize the deficiency. Paul D. Escott in his *After Secession: Jefferson Davis and the Failure of Confederate Nationalism* (1978) argues with considerable evidence that the Richmond government was unable to secure the loyalty of the mass of white southerners and so lost the war. Escott views the war as a crisis in southern society that divided yeoman farmers from the plantation elite and thus crippled the war effort. The supposedly "solid South" succumbed to class conflict, and disaffection among the plain white folk doomed the cause by provoking draft evasion, withholding of supplies, and open resistance to the Confederate government. Thus does Escott achieve much more than an extension of the Owsley thesis that the Confederacy foundered upon state rights. Escott explains why common people, as well as southern governors, came to believe that the Confederate war was a "poor man's fight" for the interests of the planter class.[20]

Confederate nationalism or its absence certainly affected the capacity of southern armies to fight the war. And historians continue to debate the issue. Those interested should consult the essays by myself, Escott, Lawrence N. Powell and Michael S. Wayne, Leon Litwack, Michael Barton, and Thomas B. Alexander in *The Old South in the Crucible of War*, edited by Harry P. Owens and James J. Cooke (1983), as well as the more recent work by Drew Gilpin Faust, *The Creation of Confederate Nationalism: Ideology and Identity in the Civil War South* (1988).[21]

A focus upon Confederate nationalism or lack of nationalism and Jefferson Davis as wartime president and commander-in-chief derives to some extent from the understanding that "overwhelming numbers and resources" triumphed in 1865. In question is the degree to which Confederate southerners were able to delay the deluge. However, the literature of southern strategy is rich with examples of analysis in the wake of Edward A. Pollard; had it not been for some flaw or failed opportunity, the Confederates might have won.

Some of the most interesting ideas have appeared in print in the series of "why-and-how books" published from 1960 to 1992. The first of these, *Why the North Won the Civil War*, edited by David Herbert Donald (1960), misleads with its title; the essays in this work are really about why the South lost. Donald, for example, refines and extends the thesis of Frank Owsley and insists: "we should write on the tombstone of the Confederacy: 'Died of Democracy.'" Donald speaks of democracy in the antiauthoritarian, protopopulist sense of that supposedly regimented institution, the Confederate army. He points out the freedom that disloyal and disaffected southerners enjoyed to act out their dissent. And Donald finds it amazing that the administration of Jefferson Davis never even attempted to defeat or punish politically recalcitrant governors, such as Zebulon Vance or Joseph E. Brown. "The real weakness of the Confederacy was that the Southern people insisted upon retaining their democratic liberties in wartime."[22]

David M. Potter renews Edward A. Pollard's critique of Jefferson Davis. In addition to observing that Davis failed to relate to other Confederate leaders, both military and political, and to the southern people, Potter charges that Davis failed to understand his role as war president. "Davis always thought in terms of what was right, rather than in terms of how to win," Potter states, and condemns Davis for creating military departments and dispersing his troops to defend the country rather than concentrating forces to defeat the Federals. All of this Potter finds in stark contrast to Abraham Lincoln's approach and concludes that "if the Union and Confederacy had exchanged presidents with one another, the Confederacy might have won its independence."[23]

In his contribution to *Why the North Won the Civil War,* T. Harry Williams mounts a frontal assault upon the reputation of Robert E. Lee. Drawing upon criticism of Lee presented by J. F. C. Fuller in *Grant & Lee: A Study in Personality and Generalship* (1933), Williams argues that Lee never functioned beyond one theater of the war and that his "preoccupation with the war in Virginia" proved a "tragic command limitation in a modern war." Moreover, Williams contends, Lee failed "to grasp the vital relationship between war and statecraft." He did not understand that war and politics are inseparable and so eschewed matters political in the name of subordination and humility. Williams ranks Lee, along with Grant and Sherman, as "great" but believes that Lee limited the scope of his operations and influence and so fell into step with "a conservative war," "almost wholly defensive," "a cordon defense." Lee and the Confederates, Williams believes, ignored the "best chance to win . . . independence," which was a "concentrated mass offensive."[24]

Next among the "why-and-how books" was *How the North Won: A Military History of the Civil War* (1983) that the authors Herman Hattaway and Archer Jones dedicated to T. Harry Williams. Jones's contribution to the collaboration is evident in the emphasis upon the Confederate West as an important theater and upon the influence of Henri Jomini and the Napoleonic heritage on both sides. Jones had already established these ideas in his earlier book, *Confederate Strategy from Shiloh to Vicksburg* (1961). Hattaway and Jones call the northern war plan the strategy of exhaustion and claim that Davis countered with a strategy of territorial defense designed to make Union conquest as costly as possible. Davis, they claim, was at his best during the period in 1862 when Lee acted as his chief of staff (March through May). Thereafter Lee became too absorbed with the Army of Northern Virginia to help Davis with grand strategy. Hattaway and Jones hold up Lee as a "master of the art of war, but essentially the commander of one army in one theater of the war." For good military reasons Davis departed from state rights and attempted to centralize his government. But in the end, the South collapsed before the North's strategy of exhaustion, and Confederates considered continuing the struggle as guerrillas but shrank from such desperation and surrendered.[25]

Archer Jones came to his collaboration with Herman Hattaway in *How the North Won* not only through his own work but also through a volume about Confederate strategy that he co-authored with Thomas Lawrence Connelly, *The Politics of Command: Factions and Ideas in Confederate Strategy* (1973). Connelly and Jones portray Jefferson Davis as a harried leader beset by personnel problems and responding to pressures and ideas generated within his organization. He moved from crisis to crisis, resolving each by choosing among the alternatives presented by his staff, politicians, officers in the field, and his own ideas. The resulting decisions were a complex of the Napoleonic-Jomini influence: the ideas of Lee, the pressures brought to bear by Beauregard, the western concentration bloc and its network of informal associations, and Davis' own changing concept of the departmental command system.[26]

Connelly and Jones develop other important themes as well. They acknowledge the capacity of Robert E. Lee to win battles in Virginia but contend that Lee became so absorbed in the Virginia theater that he failed to consider the other theaters and compounded this failure by advising Davis, in effect, to share this provincial perception of the war.

A loose association of influential men, the members of four "blocs" bound by various loyalties, connections, and resentments, nominally led by P. G. T. Beauregard, formed what Connelly and Jones call "the western concentration bloc." This faction offered a strategic vision to Davis much at odds with Lee's counsel. The western concentration bloc believed what the name implies: the West was the crucial theater, and Davis should orchestrate the destruction of Federal armies there by massing as many southern troops as possible. Confederate strategy, Connelly and Jones believe, was the product of politics. Davis responded to all manner of people and plans. The degree to which he listened to Lee, however, Connelly and Jones consider unfortunate for the Confederacy.[27]

Connelly's contribution to Confederate military history would be difficult to overstate. By the time he combined with Jones to produce *The Politics of Command,* Connelly had written a two-volume history of the Army of Tennessee that remains the classic study of the Confederacy's western army—*Army of the Heartland: The Army of Tennessee, 1861–1862* (1967) and *Autumn of Glory: The Army of Tennessee, 1862–1865* (1971). In these works Connelly anticipated the contention in *The Politics of Command* that the West was the most important theater in the war.[28]

Connelly later expanded his critique of Lee in *The Marble Man: Robert E. Lee and His Image in American Society* (1977). Ostensibly this work is a study of Lee's image from his death in 1870 to the Civil War Centennial in the 1960s. Connelly insists that Virginians and men whose reputations grew in proportion with Lee's renown invented a Lee mythology. Later generations accepted and embellished the Lee legend until he became a contortion of the man he had been in life—a marble man.[29]

To describe a Lee myth, however, it becomes important to present Lee reality with which to contrast the myth. And so Connelly concludes his work on Lee's image with observations about Lee's life. "His life was replete with frustration, self-doubt, and a feeling of failure," Connelly writes, ". . . hidden behind his legendary reserve and his credo of duty and self-control. He was actually a troubled man, convinced that he failed as a prewar career officer, parent, and moral individual."[30]

Connelly continued to explore the significance of Lee in the southern mind with Barbara L. Bellows in *God and General Longstreet: The Lost Cause and the Southern Mind* (1982). The book is an insightful collection of essays that includes an extension of Connelly's understanding of Lee. In "Robert E. Lee and the Southern Mind" Lee becomes the quintessential southerner, possessed of the same sense of alienation, "classical Christian" piety, and extremist temperament that Connelly and Bellows claim define all southerners. Yet southerners insist upon rendering Lee as a middle-class icon; "once enshrined, his nature has become obscured."[31]

Much of Connelly's revisionist critique of Lee focuses upon Lee's person and upon what people made of Lee after his death. Yet with all his emphasis in *The Marble Man* upon Lee's feelings of failure while he was alive and contrived image after he died, Connelly offers a revisionist analysis of Lee's generalship as well. Connelly echoes T. Harry Williams's claim that Lee was too preoccupied with Virginia and expands this thesis. Not only was Lee obsessed with the Virginia theater of the war; he also exerted his considerable influence with Davis to garner troops and supplies for the Army of Northern Virginia at the expense of reinforcing western armies which usually (in Connelly's estimate) needed reinforcing much more. And Lee bled the Confederacy nearly dry in his horrendous battles, so that by late 1863 too few men remained to replace southern losses anywhere.[32]

In somewhat milder form, this is the conclusion about Lee as general drawn by Russell F. Weigley in *The American Way of War: A History of United States Military Strategy and Policy* (1973). Weigley concludes his chapter about Lee and the Confederacy:

Of many of the arts of war, R. E. Lee was a consummate master. He organized his army to extract the best possible efforts from his men and his lieutenants. Within his immediate theater of war, his logistical management was excellent. His famous victories rightly made him the Southern commander most feared by his enemies. In one of them, Second Manassas, he came as close as any general since Napoleon to duplicating the Napoleonic system of battlefield victory by fixing the enemy in position with a detachment, bringing the rest of the army onto his flank and rear, and then routing him front and flank. But Lee was too Napoleonic. Like Napoleon himself, with his passion for the strategy of annihilation and the climactic, decisive battle as its expression, he destroyed in the end not the enemy armies, but his own.[33]

Not since Andrew Lytle and Allen Tate scoffed at Lee's "Sunday School morality" has the general undergone such criticism. And Lee continues to be a subject of controversy in works more recent.

If Lee were obsessed with offensive strategy, Grady McWhiney and Perry D. Jamieson would excuse him for acting out the Celtic heritage that McWhiney believes dominated southern life. McWhiney and Jamieson in *Attack and Die: Civil War Military Tactics and the Southern Heritage* (1982) contend that Confederates were not simply offensive-minded; the southerners seemed addicted to wild, desperate charges upon their enemies. Certainly the experience of the United States Army in the Mexican War conditioned those who fought or studied the battles against Santa Anna's army to believe in offensive tactics and strategy. In nearly every major engagement the troops from the United States had attacked the Mexicans and won victories. But soldiers on both sides in the Mexican War fought with muskets with an effective range of one hundred yards; in the Civil War infantrymen used rifles, and these weapons were effective at three to five hundred yards. Troops in a defensive position had an advantage over those attacking them. In addition, morale, training, and logistics among Santa Anna's soldiers were notoriously poor. In the Civil War, attackers usually confronted defenders whose spirit and supplies were equal to their own. Generals on both sides of the Civil War had to forget much of their military education and ignore a lot of conventional wisdom to adjust to circumstances that favored the defense.

McWhiney and Jamieson argue that the Confederates seemed incapable of understanding the advantage of defense warfare. Southern armies seemed determined to attack, and, because they did, they sustained enormous casualties. The source of these bloodbaths, McWhiney and Jamieson claim, was southern—the inherited traits of Celtic peoples. McWhiney and Jamieson contend that ethnically white southerners were predominately Celtic and that massive, wild charges had characterized Celtic warfare for two thousand years. Hence, "the continued devotion of Celts to their wild attacks showed that they valued tradition more than success. For more than two thousand years they relied almost exclusively upon a single tactic in warfare—the charge." McWhiney and Jamieson "contend that the Confederates bled themselves nearly to death in the first three years of the war by making costly attacks more often than did the Federals."[34]

Debate about the Celtic thesis as an explanation for Confederate defeat has been lively and might have been even more so had it not been for the publication of another "why-and-how" book—*Why the South Lost the Civil War* (1986) by Richard E. Beringer, Herman Hattaway, Archer Jones, and William N. Still, Jr. These authors devote an appendix to challenging the numbers and conclusions of *Attack and Die*.[35]

Four authors, each of whom possesses strong credentials, say many things with one voice. One of them, presumably Jones, attempts to measure the military performance of both northern and southern generals by comparing what they did to the approaches of the acknowledged "patristic fathers" of nineteenth-century warfare, Karl von Clausewitz and Antoine Henri Jomini. This analysis indicates that sources of Confederate defeat lay beyond the battlefields.[36]

Another author, probably Still, offers novel and significant credit to the Confederate Navy and its civilian counterpart, the blockade-runners. Southerners did achieve successes at sea, although the best statements of these achievements are not in *Why the South Lost the Civil War*. Still's *Iron Afloat: The Story of the Confederate Armorclads* (1971) makes a strong case for the defensive capacity of Confederate ironclads, and his *Confederate Shipbuilding* (1969) demonstrates the ingenuity of southerners in constructing vessels of war. The best work on the Confederate Navy is Raimondo Luraghi's *History of the Confederate Navy* (1996). About the blockade-runners the authority is Stephen R. Wise, who concludes his *Lifeline of the Confederacy: Blockade Running during the Civil War* (1988):

> Because of the work of the men involved in blockade running, a supply lifeline was maintained until the very last months of the war. The Confederate soldiers had the equipment and food needed to meet their adversaries. Defeat did not come from the lack of material; instead the Confederacy simply no longer had the manpower to resist, and the nation collapsed.

Still's probable contribution to *Why the South Lost the Civil War* is a reminder that ships and sailors contributed to the southern war effort.[37]

Much, if not most, of the emphasis in this collaboration concerns Confederate nationalism and the lack of it in the wartime South. The authors eventually conclude that "the Confederacy succumbed to internal rather than external causes. An insufficient nationalism failed to survive the strains imposed by lengthy hostilities." Alienated by their government, imposed upon by restrictions and regulations, afflicted by hardships and privation, and beset with the guilt of defending slavery, "Confederates, by thousands of individual decisions, abandoned the struggle for and allegiance to the Confederate States of America."[38]

Also involved in those "thousands of individual decisions" was the spiritual malaise of a people concerned on whose side God might be. If God were testing the southern white people, then perhaps a little adversity might be a good thing. But, these authors argue, adversity such as the Confederacy suffered in 1864 seemed a clear revelation of God's disfavor. And the guilt of holding slaves seems to Berringer et al. to have been a strong source of weakened will among Confederates, both soldiers and civilians.

The authors of *Why the South Lost the Civil War* acknowledge their debt to previous scholarship about Confederate defeat. Ultimately their conclusion comes down to a queer amalgam of the ideas of E. Merton Coulter and Kenneth M. Stampp. Coulter, in his massive book *The Confederate States of America, 1861–1865* (1950), finally concluded: "The forces leading to defeat were many but they may be summed up in this one fact: The people did not will hard enough and long enough to win." Stampp closed an essay entitled "The Southern Road to Appomattox" (originally a lecture delivered in 1968) this way:

> The fatal weakness of the Confederacy was that not enough of its people really thought that defeat would be a catastrophe; and, moreover, I believe that many of them unconsciously felt that the fruits of defeat would be less bitter than those of success.

Berringer, Hattaway, Jones and Still believe, "The epitaph on the Confederacy's tombstone should read, 'Died of Guilt and Failure of Will.'"[39]

In rough accord with Stampp's conclusion, the authors of *Why the South Lost the Civil War* extend their analysis beyond Appomattox and speculate about the reality that the title of their book represents. Did, in fact, the South lose the Civil War? "Southerners eventually resolved the dissonance between the world as it was and the world as they had wanted it to be by securing enough of their war aims—state rights, white supremacy, and honor—to permit them to claim their share of the victory."[40]

After *Why the South Lost the Civil War,* Archer Jones wrote another book, entitled *Civil War Command and Strategy: The Process of Victory and Defeat* (1992). He emphasizes the European authorities Napoleon and Jomini and looks backward to the sources of southern strategy. He gives Davis more credit than he had previously and praises Lee and Beauregard, too. Jones somehow manages to render Lee a defensive strategist and interprets Lee's battles, save Gettysburg, as "innovative defensive use of the turning movement and the raid."[41]

Edward Hagerman and his work *The American Civil War and the Origins of Modern Warfare* (1988) are anomalies among most of the historians and histories considered here. Hagerman is clinical, all but devoid of passion, in his analysis. Hagerman claims "two basic contributions to the understanding of the Civil War and modern military culture." He breaks "new ground in the analysis of the theory, doctrine, and practice of field fortification in the tactical evolution of trench warfare." Hagerman also offers "a new analysis of the development of field transportation and supply." These are important contributions, especially Hagerman's understanding of transportation and supply.[42]

Here is some of his insight regarding Lee and the eastern theater of the war:

> The terrible deterioration of his army when on the march was the price of moving with a transportation and supply system pushed beyond its limits. But arguably, it was the price that he had to pay to prevent the greater military disaster, namely, Union penetration of Virginia and the consequent loss of essential communications and supplies. The results indicated that he achieved his strategic objectives through Gettysburg. The consequences for his army indicated that to sustain this type of strategy under the same or deteriorating logistical circumstances would destroy that army.

And here is Hagerman's tribute to trenches:

> In this last, desperate, year-long campaign, Lee, by keeping Grant bottled up in the limited area between Washington and the James, had shown that an army fighting on interior lines, even under nearly overwhelming conditions of deprivation and against vastly superior numbers, could sustain a prolonged existence by the use of field fortification and defensive maneuver. Until its logistical base completely collapsed, the Army of Northern Virginia had successfully exploited the entrenched defense and defensive maneuver on interior lines. In the process, from the Wilderness through Cold Harbor, it had inflicted 64,000 casualties on the enemy, a number equal to

the largest size the Army of Northern Virginia attained during the year. In its defensive stand of almost eight months before Petersburg and Richmond, it inflicted approximately 50,000 more casualties, while itself suffering approximately one-third that number. In defeat and in victory, the two armies revealed the changed conditions of warfare as they affected tactical and strategic mobility, providing military thought with a great deal to digest as it sought to avoid the specter of endless trench warfare.[43]

As his title and the above passage indicates, Hagerman tends to look, forward in his analysis and project the American Civil War onto the larger stage in Europe between 1914 and 1918. This is military history for military historians. Hagerman speculates about Lee's "Celtic warrior élan," and he describes the gore of the "Bloody Angle" at Spotsylvania, "perhaps the grimmest spectacle of trench warfare in the Civil War." For the most part, though, Hagerman's book resembles in tone a bridge column in the daily newspaper—North squandered the chance to finesse the King and so never reaped advantage from South's clubs.[44]

In terms of the dichotomy between Lee's "overwhelming numbers and resources" and Pollard's emphasis upon "Confederate mal-administration," Hagerman and Jones seem to be in tune with Lee's explanation. Yet both of these historians also emphasize southern bungling, for which neither really assigns fault. Maybe the literature of southern military policy and strategy has risen above blame and the perceived need to identify some southern circumstance, which, had it been otherwise, might have enabled the Confederacy to win. At least the questions have become more analytical, concerned with how more than whom.

Charles Royster does not seem to care who won the war. In his insightful book *The Destructive War: William Tecumseh Sherman, Stonewall Jackson, and the Americans* (1991), Royster asks how the war became so destructive of life and property. Why was this war so mean, so vindictive, so productive of righteous hatred? These are Royster's queries, and his answer is disturbing. From the very beginning, he contends, many participants believed that they had to punish their enemies, make them feel sorry that they had ever entered this combat. William Tecumseh Sherman and Stonewall Jackson are Royster's principal exhibits, the combatants most committed to destruction. Royster insists that Sherman and Jackson were caricatures, exaggerated embodiments of their respective sides. "The destructive war grew from small beginnings; yet it was also present or incipient at the start of the fighting. The people who made it surprised themselves, but the surprise consisted, in part, of getting what they had asked for."[45]

Of course, Royster does not possess a monopoly on tales of gratuitous burning and bloodletting. Phillip Shaw Paludan in *Victims: A True Story of the Civil War* (1981) documents and attempts to understand the murders of thirteen suspected Unionist sympathizers from Shelton Laurel, North Carolina, in January 1863. In "The Seeds of Disaster," Lesley J. Gordon details the arbitrary execution of twenty-two "deserters" in Kinston, North Carolina, in February 1864, by George E. Pickett, "hero" of the Confederates' famous charge at Gettysburg the previous July. And Brian Steel Wills in *Battle from the Start: The Life of Nathan Bedford Forrest* is one of a number of scholars who have addressed the role of Forrest at Fort Pillow.[46]

The works mentioned are but samples of the recent emphasis upon atrocities and irregulars, especially on the southern side. Maybe Beringer, Hattaway, Jones, and Still; Coulter; and Stampp have raised an issue worth exploring further. Was the option, indeed the precedent, for a guerrilla war viable? Should Jefferson Davis's "new phase" of the war have been a final extension of Confederate strategy?

The best answer to these questions at present comes from George M. Fredrickson's Fortenbaugh Memorial Lecture at Gettysburg College published as the pamphlet "Why the Confederacy Did Not Fight a Guerrilla War after the Fall of Richmond: A Comparative View." Fredrickson compares the southern situation with that of the Afrikaners in the Boer, or South African, War. He concludes that: "The most significant and salient difference [between Afrikaners and Confederates] was not in the probable extent of racial fear or anxiety but rather in the degree of class stratification and potential class conflict among the whites in the two societies." Guerrilla warfare threatened to "turn the social order on its head by making coarse and uncivilized back country whites the leading actors in the drama." The Boers, Fredrickson states, had no basis for similar fears; for the planter elite in the South, the guerrilla option portended class suicide.[47]

The fourth and, for now, final, "why-and-how" book about southern defeat is Gabor S. Boritt, ed., *Why the Confederacy Lost* (1992). This collection of essays is the product of the Civil War Institute at Gettysburg College, one in a series of books drawn from the papers presented each summer when the institute convenes at the college. There is symmetry in the fact that the first "why-and-how book" was the product of another conference of scholars at Gettysburg more than thirty years earlier (*Why the North Won the Civil War*, ed. Donald). *Why the Confederacy Lost* is certainly one indication of the continuing interest in the Civil War among general readers and "buffs." But it is also an important book because of the scholars represented and the exciting new directions of their scholarship.[48]

James M. McPherson, whose *Battle Cry of Freedom: The Civil War Era* (1988) is clearly the best general history of the period now in print, contributes "American Victory, American Defeat," a critique of several of the reasons historians have offered for Confederate defeat. Particularly telling is McPherson's analysis of the "loss of will" thesis set forth by Beringer et al. in *Why the South Lost the Civil War*. He points out the circular nature of the logic; defeat in battle led to loss of will, which in turn led to more defeat. Defeat caused defeatism; not the other way around. Hence the answer to the question implied by the title of the book lies in military defeat, which in turn produced a loss of will to continue the war.

Then, having confronted and discounted most of the reasons most often offered for Confederate defeat, McPherson refines a theme from *Battle Cry of Freedom*—the role of "contingency." He identifies moments, most of them military, when victory or defeat hung in the balance, and the issue might easily have been resolved either way. The four "turning points" offered here are: 1) McClellan failed to capture Richmond, and suddenly the Confederates were invading the United States—Lee in Maryland, Bragg in Kentucky; 2) The Confederate twin offensive then failed—Lee at Antietam/Sharpsburg and Bragg at Perryville; 3) Confederates suffered defeats during the summer and fall of 1863—Gettysburg, Vicksburg, and Chattanooga; and 4) Federal capture of Atlanta and Philip Sheridan's successes in the Shenandoah Valley ensured Lincoln's reelection in November 1864. War compels the study of military history. Only when scholars understand how and why each contingency happened the way it did will they understand why the Confederacy did not survive.[49]

Gary W. Gallagher strikes another blow for attention to military history in his contribution, "'Upon Their Success Hang Momentous Interests': Generals." He "proceeds from the assumption that generals made a very great difference in determining the outcome of the war. Their actions decided events on the battlefield, which in turn either calmed or aggravated internal tensions that affected the ability of each government to prosecute the war."[50]

Gallagher reviews the historiographical fates of the generals assumed to have had the most influence on the outcome of the war—Grant, Sherman, and Lee. His ultimate focus is on Lee. He reviews the revisionist critiques of Lee by J. F. C. Fuller, Thomas L. Connelly, and Connelly and Archer Jones, and then he turns to the testimony of Lee's contemporaries to demonstrate the depth and intensity of Lee's influence in sustaining a Confederate will to win. Gallagher concludes about Lee: "He formulated a national strategy predicated on the probability of success in Virginia and the value of battlefield victories. The ultimate failure of his strategy neither proves that it was wrongheaded nor diminishes Lee's pivotal part in keeping Confederate resistance alive through four brutally destructive years."[51]

Gallagher's summary and commentary about Lee is essentially an extension of the process of revision and reassessment. Richard M. McMurry entered the debate with *Two Great Rebel Armies: An Essay in Confederate Military History* (1989). His title clearly suggests his conclusions about the Army of Northern Virginia and the Army of Tennessee; his research and reasoning are penetrating and profound. McMurray's final chapter, "Historians and Generals," answers the Connelly and Connelly-Jones revisions of Lee point by point. McMurray is convincing.[52]

By the time McMurry's book had gained the recognition of scholars, another revisionist assault on Lee was available in libraries and bookstores. Alan T. Nolan's *Lee Considered: General Robert E. Lee and Civil War History* (1991) is an imitation, albeit pale, of Connelly's *The Marble Man*. Nolan contends that Lee was significantly less an officer and a gentleman than his myth avers. As a general, Lee, Nolan accuses, squandered Confederate blood and resources in campaigns and battles that did not resolve anything and, worse, precluded victory. Nolan's book reveals a spirit mean and sad, and neither of these adjectives applies to Lee.[53]

In the face of Connelly's criticism, Nolan's cant, and a tide of revision, Charles P. Roland published *Reflections on Lee: A Historian's Assessment* (1995). "Notwithstanding Lee's mistakes and weaknesses, whether real or imagined, his generalship was the crux of the Confederacy's extraordinary military effort. Massively outnumbered in the field and operating under virtually every other handicap known to war, he repeatedly brought the Union to the edge of despair. That anyone else could have done more is beyond demonstration. It challenges credibility."[54]

In the same year that Roland's *Reflections* appeared, I published *Robert E. Lee: A Biography* (1995). I attempt to present Lee whole—as a person who achieved greatness out of the human condition. One of the most admirable qualities I find in Lee was his capacity to make the best of any circumstance in which he found himself. Certainly he did this when he commanded the Army of Northern Virginia; his greatest victories emerged from desperate situations.

Lee's experience during the first year of the war was important to his strategic understanding of this war and of Confederate prospects. From the time he accepted command of Virginia forces in April 1861 until he assumed command of the Army of Northern Virginia on June 1, 1862, Lee held no combat command. He experienced frustration—in western Virginia, on the coasts of South Carolina, Georgia, and Florida, and in Richmond as adviser/chief of staff to Jefferson Davis. As a result he became convinced that the Confederacy would have to win decisive, climactic battles, annihilate at least one enemy army if the southern nation were to have any chance to win. And this annihilation had better occur sooner rather than later because the enemy would become stronger in men and resources at the same time the Confederacy became weaker. Lee's appropriation of the offensive-defense emphasized offense.

Jefferson Davis had a different emphasis. He favored the defense in the belief that the Confederacy would win a war of wills with the United States. Lee realized that he and the president did not share like visions of victory; Lee also knew that he could not oppose the commander-in-chief overtly and retain command. So Lee sought his climactic battle without revealing the scale of his intentions to Davis. For his part, Davis never quite grasped the depth of difference between Lee and himself.

But ideas had consequences. Lee may well have accepted battles at disadvantage because he feared that not only the enemy but Davis as well might not offer him as good an opportunity thereafter. Davis often withheld reinforcements (during the Gettysburg campaign, for example) and so limited Lee's capacity to render his strategy as grand as he planned. Because Davis and Lee sometimes worked at cross-purposes, their unspoken, thus unresolved, conflict diminished chances for victory.[55]

Very soon after my biography of Lee appeared, Steven E. Woodworth published *Davis and Lee at War* (1995). Woodworth's book is a companion to his outstanding study of Davis and the western theater, *Jefferson Davis and His Generals: The Failure of Confederate Command in the West* (1990), and together these two works form the best military analysis of Davis available. Woodworth is bold in his judgements, and his insight and understanding are important. The conclusions about Davis in his first book focus on the Confederate president's inability "to make excruciatingly difficult decisions quickly, surely, and correctly." Woodworth speculates that at the base of Davis's troubles lay "basic insecurity" and concludes:

> Davis did not have the confidence in himself, in God, in Providence, or whatever, that might have enabled him to overcome each of these shortcomings. Taken together with his many and considerable strengths both of character and intelligence, Davis's shortcomings are few and small. They loom large only insofar as they prevented

him from achieving the level of greatness necessary to complete the enormous task he almost carried the distance. Far from mediocrity, Jefferson Davis was a man of remarkable talents who fell short only by the narrowest of margins. Perhaps that, after all, is as good an epitaph as any for the Old South: It produced some great men who, in the end, were not quite great enough.[56]

Woodworth intends the double meaning in the title of *Davis and Lee at War*. His conclusions, reached independently, are very nearly the same as mine in *Robert E. Lee: A Biography*. Since Woodworth's book is a study of command and strategy, his military narrative is more intricate than mine. Moreover, his focus is Davis; mine is Lee. So we complement each other in presenting variations on the same theme.[57]

*Why the Confederacy Lost* contains still more fresh ideas and new directions for understanding southern military policy and strategy. Archer Jones, for example, offers "Military Means, Political Ends: Strategy" and reinforces the link between war and politics. Whether or not members of the Confederate high command had ever read or digested the military wisdom of Clausewitz, they acted out his truism that war is an extension of politics. And because they did, the connection between strategy and policy was important—indeed more important than the paucity of recent studies of Confederate politics indicates.[58]

Reid Mitchell's contribution to *Why the Confederacy Lost* is "The Perseverance of Soldiers," in which he acknowledges the significance of the northern will to continue the war to victory as reflected in the commitment of common soldiers in the armies of the United States. Mitchell also focuses on the ambivalence exhibited by the Confederate rank and file and expressed in war-weariness and desertion. To some extent, Mitchell opens himself to the charge that he is simply setting forth another version of the "failure of will" contention, in this case directly related to the circular logic (defeat begets defeatism) that is its serious flaw. Yet Mitchell's point is important. He began making that point in his *Civil War Soldiers* (1988), refined it significantly in *The Vacant Chair: The Northern Soldier Leaves Home* (1993), and makes it once more (sometimes in the same words) in *Why the Confederacy Lost*.[59]

"The Union was a man's family writ large," Mitchell writes in *The Vacant Chair*, and he suggests that domestic values transferred to military units, companies, and such girded Federal soldiers' ideological understanding of their cause. Confederate soldiers, too, Mitchell posits, fought for hearth, home, motherhood, womanhood, and family. But as Confederate armies became less able to protect these institutions, as the Confederate government imposed upon the integrity of domestic stability in the name of greater sacrifice for the cause, and as southern slaves began acting out freedom in the countryside, Confederate soldiers began to chose loyalty to home and family over loyalty to the Confederate cause. As a consequence the heaviest battalions remained heavy, and Confederate ranks shrank from desertion.[60]

A similar idea is Drew Gilpin Faust's suggestion that southern women really had the most to do with Confederate defeat. She writes about female frustration during final two years of war:

> The traditional narrative of war had come to seem meaningless to many women; the Confederacy offered them no acceptable terms in which to cast their experience. Women had consented to subordination and had embraced the attendant ideology of sacrifice as part of a larger scheme of paternalistic assumptions. But the system of reciprocity central to this understanding of social power had been violated by the wartime failure of white southern males to provide the services and support understood as requisite to their dominance.

And so Faust concludes:

> Historians have wondered in recent years why the Confederacy did not endure longer. In considerable measure, I would suggest, it was because so many women did not want it to. The way in which their interests in the war were publicly defined—in a very real sense denied—gave women little reason to sustain the commitment modern war required. It may well have been because of its women that the South lost the Civil War.

It becomes very difficult to formulate military policy and strategy if there are no soldiers.[61]

The final essay in *Why the Confederacy Lost* is Joseph T. Glatthaar's "Black Glory: The African-American Role in Union Victory." Glatthaar is the author of *The March to the Sea and Beyond: Sherman's Troops in the Savannah and Carolinas Campaigns* (1985), a social history of a principal Union army. He has also written *Forged in Battle: The Civil War Alliance of Black Soldiers and White Officers* (1990) and *Partners in Command: The Relationships between Leaders in the Civil War* (1994). His essay in *Why the Confederacy Lost* makes the point, so obvious as to be easily overlooked, that the massive influx of African American troops during the last two years of the war had a significant impact upon the outcome. "The impact of blacks on the Civil War is comparable to the American experience in the First World War. To insist that blacks defeated the Confederacy, like assertions that the Americans defeated Germany, dismisses the efforts of all those others who had fought long and hard during the war. But like the doughboys in World War I, blacks helped to make the difference between victory and stalemate or defeat. They arrived in great numbers at the critical moment, and their contributions on and off the battlefield, in conjunction with those of whites, were enough to force the enemy to capitulate."[62]

Conclusions like those sketched above and throughout this essay are expansive indeed. They emerge in response to the primal fact of southern defeat and questions about why and how Confederate armed forces failed. Within such a context any factor and all factors affecting Confederate efforts to secure independence are germane. [63] The scope of the historiographic debate about Confederate conduct of the war has been a decidedly mixed blessing. It has become quite possible, indeed most respectable, to discuss victory and defeat in the American Civil War without mentioning a single battle or general. Yet expansive thought has too often been missing-in-action within the narrow, jargon-infested tomes that regularly pass for military history in the United States.[64]

Military history is or ought to be about the experience of a people at war. By definition war is crisis; people and peoples reveal themselves in circumstances of crisis—hence the appeal of extra innings, twelve-point tiebreakers, "sudden death," "shoot-outs," as well as presidential debates, job interviews, and deadlines. To the degree to which the Civil War was or became "total," the experience rendered warfare and the southern people, white and black, essentially inseparable. So issues as apparently disparate as generals and gender, guerrillas and Jomini, offense and defense, Celts and contingency, logistics and loss of will, democracy and the draft, nationalism and Nashville, guilt and Gettysburg, slavery and state rights—all of these and more have been fair game for discussion as factors affecting the southern trial by battle.

# BATTLEFIELD TACTICS

## JOSEPH T. GLATTHAAR

As the morning fog ascended on the thirteenth of December in 1862, the Confederate Army of Northern Virginia gazed down from the heights on the small community of Fredericksburg. There, in the streets below and on the expansive grounds to the east, they observed column after column of Federal infantrymen, handsomely adorned in rich blue coats and pale blue slacks, waiting anxiously for the order to advance.

In town, an epidemic of apprehension spread through the Yankee ranks as they scanned the objective above them, Marye's Heights. The plan called for waves of Union forces to strike in column and seize the Rebel position by storm. Untested soldiers wisely feared the unknown. Veterans who had slugged it out on half a dozen major battlefields could forecast the results with extraordinary accuracy. They had to charge over open terrain against a well-trained enemy posted on high ground and secure behind a stone wall and fortifications. Worse, the defenders stood several lines deep, armed with rifled muskets and supported by ample artillery. An assault offered dim prospects for success. Yet when the directive came to advance, the Yankees performed their duty to the utmost. Drawing deeply on their commitment to the cause and their obligations to their comrades, they passed through the town and pressed toward the enemy.

From their elevated position, quite a few Confederates detached themselves enough from the impending battle to notice the peculiar splendor of the event. Elegant rows of tightly packed Union troops, emerging from the quaint village and parading up the slopes south of Fredericksburg, offered a rare spectacle of the bizarre beauty of military operations. Then, suddenly, walls of Confederate flame transformed the visual feast into a chamber of horrors. A thunderous eruption of shot, shell, and bullet ripped through those glorious blue ranks. The front lines staggered and dropped. Succeeding waves stumbled amid fire and bodies. Ranks bunched up, becoming even more inviting targets for Confederates.

To all witnesses, the gaping holes in Yankee lines offered telling re-minders of their dreadful losses. As soldiers fell, the attack lost its steam, and thousands of bluecoats hugged the ground, recognizing the insanity of further advance. More resolute comrades refused to halt and sacrificed their bodies in vain. By the late-afternoon sunset, 8,500 Federals lay dead or wounded before Marye's Heights. A solitary Yankee fell within thirty yards of the wall; no one else came closer than a hundred yards. Like so many Civil War battles, it was a day for the defenders.

Only in a marshy sector of the Rebel line, where deployment in strength was impossible, did Federals gain any headway. Confederate defenders fell back, but in a matter of moments, that fiendish Rebel yell signaled the arrival of reinforcements, and a vicious counterattack quickly snuffed out the penetration.

From a commanding position to the northwest, Confederate general Robert E. Lee peered through the misty haze to witness the grand counter assault. Lines of men, attired in ragged, butternut-colored garb, swept from the swampy woods in close pursuit of the fleeing Yankees. At that instant, Lee turned to one of his key subordinates, Maj. Gen. James Longstreet, and uttered words that precisely characterized the physical and emotional contradictions of the moment. "It is well this is so ter-rible!," he articulated, "we should grow too fond of it!"[1]

As Lee well knew, the advantages lay with the defenders. At the Battle of Fredericksburg, Lee and his subordinates demonstrated superior tac-tics—the ability to transform potential combat power into a successful battle. The Confederates protected themselves by seizing high ground and securing positions behind walls and field fortifications, while the Federals had to assault over open terrain. By establishing a semicircular line that anchored at both ends along the Rappahannock River, Lee stripped the maneuver options from the Yankees. If those Union forces south of the river wanted to fight, they had to launch frontal assaults. Since both sides possessed the same weapons, then the high ground and fortifications of-fered a huge firepower advantage to the Confederates. From greater heights Confederate weapons had superior range, and fortifications, walls, and woods offered concealment, which the Federals lacked. The leadership edge, too, rested with Lee and his army. The renowned Confederate gen-eral dictated the options to the Union army commander, Maj. Gen. Ambrose E. Burnside, and he stripped away alternatives from Federal sub-ordinates. All they could draw on was courage in their frontal attack, while Confederate officers simply encouraged their men to aim and fire. Thus, Lee converted potential combat power—protection, maneuver, fire-power, and leadership—into a lopsided victory for the Confederacy.

That December day, some 18,000 soldiers on both sides fell killed or wounded, three times as many casualties as the United States suffered on D-Day in World War II. Yet these Civil War armies demonstrated remarkable resiliency. Five months later, the same forces fought a major battle with 30,000 more casualties, and two months after that, at Gettysburg, they lost two and a half times as many men as at Fredericksburg.

In magnitude, the Civil War overwhelmingly eclipsed anything Americans had experienced previously. All told, over 200,000 soldiers on both sides died in combat, and perhaps half a million or more sustained wounds. Approximately three million people served in uniform. Only by exploiting two powerful forces in society, nationalism and industrialization, could the Civil War achieve this extraordinary scale and scope of warfare.

In the eighteenth century, French philosopher Jean-Jacques Rousseau and French military theorist François-Apolline, Comte de Guibert, anticipated the impact of the burgeoning concept of nationalism on warfare. They foresaw the creation of huge armies of citizen soldiers, fighting not for pay but for a cause. If properly trained and led, an army composed of such warriors, they believed, could endure untold hardships, fight with unusual tenacity and purpose, and outmarch and outmaneuver professional commands. When opposing sides tapped into this storehouse of power called nationalism, as occurred in the Napoleonic and American Civil Wars, warfare attained mammoth proportions.[2]

Both the Union and Confederate armies benefited additionally from the advent of industrialization. In the northern states, machinery produced prodigious quantities of uniform weapons, ammunition, and military accouterments with fewer laborers. Reliance on farm machinery, too, fed the northern populace and its massive armies by increasing prewar harvest levels while freeing up hundreds of thousands of men for military service. In the Confederacy, its infant industries expanded to produce considerable wartime matériel, and its free and slave labor in the fields filled the void reasonably well when young white males rushed off to war. The seceding states also profited from equipment manufactured abroad and smuggled past the Federal blockade.

Not only were Civil War armies dramatically larger than any the unified nation had ever organized, but technological developments also provided these soldiers with superior weapons. Since the days of the American Revolution, nearly all infantrymen carried smoothbore muskets and fired round projectiles of lead. The muskets were hand-held weapons, approximately four feet in length, that soldiers loaded by dumping gunpowder down the barrel followed by a round ball and using a long pole called a ramrod to pack everything down tightly. They then poured gunpowder into a small metal dish called a flashpan. By cocking the piece and pulling the trigger, either a smoldering wick or a spark from the friction of flint striking metal flared the gunpowder in the flashpan, which ignited the powder in the barrel, causing an explosion that hurled the projectile outward. In wind, rain, or snow, these flashpans proved deficient.

Very few units employed rifled muskets. Because of spiral grooves carved in the barrel, called rifling, the projectile took on a spin which enabled it to fly farther and straighter. Unfortunately, these rifled weapons were more cumbersome to wield and load, reducing their usefulness in battle.

Two technological developments altered the type and effectiveness of the shoulder weapon. By the time of the War with Mexico, the creation of a percussion cap—a tiny copper container with some explosive material in it—eliminated the need for a flashpan or flint and made wider use of rifled muskets more practical. After loading the powder and round, one merely placed a percussion cap on the firing nipple and pulled the trigger, which drove the hammer down on the percussion cap, causing an explosion that ignited the powder in the barrel. In the Civil War, these percussion caps held fulminate of mercury.

The second invention, which Carl L. Davis describes in *Arming the Union* (1973), was the conoidal-shaped projectile commonly known as the minié ball. Originally created by a French officer named Claude Etienne Minié, this "ball" resembled a bullet in shape, with a wooden plug at the base. Upon explosion, the wooden plug expanded, thereby harnessing more of that combustible power and also gripping the walls of the barrel better for a tighter spin. With its conoidal shape, the projectile literally cut through the air, traveling much farther and more accurately than a ball. An American named James H. Burton modified Minié's projectile considerably by eliminating the plug and hollowing the base of the lead object. It was quicker and simpler to manufacture and fit easier down the barrel. Its hollow base expanded upon explosion, which trapped the force of the blast well and gripped the rifling grooves for a tight spin. The double misnomer, however, remained, and Civil War soldiers referred to Burton's bullet as a minié ball.[3]

Union lieutenant general Ulysses S. Grant claimed in *Personal Memoirs* that someone could fire at you with a smoothbore musket and ball from several hundred yards "all day without you finding it out." Grant, of course, exaggerated for effect, but the evidence of the inaccuracy of those smoothbores compared to Civil War rifled muskets corroborates the general's claims. For his article entitled "Civil War Minie Rifles Prove Quite Accurate," small-arms expert Jac Weller tested a variety of shoulder weapons used before and during the Civil War. With smoothbores and round shot, "if I could get five consecutive shots into a group less than 36" across at 100 yds., I reckoned it most lucky." At four hundred yards, they had no accuracy. By contrast, Weller determined that Civil War rifled muskets with Burton's bullets performed extremely well. At one hundred yards, he could group all ten rounds within a ten-inch diameter; from four hundred yards away, he could hit a six-foot-square target with considerable regularity; and at one thousand yards, he discovered "some accuracy," with the ability to drop rounds into an area the size of an artillery battery frequently.[4]

Although Civil War infantrymen carried a variety of weapons into the field with them, the standard arms were the Springfield or Enfield rifled muskets. The Enfield, manufactured originally in Great Britain, was approximately four-and-a-half feet in length, weighed a little over nine pounds, and had a bore diameter of .577 inches. The American-made Springfield rifled musket, the most common infantry weapon in the war, was approximately an inch longer, weighed slightly less, and had a .58–inch bore diameter. Both weapons fired identical rounds and had bayonets that fixed to them. According to Weller's tests, the Enfield fired more accurately. Its slightly narrower barrel provided a tighter fit for the round, and the level of precision craftsmanship of the Enfield surpassed the Springfield. Yet Civil War infantrymen preferred the Springfield to the Enfield. Its durability better suited the rough and tumble world of soldiering, it was lighter on the march, and because of its wider barrel, it required less frequent cleaning, a huge advantage in combat.[5]

For cavalrymen, technology improved the quality of their weapons as well. In the years before the war, horse soldiers had fought with carbines or musketoons—shorter versions of infantry arms—which proved more manageable on a mount than the long and cumbersome rifled musket. The Confederacy armed its horsemen with the rifled Enfield musketoon, a muzzle loader that Weller deemed an excellent weapon, even at one thousand yards. It also offered the convenience of firing the same round as the rifled musket.

As the war broke out, so Robert V. Bruce writes in his timeless classic *Lincoln and the Tools of War* (1956), the Federals shifted to a breech-loading rifled carbine. Since cavalrymen loaded it in the rear or breech instead of in the muzzle, it proved much more serviceable to men on horseback. A soldier could fire three times as many rounds per minute as he could with a muzzle loader. By 1864, the Union had shifted completely to the seven-shot Spencer repeating carbine for its horse soldiers, on the direction of Abraham Lincoln and over the objections of Chief of Ordnance

James W. Ripley. The Spencer accommodated seven self-contained .52 caliber cartridges that cavalrymen loaded through the butt of the stock. Additional magazines enabled mounted men to fire up to seventy rounds accurately in five minutes without cleaning the weapon, which provided them with an extraordinary advantage over their Confederate counterparts.[6]

Unfortunately, Bruce argues, Ripley rejected repeating rifles for infantrymen, primarily because he believed that using them would lead to an unprecedented waste of ammunition. Again, on Lincoln's insistence, selected mounted infantrymen received Spencer repeating rifles, and, according to Theodore Upson, whose letters, journals, and reminiscences were edited by Oscar Osburn Winther and published under the title *With Sherman to the Sea* (1943), thousands of infantrymen spent their own money to purchase repeaters. In fairness to Ripley, the Union could not produce the metallic cartridges necessary for repeaters in sufficient numbers early in the war, nor could inexperienced Federal logisticians haul much more ammunition than they did without serious complications. Still, soldiers on both sides recognized the tremendous advantage of this increased firepower, and events proved that infantrymen and cavalrymen armed with repeaters expended their ammunition sensibly. So important as an element of superiority were repeating rifles that both Bruce and Fred Albert Shannon in *The Organization and Administration of the Union Army, 1861–1865* (1928) believe that the Union could have won the war in 1862 with their widespread use.[7]

According to L. Van Loan Naisawald in *Grape and Canister,* rifling altered weapons in the field artillery the least. The most popular cannon on both sides was the 12-pounder Napoleon, a muzzle-loading smoothbore, based on a model of Napoleon III's. The Union forged all its Napoleons of bronze; when Confederates encountered difficulties procuring copper and tin, they shifted to Napoleons cast of iron. Under ideal conditions, Napoleons had a range of almost a mile. Their large bore size and versatility in the use of ammunition made them a particularly lethal weapon.[8]

Napoleons fired four types of ammunition. Solid shot caused the least damage but provided the greatest range, nearly a mile. Shells, which exploded by timed fuses over the heads of the enemy, could travel three-quarters of a mile. Spherical case shot consisted of marble-sized balls packed in a thin iron container. A fuse ignited an explosive charge that scattered the balls up to eight hundred yards away. The last and most lethal ammunition was canister, a tin container filled with large balls of lead. The container ripped apart as it traveled down the cannon barrel and sprayed those balls much like a giant shotgun blast. Its optimum range was two hundred yards or less. Under critical circumstances, cannoneers could fire two canister rounds at once.

Attempts to rifle guns made of bronze so weakened the tube that they frequently exploded. Instead, the most famous rifled guns, the three-inch Ordnance Gun and the 10-pounder Parrot, notorious for its sleeve wrapped around the breech for additional strength, were made from iron. Despite their accuracy and increased range of up to four thousand yards, most artillerists preferred the Napoleon. Combat situations seldom offered opportunities to fire guns more than a mile, and the narrower bore size of rifled cannons required smaller rounds. Union armies relied more heavily on rifled artillery guns than the Confederates.[9]

An artillery battery of four or six guns had anywhere between eighty and one hundred and fifty-six officers and men, although losses sometimes brought them below the minimum size. Civil War soldiers fired cannons by dropping charges of gunpowder, already in bags, down the tube and ramming in a projectile. At the back end of the gun, another man placed a friction primer in a small opening. When a soldier pulled the lanyard, it yanked part of a friction primer hard enough to ignite powder in its stem. This fire lit the powder bags, and the explosion hurled the projectile out of the tube. Someone then swapped out the barrel with water to extinguish any sparks and clean out a bit of powder residue before the gunners could load the cannon again.

In the days of Napoleon Bonaparte, the three arms of the service—infantry, cavalry, and artillery—checkmated one another. Much as in the children's game of rock, paper, and scissors, each arm proved highly effective against one and extremely vulnerable against another. Cannon blasts tore huge gaps through tightly packed infantry lines. (Paper covers rock.) By exploiting its extreme speed, cavalry could outmaneuver artillerists and drive them from their guns. (Scissors cuts paper.) Infantry, however, formed squares, which enabled its men to fire at cavalry attacking from any direction and presented a solid wall that intimidated the animals. (Rock blunts scissors.)

Because of the limited range and inaccuracy of smoothbore muskets, compounded by their slow rate of fire, officers in Napoleon's day feared the bayonet and saber more. They assembled their troops in concentrated formations, to repel blade attacks and launch effective assaults of their own. Charges with bayonets and sabers provided an incomparable shock value in Napoleonic warfare. They forced soldiers and cavalrymen to close with the enemy, and breaks in the line could lead to a rout and the destruction of an enemy's command.

By the time of the Civil War, John K. Mahon asserts in his article entitled "Civil War Infantry Assault Tactics," the impact of rifling and conoidal projectiles had dramatically changed warfare. The combined technologies stretched the battlefield, compelled armies to assemble farther apart, reduced the density of men in the combat zone, and diminished the value of shock action, such as assaults.

Mahon contends that battles now became longer and less decisive, with the defensive elevated over the offensive. Attack formations usually retained a key element from Napoleon's days, a belief that the bayonet would be a critical weapon. Yet rifled muskets stripped the effectiveness of bladed weapons, except for their psychological value. Civil War medical branches tabulated very few wounds from bayonets or sabers. Because of the range of rifled muskets, armies formed farther apart, which meant that attackers had to cover greater distances, all the while exposed to the fire of defenders. Under the increased range of these new weapons, pursuits proved more ineffectual. Retreating soldiers employed the defensive advantages of rifled muskets and artillery to protect themselves, thus making battles less decisive.

Tactical efforts to lessen the impact of these weapons are the subject of Edward Hagerman's frequently cited doctoral dissertation of the 1960s, finally published in 1988 under the title *The American Civil War and the Origins of Modern War*. Hagerman notes that the distinguished professor of the United States Military Academy, Dennis Hart Mahan, instructed his students in the use of field fortifications and the limitations of frontal assaults even before the advent of the minié ball. Mahan concluded that Napoleonic assaults wasted citizen soldiers, who were valuable members of society. With the introduction of rifled weapons, these inexperienced troops fought better on the tactical defensive. Some of Mahan's students employed field works early in the conflict, while others adopted them more reluctantly, but by the latter half of the war, soldiers threw up impressive trenches on their own initiative. Personal experience proved time after time the value of defensive fortifications.[10]

In *Attack and Die,* Grady McWhiney and Perry D. Jamieson agree with John Mahon and Hagerman on the impact of rifled muskets and minié balls on fighting in the Civil War, arguing that these technological changes provided tremendous advantages to the defender. But while Federals adapted to the new advances in weaponry, they insist, Confederates failed to do so, employing the same aggressive tactics and offensive predilections that Napoleon had used in Europe over half a century earlier and the Americans in Mexico had done nearly a decade and a half ago. The consequences were disastrous, as the Confederacy literally bled itself to death in the first three years of war. McWhiney and Jamieson place the blame on an overpowering cultural consideration: Southern heritage, derived from their Celtic ancestors, predisposed them to offensive warfare.[11]

The Celtic origins of Confederate aggressiveness and the notion that the Confederacy bled itself to death have caused a firestorm of debate which, unfortunately, has camouflaged the great contributions of the book. McWhiney and Jamieson provide us with the best survey of American tactical thought from the Napoleonic era into the Civil War. Despite the army's habit of deriving military ideas and tactical manuals from Europeans, quite a few United States officers had assessed the impact of this increased range and accuracy on infantry tactics before the war. Modifications in William J. Hardee's *Rifle and Light Infantry Tactics* (1855), the prewar infantry manual of the U.S. Army, called for more rapid deployment of infantry from the march into the attack and increased speed while advancing on the enemy. Yet very few anticipated the negative impact of the rifle on tactical offensives, and even after four years of fighting, thoughtful soldiers could not agree on how to overcome it.

Among the most prominent critics of *Attack and Die* are Herman Hattaway and Archer Jones. In their book *How the North Won*, the best single volume on the military history of the war, Hattaway and Jones offer an introduction to Civil War tactics and a primer on the impact of rifles, devoting considerable attention to flanking movements that enabled forces to avoid frontal assaults. Even Lee, notorious for his massive battles, consciously employed turning movements to reduce losses. In *Why the South Lost the Civil War*, which Hattaway and Jones co-authored with Richard E. Beringer and William N. Still, Jr., the four historians devote an appendix to refuting the *Attack and Die* thesis. The authors insist that the Celtic frontal assaults were more a product of swords and spears than culture, and that all armies attacked frontally with those weapons. From a statistical standpoint, they examine thirty battles from 1861 to 1863. The Confederacy attacked in only thirteen of them, and their losses in all thirty fights were almost identical to Union casualties. Strategic considerations, rather than culture, these scholars suggest, often determined whether an army attacked or defended.[12]

Albert Castel, in a sensibly argued article with the peculiar title "Mars and the Reverend Longstreet" (1987), challenges the *Attack and Die* claims by placing assaults in the perspective of available options. He dismisses the Celtic origins of frontal attacks as "a debatable theory, to put it mildly," and attempts to explain why the assaults took place. Once enemies engage in combat, commanders have four options: fight on the defensive;

attack on a broad front; assault the enemy directly, but on a narrow front; and attempt to strike the opponent's flank or flanks with a turning movement. Those who fight on the defensive surrender the initiative. They must rely on their opponent to strike them, and supply problems may deprive them of the luxury of waiting for the enemy to attack. Furthermore, armies on the strategic offensive must seek a decision on the battlefield, which often requires the tactical offensive. A broad frontal attack works only when the aggressor has an overwhelming military advantage. Flanking movements demand a high level of execution, which inexperienced officers and men struggle to meet. They also rely on the element of surprise, and a commander who attempts one assumes a high risk of disaster. Terrain, too, might preclude the possibility of a turning movement. Thus, in many instances the frontal assault appears as the only viable option.[13]

Whether historians agree or disagree with the McWhiney-Jamieson thesis, scholars from Mahon to Castel endorse the idea that the rifle and minié ball altered warfare dramatically. Paddy Griffith not only challenges the impact of the rifle; he also stands the *Attack and Die* thesis on its head in his *Battle Tactics of the Civil War* (1989). Griffith refutes the claim of the Civil War as the first modern war, insisting that it more properly ranks as the last Napoleonic war. The smoothbore had already tilted the advantage to soldiers on the tactical defensive. Compact formations and field fortifications resembled those of Napoleon's era, and the close fighting nullified the benefit of rifling and minié balls. With proper training and leadership, frontal assaults would have worked, as they did more than half a century earlier. Blame for tactical failure rested not with the rifle but with the poorly disciplined citizen soldier and his inadequately schooled officer corps. A subsequent study by Earl J. Hess entitled *The Union Soldier in Battle* (1997) endorses Griffith's basic arguments.[14]

Griffith proposes an intriguing thesis, but his arguments fail to stand up to careful scrutiny. Whether the Civil War was the last Napoleonic war or the first modern war is a semantic question—much like whether it was an example of total war or not. The answer depends on how one defines modern (or total) war. His calculation of ranges for infantry fights are unsystematic at best. Yet relying on Griffith's data, the average distance of infantry fights was 127 yards, well outside the accurate range of smooth bore and round shot, according to Weller. Furthermore, that average of 127 yards indicates that many fights took place at greater distances.[15]

Perhaps, too, more disciplined soldiers and superior leadership would have enabled frontal assaults to work, but that question will never be answered. Nor is it likely that mid-nineteenth-century Americans would have tolerated a more strict military establishment. That lack of discipline was a product of their democratic-republican environment. With the exception of most black soldiers, it was a war fought by participants in or about to become part of the political process. American society, James M. McPherson explains in *For Cause and Comrades* (1997), "prized individualism, self-reliance, and freedom from coercive authority." The army could strip these citizen soldiers of some individualism, but they would never become disciplined military cogs.[16]

Certainly frontal assaults did work in the Civil War. Hood's Texans carried the Union position at Gaines Mill in June 1862, and, as late as May 1864, Emory Upton directed an assault at Spotsylvania that popped through the Confederate works. Nor were they the only successful frontal assaults in the war. But the Union disaster at Fredericksburg and Lee's catastrophic repulse on the third day at Gettysburg were much more representative of the outcome when Civil War soldiers attacked a well-defended, lightly fortified position. Even the successful charges at Gaines Mill and Spotsylvania occurred under unusual circumstances. For all their heroics, Hood's men still benefited from stampeding Union cavalry, which disrupted the defensive position. At Spotsylvania, Upton planned his attack meticulously, arranged his assault regiments carefully, and coached his lead elements on how to fan out as they penetrated the Confederate works. Nonetheless, his men emerged from a protected woods and had to cross over an open area of only two hundred yards, against a Confederate line denuded of nearly all its artillery. With proper artillery support alone, Upton's assault may have failed.

Because the tightly packed lines and columns made such easy targets for defenders armed with rifled muskets, as Edward Hagerman explains, some progressive thinkers experimented with loose-order skirmish line attacks. Soldiers advanced in scattered formations, taking advantage of rocks, trees, and underbrush for concealment. This tactical adaptation reduced casualties but stripped the attacking force of its might. By dispersing manpower, the commander also diluted his firepower and reduced his ability to command his forces effectively. Only under certain conditions, with experienced officers and soldiers armed with repeating rifles, would such a tactical solution work.

The problem that Civil War commanders confronted, as James M. McPherson suggests in *Battle Cry of Freedom,* was technological improvements in weaponry, without comparable gains in communication. To counter advances in the range and accuracy of rifled weapons and even artillery, officers needed to disperse their forces to make their soldiers less inviting targets, while at the same time preserving control to ensure a concentration of fire and coordination among forces to secure objectives.

Unfortunately, commanders in battle communicated the same way their ancestors had done hundreds of years ago: through voice, the use of flags, handwritten messages, and musical instruments such as bugles and drums. The deafening cacophony of battlefield sounds—the sonic boom of cannon, the crack of tens of thousands of muskets, and shouts of joy, fear, and pain—drowned out voices and bugles, and huge clouds of smoke from black powdered weapons often obscured flags and concealed officers from couriers. Under these conditions, talented Civil War leaders could barely command and control their men in compact formations. To disburse them in battle would guarantee an absence of proper direction and would squander their combat strength. Not until World War II, with the introduction of the radio, could officers scatter their forces and still control them adequately.[17]

Like infantry, most scholars agree, artillery in the attack suffered at the expense of rifled muskets. In the Mexican War, the United States used cannon as offensive weapons, positioning them in front to lead attacks. But technological improvements since then favored the infantry. Seldom did the terrain offer an opportunity to exploit the advantages of rifled artillery guns, and the small projectiles limited their impact on the battlefield. The most effective ammunition for smoothbore Napoleons, canister, was well within deadly range of infantrymen, and even at distances for spherical case shot, rifle volleys could wreak havoc on an artillery battery.

Augmenting the problem of offensive support was the fact that, except in a handful of instances, Civil War artillerists had to fire directly on the target. The erratic performance of guns and ammunition discouraged most attempts to fire indirectly—over their own troops to strike at the enemy—as they did in World War I. In his memoirs, edited by Gary W. Gallagher under the title *Fighting for the Confederacy,* Brig. Gen. Edward Porter Alexander discussed at length the single greatest obstacle to use of indirect fire, defective ammunition. Shells exploded so frequently as they emerged from the cannon among Confederates, and often enough with Federals, that infantrymen refused to permit their gunners to fire overhead with anything except mortars, or siege guns, which lofted huge explosive rounds high into the air to drop them into enemy trenches. Even oblique or angled fire during an attack was an exacting proposition in the Civil War. On the third day at Gettysburg, Alexander attempted to push some artillery forward during the assault to support the attackers with oblique fire. Despite his use of veteran gunners, it proved too dangerous, confusing, and complex to execute effectively.[18]

Artillery's primary use, then, was as a defensive tool, firing solid shot, shell, and finally canister into assaulting lines. According to Naisawald in

*Grape and Canister*, field artillery "was a potent force—but only defensively. No offensive operation on either side was decisively affected by the use of artillery; it was beyond the capabilities of the materiel and fire control systems of that era." Yet artillery proved its worth above and beyond the casualties its fire inflicted. It still retained a psychological component, a shock value that fortified its friends and frightened its foe. In warfare against ground troops, who drew heavily upon character and courage to advance, artillery played a powerful role. As Jennings Cropper Wise wrote in his partisan yet still quite useful study, *The Long Arm of Lee* (1915): "Not only do the guns exert a tremendous moral effect in support of their infantry, and adverse to the enemy, but they do far more." Artillery often discouraged infantry from assaulting and induced enemy ground forces to seek cover and helped to check their fire.[19]

In time, military leaders realized that for optimum utility, they needed to mass their guns and fight them in combination with infantry. Commanders on both sides squandered the might of artillery by parceling a battery to each brigade, thereby losing the ability to concentrate artillery blasts on specific points of the enemy position to aid infantrymen best. Very early in the war, Wise asserts, Alexander formed the first artillery battalion in an effort to mass fire. The Confederacy, however, drifted away from this approach, and not until reforms in September 1862 and modifications in late May 1863 did Lee's army create artillery battalions assigned to each infantry division, with an artillery reserve for each corps. In the Union Army of the Potomac, according to Naisawald, Maj. Gen. George B. McClellan established a system of four batteries per division. When divisions combined into corps, half the batteries would comprise the corps reserve artillery, and there was also an army reserve. Later, the Union authorities addressed a significant problem: artillery from uncommitted divisions remained idle in battle. They solved this problem by creating artillery brigades of four to eight batteries assigned to each corps, and about one-third of all batteries remained with the army reserve.

Out West, the more disorganized nature of artillery is reflected in the quality of scholarship. Larry J. Daniel's *Cannoneers in Gray* (1984) is the only strong, comprehensive book on artillery west of the Appalachians. The Confederate Army of Tennessee, so Daniel writes, suffered from inadequate equipment and a lack of knowledgeable artillerymen. Like the eastern armies, it dissipated firepower by assigning batteries to brigades. Army commander Gen. Braxton Bragg created a battalion structure on paper in 1862; individual batteries continued to function in conjunction with infantry brigades. In 1864, after Gen. Joseph E. Johnston took over for Bragg, the Confederates created true battalions of artillery and formed these battalions into artillery regiments assigned to each corps, with some artillery batteries held in reserve at the army level. The Army of Tennessee was a year behind its eastern counterpart, and at the time it was creating an army reserve, both eastern armies and Sherman's army were breaking them up for better usage.[20] According to Paddy Griffith, this shift in artillery organization indicated a movement back to Napoleon's days. Napoleon had determined the value of concentrated artillery fire and had massed guns on the divisional level. In the intervening five decades, the trend had been to disperse artillery, but experience in the Civil War resurrected the French artillerist's views, with improved results.

The third arm, cavalry, lost much of its traditional function on the Civil War battlefield, contends Mahon in "Civil War Infantry Assault Tactics." Napoleon employed his horsemen as shock forces to strike just as the enemy exhibited signs of wavering. In the Civil War, cavalry retained its offensive element, due to speed and mobility, although its strength in combat rested with the ability to ride to battlefields and fight like infantrymen. Just as rifled weapons had diminished the impact of bayonets for infantrymen, so they reduced the utility of sabers for horsemen. While cavalrymen performed much of their traditional role in reconnaissance, screening army advances, and strategic raiding, their true contribution rested with that novel combination of mobility and firepower.

Stephen Z. Starr, however, disagrees with Mahon on the origins of using cavalry as mounted infantry. In his three-volume classic, *The Union Cavalry in the Civil War* (1979–1985), Starr sees the break with more traditional European uses of cavalry as much more complicated and unintentional than Mahon and others claim. Officers and enlistees in Union cavalry regiments intended to fight not like U.S. Army dragoons—troops armed with musketoons, sabers, and pistols, who were expected to battle on horseback and on foot as infantry—but like traditional European cavalrymen. Unfortunately, neither the horses nor the men had enough training to fight on horseback with sabers. Without adequate numbers of skilled cavalrymen, those shock attacks with sabers made little sense.[21]

When Union leaders attempted to expand the size of their cavalry in the West, Starr explains, they had to tap infantry regiments for manpower. Since these men felt much more comfortable fighting on foot, they did so, using the horses for mobility and dedicating one in every four as a horseholder during combat. Once the War Department placed Spencer repeating carbines in their hands, that increased firepower easily compensated for that one-fourth reduction in battle strength. Thus, the true transformation in the cavalry derived more from accident and necessity than from conscious alteration.

No doubt, Brian Steel Wills agrees with Starr's concept in his biography of the Confederate cavalryman Nathan Bedford Forrest entitled *A Battle from the Start* (1992). Forrest and his horsemen shattered all stereotypes about cavalry as the glamour service simply because Forrest, a natural-born leader, drew on his personal aggressiveness and good sense to offset his lack of formal cavalry training. In time, Forrest's horsemen honed their skills and demonstrated extraordinary versatility. They fought mounted or on foot against cavalry and infantry, endured unusual hardships, campaigned long and hard, gobbled up garrisons, destroyed rail lines, seized military supplies, and generally made life miserable for Union commanders in the West. An offensive weapon like no other, Forrest lived up to his simple combat philosophy, "Get there first with the most."[22]

While Forrest proved himself the "Wizard of the Saddle" for the Confederates, Federals began to adapt themselves to the same type of warfare, except their horsemen carried seven-shot Spencer repeating carbines. Maj. Gen. Philip Sheridan demonstrated this overwhelming firepower superiority in his Valley Campaign of 1864 against Jubal Early's raiders, a subject that requires additional study. In *Yankee Blitzkrieg* (1976), James Pickett Jones describes the lightning speed and thunderous blows that Maj. Gen. James H. Wilson's cavalry corps—armed with repeaters—delivered in his raid on Selma, Alabama, in 1865. Even Forrest, whom Wilson bested at Ebenezer Creek, admitted he was whipped for the first time in the war.[23]

Because cavalrymen frequently fought as mounted infantry against other ground troops, they relied frequently on artillery to sustain them in battle. Lighter, more mobile guns called horse artillery bolstered cavalry on both the tactical offensive and defensive. According to Wise, the traditional purpose of horse artillery was to clear roads for cavalry advances and to check pursuits. Civil War commanders discovered, however, that the combined arms of highly mobile artillery and cavalry fighting as infantry blended well on the battlefield. Not only did it render additional fire support, but well-directed cannon fire also added that psychological dimension of unnerving the enemy.

Whether one agrees or not with the *Attack and Die* thesis, McWhiney and Jamieson have hit upon an important concept—that national and regional character influences how and where armies fight. Culture and society shape collective attitudes and foster the development of mutual beliefs that affect the causation and the execution of war, both on a national and an individual basis. In *Embattled Courage* (1987), Gerald F. Linderman perceives courage as the glue that kept men together, bonded them, and enabled them to endure the rigors of combat early in the war. Social standards in the North and South promoted courage as the proper moral behavior for soldiers to exhibit. Over time, as losses and hardships compounded, most soldiers discarded notions of courage as arcane and adopted a harder approach to war, so Linderman insists.[24]

In a brilliant yet complex book entitled *The Destructive War* (1991), Charles Royster detects strong elements of aggressiveness and a demand for massive destruction in both northern and southern society. He reveals these collective impulses through Thomas Jonathan "Stonewall" Jackson and William T. Sherman. Jackson, perhaps before others, called for an offensive war that would inflict terrible pain on the Union for its audacity in attempting to coerce southerners into remaining in the Union. Sherman, who arrived at the concept of wholesale aggressiveness and massive destruction a bit slower, hoped to punish the South for rushing to war against the finest government on earth. In one of the war's great anomalies, neither the Union nor the Confederacy would admit it wanted the war, but both sides hoped to devastate the other.[25]

Other studies seem to support Royster's arguments. Gary W. Gallagher argues in *The Confederate War* (1997) that aggressive Rebel strategy reflected the expectations of the southern people. As often happens in a democratic society, citizens insisted that strategy and tactics ratify their nationalistic objectives. The Confederacy had to prove its independence on the battlefield by punishing northerners into conceding that the price for restoring the Union was too great, even though such battles depleted their limited manpower and resources. Lee, in his audacious style of warfare, merely fulfilled societal demands.[26]

From the Union standpoint, Mark Grimsley's *The Hard Hand of War* (1995) demonstrates the evolution of the Union policy from a limited conflict to a destructive war. In a book that blends handsomely with Royster's social and cultural arguments, Grimsley traces the transition of the northern war effort from conciliation to pragmatism to "hard war." Yet, as Grimsley asserts, even in their most destructive phase, northern morality imposed limits on soldiers' behavior. In my *March to the Sea and Beyond* (1985), I explore the results of that hardening process in Sherman's army on the Savannah and Carolinas Campaigns. After two years of attempting to squeeze his volunteers into a disciplined, conventional fighting force, Sherman adapted his approach to the war to exploit their true assets, an unwavering commitment to the Union cause and a broad array of wartime and peacetime experiences. He directed his citizen soldiers on extensive raids that struck at the heart of the Confederacy. During these expeditions, Sherman dispersed his forces, relying on the military know-how of veterans and the moral sense of restraint from civil life to accomplish his objectives. While both Grimsley and I discover substantial and sometimes massive destruction of property and some petty thievery, especially in South Carolina, neither of us uncovers evidence of widespread or systematic murder or rape.[27]

Sherman's troops, however, boasted no monopoly on a vigorous commitment to their cause. Those soldiers who rushed Marye's Heights that brisk December day demonstrated an unsurpassed level of valor and devotion, as did men on both sides in hundreds of other fights over those four years of combat. Such extraordinary conduct on battlefield after battlefield invokes the question: In the face of such limited tactical options, lethal weapons, and unyielding hardships, how could Civil War soldiers display such dedication? In *Civil War Soldiers* (1988), Reid Mitchell attributes that tenacity of purpose to a deep and rich ideology. Interestingly, Mitchell perceives common themes among the belligerents such as their Revolutionary heritage, their sense of masculine identity, and their devotion to liberty, yet they split over such issues as Union and secession or freedom and slavery. Several years later, in his book *The Vacant Chair* (1993), Mitchell spins off another theme, the image of home and the values it represented, to indicate the power of northern commitment.[28]

By expanding on Mitchell's themes, James M. McPherson recognizes a variety of factors working together to attract soldiers to the cause, to sustain them in the service, and to fortify them in their hour of greatest need, through combat. In *For Cause and Comrades* McPherson contends that a host of concepts—duty, honor, comradeship, patriotism, ideology, perceptions of manhood, and community pressure—interacted to provide Civil War soldiers with the strength to serve through boredom and tragedy. Yet those concepts, as McPherson points out early in his book, were neither shared universally throughout the army nor preserved consistently over four years of fighting. Emotions and levels of commitment waxed and waned. Fulfilling one's obligations did not necessarily mean a soldier still ratified the cause or endorsed its course, just as desertion did not necessarily mean a loss of that commitment. Soldiers left the army for all sorts of reasons, William Blair elucidates in his *Virginia's Private War* (1998), particularly during times of idleness, and many of them came back in time for campaigning.[29]

As the very last of the citizen soldiers returned home, long after they had laid the fallen at Fredericksburg to rest, the United States and the European powers wrestled with the tactical lessons of the Civil War. Perry D. Jamieson in *Crossing the Deadly Ground* (1994) explains that American military leaders realized that rifles, artillery, and field fortifications weighed heavily on the side of defenders. What U.S. Army personnel wrestled with over the next few decades was how to restore the tactical offensive to warfare. Emory Upton, the artillery officer who earned a reputation for his infantry assault and who commanded a division of cavalry on Wilson's Selma Raid, prepared an infantry manual which called for single-line formations and greater dispersion and mobility, to reduce the impact of defensive weapons. These tactics marked an important step by devolving more responsibility on company-grade officers and non-commissioned officers. Upton also attempted to assimilate tactics among the three branches, so that artillery, infantry, and cavalry functioned more compatibly. Yet the army never fully absorbed the lessons of the war, Jamieson contends, because of dissension among the officer corps and the relentless digressions from unconventional Indian wars.[30]

Despite creditable reporting by European military observers, Jay Luvaas notes in his admirable study *The Military Legacy of the Civil War* (1959), few tactical lessons took hold among the great Western powers— England, France, and Germany—in the next two decades after 1865. The bumbling performance of volunteer soldiers early in the war soured many military experts, while in the minds of others the widespread European adoption of breech-loading small arms constituted all previous wars obsolete. Then, too, the Austro-Prussian and Franco-Prussian Wars dominated the European scene. With their lightning offensives and decisive campaigns, those experiences readily eclipsed any insights into future conflicts from the Civil War. Analysts failed to grasp the enhanced power of the defensive and the resilience of field works. Disregarded as well were lessons from cavalry serving as mounted infantry. By the end of the century, some European officers intuited benefits from studying Civil War tactics, but not enough to anticipate the bloody harvest in World War I.[31]

Although the numbers of books on Civil War tactics may surprise some readers, in fact the scholarship has barely scratched the surface. In his *American Way of War*, Russell F. Weigley sees a direct link between the strategy of Ulysses S. Grant and that employed by the United States in World War II. Does tactics have a comparable impact? Perry Jamieson has explored its influence on tactics in the post–Civil War army, but how have Civil War tactics and battles provided insights for military personnel in the past century and a third? In what ways have they affected the planning and execution of battles and campaigns?

For too long, scholars have downplayed the importance of the combined arms concept in the Civil War. Artillery buoyed friendly infantry through technical and psychological power, while striking physical and emotional fear in the bodies and minds of its enemies. Yet artillery in the Civil War could not stand alone. It demanded infantry or cavalry support to survive on the battlefield. No branch of service underwent a greater transformation in the war than cavalry. It learned to fight like infantry, especially with Spencer repeating carbines, while preserving the speed and mobility of horse soldiers. Against other cavalry, horse artillery was an asset; against enemy infantry, it was imperative for dismounted horsemen. This interdependence in combat and the development of individual branches of service have attracted too little scholarly attention.

The Civil War took place at a critical moment of technological change, with major social and tactical repercussions. In place of smoothbores and round balls, Civil War soldiers fired rifled muskets and conoidal projectiles, and some even used repeating rifles and carbines. Firing with a smoothbore and a ball was an art. Only those with true talent could do so accurately from a hundred yards or more. But technological advances help to convert an art into a science. Suddenly, anyone with a bit of training could fire accurately at 150 or 200 yards, and those with repeating rifles had seven rounds to compensate for their lack of talent. How did this technology alter the social dynamics within units? Did outstanding marksmen lose stature? What impact did it have on personnel assignments and replacements? Certainly an examination of Regular Army units could provide answers, but so could volunteer regiments, especially those that joined early in the war and received smoothbore weapons. Since cavalrymen now fought dismounted, did perceptions of the mounted service change? How did this development influence status within cavalry commands? And what about artillery, which employed smoothbore and much more accurate rifled guns: Were there social and cultural implications, too?

Campaign and battle books, a genre that has attracted the interest of both scholars and buffs alike over the years, should be a fount of information on tactics. In recent years, however, these volumes have grown stale. Many are potboiler publications, hoping to tap the exploding Civil War book market. They attempt to compensate for lack of originality, pedestrian analysis, and inadequate research with slick writing. Invariably, these volumes drag down the quality of this vital field of study and fuel the contention in academic circles that military history lacks rigor.

Fortunately, a handful of authors have helped to salvage this declining art. Among the few academics who have written skillful studies of campaigns are William L. Shea and Earl J. Hess. Their book *Pea Ridge* (1992) is a careful work, based on extensive research, and a painstaking exploration of the battlefield itself. The contours of the ground, long-forgotten roads, and even remnants of fences have provided evidence for a detailed re-creation of several eventful days in March 1862.[32]

By and large, professional historians at the National Park Service author the best campaign and battle books today. Robert K. Krick, Harry W. Pfanz, and John J. Hennessy, to name just three, have blended rare knowledge of battlefields with intensive primary-source research and skillful writing to prepare studies that rival such classics as John Bigelow's *The Campaign of Chancellorsville* (1910) and Richard J. Sommers's *Richmond Redeemed* (1981). More volumes of this ilk would provide us with greater tactical insights and help to restore the reputation of this area of scholarship.[33]

In 1976, John Keegan published a revolutionary book entitled *The Face of Battle* in which he began by chiding scholars for their unrealistic portrayals of combat. There were various levels of experience in battle, Keegan insisted, and what individuals encountered in one area might be very different from what soldiers a hundred yards away were called upon to face. By drawing on a rich knowledge of the battlefields, weapons, tactics, equipment, and organization, he depicted the battles of Agincourt, Waterloo, and the Somme in terms much fuller than previous scholars had used.[34]

Civil War historians have paid mere lip service to Keegan's ideas. Take, for example, the rifled musket. Since most Civil War engagements took place in the South during warm-weather months, a soldier's gun barrel would be hot even before he fired, especially on a sunny day. A skilled infantryman could deliver about three rounds in a minute. After he fired eight times consecutively, his barrel would become extremely hot from the explosion and friction of the ball gripping those rifled grooves at such high speed. By twelve shots, he could no longer touch the barrel, even with his shirt sleeve covering his hand. Within four minutes of beginning intense firing, then, he was out of action temporarily, unless he picked up the weapon of a fallen comrade. The enemy, however, still fired at him.

After ten rounds with a black powder weapon, the residue impaired a soldier's ability to reload. A crust of burnt gunpowder would line the inside of his barrel, and with each shot, the minié ball fit more and more tightly. The soldier needed to apply tremendous force to ram down each round. Since the spiral grooves filled with residue first, shots benefited less and less from the rifling and would become more and more errant. By a dozen or so firings, the musket would foul so terribly that it proved unusable. Federal soldiers carried Williams cleaners, cartridges that supposedly scoured the filth from the rifle barrel. They did not work particularly well, and in 1864 the army halted its purchase of them. Thus, troops on both sides eventually had to pick up other weapons from the battlefield or clean their own weapons, either while lying down or while hiding behind a tree. The cleaning process required water, patches, and percussion caps and took several minutes, often under enemy fire. Units that suffered from water shortages, then, placed themselves in a precarious position in battle.[35]

In fact, Civil War soldiers seldom mentioned the scorching heat of their barrels and rarely discussed cleaning their weapons, because these were such commonplace occurrences that few thought them worthy of mention. The impact on the battlefield, though, was unmistakable, and scholars have overlooked this aspect of combat and its repercussions completely. If Blair is correct that there were many reasons for desertion and that scholars cannot assume that it was a reflection of support for the war effort, then perhaps historians should revise their assumptions about the motives of those soldiers who fell behind in the attack or temporarily drifted away from their regiments on the battlefield. Ultimately, Keegan's concepts and approach may well retain their validity today.

The suggestions made in this essay are just that—mere suggestions of a few possible areas in which historians may perceive opportunities to expand our knowledge of events. They are not offered to dictate the future direction of Civil War studies. But if we hope get the "real war" into the books, as Walt Whitman challenged generations of authors to do, then we must alter our approach and pay more careful attention to Civil War tactics and combat.

The objective of history is to tell us what happened and why it occurred, to make some sense from a jumble of events and to explain and analyze what life was really like in previous times. It is to provide us with both a glimpse and an understanding of those events and people who shaped our world today. If we ever hope to grasp the true experiences of those brave men who sacrificed their lives in the vain assault up Marye's Heights or perceive how it looked and felt to Confederates as they waited to open fire on those elegant columns of blue-coated attackers, then we must come to terms with Civil War tactics. Despite its inherent tragedy and seeming futility, these tactics determined how troops trained and fought, prescribed the sorts of experiences that Civil War soldiers encountered, and to a large extent dictated the astounding losses in America's costliest conflict.

Most scholars agree that the Civil War was the defining moment in our nation's history, a watershed event that transformed the United States and continues to influence the course of the country today. To disregard the way in which soldiers engaged their enemy, to dismiss the importance of weapons and field fortifications and how they used them, is to provide an incomplete portrait of the men's experiences and to diminish the extraordinary achievements and sacrifices they made on behalf of future generations.

# "NOT THE GENERAL BUT THE SOLDIER"

## The Study of Civil War Soldiers

### REID MITCHELL

Fortunately, with us, the soldiers make the officers,
& not the officers the soldiers.
—William Pegram, discussing the death of Stonewall Jackson.
William Pegram to his sister, May 11, 1863. Pegram-Johnson-
McIntosh Papers, Virginia Historical Society.

We have waged this war not by strategy but by fighting,
and the hero of it is not the general but the soldier.
—A Synopsis of the Art of War. Dedicated to the Junior Officers
of the Confederate Army (Columbia, S. C., 1864)

The anonymous author of *A Synopsis of the Art of War* may have overstated his case when he said "We have waged this war not by strategy but by fighting, and the hero of it is not the general but the soldier," but he did identify a key truth about the Civil War. Despite the status of Grant, Lee, and Sherman among American generals, the war was not won by strategic brilliance. Both sides displayed roughly the same level of competence, and both thought about matters military in the same way. Neither side solved one of the greatest dilemmas of the war: how to launch a tactical assault without enduring losses that today would be viewed as unacceptable. There was nothing in the Civil War comparable to the innovations in tactical thinking that distinguished the last years of World War I. For the Union army as well as the Confederate, the war was waged by fighting, and the soldiers paid the cost. Any analysis of the military course of the war that takes soldiers' morale for granted belongs more properly in a computer simulation than a work of history.

The Union and the Confederacy alike created mass armies out of an overwhelmingly citizen population. The attitude of the rank-and-file on each side probably represented the majority attitudes of each society as a whole. Furthermore, the soldiers left behind a wealth of sources—letters, diaries, regimental histories, and memoirs. So while there are better avenues for the study of formal ideology, the study of the soldier reveals much about politics and culture during the war.

As a field, the study of Civil War soldiers is just reaching maturity. Except for the history of women and gender, that can be said of no other field considered in this volume. Indeed, in this essay we will proceed year-by-year while discussing scholarship. Two signs of the maturation are the appearance of the first book that attempts to synthesize the existing literature—Larry M. Logue, *To Appomattox and Beyond: The Civil War Soldier in War and Peace* (1996)—and the emergence of two significant debates, the first over the question of ideology and soldier motivation, the second over the psychological impact of the soldiering experience.

Beginning with Lloyd Lewis and Bruce Catton, many historians have used regimental histories and other sources left by the common soldiers to enliven their narratives of the war. Often such narratives have helped us better understand what motivated soldiers and how they perceived the war. A stellar example is the third volume of Bruce Catton's Army of the Potomac trilogy, *A Stillness at Appomattox* (1953), which discusses soldier reenlistment.[1]

Nonetheless, it is no overstatement to say that the scholarly study of Civil War soldiers as a field in itself started with one man, Bell Irvin Wiley. Indeed, his accomplishment in this field was so imposing that for a generation it was also safe to say that the scholarly study of Civil War soldiers stopped with Bell Irvin Wiley. His two books, *The Life of Johnny Reb: The Common Soldier of the Confederacy* (1943) and *The Life of Billy Yank: The Common Soldier of the Union* (1952), opened and closed the field, and they still provide the scholarly framework within which many, although not all, historians of the soldiers' experience work. In some ways, most subsequent scholarship has been a gloss on Wiley.[2]

Wiley wrote *The Life of Johnny Reb* almost as an act of filial devotion; he had grown up surrounded by aging Confederate veterans. He later described himself as "one who was nurtured in Confederate tradition." Nonetheless, he was also determined to bring a new level of honesty to the discussion of Confederate soldiery.[3] Wiley particularly concentrated on the material circumstances of soldiering. He devoted chapters to uniforms, food, and weapons. He also discussed how soldiers passed their time, not just in battle but in winter camps, and described the games they played, the letters they read and wrote, the music to which they listened, the drinking, gambling, and whoring some of them did. But compared to later historians, Wiley was less interested in the ideology and attitudes of Confederate soldiers—which is not to say that he neglected the subject entirely.

According to Wiley, at the beginning of the war, hatred for the Yankees, particularly over the issue of slavery, and the desire for adventures motivated the men who joined the Confederate army. Of the nearly four hundred pages of text, Wiley spends only four considering the reasons men enlisted in the Confederate army. Wiley does not even mention the issue that many later historians have thought crucial—the southern understanding of liberty.

Wiley organized *The Life of Billy Yank* along the same lines as his earlier book on "Johnny Reb." Once again, there were chapters on diversions, battles, winter quarters, weapons, food, and the like. Sometimes the superior logistical capacity of the Union is responsible for the only differences between chapters in *Billy Yank* and those on the same subjects in *Johnny Reb*. Wiley did not believe that the psychology or behavior of Billy Yank differed much from those of Johnny Reb. He did argue that Yankees were more literate, more concerned with politics, and more practical than Confederates, and that rebel soldiers were more religious and more imaginative than northerners. He also thought that Confederates cared more deeply about the war and that Union soldiers were more concerned with money. But these are few differences to emerge from two long volumes on Federals and Confederates, and Wiley concluded that Johnny Reb and Billy Yank were basically alike. He admitted that "the two were so much alike that the task of giving this book a flavor and character distinct from *The Life of Johnny Reb* has at times been a difficult one."[4]

What may delight or infuriate Wiley's reader is his reluctance to draw conclusions from his masterfully presented evidence. Nobody doubts that Wiley knew the Civil War soldier as well as any historian has. Yet in *Johnny Reb* and *Billy Yank* he was often reluctant to push beyond description. While it may be heresy to suggest it, *Johnny Reb* and *Billy Yank* are not among Wiley's strongest works. *Southern Negroes* (1938), *The Road to Appomattox* (1956), and *The Plain People of the Confederacy* (1944) all surpass them as works of analysis. *The Plain People of the Confederacy* attempts to present the experience of Confederate soldiers, nonslaveholding white southerners, and enslaved African Americans. Furthermore, anticipating the conclusions of more recent scholarship, Wiley concludes that the disaffection of white yeoman families because of conscription and speculation may have been the cause of Confederate defeat. "Long before the finale at Appomattox," he writes, "the doom of the Confederacy had been firmly sealed by the wide-spread defection of her humblest subjects."[5]

The chapter "The Common Soldier" in *The Plain People of the Confederacy* is Wiley's single best treatment of soldiers. To be sure, to a large extent it is simply an encapsulation of *Johnny Reb,* discussing food, clothing, illness, and so on. But the critical issue of morale, which was somewhat buried in *Johnny Reb,* is made central to *The Plain People.* Wiley argues that morale "sank to a very low ebb during the latter half of the war." He explains this less as a result of battlefield defeat than because of "reports of hunger, raggedness, and sickness . . . from loved ones at home." These reports caused many soldiers to desert and the majority who stayed sometimes to despair. This analysis, still current in the literature today, even among historians who overlook its origins with Wiley, is the farthest Wiley went in linking his work on soldiers to either social history in general or to the ultimate outcome of the war.[6]

For a generation after Bell Wiley's pioneering studies, there was little written about the common soldiers. Case closed. Then, in the 1980s, historians reopened the field—if the work of one scholar constitutes a field—with a series of new studies. The first new book on Civil War soldiers to appear was the least influential and perhaps the oddest: Michael Barton, *Goodmen: The Character of Civil War Soldiers* (1981).[7]

Barton uses social science methods, particularly content analysis, to discuss letters and diaries of soldiers. Few other scholars, except for Joseph Allan Frank and George A. Reaves, have followed suit—to be frank, partly because the methods have seemed trivial and partly because Barton neglected manuscript sources and thus arrived at some dubious conclusions. (Most famously, he claimed that northern officers did not write letters of consolation, which is simply wrong.) In general, however, Barton's work supports both Wiley and more recent historians; he finds commonalities among American soldiers no matter what their rank or political allegiance.

More representative of the emerging work on soldiers was the next to appear in print, Joseph T. Glatthaar's *The March to the Sea and Beyond: Sherman's Troops in the Savannah and Carolinas Campaigns* (1985). All Glatthaar claimed to have done was extend Wiley's analysis of the Union soldier, which focused heavily on the Army of the Potomac, to Sherman's army. Actually, Glatthaar raised the study of the common soldier to a new level of sophistication by taking the soldier's attitudes toward the war, toward African Americans, and toward white southerners much more seriously than Wiley had. In other respects, Glatthaar stuck to Wiley's model. Like Wiley, Glatthaar paid great attention to the material circumstances of soldiering. His chapter on camp life is very much in Wiley's vein.[8]

Reenlisted veterans, men who supported Lincoln's reelection, composed the bulk of Sherman's army. Furthermore, because of the nature of the March, they depended on their own initiative and escaped the supervision of senior officers to an extraordinary degree. Glatthaar shows them to have had a strong commitment to Union, a hatred for southern society, which they perceived as not only treasonous but antidemocratic as well, and a hatred of slavery as an institution—although often accompanied by prejudice against African Americans and doubts about their place in America after emancipation. Beyond ideological motivations, Glatthaar also explicates the extreme self-confidence and self-reliance of Sherman's men, arguing that no other army could have made the March. (Here it might be added that the March would have been unthinkable in traditional European warfare; a European commander would have assumed that such a loosely controlled army would evaporate as its soldiers deserted.)

Probably *The March to the Sea and Beyond* did not influence the work that appeared immediately after its publication; for a work of scholarship to be absorbed requires more time, and some of us deliberately avoided reading it while we revised our dissertations for publication. But Glatthaar, building on Wiley's pioneering volumes, identified the issues with which historians of the soldiers have been most concerned—ideology, race relations, motivation, and how to fit new work into Wiley's legacy.

While *The March to the Sea and Beyond* represents the new mainstream, in retrospect the most significant book published on Civil War soldiers during the 1980s is Gerald F. Linderman, *Embattled Courage: The Experience of Combat in the American Civil War* (1987). Certainly it has created the most debate.[9] Linderman's portrayal of the Civil War is the bleakest in the literature. "Every war begins as one war and becomes two, that watched by civilians and that fought by soldiers." Linderman argues that during the Civil War, as during other wars, civilians keep alive romantic concepts of combat long after soldiers have lost them. The romantic concept of war most important to Linderman is courage, which for him is a "constellation of values," including honor, godliness, and manliness. Courage itself, he argues, had a narrow meaning for the soldiers of 1861—heroic action without fear—but as a central cultural icon, its importance went far beyond the battlefield. In the absence of discipline, courage held armies together. According to Linderman, men both north and south understood the war and its meaning through courage more than through ideology.[10]

Linderman presents the war as totally destructive of the naive ideals of Union and Confederate volunteers. Expectations of combat, ties to home, convictions about courage—the war diminished all of these. By the time the war was over, Linderman suggests, the gap between civilian fantasy and soldier reality could not be bridged. Yet, despite their disillusionment, veterans failed to tell the truth about the war; instead they were melted into the general late-nineteenth-century celebration.

Whatever its merits, which were considerable, Linderman's interpretation ran against the emerging trend in the study of Civil War soldiers. By relying so heavily on published materials, particularly memoirs, Linderman left himself open to attacks on his research as well as on his interpretation. I would argue that even given his broad-based definition, *courage* is too narrow a concept to symbolize the worldview of the soldiers. But Linderman should be congratulated for raising tough questions about the nature of the Civil War.

James I. Robertson, Jr.'s *Soldiers Blue and Gray* (1988) studiously avoided tough questions—and new ones. Robertson, a doctoral student of Bell Wiley, is also his most self-conscious heir. The purpose of this *Soldiers Blue and Gray* was to "supplement" Wiley by drawing on the large amount of primary material published since Wiley wrote *Johnny Reb* and *Billy Yank*. Breaking little new ground, Robertson offers the reader a fine, one-volume study that reaches many of the same conclusions that Wiley did. Like *Johnny Reb* and *Billy Yank, Soldiers Blue and Gray* is largely descriptive; Robertson does little to place soldier experience into any larger context. Robertson's organization of his material is most similar to Wiley's; there are chapters on enlisting, camp life, diversions, religion, and so on. If anything, Robertson is more celebratory than Wiley. "This study concentrates on that bulk of nineteenth century manhood," he writes, "the Johnny Rebs and Billy Yanks who, through service and sacrifice, bequeathed to all Americans an unforgettable legacy." Robertson does not neglect some of the less heroic aspects of war, but he is interested only in heroes. He explicitly excludes from consideration those men who "in general were unworthy of the soldier status they possessed." Rarely has a historian so openly shucked his responsibility to represent the past fully.[11]

Where Robertson surpasses Wiley is in his treatment of the United States Colored Troops. While Wiley was a pioneering historian not only of Civil War soldiers but of African Americans during the war as well, he discusses black soldiers only from the viewpoint of white soldiers. Robertson addresses the meaning of the war for black troops. But, in general, Robertson is Wiley Redux.

The year 1988 saw the publication of four books on Civil War soldiers. Besides *Soldiers Blue and Gray,* there were Randall C. Jimerson, *The Private Civil War;* Earl J. Hess, *Liberty, Virtue, and Progress;* and my *Civil War Soldiers.* While Hess considers only northern soldiers, Jimerson and I both compare Confederate and Yankee experiences and find in them a common American culture. It is worth noting that three of these books—Jimerson's, Hess's, and mine—were originally dissertations, as was Glatthaar's *March to the Sea and Beyond.*[12]

Earl J. Hess's *Liberty, Virtue, and Progress: Northerners and Their War for the Union* describes northern culture in general but considers the beliefs of Union soldiers in particular. He explains in his introduction that "This study grew from a desire to understand how a society emotionally conducts a long, costly war effort." *Liberty, Virtue, and Progress* is a study of ideology both as a set of ideas and a set of "cultural values"— what Clifford Gertz identified as "ideology as a cultural system." The values that Hess identifies as central to northern soldiers are "self-government, democracy, individualism, egalitarianism, and self-control." Furthermore, Hess insists that "the war's successful close reinforced the values of liberty in the North as no other event did."[13] Rather than changing them, the war perpetuated antebellum ideology and ideals. In this book—though not in his later *The Union Soldier in Battle* (1997)—Hess, like Linderman, draws on postwar memoirs and speeches as well as contemporary letters and diaries as sources for understanding the soldiers. While I have no major disagreements with his conclusions, occasionally I worry that, having used postwar sources to establish prewar beliefs, his emphasis on continuity becomes suspect. Nonetheless, *Liberty, Virtue, and Progress* is a brilliant book that failed to attract the notice it deserved.

Randall C. Jimerson acknowledges Bell Wiley and Bruce Catton as key to his "approach to understanding the Civil War." While Jimerson, a student of Gerald Linderman, considers civilians as well as soldiers in *The Private Civil War: Popular Thought during the Sectional Conflict,* this book, which draws on the letters and diaries of officers and enlisted men, is a major contribution to the study of the common soldier. Although Jimerson's book did not appear until the late 1980s, his dissertation, which I consulted for my book *Civil War Soldiers,* was accepted by the University of Michigan graduate school in 1977, which easily makes him the first of the post-Wiley generation.

Arguing that "belief in sectional difference overpowered the reality of cultural homogeneity," Jimerson concentrates on the shared cultural values of Confederate and Union soldiers. Both believed that they were fighting a war for freedom; but as Jimerson notes, "The similarities between northern and southern declarations about preserving liberty are striking, yet there are also subtle but significant differences of meaning." When they considered government, Confederates feared its power to interfere, while Unionists welcomed its power to protect liberty. Nonetheless, Jimerson's overall conclusion, one that I share, is that "the war thus reveals not two different civilizations, but one people divided by conflicting interpretations of common American values."

My own *Civil War Soldiers* reinforces many of Jimerson's conclusions. I argue for a shared American culture, which revealed itself in perceptions of the enemy, political rhetoric, the transformation of soldier to veteran, and so on. Like Jimerson and others, I posit ideology as the most significant reason for the enthusiastic volunteering at the start of the war. Along the lines of Wiley's *Plain People of the Confederacy,* I try to investigate some of the meaning that Confederate mishandling of the war had for soldiers. My most ambitious analysis is of what I termed "the landscape of war"—what I sometimes think of as "the *Heart of Darkness* chapter." Here I try to explore the Union soldier's sense that the South was a foreign country. Whatever differences in nuance between my interpretation and the work of Jimerson, Robertson, Linderman, Glatthaar, and Hess, my work fits easily into their broad analysis of soldiering.

Joseph Allan Frank, a political scientist, and George A. Reaves, longtime National Park historian at the Shiloh Battlefield, joined to write *"Seeing the Elephant"* (1989). Frank and Reaves had two purposes in this monograph. The first was to test the sweeping generalizations about Civil War soldiers made by two generations of scholars, from Bell Wiley on down, by focusing more narrowly on one specific group—Union and Confederate recruits at Shiloh, the first great battle of the war. The second was to apply "content analysis" to the social history of the soldiers.[14]

On the one hand, Frank and Reaves succeed in doing what those who employ social science methods do: "proving" the obvious. Few conclusions of *"Seeing the Elephant"* will surprise readers of the earlier literature; and if such readers choose to believe that these conclusions have been demonstrated more scientifically, I think they are naive. As Joseph T. Glatthaar observed of earlier "scientific" work on the soldiers, scholars "must rely ultimately on impression in deciding what words or phrases to count and how to interpret them." Despite its bogus airs of scientific respectability, "content analysis" is hardly scientific.[15]

On the other hand, *"Seeing the Elephant"* is rich in details and judicious in conclusions. Frank and Reaves consider issues beyond the first experience of combat. Like many others, they are particularly concerned to explain soldier motivation. Furthermore, as other scholars have, they identify surprisingly few significant differences between Union and Confederate soldiers.

Two more books, both of which appeared in the 1990s, should be considered as an extension of the literature of the 1980s. Larry J. Daniel's *Soldiering in the Army of Tennessee: A Portrait of Life in a Confederate Army* (1991) and James M. McPherson's *What They Fought For, 1861–1865* (1994) are also part of the emerging consensus on Civil War soldiers.[16]

Like Glatthaar, Larry J. Daniel provides additional insight into the soldier experience by focusing on one army. Furthermore, by choosing a western army, the Army of Tennessee, he helps shift the focus away from Lee's army, whose soldiers are overly represented in general surveys. Daniel does not argue that the western Confederates were fundamentally different from those of the east, although he does find they were less "refined." His principal interest is how an army that was more conversant with defeat than victory managed to keep its morale at fighting level. The "unity of the army," he says, can only be explained "from the bottom up."[17] The Army of Tennessee's morale depended on discipline—Braxton Bragg in particular was something of a martinet; the religious revivals around Dalton, Georgia, after the battle of Missionary Ridge; the nineteenth-century attitude toward battlefield deaths; and the emotional bonds of shared suffering. Quoting Union general John M. Schofield, Daniel concludes, "I doubt if any soldiers in the world ever needed so much cumulative evidence to convince them that they were beaten."[18]

James M. McPherson's *What They Fought For* is a teaser for his fuller treatment of Civil War soldiers, *For Cause and Comrades: Why Men Fought in the Civil War* (1997). In the longer work, McPherson examines a broad array of motives for service in the Union and Confederate armies; in *What They Fought For,* he concentrates on the ideological understanding of the war among the soldiers. The scholars for whom his attack is particularly relevant are Bell Wiley and Gerald Linderman. But McPherson is wrong to insist that scholars have neglected the ideology of Civil War soldiers. The works of Glatthaar, Jimerson, and myself all put ideology at the center of volunteerism; even Linderman admits that volunteers were ideologically motivated, although he believes that part of the process of turning into soldiers was losing such motivation.

McPherson breaks new ground in his effort to provide a statistical background of the men holding these attitudes and in his attempts to trace ideology over time. For example, among Confederate troops, he takes into account regional and class variations, finding that "a larger proportion of soldiers from the lower-South cotton states expressed strong patriotic and ideological motives than of those from the upper South." He argues that there was "a greater democratization of ideological purpose among Union soldiers." Disagreeing with Linderman, McPherson argues that there was no decline in ideological motivation among Union soldiers as the war progressed.[19]

After the initial round of publications on Civil War soldiers, some of the historians involved, as well as others, have extended the study by writing on additional groups or by focusing on a different set of issues. Examples of the first are Glatthaar's *Forged in Battle* (1990), which considers African American soldiers, Stuart McConnell's *Glorious Contentment* (1992), which looks at Union veterans, and Michael Fellman's *Inside War* (1989), a study of guerrillas; examples of the second include my *Vacant Chair* (1993), which draws on gender studies, and recent work by others concentrating more narrowly on soldier motivation.[20]

Joseph T. Glatthaar established himself as one of the leading historians of the soldier experience with his study of Sherman's army. His second book, *Forged in Battle: The Civil War Alliance of Black Soldiers and White Officers*, was more difficult to research but as fine as his first. With the exception of immigrants, white soldiers left a marvelous body of evidence behind them; black soldiers, the overwhelming majority of whom had been enslaved and denied even minimal education, did not.

Glatthaar argues that while some officers in the United States Colored Troops were men-on-the-make, that is, enlisted men who wanted to become officers, in general the officers were of high quality in terms of their commitment to antislavery, religious belief, past education, and political savvy. At least as important, most of them were experienced soldiers. They were men willing to endure social ostracism to command black troops. On the average, the soldiers of the USCT may have had better officers than their white counterparts. Glatthaar also reveals the limits of the wartime alliance of black soldiers and white officers. Once the war was won and slavery abolished, as a rule white officers did not support equal rights or black suffrage.

Glatthaar's portrayal of the limits of even USCT officers' allegiance to black rights agrees with the general discussion of Union veterans in Stuart McConnell's *Glorious Contentment: The Grand Army of the Re-*

*public*. McConnell analyzes how one group of veterans tried to deal with memories of the war. "I have tried to cast my net widely," McConnell writes, "to recapture the social and cultural meaning of Grand Army membership." While he hardly neglects the GAR's role as a pension lobby, so ably described by Mary R. Dearing's *Veterans in Politics: The Story of the GAR* (1952), McConnell shows how northern veterans congratulated themselves for saving the Union. According to McConnell, the GAR spent far less time commemorating the soldiers' destruction of slavery, and despite its support of the Grand Old Party, as the century closed the veterans fully supported sectional reconciliation. Hess's *Liberty, Virtue, and Progress* and McConnell's *Glorious Contentment* agree on the continuity of Union idealism, but McConnell sees this continuity as a far more conservative phenomenon than does Hess.[21]

Michael Fellman's *Inside War: The Guerrilla Conflict in Missouri during the American Civil War* considers one category of fighting men that Robertson in *Soldiers Blue and Gray* deliberately eschewed: guerrillas. Fellman analyzes if not the ideology the ethos of guerrillas and counterinsurgents in the Missouri war. This was a vicious, nasty war that Americans rarely choose to remember and now find impossible to celebrate. But as Fellman shows, Missouri guerrillas, including Quantrill's raiders, held veterans' reunions like everybody else. Arguing that "real war assaults, diminishes, and embitters participants," Fellman's account of insurgency and counterinsurgency and the hell that combatants of both sides created for civilians caught in the middle reveals the dynamics of what he calls "self-organized combat."[22]

My own book, *The Vacant Chair: The Northern Soldier Leaves Home* studies northern culture, and although I framed questions differently from the way Hess did, I concur with many of his conclusions in *Liberty, Virtue, and Progress*. Arguing that conceptions of domesticity and family roles influenced the way northerners perceived the world and thus the war, I tried to link gender studies with the social history of the northern soldier. Clearly, the relationship between masculinity and soldiering is an important one. It is not, however, necessarily the most important domestic concern for understanding the war. Northern men prided themselves on their manly self-restraint; a new understanding of true manhood had emerged from the social transformation of the antebellum era. Northerners also prided themselves on the stability of their homes and families, the crucible in which these "true men" were forged. When they looked south, they saw men who "unmanned" themselves with their lack of self-restraint and homes that interracial sexual license had made unworthy of the designation. They saw what we might call the domestic preconditions of rebellion. When northerners compared themselves to southerners, they imagined a culture prone to license that threatened to make war on a culture based on virtue, self-restraint, and patriotism—values they believed were inculcated by the virtuous and patriotic mothers of the North.

Mark Grimsley's *The Hard Hand of War* (1995) is primarily a nuanced presentation and appreciation of Union policy toward civilians, but its argument depends heavily on the author's understanding of Union soldiers and their concept of self-control. Union military policy of directed severity "survived because tens of thousands of Union soldiers—toughened by war, hungry for creature comforts, and often angry at civilians in their midst—nevertheless understood the logic and abided by it." Grimsley shows that Union soldiers resisted the policy of conciliation that characterized the first years of the war but that the bulk of them did observe restraint in the war upon civilians.[23]

Following the lead of Lloyd Lewis and Bruce Catton, historians continue to consider the experience of soldiers when describing battles and campaigns. They draw on manuscript sources far more than Lewis and Catton did, and the integration of the soldier's viewpoint with the general's has become more sophisticated. Four examples among the dozens I could cite: Charles Royster, *The Destructive War: William Tecumseh Sherman, Stonewall Jackson, and the Americans* (1991), John J. Hennessy, *Return to Bull Run: The Campaign and Battle of Second Manassas* (1993), Stephen W. Sears, *To the Gates of Richmond: The Peninsula Campaign* (1992), and Harry W. Pfanz, *Gettysburg: The Second Day* (1987). Perhaps it is worth mentioning that Hennessy and Pfanz are National Park Service historians whose familiarity with the battles they discuss exceeds that of many academic scholars for their subjects.[24]

The first attempt to synthesize recent literature—and to extend it—is Larry M. Logue's provocative *To Appomattox and Beyond: The Civil War Soldier in War and Peace* (1996). Logue's starting place is his understanding of the difference between northern and southern societies. Logue goes further than any of the historians previously discussed in distinguishing Union and Confederate soldiers. Furthermore, he carries the story well past the end of the war.

Carefully putting the soldier's experience in the context of American social change, Logue argues that self-control, inculcated by a modernizing society, was the essential cultural value for northern soldiers. According to Logue, honor and feeling influenced southern soldiers more. Logue also emphasizes the difference between Confederate and Union veterans' experiences, suggesting that Confederate veterans had greater influence on politics in the South than Union veterans had in the North or in the nation as a whole. Logue's "synthesis" poses a challenge to one of the general conclusions of historians in the field: the cultural similarity of the Union and Confederate soldiers.

None of Bell Wiley's children has been oedipal. Not only does the father still live; nobody has tried to kill him either. There is only one area of great disagreement between the generations and that is the importance of ideology as a motivating factor in the enlistment and subsequent service of the common soldier. It seems to be the case that scholarship on the soldier can be divided into that written by the World War II generation and that by the Vietnam War generation. *Johnny Reb* appeared during World War II and *Billy Yank* in 1952. Wiley, in fact, was one of the authors of the U. S. Army's "green book" on creating the World War II army. Perhaps his understanding of the American soldier in that war distorted Wiley's interpretation of the Civil War generation. It is hard otherwise to explain his insistence that Civil War soldiers rarely thought about the political issues of the war when their correspondence, which Wiley knew as well as any scholar, is full of discussion of just such issues. World War II veterans seem particularly prone to denigrate the influence of soldiers' ideology.[25]

Until recently, historians have not been fratricidal either. Despite differences in interpretation, practitioners in our field have refrained from squabbling among themselves, and perhaps the latent disagreements strike few of us as serious. After all, there is general consensus that soldiers were ideologically motivated, at least initially, and most of us identify roughly the same set of motivations.

The reluctance to quarrel has reached its end. The scholar whose work has drawn the most fire is Gerald Linderman. Two books published in 1997 disagree vigorously with the interpretation offered by Linderman's *Embattled Courage*—James M. McPherson's *For Cause and Comrades* and Earl J. Hess's *The Union Soldier in Battle*.[26]

McPherson rejects Linderman's portrayal of war-weary veterans out of hand. McPherson's two most notable contributions are his care at delineating soldier ideology over the course of the war and his importation from French history of John A. Lynn's conceptual framework. Lynn subdivided soldier motivation into three categories: initial motivation, sustaining motivation, and combat motivation. The use of Lynn's categories lets McPherson write far more carefully of motivation than any of his predecessors. McPherson finds ideology as key to both initial and sustaining motivation. He also considers religion, regional pride, and other factors as part of sustaining motivation. Like many historians of World War II, McPherson finds "primary group cohesion" crucial to combat motivation, but he emphasizes that, whatever prompted men in battle, without sustaining motivation—belief in the cause—there would be no armies to bring to the battlefield. Like Linderman, McPherson pays particular attention to the last portion of the war; unlike Linderman, he finds no diminishment of ideological motivation for either Confederate or Union soldiers. *For Cause and Comrades* deftly summarizes the field, treats with greater sophistication issues raised earlier, and adds to the debate that Linderman initiated.

Many of us who write about Civil War soldiers pay lip service to Keegan's *Face of Battle.* Hess is the only one who has actually employed Keegan's methods. *The Union Soldier in Battle* is a *Face of Battle* for the Civil War; there is no better book on combat during that war. But Hess goes far beyond Keegan in his assessment of soldier motivation and soldier memory of battle.

Hess's thesis is that rather than victims, as portrayed by Linderman, Union soldiers were "victors over the horrors of combat." Whereas Linderman sees nothing but the destruction of early ideals, Hess finds their transformation and retention. Hess attributes the perseverance of Union soldiers to a variety of reasons, including ideology and religion, comradeship—and linear tactical formations—support from home, and pragmatic working-class habits. He argues that the soldiers shaped the battle experience into something manageable and that most did not let war change their characters. The overwhelming majority of Union veterans, Hess says, did not suffer from disillusionment. Instead, they took pride in both the cause and their sacrifices for it.[27]

The debate over *Embattled Courage* should be only a beginning. There are numerous fault lines in the literature. For example, one implicit debate concerns the nature of ideology. Here the studies of James M. McPherson and Gerald Linderman represent the two poles. McPherson goes the farthest in understanding ideology as a system of explicit ideas; Linderman, along with me to a far lesser extent, treats ideology primarily as a cultural system. What constitutes ideology? Is "patriotism," for example, a set of ideas and ideals, an emotional allegiance, a symbolic system? What does it mean to say that soldiers on both sides were influenced by patriotism? At what point, if any, is it useful to criticize soldiers' beliefs? Nobody, I trust, is prepared to defend the Confederate soldier's pro-slavery beliefs. But when a Union soldier says that the Confederacy plans to enslave the North or a Confederate says that Yankees advocate racial intermarriage—both wildly untrue—should we call this paranoia? How do we discuss such beliefs without using slippery and misleading psychological terms? Is paranoia ideology?

Another question, historiographical rather than historical, is the intellectual origins of this literature. Since I was moved to study Civil War soldiers, partly by the resurgence in the study of war and society associated with Keegan's *The Face of Battle* and Paul Fussell's *The Great War and Modern Memory*, I have always assumed that those two studies influenced most others in the field—not as models but as inspirations. I have said as much in print.[28]

Now I am not so sure. James M. McPherson cites Fussell and Keegan in his two studies; Glatthaar cites Keegan, although not Fussell, in *The March to the Sea and Beyond*, and Gerald Linderman also cites Keegan alone. Despite all the clamor for a "Face of Battle" for the Civil War, only Hess has made the attempt to portray one, and even his vivid description of the physicality of war fails to deal as precisely with the application of force on human bodies as Keegan did. As for the rest of us, we agree that battle was really awful and people got killed. This does *not* constitute a "Face of Battle for the Civil War."

Another implicit debate that particularly interests me has to do with the experience of war. Students of the war experience profoundly disagree over the psychological impact of soldiering. The question, put bluntly, is, Did the war screw up soldiers? Rather than divide the scholars into two separate camps, it might be better to consider positions on a continuum. On the far end of the spectrum, those who find little psychological damage are James I. Robertson, Earl J. Hess, and, I think, James M. McPherson. On the other end, those who suspect the war played havoc with men's psyches are Linderman and perhaps Michael Fellman ("real war assaults, diminishes, and embitters participants"). Joseph T. Glatthaar, who considered the postwar careers of white officers with the USCT, and I are somewhere near the middle of the spectrum. My skepticism may be little more than emotional—I find it hard to believe that the experience of soldiering does not have a deleterious effect on the human psyche, and if the short stories of Ambrose Bierce do not establish that it did, a plethora of GAR orations do not prove that it did not.[29]

Maybe it all comes down to how we view war and human nature. There is one thing that none of us would deny: the evidence is abundant, and you can ask as many questions as you care to ask about historical trauma, human experience, and the individual heart. And the questions will be old ones. Homer began the *Iliad* with "Anger now be thy song;" and Virgil the *Aeneid* with "I sing of arms and the man." After Cain killed Abel and God caught him, the Lord said—in the words of the King James Version of the Bible that so many Civil War soldiers read and cherished—"What hast thou done? the voice of thy brother's blood crieth unto me from the ground." And after the Lord cursed him, Cain answered: "my punishment is greater than I can bear."

# ABRAHAM LINCOLN VS. JEFFERSON DAVIS

## Comparing Presidential Leadership in the Civil War

### MARK E. NEELY, JR.

In 1960, on the threshold of the twentieth-century presidency's most glamorous period, modern historiography on presidential leadership in the Civil War enjoyed a promising beginning with the publication of David M. Potter's essay "Jefferson Davis and the Political Factors in Confederate Defeat."[1] Potter, among the greatest of American historians in the twentieth century, asserted that "it hardly seems unrealistic to suppose that if the Union and the Confederacy had exchanged presidents with one another, the Confederacy might have won its independence."[2] Yet, a generation later, in a volume of essays entitled *Abraham Lincoln: Sources and Style of Leadership* and published in 1994, Jefferson Davis is mentioned in only three sentences. The references to Davis are incidental and have nothing to do with the comparative leadership abilities of the two presidents.[3]

In a sense, then, the comparative historiography of presidential leadership in the Civil War both began and ended with Potter's essay. One attempt to compare Lincoln and Davis has appeared since Potter's, but it was of article length, and, the author, after showing promising insights, ultimately fell prey to a sarcasm that displaced sober analysis.[4] Dozens of Civil War articles and books written after 1960 contain a sentence or a paragraph or two comparing Lincoln and Davis. But serious attempts of greater length than Potter's, based on close historical reading of the sources, to compare presidential leadership in the North and South in the Civil War do not exist. Nor have all the books written about Lincoln or Davis since 1960 attempted to assess the question of presidential leadership.

With little substantial literature comparing presidential leadership in the Civil War, this essay cannot rest on an obvious, well-defined body of works. Another author might well tackle this subject by discussing an entirely different array. Works that focus primarily on military strategy are excluded from this essay, as they belong with other essays in this volume.[5]

## THE LIMITATIONS OF THE EXISTING LITERATURE

Limitations and problems of the existing literature include the following: a gross imbalance between the amounts of scholarship on the two figures; a turning away from study of the presidential administration of Lincoln in modern times; the irrelevance of much early literature on Davis because of dated racial assumptions; and the absorption in trivial subjects in the early literature on both men.

Any assessment of the literature risks imbalance, for the number and quality of the works on Abraham Lincoln dwarf those on Jefferson Davis. To write about Davis as a historiographically equal subject of necessity slights some of the Lincoln works. Moreover, recent literature on Lincoln is not the best to use in judging his leadership. Nothing equals in exhaustiveness James G. Randall's four-volume *Lincoln the President* (completed after Randall's death by Richard N. Current in 1955), the early volumes of which appeared at the end of World War II. Nor would any assessment be complete without reference to the ten-volume history co-authored by Lincoln's private secretaries, John G. Nicolay and John Hay, which appeared before the end of the nineteenth century.[6]

Unlike the older Lincoln scholarship, the older Davis scholarship is severely limited in relevance, much of it outmoded by radically altered assumptions about race in the post-1960 era. For example, Hamilton James Eckenrode's *Jefferson Davis, President of the South,* published in 1923, was inspired by the ideas of the popular racialist writer Madison Grant and depicted the Confederate president as the last best hope of the Nordic race.[7]

The older literature on Davis shares with that on Lincoln another limitation: the preoccupation with popular subjects. Both these figures in the past held status as popular icons and symbols as well as historical figures whose presidential policies, administrative actions, and political ideas attracted serious scholarly study. A glance at a Davis bibliography from the 1930s reveals how many works focused on popular questions: whether he was wearing women's clothes when he was captured at the end of the war, whether late in life he endorsed prohibition of alcoholic beverages, and what role he played in the conspiracy to assassinate

Abraham Lincoln. These unfortunate preoccupations have left many serious subjects unstudied or incompletely assessed; among them are the
economic thought of Jefferson Davis, his constitutional ideas, and even
his racial views.[8]

An older work on Davis, as thoughtful as any ever written, serves to
point up the general neglect of Davis as a serious subject of study. In
1915, Nathaniel W. Stephenson published in the *American Historical
Review* a speculative article called "A Theory of Jefferson Davis."
Stephenson, among the first academic historians to write on Lincoln and
Davis, also took an early interest in applying psychology to history. He
argued that Davis's youth was not shaped by those local institutions that
made southerners naturally fond of state rights. Instead, he was almost a
man without a state. Until he reached the age of twenty-seven, his was a
peculiarly national career, much of it spent far from home influences. At
age seven he trekked off to preparatory school in Kentucky hundreds of
miles north of his childhood home in Mississippi. It was a Catholic school
at that, offering an intellectual atmosphere as different from his Baptist
home environment as could be found anywhere in the slave states. The
completion of his college education, begun at Transylvania in Kentucky,
came at the United States Military Academy at West Point, New York,
one of only two national schools in the country. Military assignments
followed, several of them in bleakly cold, faraway northern outposts.[9]

He settled down to a Deep South plantation environment only after
his first marriage in 1835. After his wife's early death, he continued to live
near his brother Joseph E. Davis in Mississippi and planted and talked
politics. Stephenson surmised that Davis never internalized the state rights
theories he later espoused as a sectionalist politician in the 1850s. His
state rights career was a "self deception," and he was a state rights "thinker
at second hand" only. When he became president of the Confederacy in
1861, he quickly cast off these ideas for nationalistic ones and thus returned to his "basal impulses."[10]

Stephenson's intriguing invitation to assess Davis's psychology was
never fully accepted.[11] By contrast, Abraham Lincoln, as healthy-minded
and robust a president as ever occupied the White House, has been the
subject of many strained psychological inquiries, especially in recent years,
and even his physical health has undergone skeptical scrutiny. Jefferson
Davis, not Lincoln, was the likely subject for the medical historian's scal-
pel and the psychohistorian's couch, as Stephenson recognized over eighty
years ago. Davis, who essentially disappeared from history for a decade
after the death of his first wife, and who emerged from this exile to marry
a woman about half his age and enter politics, ever after exhibited a mass

of physiological and psychological pains and tics.

His physical health was demonstrably poorer than Lincoln's. He was by the time of the war virtually blind in one eye. In Mississippi he had contracted malaria—a recurrent malady, especially debilitating in late summer, a time when the commander-in-chief's attention was most needed for coordinating military campaigns.[12] He suffered also from facial neuralgia, poor digestion, insomnia, and nervous exhaustion. Whatever the source and extent of Davis's physical or psychological problems, they affected his leadership, causing loss of work days to illness and a marked inability to deal at all times agreeably and patiently with politicians, generals, critics, and the general public.[13]

By way of ironic contrast, the current fascination with Lincoln's private life has led historians away from the presidential years and the studies of policy and administration that would make possible new assessments of his leadership following modern models borrowed from political science. Instead, typical modern studies deal with psychology and intimate biography.[14]

## JEFFERSON DAVIS AND LEADERSHIP OF THE CONFEDERACY

Modern developments in scholarship on the Confederacy, racial questions aside, at first favored a rise in Davis's reputation as president. What might be called the modernist school of Confederate history has benefited him, beginning with the work of Frank E. Vandiver and continuing with his graduate students and other historians inspired by his arguments. Vandiver's *Jefferson Davis and the Confederate State,* his 1964 Harmsworth lecture, drawing on his earlier research on Confederate manufacturing, supply, and armament, came up with an image of Davis as modernizer:

> The techniques of administration and business management Davis adopted during the war, the experiment he conducted in rudimentary economic planning, in social control, in national mobilization, all represented fundamental changes in the South—changes which wrenched it rudely into modern times. . . . All of which is to say that when the Confederate dream ended at Appomattox, Dixie was far more modern, far more compatible with the North than ever before.

Vandiver later extended the insight to a comparative piece entitled "The Civil War as an Institutionalizing Force" (1968).[15]

Vandiver's student, Emory M. Thomas, instead of invoking "modernization" or "institutionalizing," hit upon "revolutionary" as the rubric to describe a similar phenomenon in his influential book *The Confederacy as a Revolutionary Experience* (1971). He pictured a Confederate "revolution" somewhat out of the control of its instigators and propelling dramatic changes in the South:

> The Confederate government, albeit unwittingly, transformed the South from a state rights confederation into a centralized, national state. In so doing the government, or more usually Jefferson Davis as leader and symbol of the civilian Confederacy, incurred the displeasure of those who felt the government had gone too far and of those who thought it had not gone far enough. Within the limits of its ability the Davis administration dragged Southerners kicking and screaming into the nineteenth century.[16]

Since what Thomas described was an "unwitting" revolution, perhaps it would be wrong to weigh this heavily on the side of raising the estimate of Jefferson Davis's leadership. Thomas himself refused to "harangue on the merits of Jefferson Davis" but nevertheless felt the "need to respond to Davis' critics on some points."[17]

The Vandiver-Thomas revolution in Confederate history raised the reputation of Jefferson Davis, though that was hardly its intent or starting-point. The viewpoint has influenced the biographies of Davis that have appeared since 1960. Clement Eaton's *Jefferson Davis* (1977), a book unequal to its distinguished author's reputation, put forward no clear message. Though Eaton seems never to have made up his mind about Davis, he did credit him with growth in the presidency, "especially in freeing himself from the incubus of his original state rights obsession and arising as a true statesman to a conception of the growth of an organic nation and the development of realistic policies to attain Southern nationalism."[18] William C. Davis's *Jefferson Davis: The Man and His Hour* (1991), longer and more diffuse than Eaton's work, likewise retained the modernizing view:

> More than anyone else, Jefferson Davis built the system and organization that kept those armies in the field another four years. Cajoling the governors, dominating Congress, having the courage to call for and enforce conscription, taxation, and the impressment of agricultural produce did not make him popular, but it kept the legions manned, armed, fed, and moving. Moreover it was Davis who, more than anyone else, accounted for what little sense of Confederate nationalism grew in the South. It came at the price of some of his

cherished states' rights beliefs, and cost him the goodwill of men like Stephens, Brown, Toombs, Vance, and more.[19]

*System* and *organization* were not words that came readily to mind in writing about Jefferson Davis in the nineteenth century, but after Vandiver and Thomas wrote, they commonly appeared in works about his presidency.[20]

The Vandiver-Thomas modernist school was soon challenged, however, by the appearance of the best book on Jefferson Davis written since 1960 and perhaps the best ever written about him: Paul D. Escott's *After Secession: Jefferson Davis and the Failure of Confederate Nationalism* (1978). The very title signaled Escott's dissent from the Vandiver-Thomas school. Whereas Thomas wrote a history of the Confederacy entitled *The Confederate Nation, 1861–1865,* Escott put the focus on the *failure* of Confederate nationalism. Along the way, he made important points about the leadership of the Confederate president.

Escott managed to salvage the insight that lay in Stephenson's "theory" without heavy-handed imputations of Davis's insincerity and without psychological speculation. Instead, he kept in mind the political problems faced by Davis and the Confederacy. Escott depicted Davis as a conscious, intelligent, and subtle molder of Confederate ideology. The result is the most serious consideration of Davis's developing political thought during the Civil War.

Escott marks Davis's political thought as president carefully against the key events in Confederate history. In the beginning, he argues, Davis made a shrewd move away from slavery apologetics to an ideology that stressed the continuity of American history from the era of the Articles of Confederation to the Confederate States of America, which now alone, according to Davis, carried the promise of constitutional liberty from the era of the founders. Defending slavery—even mentioning it in political rhetoric, as the tone-deaf and perverse Alexander H. Stephens had done in his disastrous "cornerstone" speech—was divisive in the South, helpful to the Republicans in the North, and likely harmful to the reputation of the Confederacy in world opinion. Above all, it reminded the majority of nonslaveholders in the Confederacy of the sacrifices they were making for the slaveholders' property rights.

Thus, stressing liberty or southern rights and avoiding slavery apologetics served the Confederate cause well, but it was not enough, Escott argued, when the military fortunes of the South turned desperate. Then Davis did not prove adaptable enough to find new doctrines to keep up the people's morale. After Gettysburg and Vicksburg, Escott said, "Confederate ideology . . . practically ceased to exist as an ideology. No organized body of doctrine, principles, and goals remained, only the prod of fear." Davis offered the people from then on, Escott asserted, only threats, grim predictions, denunciations of the malignant rage of the enemy, and the specter of servile insurrection.[21]

What the Confederacy needed was a fresh turn in ideology toward policies that would offer relief to the common people for their extraordinary sacrifices for the war effort. Because he was himself a planter and because he represented the planter class that controlled the Confederate state, Escott suggested, Davis had nothing to offer the common people. "Ideology," Escott said, "meant less . . . to the common people of the Confederacy. Their prime need was immediate economic assistance, and they did not hesitate to seek or accept it whenever it was offered."[22] In the final analysis, Escott concluded:

> any assessment of him as Confederate president must rest to a great degree upon his sensitivity to problems of morale and his effectiveness in eliciting the enthusiasm and energies of the people. It is in this area that the judgment of Davis must be most harsh.
>
> The Confederacy's chief executive proved insensitive to the problems of ordinary southerners, who suffered greatly from inflation, shortages, speculation, and impressment.[23]

What Escott offered, without saying it in so many words, was the dialectical answer to the modernist view of Jefferson Davis. The Vandiver-Thomas school, one realizes after reading Escott, was preoccupied with the innovations of the Confederate elite—"rudimentary economic planning," "social control," and "national mobilization"—and did not take fully into account the lot of those citizens who were controlled, mobilized, and fit into others' plans, though they be "kicking" and "screaming." The common people suffered and went hungry and died, and because Davis and the planters would not adequately provide for their relief, Confederate nationalism failed.[24]

Thanks especially to the Vandiver-Thomas school and Escott's response to it, the theoretical stage is now set for fruitful debate on Davis's leadership. Lamentably, it will likely be a long time coming. It seems doubtful that the debate will advance rapidly without a readily available and reliable edition of Jefferson Davis's works. The publication of the first collection of Davis's letters and papers to benefit from modern documentary editorial standards is under way and has to date reached a bit beyond the half-way point of his presidential years.[25] Lincoln's works have been available since 1955. By this crude measure, Davis scholarship is at least forty years, more than a generation, behind. The editorial team at the Davis Papers project bears an awesome responsibility for the future of scholarship on the Confederacy.

In the end, although Davis scholarship has been immensely enriched in recent times, the dialogue has proved to be an internal one, among southern historians and historians of the Confederacy. The wider impact is hardly detectable. It would be difficult to imagine, even some thirty-eight years and several revisionist works after David Potter's celebrated essay on political leadership, the publication of a volume analogous to the one on Lincoln mentioned in the first paragraph of this article, called *Jefferson Davis: Sources and Style of Leadership*.

## ABRAHAM LINCOLN AND LEADERSHIP OF THE UNITED STATES

Lincoln scholarship has shown in the period since the appearance of Potter's essay little deviation from the general twentieth-century judgment that his presidential leadership deserved the highest marks.[26] Nevertheless, there were changes on questions of race, slavery, and politics. Earlier in this century historians emphasized the differences between Lincoln's ideal of emancipation and race adjustment and the policies his administration actually imposed during the Civil War. James G. Randall, for example, always took pains to show that Lincoln desired a gradual and compensated emancipation that bore little resemblance to wartime emancipation by presidential proclamation. The view prevailed that the immediate and uncompensated scheme represented in the Emancipation Proclamation was forced on him by the radical wing of the Republican party—a view which, implicitly if not explicitly, proved that Lincoln was not the political master of his own house.

The rashest statement of the case came in T. Harry Williams's *Lincoln and the Radicals* (1941). Williams, who often used similes best left in the barracks, put the political relationship between Lincoln and the Radical Republicans this way: "The wily Lincoln surrendered to the conquering Jacobins in every controversy before they could publicly inflict upon him a damaging reverse. Like the fair Lucretia threatened with ravishment, he averted his fate by instant compliance."[27] Of the developments leading up to the Emancipation Proclamation, Williams said the following, and it typified the judgments of his generation:

bulking larger in Lincoln's thoughts than the uncertainties of diplomatic developments were the grave issues of domestic politics. The

strongest cornerstone of his program had been the all-parties coalition of Republicans, Democrats, and loyal slaveholders, to fight the
war to a conclusion. To hold this discordant conglomeration together it was imperative that he be able to repress the abolitionist
instincts of his own party. This Lincoln could not do. . . . While he
had hoped to build an inclusive political alliance to sustain his efforts to restore the Union, it was important above all else that he
have the support of his own ardent followers. Without their aid he
could not preserve the American experiment in government. Nor
was he blind to the mounting Jacobinism among the people whose
tribune he always considered himself to be. If they demanded that
the Union be saved through emancipation, Abraham Lincoln would
save it that way.[28]

Since 1960 ideas have altered dramatically, and Lincoln's claims to
leadership, especially on the question of slavery, are anchored in various
able monographs and articles, the most tightly argued of which is LaWanda
Cox's *Lincoln and Black Freedom: A Study in Presidential Leadership*
(1981).[29] The subtitle was significant: Professor Cox dealt seriously with
the issue of leadership and was intent on reversing the image left by the
revisionist historians like Randall and Williams:

When war opened possibilities unapproachable in the 1850s,
Lincoln's reach was not found wanting. Indeed, there is something
breathtaking in his advance from prewar advocacy of restricting
slavery's spread to foremost responsibility for slavery's total, immediate, uncompensated destruction by constitutional amendment. The
progression represented a positive exercise of leadership. It has often been viewed as a reluctant accommodation to pressures; it can
better be understood as a ready response to opportunity. Willing to
settle for what was practicable, provided it pointed in the right direction, Lincoln was alert to the expanding potential created by war.
Military needs, foreign policy, Radical agitation did not force him
upon an alien course but rather helped clear a path toward a long-
desired but intractable objective.[30]

Because she focused on slavery and race—mainly on reconstruction
in Louisiana—Cox compared Lincoln not with Jefferson Davis but with
Andrew Johnson. She also devoted almost a fourth of her text to a chapter entitled "Reflections on the Limits of the Possible." She answered
political scientist James MacGregor Burns's naive criticism of Lincoln's

leadership. Burns faulted Lincoln for absorption in "operationalism" and for leaving the country visionless at his death so that Reconstruction efforts to bring black equality failed. "What the South needed," Burns wrote, "was . . . long-run development programs sponsored by the federal government, like those that have become familiar to us in recent years and that were not unknown to men of vision in the 1860's."[31] Cox, by contrast, took note of the state of scientific opinion on race, the lack of national consensus and consequent confinement of progressive goals for the black population to the Republican party alone, and other limits imposed by the intellectual assumptions of the nineteenth century:

> The years of political Reconstruction, to borrow an apt phrase from Thomas B. Alexander's study of Tennessee, offered no "narrowly missed opportunities to leap a century forward in reform." Not even a Lincoln could have wrought such a miracle. To have secured something less, yet something substantially more than blacks had gained by the end of the nineteenth century, did not lie beyond the limits of the possible given a president who at war's end would have joined party in an effort to realize "as nearly as we can" the fullness of freedom for blacks.[32]

In praising Lincoln's vision and political skills to Andrew Johnson's disadvantage, Cox did note one curious and off-putting feature, that "Lincoln's presidential style" was "at odds with that forthrightness which stands high in twentieth-century criteria for presidential leadership."[33] Sometimes it served to gain grudging support gradually for ambitious goals, but the fact remains that he preferred often to work deviously, leading politicians and people alike to think he was not going to do what he had already in fact decided to do (as was the case with emancipation itself in the summer of 1862).

Cox's penetrating critique of revisionist views of emancipation and wartime reconstruction failed to anticipate the next development in scholarship on this question. She pointed out the obstacles that faced Lincoln and Johnson in the First Reconstruction. These obstacles made the Second Reconstruction of the 1960s a "false model" for historians attempting to measure what had been possible in the 1860s. Cox mentioned among other things the role of African Americans:

> In the creation of the national consensus of the 1950s blacks themselves played a key role beyond that open to them a century earlier. Their political influence in the North was considerable because of

the numbers who had moved out of the South to fill northern labor needs. The distance from slavery allowed their leaders, South as well as North, to operate with formidable resources, skills, and organization and to present a case that could no longer be evaded by a show of scientific or social justification. They made inescapably visible to white America the injustices piled high during the postemancipation decades.[34]

For some historians this judgment underestimated the contribution of African Americans to their own freedom during the Civil War and, implicitly, exaggerated Lincoln's.

Like the dialectical response to the modernist school in Jefferson Davis historiography, a competing view of emancipation arose among black and radical historians. This new theory, which may be called the theory of self-emancipation, once again relegated Lincoln to a follower's role. Now, however, he appeared to succumb not to the radicals in Congress but to the overwhelming fact of emancipation realized by nameless slaves who left the loosely guarded and sparsely populated plantations during the war to meet Union armies or arrive in northern-controlled areas. Their anomalous presence demanded administration policies to deal with them and define their status. The overall result of this idea for Lincoln scholarship was similar to that for Davis in the Escott book: the common people were inserted into a historical scheme previously dominated by members of the political elite only. The purpose was rather different. The focus in the case of emancipation was not, as it was in the case of the common white people of the Confederacy, on injustice, social class, and the suffering of these people. The point was the agency of the African Americans, their being the shapers of their own destiny and not the passive objects of government policy.

The new view offered a valuable corrective, based on the method of social history. Lincoln biographers had long admitted that the Emancipation Proclamation, a piece of paper on a desk in Washington, at first did not actually free anyone. To realize the free status it offered, slaves had somehow to come under the control of the Union, and thousands did so by their own efforts, fleeing plantations to come into Union lines. Such efforts were not easy, and the myriad acts of individual courage demonstrated by slaves have been until recent times ignored completely by history—and to some degree unfairly overshadowed by veneration of the Great Emancipator. That injustice has been corrected without diminishing Lincoln's reputation as leader except in areas where it was already stunted—among black and radical historians. The Emancipation Proclamation blazed the trail, but it often required the courage and initiative of ordinary slaves to follow it to actual freedom.

The developments in the study of emancipation policy during the Civil War illustrate an important point about the study of presidential leadership in the Civil War: that study was essentially born dead with Potter's essay, and it is likely to remain dead as a question framed in Potter's terms. It seems significant that the major challenge to the idea of Lincoln as leader on emancipation, the self-emancipation theory, cannot be located in any work on the president or, indeed, in any single work at all. Instead, the idea welled up from several studies of the impact of African Americans on the Civil War. The first and most circumspect was Leon F. Litwack's *Been in the Storm So Long: The Aftermath of Slavery* (1979), but also important were the thick volumes published by the project for the Documentary History of Emancipation and Barbara J. Fields's book, *Slavery and Freedom on the Middle Ground: Maryland during the Nineteenth Century* (1985).[35] It is easier to find responses to the theory from Lincoln's defenders than to find the theory of self-emancipation itself systematically spelled out as scholarly theories usually are and buttressed with appropriate evidence.[36]

The theory of self-emancipation implies that Lincoln offered no leadership, but no one explicitly argued that position, and, by and large, Lincoln's reputation as leader survived. His abilities as political leader especially enjoyed steady praise, beginning, a little before Potter's essay, with David Donald's *Lincoln Reconsidered: Essays on the Civil War Era* (1956) and continuing through the work of LaWanda Cox.[37]

Potter's old question of whether an exchange of presidents between the Confederacy and the Union would have reversed the outcome of the war is not likely to inspire new works on the presidency of Lincoln or Davis. That was a question that loomed large only in an era when the "great man" theory of history still thrived. In current historical writing such a view of individual greatness is usually the product of emphasis on constitutional history and on the traditional source of political history, the state papers, speeches, and letters of political elites. Such an approach is best seen in Phillip Shaw Paludan's *Presidency of Abraham Lincoln* (1994), a volume in a series on the U.S. presidents.

Paludan's assessment relies on traditional sources and to a surprising degree on a forthrightly sunny outlook on American constitutional history. "The underlying premise of the book," he says, "is that the political-constitutional system, conceived and operated at its best, inescapably leads to equality." Paludan admits being "particularly interested in what Lincoln said, for the most important power of a president . . . is the power to persuade." The principal original contribution to Lincoln historiography of *The Presidency of Abraham Lincoln* is an assessment of "how Lincoln managed to shape a public understanding." Here Paludan follows a trail blazed by James M. McPherson, but the underlying conception of the presidency in this scheme is essentially anachronistic. Politicians in the nineteenth century had scant notion of public opinion apart from political opportunity and electioneering occasion. The idea of "propaganda" as advertising or public relations for the state, distinct from advocacy for the party in a political canvass, was not clear enough to mark the distinguishing quality of Lincoln's leadership.[38]

In other words, the arena of ideas is not the place to find explanation of Civil War leadership. Social history and the history of party systems reflect today's historians' sense of the inadequacies of a traditional approach. Potter's famous essay, even as it marked the passing of an older view of the role of great men in history, ushered in a new approach as well. The article was influential in two ways. Although Potter argued that "the factors of personality played an important part in guiding the impact of the impersonal social and economic forces," near the end of his essay he admitted that a "political scientist might well object that it is superficial to emphasize these factors of personality without considering the question of what there was in the political system of the South that prevented the development of any viable alternative to the leadership of Davis."[39] For his day, few historians were more interested in the uses of social science in history than Potter, and his insight about institutional explanations of the failure of Confederate political leadership was so powerful that for some it erased the effects of his comparison of Davis and Lincoln as presidents. Potter offered in the next-to-the-last paragraph of his essay a speculation more influential than all that had come before it: "There is another suggestion which comes to mind. This is the possibility that the Confederacy may have suffered real and direct damage from the fact that its political organization lacked a two-party system."[40]

Later, the historian Eric L. McKitrick developed the idea in a long essay called "Party Politics and the Union and Confederate War Efforts," published in a volume entitled *The American Party Systems* which revealed, in the words of the foreword, that "many historians have come to believe that party history can . . . be informed by the conceptual and theoretical tools that have been developed by the social sciences, including political science."[41] McKitrick invoked Potter's inspiration as "the most original single idea to emerge from the mass of writing . . . on the Civil War in many years" and explained its significance:

It implicitly challenges two of our most formidable and consistently held assumptions regarding political life of the time, assumptions which until recently have gone unquestioned. One is that Lincoln's leadership of the Union war effort was severely and dangerously hampered by political partisanship—that is, by obstructions put in his path by Democrats on the one hand and, on the other, by extremists within his own Republican party. The other assumption is that Davis and the Confederate government, by deliberately setting aside partisanship, avoided this difficulty.[42]

McKitrick's own essay was thereafter frequently invoked as a sweeping explanation of important developments in the Civil War.[43]

McKitrick's principal critic from the standpoint of Confederate history is George C. Rable, whose book *The Confederate Republic: A Revolution against Politics* (1994) focuses on antiparty sentiment in the Confederacy. Sincere antiparty sentiment caused Jefferson Davis to regard opposition as unpatriotic and made his critics, sometimes depicted in Rable's book as fanatical libertarians, reluctant to organize against the government they feared. Ironically, Rable points out, antiparty sentiment was one belief that the two "political cultures" of nationalism (Davis) and individualism (Davis's libertarian critics) shared. For Potter, the importance of lack of parties in the Confederacy carried implicit criticism of Jefferson Davis: Potter thought the Confederate political system should have come up with someone better than Davis to lead the nation. The absence of political parties explained that failure to Potter and McKitrick. In the end, Rable attempts to explain both Davis's unresponsiveness and his critics' shrill denunciations of him as products of the Confederacy's anti-party ideal, but the two sides seem so bitterly divided as to make that not quite believable.[44]

The impact of social science on history and the rise of social history with its implicit assumption that "great men" have not the influence earlier generations imagined have already had some impact on Lincoln biography.[45] David Herbert Donald's *Lincoln,* published in 1995, is notable for its view that Abraham Lincoln was controlled by events.[46] Facing the dedication page there stands alone in block letters not the words of the Gettysburg Address or the Second Inaugural Address but these: "I CLAIM NOT TO HAVE CONTROLLED EVENTS, BUT CONFESS PLAINLY THAT EVENTS HAVE CONTROLLED ME. Abraham Lincoln to Albert G. Hodges, *April 4, 1864.*" Indeed, the book's dissent from a view of Lincoln as vigorous leader has lashed some critics into a virtual fury of disagreement. But it is a sign of the times.

Donald early in his career in writing history crusaded for the application of social science methods to history, among them statistics and computers. In 1965 he wrote:

> To explain Lincoln's success, and to explain his policy, it is . . . not necessary to resort to biography, and it is not even relevant to speak of his great charm, his passion for funny stories, or his inspiring eloquence. A rather simple computer installed in the White House, fed the elementary statistical information about election returns and programed to solve the recurrent problem of winning reelection, would emerge with the same strategies and the same solutions.[47]

Of course, Donald changed his mind about resorting to Lincoln biography in the succeeding twenty years, but he too had felt the impulse that inspired Potter to defer to political science at the end of his essay on presidential leadership in the Civil War. Donald understood the methods and conclusions of modern social and political historians too well to write a biography in the old "great man"-leadership mold.

Thus David M. Potter showed in his famous essay on Jefferson Davis and the "political factors in Confederate defeat" the Janus-faced quality that has given his work long life and high esteem in the history profession. He was among the last and greatest of the masters of the old history, mostly political and mostly written from the letters, speeches, and congressional votes of the elite. But his work also looked forward to the time when historical writing would be inspired by social scientific models and when many historians would regard as "superficial," the word Potter himself used, assessments of leadership based on personality and would look beyond political elites for historical sources. In this single essay both qualities were united, so that Potter at once presided over the birth and the burial of comparative assessments of presidential leadership in the American Civil War.

Potter's famous essay and this much less important one surveying the literature on Civil War presidential leadership bracket the period of the twentieth century in which the American presidency soared to what some regarded as dangerous, "imperial," even "monarchical" heights of power and fell again in tragic hubris into a "twilight" or "beleaguered"[48] state. Although the historical literature discussed in this essay was driven by the internal dynamics of history—sources, methodologies, provocative interpretations, it would be shortsighted to ignore the parallel developments in the general view taken of the American presidency today. Disillusionment with modern presidential power and the reluctant recognition that the

American people should not allow presidents as much power as they have recently enjoyed did not lead to disillusionment with powerful presidential leaders of the past, such as Lincoln. But modern disillusionment surely took some of the bloom off the rose of presidential study and fostered an atmosphere in which historical curiosity might seek answers to questions about the Civil War in other areas. Historians have been looking more deeply and more broadly for answers, their interest in presidential leadership declining with the decline of the presidency in modern times.

# AN ELUSIVE SYNTHESIS

## Northern Politics during the Civil War

### MICHAEL F. HOLT

In his lucid and astute 1989 study of Civil War congressmen, Allan G. Bogue noted that while historians have investigated Congress in various ways, they "have shown less interest in putting the various approaches together and in developing broader conceptions of how the congressional machinery actually worked during the Civil War years."[1] As this essay attempts to demonstrate, Bogue's stricture about the failure to integrate divergent tacks and foci into a coherent and conceptually fresh whole applies with equal validity to the entire corpus of literature on northern Civil War politics written since the mid-1960s. Since then, indeed, the only general overview has been James A. Rawley's valuable, but brief and unannotated, *The Politics of Union,* published in 1974, before much of the most methodologically innovative and sophisticated work on northern politics appeared.[2] This essay, therefore, seeks primarily to explain why an up-to-date, integrated synthesis has proved so elusive and to suggest some possible avenues toward achieving one.

Since many readers of this volume are probably more familiar with—and interested in—military aspects of the Civil War than with its politics or with political history in general, it is necessary, first, to stipulate what I mean by *fragmentation* and what an integrated political synthesis might look like. Since 1960, historians have written about Congress, Abraham Lincoln's administration, state politics, Republican and Democratic factionalism, political culture and ideas, specific social groups' involvement in politics, the growth and exercise of governmental power, and other topics covered by the capacious term *politics*. But they have usually analyzed them in isolation from each other. Studies that focus on factionalism within the Republican party, for example, usually ignore the Democratic party altogether, and vice versa. Studies of Lincoln's relationship with

Republicans in Congress and the states and of his simultaneous dealings with Democrats often stand independent of each other. Scholars who assess roll-call voting patterns in, or the content and thrust of policies enacted by, Congress during the war usually say little or nothing about popular voting behavior or the societal impact of those policies, while students of grassroots voting behavior usually eschew any systematic analysis of policy-making by Congress or state legislatures. With a few outstanding exceptions, indeed, governance during the war—the actions of executive, legislative, and judicial branches of government—at the local and state levels, on the one hand, and in Washington, on the other, has been treated as though its various manifestations took place on different planets. An integrated synthesis of northern Civil War politics, conversely, would systematically address the interactions among these and other dimensions of politics and, when appropriate, link them as well to the chronological course of the war.

At least four factors have generated the fragmented diversity of political historiography about the war, although other scholars could probably add their own candidates to the suspects identified here. First, and predictably, scholars who have studied the same specific topic—say, the northern Democratic party—often advance different interpretations, and it is difficult to pull parts together into a coherent whole without agreement on the individual parts themselves. At the very least, historians interested in synthesis must select from divergent interpretations of different political phenomena those that are most conducive to their integration.

Second, at least two inherited interpretive controversies about Civil War politics have influenced the agenda of historians writing since 1965, and each controversy has focused attention on one of the major political parties rather than on the interaction between them. One concerns the validity of Republican charges during and after the war that most northern Democrats were Copperhead traitors to the Union cause.[3] The other was a contentious debate, conducted prior to 1965 primarily between T. Harry Williams and David Donald, about the validity of Williams's thesis that the major axis of partisan political conflict during the Civil War was not between Democrats and Republicans but between Lincoln and the Radical faction of his own Republican party.[4]

The third factor contributing to the fragmentation of recent literature has been a shift in the training, interests, and research agendas of many scholars studying Civil War politics since the mid-1960s. Fourth—and inextricably linked to this reorientation—have been trends in the broader field of political history that have shaped much recent writing about wartime politics.

The disjointed state of recent scholarship on Civil War politics is hardly unique. It stems primarily from the current disarray in the field of nineteenth-century American political history in general. Prior to the mid-1960s, much of the most significant work on northern Civil War politics was produced by such historians as Williams and Donald, giants of Civil War historiography who were experts on the Civil War era as a whole, who were just as comfortable and prolific in writing about the military aspects of the war as about its politics, and who were primarily interested in whether and how northern politics helped or hindered the Union war effort. The conduct and outcome of the war, in sum, were their chief subjects; politics was one means, among many, of addressing them.

To be sure, some writers about Civil War politics since 1965, including Donald himself as well as other biographers of Lincoln, have continued to stress the interaction among military developments, political maneuvers, and northern victory.[5] Certain political events, such as Lincoln's reelection in 1864, have long been connected to battlefield outcomes like Sherman's capture of Atlanta.[6] Virtually all recent authors, moreover, exhibit considerable expertise about those aspects of the war on which they have focused. Nonetheless, the most influential writers since 1965 were usually trained as political historians or political scientists, not Civil War experts. In most cases, they have left military history to others. And they have not studied wartime political developments primarily in order to explain why the North won the war. Instead, they have focused on those developments either as a prelude to postwar federal policies for blacks and Reconstruction, as steps toward the emergence of a modern economy or a powerful state, or, more frequently, as a laboratory to test certain methodological approaches and hypotheses of current interest to political historians and political scientists, but not necessarily to specialists on the Civil War. Note, for example, that Allan Bogue, one of the leading practitioners of the new approaches to political history that emerged in the 1960s, refers in the previously quoted passage to the key problem as one of "how the machinery of Congress actually worked during the war years," not how congressional action contributed to or hindered northern victory in the war.

This shift in the analytical purposes of the scholars who have produced the most influential recent literature on northern politics is crucial in explaining the impasse that inhibits a modern synthesis of it. Since 1960, political historians have experimented with a number of methodological approaches and interpretive frameworks to gain an understanding of the rhythms and patterns of American politics, almost all of which have shaped and helped fragment recent writing about Civil War politics.

*Experimented* is the operative term. Through a trial-and-error process during the last four decades political historians have repeatedly seized on one approach or paradigm as a kind of Rosetta Stone that would unlock the mysteries of the political system, and then, either quickly or reluctantly, they have abandoned it for a different one. There has been no consensus about what aspect of political life most merits attention or how best to study it. Rather than marching in lock step or even pursuing seemingly fruitful paths blazed by colleagues in the field, political historians have followed different drummers and often veered off in new directions. As a result, the literature on nineteenth-century American political history in general, like that on northern politics during the Civil War in particular, adds up to a cacophony rather than a symphony, or, to switch metaphors, to a kaleidoscopic jumble of shards rather than a coordinated and coherent portrait of the whole.

Lamentations about this fragmentation abound as do calls for a new "total political history" or at the least a reintegration of political narrative with social history.[7] These, too, have helped shape recent writing about northern Civil War politics and helped create obstacles to synthesizing it. At the same time, the insights of these new approaches establish the modern benchmarks of what an integrated or comprehensive political history should include. Combined in ways that many individual authors might resist, finally, these new approaches suggest routes toward a possible reintegration of the field.

If political historians have never worked in complete unison, for ten or fifteen years after 1965 many of them shared a common faith about how best to study and comprehend America's political past. Those years witnessed the emergence of the so-called new political history in tandem with the party system/realignment synthesis that provided a way to reperiodize and reconceptualize American political history from the 1790s to the present.[8] At the theoretical cutting edge of both political history and political science, together they were eagerly embraced with the zeal of converts discovering new truth by both freshly minted Ph.D.'s and retooled veterans. Of great importance in shaping the subject matter for political historians, moreover, both approaches rested implicitly and often explicitly on a critical central tenet. This held that, particularly during the nineteenth century, political parties, rather than other forms of political participation or other kinds of political institutions, were absolutely crucial in channeling and shaping the political behavior of both leaders and followers and in bringing about historical change. Thus, political parties, their component parts, belief-systems, and actions, became the chief focus of scholarship.[9]

Rejecting narrative political history as episodic and unsystematic, the "new political history," now well past middle age, advocated that historians incorporate and help refine behavioral theories from sociology and political science and use quantitative or statistical techniques to identify underlying and enduring patterns of aggregate, rather than individual or elite, political behavior, patterns that would then become the subject matter for explanation. In practice, this prospectus led to a series of quantitative analyses of the partisan, regional, and factional dimensions of roll-call voting patterns in Congress and state legislatures as well as to statistical analyses of popular voting behavior that sought to measure the rigidity or mutability of partisan cleavages in the electorate and to identify the different population groups that consistently supported rival political parties. Allan Bogue, Michael Les Benedict, Joel H. Silbey, Jean H. Baker, Paul Kleppner, and Dale E. Baum, among others, applied one or more of these approaches to the study of northern Civil War politics.

The concomitant realignment/party system synthesis argued that American political history from the 1790s to at least the 1960s could best be understood in terms of five successive two-party systems that were distinguished from one another less by the content of the issues and policies over which their constituent parties fought than by the durability of voter allegiance to the rival parties. What demarcated these systems from one another, what signaled the end of one two-party system and launched a new one, that is, was *not* just a change of party labels. Rather, it was sets of contiguous elections during a period in which a large minority of the electorate permanently switched or realigned their partisan affiliations, thus creating both a new majority coalition and a new two-party system. What kept the new majority party and the new two-party voter cleavage intact until the next realignment thirty to forty years later, in turn, were the actions of government. The new majority coalition created by the voter realignment seized control of national and state governments and used that control to enact policies that, by redressing the grievances of voters that had originally fueled the realignment, cemented both the allegiance of its new supporters and its status as the majority party, even as those same policies further alienated the majority's partisan rivals.

The realignment/party system paradigm contains crucial implications for the study of Civil War politics because it posits that major voter realignments occurred in the 1850s, the 1890s, and 1930s. Proponents of the paradigm also maintain that the 1850s realignment inaugurated the so-called Third or Civil War party system, which displaced the second system of interparty competition between Whigs and Jacksonian Democrats. The very titles of the three major book-length studies of this new party system reflect belief in this shift—Paul Kleppner, *The Third Electoral System, 1853–1892: Parties, Voters, and Political Cultures* (1979); Stephen L. Hansen, *The Making of the Third Party System: Voters and Parties in Illinois, 1850–1876* (1980); and Dale E. Baum, *The Civil War Party System: The Case of Massachusetts, 1848–1876* (1984).[10] Of particular significance for the analysis of wartime politics, proponents of the model explicitly assert or implicitly believe that it was the Republicans' responsibility for and management of the North's successful war effort that cemented their status as the nation's new majority party until at least the mid-1870s.

Here, then, was a conceptual framework with seemingly great potential for integrating different aspects of Civil War politics. With it one could link policymakers and governance to voters. Since it was the requirements of the North's war effort that evoked the voter-solidifying and partisan-polarizing Republican policies from 1861 to 1865, with this framework one could also link partisan politics to the rhythms, military conduct, and outcome of the war itself. In fact, however, this promise went unfulfilled. Adoption of a common framework for analysis did not guarantee a coordinated research agenda or common conclusions. In fact, juxtaposition of important theoretical components of the realignment/party system model to actual applications of it by students of Civil War politics only underscores the disarray, not the coherence, of their studies.

After 1965, the very first application of the model to the Civil War years exemplified its promise for generating new insights, yet it also showed how quickly that promise could go glimmering if other historians failed to pursue those intriguing leads. In a stunningly imaginative, original, and ultimately idiosyncratic essay entitled "Party Politics and the Union and Confederate War Efforts," published in 1967, Eric McKitrick deployed the party-system concept to help explain why the North won the war. Ignoring the theory's realignment and popular voting components, McKitrick seized instead on an equally critical aspect of the model, namely, that the very concept of a two-party *system* highlights conflict between its constituent parties as the system's central dynamic. Thus, he brilliantly argued that the continuation of two-party competition in the North throughout the war and its absence from the Confederacy gave the North its decisive advantage over the South. Constant Democratic attacks on the record of the Lincoln administration and the Republican-controlled Congress forced Republicans of all kinds to rally in defense of that record in order to win elections. Since the Republicans were the new majority party, that necessity kept most of the North united behind the Republican government's war effort long enough for the North to win, whereas the partyless Confederacy succumbed to fractious division, discord, and de-moralization.[11]

Aside from its breathtakingly ingenious argument, what is most note-worthy about McKitrick's essay is its appalling lack of influence on subsequent writing about northern Civil War politics. In general studies of the war and of specific northern states, a few scholars incorporated his point that two-party competition gave the North an edge over the Con-federacy. I have quibbled with his explanation of how, but not whether, two-party competition contributed to northern victory in an essay on Lincoln's wartime political strategy that has had even less impact on sub-sequent literature than McKitrick's piece.[12] Perhaps because developing or testing McKitrick's argument required a systematic comparison of south-ern and northern politics or because it implicitly minimized the significance of intraparty factional divisions others found central to Civil War politics, however, most political historians have not followed McKitrick's lead or been concerned with explaining northern victory. Quite unlike him, they have been primarily interested in the realignment component of the model, and in most of their studies the war itself constitutes only a brief episode of a much longer period or a background context for a quite different focus of attention. Yet it is in those politically oriented studies that inter-pretive disarray is often most glaring.

For example, whereas the realignment/party system model posits a link between policy output and popular voting behavior, that connection has been asserted, not demonstrated. As noted earlier, historians inter-ested primarily in the emergence of new voting alignments in the electorate—Kleppner and Baum, for instance—do not systematically as-sess the partisan dimensions or even the content of policy output from Congress or (in Baum's case) the Massachusetts state legislature. Nor do analysts of Congress link its actions to subsequent elections.[13] And the discrepancies between theory and application do not end there.

For one thing, according to the most sophisticated theoretical formu-lations of the realignment/party system model, realignments allow new majority parties to capture control not just of the national government but of state governments as well, and it is policies enacted *at both levels of the federal system,* not just in Washington, that cement the new parties' majority status.[14] However, aside from work on Connecticut and New Hampshire by Lex Renda and a dissertation-in-progress by John R. Kirn on the Civil War party system in New York, I know of no studies that systematically examine the partisan dimensions of roll-call voting pat-terns in, and the substantive dimensions of policies enacted by, northern state legislatures in the late 1850s or during the Civil War.[15] This gap in our knowledge offers one of the greatest opportunities for fresh work on northern Civil War politics.

But that gap also relates to another disjuncture between realignment theory and its past applications to the Civil War period. According to the theory, realigning periods were characterized by unusually intense ideological polarization between the major parties *and* by unusually high or sharp levels of *inter*party conflict, as opposed to *intra*party factional division, over policy output in legislative bodies. A corollary axiom of the party system paradigm—one central to McKitrick's essay—is that during the existence of any two-party system the two major parties were locked in a synergistic relationship with each other and can only be fully understood in terms of that reciprocal interaction. As Jean H. Baker once put it, "The majority Republicans were inextricably linked in strategy, motives and ideals to their [Democratic] opponents, and, like ballroom dancers, cannot be appreciated without their partners."[16] In short, no study of the Republican or Democratic party during the war that treats it in isolation from the other is complete.

Almost every political historian writing since the 1960s affirms a belief in both of these propositions. Baum's study of the Civil War party system in Massachusetts, for example, pivots on the intensity of ideological polarization over war issues and concomitant matters concerning emancipation and blacks during the 1860s, and both he and Kleppner go to great lengths to explain how and why the Republican and Democratic electorates differed. Many other recent studies of Civil War politics explicitly acknowledge the imperatives of interparty competition as a background context. Yet the incontrovertible—and, in light of these professions, surprising—fact is that the great bulk of recent work on political parties during the Civil War, including a brilliant book on the Democratic party by Jean Baker herself, focuses on one party in isolation rather than on the interaction between two parties. Most of those books and articles—and especially quantitative studies of roll-call voting patterns in Congress—emphasize the exacerbation of *intra*party factionalism, not the intensification of *inter*party conflict, as the most important aspect of Civil War political life.[17]

As already mentioned, interpretive controversies inherited from a previous generation of historians in part accounts for this seemingly incomplete unifocal perspective, but those controversies engendered emphasis upon internal party divisions for somewhat different reasons. Republican factionalism was intrinsic to the Lincoln-versus-the-Radicals debate, for T. Harry Williams in his original formulation of the thesis, as well as others who extended it to the postwar years by asserting Radical responsibility for Reconstruction legislation, always admitted that the Radicals constituted only one wing of the Republican party. For them, however, the Radicals were not just the party's dominant wing in terms of influence if not numbers. They were also the most militantly and vindictively antisouthern Republicans who demanded confiscation, emancipation, and the use of black troops and who rejected Lincoln's healing proposals for Reconstruction in order to crush and humiliate the South's planter elite. They acted, in short, not out of altruistic concerns for restoring the Union or advancing black rights, as supposedly did the magnanimous Lincoln and non-Radical Republicans, but from a selfish partisan determination to keep the Republican party in power in order to protect and advance its probusiness economic agenda behind a smokescreen of anti-Confederate and ostensibly antislavery measures and rhetoric. And in the end, according to the original thesis, they triumphed over Lincoln and moderate Republicans on virtually every front during the war and the subsequent Reconstruction.

In his original attempts to refute this dramatic scenario of intraparty division, David Donald argued not only that Lincoln personally enjoyed good relations with individual Radicals such as Charles Sumner. He also minimized the significance of Republican factionalism. Beyond a few well-known individuals, Donald asserted, a discernible Radical faction was difficult to identify. Those few Radicals, like all Republicans, moreover, were internally divided over the economic policies Radicals were supposedly intent on protecting, and virtually all Republicans, not just Radicals, were determined to preserve the party's control of the national and state governments. In the most celebrated conflicts between Lincoln and congressional Republicans—over Congress's early demands for confiscation, emancipation, and the enrollment of black troops, Senate Republicans' attempt to purge Seward from the cabinet or support for the Wade-Davis bill which Lincoln pocket-vetoed, for example—virtually all congressional Republicans, not just Radicals, were at odds with the president.[18]

The controversy about Radical Republicans inherited by political historians in the mid-1960s, in sum, was shaped by Donald as much as by Williams. It entailed not just an unresolved dispute about the nature of Lincoln's relationship with congressional Republicans but equally fundamental questions about whether Radical and non-Radical or moderate factions of the Republicans existed, and if so, exactly how and over what they differed, and how those factional antagonisms influenced policy formation during the war and Reconstruction. Whatever other historians were asserting about the critical importance of interparty interaction in two-party systems, answering these particular questions did not seem to require paying much attention to the congressional Democratic minority. The "action" in historiographical terms was in internal relations within the Republican party alone.

During the 1960s and 1970s, therefore, many able scholars, though disagreeing with one other on some things, concluded that neither Williams's dramatic scenario of Lincoln's being overpowered by a malicious Radical faction of his party nor Donald's attempt to pooh-pooh the existence of Radical and Moderate Republican factions was tenable—as, indeed, did Donald himself in study published as early as 1965.[19] Simultaneously, their studies exemplified how much questions regarding blacks, race relations, and Reconstruction preempted the attention of historians in those decades. Of those who reassessed Lincoln's relations with congressional Republicans, for example, Hans Trefousse found Lincoln perfectly in accord with congressional Radicals, whom he characterized as sincere antislavery zealots motivated by principle, not just narrow partisan self-interest. The Radicals, Trefousee maintained, were Lincoln's "vanguard for racial justice" whom Lincoln happily allowed to blaze a trail toward black freedom and equality. Subsequently LaWanda Cox upped the ante by arguing that Lincoln actually led rather than followed congressional Republicans in the eradication of slavery, while still more recent students of Lincoln disagree as to whether ending slavery had equal or lesser priority for him than winning the war and preserving the Union.[20]

In their positive appreciation of Radical motives, these studies mirrored important analyses of congressional Republicans that often employed the statistical methods of the "new political history" by Bogue, Herman Belz, Michael Les Benedict, Glen M. Linden, and others.[21] Together they demonstrated that congressional Republicans were indeed divided into Radical and Moderate factions throughout the war, that Moderates (and a few Conservatives), who differed with Radicals primarily about the pace and political cost, not the goals, of antislavery and problack action, usually had greater influence on legislation, and that the two camps disagreed primarily about matters involving race and Reconstruction, not economic or war-mobilization issues. Simultaneously, however, the same studies warned, as Donald once had, that the influence of these factional divisions should not be exaggerated. On most congressional business, conflict between Democrats and Republicans was sharper than between Republicans themselves, and almost all congressional Republicans, not just the Radicals, were at odds with Lincoln during disputes between the executive and legislative branches.

Despite the portrait of harmony between Lincoln and congressional Republicans drawn by Trefousse and Cox and of Republican unity stressed by McKitrick, most of the new studies of Congress emphasized that Lincoln and congressional Republicans did indeed disagree on some important matters.[22] Yet they also showed that no single actor or group had complete charge of the situation. As Bogue thoughtfully concluded, "Legislation did not emerge during the Civil War because Lincoln single-handedly conceived and guided it through Congress, nor did the radical Republicans of that body chart the course of war policy unhindered. Within Congress [and within Lincoln's administration itself] the interplay of radical, moderate, and conservative politicians shaped public measures."[23]

Glaringly absent from this equation, though usually not from the studies of Congress by Bogue and others, are northern Democrats. In part, this omission stems from the tiny number of Democrats in the Thirty-seventh Congress (1861–1863), for they indeed had little influence in shaping legislation. Yet the omission also reflects the fact that recent studies of the Democrats have proceeded in isolation from the work on Republicans. While the inherited historiographical controversy about Radical Republicans necessarily focused historians' attention on internal Republican factionalism, such was not the case with the preexisting interpretive debate that spurred much of the new scholarship on Democrats after 1965—whether or not most Democrats were Copperhead traitors who publicly demanded peace at any price, even the price of permanent disunion, resisted necessary war measures in Congress, and secretly plotted to aid the Confederates' war effort.

Virtually every historian writing about the wartime Democratic party since 1960 rejects this exaggerated stereotype and insists that Democrats were loyal supporters of the war effort and the goal of reunion. Democrats, they argue, sharply distinguished between those goals and partisan opposition to certain Republican war aims and measures which they abhorred as outrageous and unconstitutional violations of state rights, individual liberty, and, these studies emphatically demonstrate, white supremacy to which intensely Negrophobic Democrats were intransigently committed. Equally noteworthy, however, during the late 1960s and early 1970s, defenders of the Democrats treated the party as a unit rather than focusing on its internal divisions. Building on his 1960 revisionist study of midwestern Copperheadism, Frank L. Klement, for example, argued that Democratic secret societies had partisan, not antigovernment or antiwar, goals, that they were the equivalent of Republican Union leagues, and that they were formed to combat feared military suppression of Democratic voters in elections. Analyzing roll-call votes in the House and Senate between 1861 and 1863, Leonard P. Curry and Jean H. Baker demonstrated that most Democrats supported Republicans in backing necessary war measures and a surprising amount of nonmilitary legislation as well. Only on matters concerning blacks, confiscation, and approval of some of Lincoln's executive actions that infringed on individual rights did Democrats solidly oppose the Republican majority, although Baker also found considerable partisan conflict on economic measures. Of great importance, both Curry and Baker also discovered high levels of internal cohesion among congressional Democrats on most votes, in contrast to the Republicans' internal factional divisions, and Baker openly questioned the utility of distinguishing among Democrats in terms of their pro- and antiwar commitments.[24]

Two kinds of evidence, however, challenge this rosy revisionist portrait of unified Democratic loyalty. Unearthed only during the past five years, the first may well have more impact on future writing about wartime politics than it has had on the literature discussed in this essay. The case for loyal Democratic support of the nonracially related measures necessary to fight and win the war—taxes, bond issues, appropriations to pay troops and purchase supplies, troop requisitions, and the like—rests solely on studies of congressional votes. It may, in fact, distort the Democratic party's position. While we know far too little about what transpired in northern states during the war, Renda's comprehensive account of roll-call votes in the Connecticut and New Hampshire legislatures indicates that most Democrats consistently opposed the taxes and bond issues necessary to pay and supply volunteers raised in those states as well as measures to allow soldier voting in the field. In addition, studies of localities in the latter state indicate far lower levels of volunteering and much more resistance to raising taxes to fund volunteer bounties in towns controlled by Democrats than in those the Republicans dominated, just as Iver Bernstein's superb account of the New York City draft riots reemphasizes some Democrats' intransigent aversion to the war.[25] At the subnational level, in sum, Democratic opposition to the Republican war effort may have been far broader than resistance to measures concerning black rights, punishment of the South, or individual civil liberties.

Second, even without knowledge of this very recent research, historians intent upon refuting the legend of Democratic Copperheadism could not deny the embarrassing presence of strident antiwar Democrats such as Ohio's Clement L. Vallandigham, Pennsylvania's George Woodward, and Connecticut's Thomas Seymour, all of whom captured Democratic gubernatorial nominations in 1863. Their solution to this dilemma was to adopt the tack followed by historians working on the Republicans—namely, to stress intraparty factional divisions between Peace and War (or Union) Democrats at the expense of attention to the dimensions of interparty combat. There were Peace Democrats, these historians admitted, but they were a minority who were constantly at odds with the loyalist Democratic majority. Prowar, but still antiadministration, Democrats dominated the party. They were chiefly responsible for and the chief beneficiaries of the sweeping Democratic comeback in the state and congressional elections of 1862. And only a misreading of those 1862 triumphs—rather like the modern Republicans' misinterpretation of the 1994 congressional elections—allowed Peace Democrats to surge to temporary prominence in the party in 1863.[26] In sum, historians of the Democratic party focused on intraparty factionalism because it provided an efficacious way to defend Democrats from charges of disloyalty.

This stress on "the internal dynamics of the party" as the central force shaping Democrats' history during the Civil War provided the analytical framework for one of the two best studies of the wartime Democracy to appear since 1965—Joel H. Silbey's *A Respectable Minority*. Assigning the tag War Democrats to the tiny minority of Democrats willing to cooperate with Republicans in a supposedly bipartisan "Union" coalition, Silbey finds the main division between Democrats not over peace or war but over how best to compete with Republicans for voter support. "Purists" hoped to mobilize the die-hard Democratic rank-and-file by stressing traditional Democratic principles and aggressively denouncing Republican war measures and war goals, even at the risk of appearing disloyal. "Legitimists," in contrast, feared that too strident an antiwar stance would depress Democratic turnout and, more important, ruin any chance that Democrats could enlarge their electoral support by winning over, not Republicans, but non-Democratic conservatives like men who had voted for John Bell or abstained in 1860.[27]

Republicans are always a background presence in Silbey's book, if only because their policies enraged Democrats, but his analysis remains focused upon Democrats' internal divisions. This stress is surprising, for Silbey is one of the leading practitioners of the "new political history" who has frequently espoused the axiom that it is the interaction between rival parties in any two-party system, not one party alone, that should be the subject matter of political historians. One might cite the space limitations of the series in which his book appeared to explain this anomaly. But it springs primarily, I believe, from another internal contradiction in, or at least evidentiary disagreement about, the realignment/party system model that has helped prevent a modern synthesis integrating studies of Civil War politics.

Historians who agree that the 1850s voter realignment launched a new Civil War party system sharply differ with one another about the chronological boundaries between its realigning stage, when voter affiliation was fluctuating and voters were thus up for grabs by competing parties, and its stable phase, when voter allegiance to one or the other of the major parties was fixed and rigid. According to Kleppner's region-wide analysis of the entire third-party system, on the one hand, the voter fluctuation that began in the 1850s continued, with a brief interruption during the mid-1860s, into the 1870s, and the system's stable phase began only in 1876. Baum argues, on the other hand, that realignment was complete by 1860, that the entire decade of the 1860s witnessed rigidly polarized electoral cleavages in Massachusetts, and that there a new realignment began in the 1870s when the salience of Civil War and Reconstruction issues declined. Silbey adopts the same chronology as Baum. "By 1860 the electorate had become locked in," he asserts. "The popular voting situation observable in the war had been established in the 1850s, and not much shaken thereafter. The war apparently did not create many new Republican or Democratic voters or else created them in equal numbers."[28]

At stake here is not just a quibble over semantics or over whose statistical coefficients are more reliable. How one interprets Civil War politics and what one focuses on depend intrinsically on how much partisan fluidity among leaders and voters existed. If the strength and component parts of the rival major parties are set in cement, then it may make sense to identify internal factional rivalries within a single party as the most important dynamic element in the system. In contrast, if voters are up for grabs—or more precisely, if political leaders *believe* they are up for grabs— then a focus on the strategies of interparty competition to win over new voters is arguably the better approach.

The degree of fluidity—that is, voter movability—in the system also has crucial implications for how one interprets the Union party movement that emerged during the war, claimed to be distinct from the Republican party of 1860, and sought to unite prowar Republicans and Democrats in a new organization. Silbey dismisses, and argues that virtually all Democrats during the war dismissed, this effort as a transparently cynical Republican trick to lure gullible Democrats into committing party suicide. In contrast, citing evidence of virulent Republican hostility to the Union party, Christopher Dell in his *Lincoln and the War Democrats,* treats it as a serious threat to Democratic unity, although his hyperbolic assertion that "as the spiritual father of the wartime Union party," "Abraham Lincoln was the Pied Piper of Civil War politics who lured unwary Democrats with Conservative phraseology and Radical intent" approaches the surreal.[29]

I have in the past and continue to regard the Union party as more than a cosmetic Republican device, but my point here is not to refight apparently lost causes.[30] Rather, I believe that this question about the openness or "closedness" of northern Civil War politics to partisan change by both voters and leaders provides the single most important key to writing a cohesive synthesis about that politics. The heart of the matter is the critical difference between contemporary perceptions and twentieth-century historians' analyses.

No matter whose statistical evidence about when the voter realignment that inaugurated the third-party system ended is more accurate, the fact is that those who lived during the nineteenth century never knew they were experiencing the realigning or stable phase of a party system. The realignment/party system model is based on modern statistical analyses that show continuity in the partisan preferences of voters (or the geographical units that recorded votes) in successive elections—say, 1860, 1862, 1864, 1866, and 1868. What historians and political scientists have defined as realignments, as distinct from normal voter turbulence, is the permanence of voter change over time. Yet that permanence can only be measured in hindsight. Neither voters nor politicians living between 1860 and 1865 knew in advance how people would vote in 1861, 1862, 1863, and 1864. What they knew was that an older system of conflict between Whigs and Democrats had collapsed by the fall of 1854 and that since then chaos had ensued.

Neither northern voters nor politicians living during the Civil War, in sum, could be sure that either the voter alignments of 1860 *or the existing political parties* that had contested that presidential election would endure. An appreciation and exploitation of that uncertainty, I believe, offers the best chance of synthesizing the diverse literature written by "new political historians" and fans of the realignment/party system paradigm. To cite but one example, if one posits a perception of political flux and uncertainty during the war years, one can link the literature on Lincoln's relations with congressional Republicans and on splits between Radical and Moderate congressional Republicans to the literature on Democratic factionalism. One might argue, as Michael Perman has done so brilliantly in his study of southern political parties from 1869 to 1879,[31] that all three internal divisions entailed disagreements about competitive interparty strategies that in turn stemmed from disagreements about whether nominal supporters of the rival parties could be converted. Even more important, perhaps, this interpretive stance provides the best chance for synthesizing the work of the "new political historians" with other kinds of political history written since the mid-1960s, often in explicit rejection of that work.

Many historians of Civil War politics, especially those interested in the substance of wartime federal policies, had never shown much interest in the "new political history," but by the mid- and late-1970s it and the party-system paradigm were increasingly coming under hostile fire. Their emphasis on quantifiable data seemed excessively mechanistic and narrow, excluding a focus on ideas and values. Their privileging of political parties precluded investigation of other forms of political expression and other political institutions. They seemed to ignore subjects like class formation and class conflict that were so important to social historians. More fundamentally, they seemed incapable of saying anything new. Thus, some political historians struck out in a variety of new directions while others probed more deeply along traditional paths.

One of the most important of the new directions reflected a revived interest in political ideology and in its newly discovered offshoot, political culture. By far the outstanding example of this latter approach for the Civil War years—indeed the best book on the subject for all of American history—is Jean H. Baker's marvelous *Affairs of Party: The Political Culture of Northern Democrats in the Mid-Nineteenth Century,* a study not of formal political behavior but of "the system of empirical beliefs, expressive symbols, and values which defines the situation in which political action takes place." Although Baker had used the quantitative techniques of the "new political history" in previous studies, here she explicitly rejects that approach as having reached its interpretive limits. Interested primarily in how men became Democrats and what it meant to have that affiliation, she similarly rejects Silbey's stress on Democratic factionalism, just as she eschews formal comparison with the Republicans on the ground that the party was still too young during the war to have a "culture." Baker's splendid book, in short, is truly *sui generis.* Nothing like it has ever been written, although Earl J. Hess's slender study of northern political values during the war invokes some of the same themes of republicanism, racism, and Americanism. One can, then, admire Baker's brilliant achievement, yet still doubt that a focus on political culture provides a practicable way to synthesize the literature on Civil War politics.[32]

Since the 1970s, still other historians of Civil War politics have followed the call of labor historians to integrate social and political history by assessing the broad political aspirations of workers, the different ways outside of formal political parties those aspirations were expressed, and how workers' class foes often used governmental power to frustrate them. Grace Palladino's prize-winning study of class conflict in Pennsylvania's anthracite coal regions, for example, demonstrated how mine owners exploited their connections with the Republican state and national administrations to secure the intervention of federal troops and state militia to break up strikes.[33]

By far the most impressive and suggestive study of this ilk, and perhaps the most successful attempt to integrate social and political history yet written, is Iver Bernstein's *The New York City Draft Riots: Their Significance for American Society and Politics in the Age of the Civil War* (1990).[34] Bernstein not only demonstrates that the riots had a political and not simply a class or racist objective and that different kinds of workers had different goals depending upon their employment and social experiences. He also shows how divided partisan control of governments at different levels of the federal system helped to precipitate and to resolve the crisis, thus illustrating how explicit attention to federalism might link local studies with those of national politics. Put briefly, Bernstein argues that workers took to the streets to stop the draft only because local Democratic authorities, who controlled the city government, lacked the power to prevent national Republican authorities from implementing it. Yet those local Democratic politicians also helped dissipate the crisis, first by persuading the Lincoln administration to use state, rather than federal, troops under the command of a prominent Democrat to restore order, then by persuading the administration to suspend implementation of the draft, and, most important, by floating city bond issues to raise money to give to drafted New Yorkers so that they could pay commutation fees or hire substitutes and thus avoid military service. Social conflict among New York's classes and races was therefore intrinsic to the riots, but the riots also pitted the jurisdictional authority and resources of the municipal and national governments against each other because different *political parties* controlled those governments.

Palladino's and especially Bernstein's study thus show that governmental policies have direct impact on social experience and that the Republican and Democratic parties used governmental power in different ways. Thus they implicitly link popular elections that determined which party controlled government to the actions of government itself and suggest that a focus on interparty interaction during the war could incorporate such studies just as it can intraparty factionalism if one allows for the plasticity of the political situation. For similar reasons, the same approach can encompass the final category of recent literature about Civil War politics discussed here—that which focuses on the growth of the state and the nature of Civil War governance.

Well before 1965 numerous historians noted that the Civil War required an unprecedented increase in the size of the national government and the exercise of unprecedented powers by that government. Simultaneously, the absence of southerners from Congress allowed passage of economic legislation that enormously increased Washington's intervention into economic life. Historians often noted the Republicans' responsibility for these changes, but they cited them primarily as evidence that the Civil War was a turning point in that power was permanently centralized in the national government—a "leviathan," some called it—at the expense of the states, which lost jurisdictional authority over "a host of domestic institutions and concerns, once strictly and admittedly within the[ir] domain," while the new congressional economic policies laid out a "Blueprint for Modern America." Occasionally, as well, some scholars contrasted this consolidation of authority with the Confederacy's supposedly decentralized war effort resulting from excessive state rights zeal to help explain northern victory in the war.[35]

Fifty years ago, for example, William B. Hesseltine argued in *Lincoln and the War Governors* that during the war "the nation had emerged victorious over the states" in the North as well as the South because "Lincoln had triumphed over the [northern] governors." Lincoln's superior intellect and political acumen largely accounted for his success, Hesseltine contended, but the instrument through which he won was the Republican party. In 1860, governors had controlled that decentralized organization and elected Lincoln on their coattails. But Lincoln had used the exigencies of war to centralize authority in Washington and take command of the Republican party, reduce once-proud governors to his recruiting agents, and elect them on his own coattails in 1864.[36]

In contrast, Leonard P. Curry stressed congressional initiative not Lincoln's genius in his intricately detailed history of the nonmilitary legislation passed by the Thirty-seventh Congress. But he, too, posited a change in "the American governmental concept from one of federalism to one of nationalism" to account for Congress's abolition of slavery in the District of Columbia and federal territories, the chartering of the Union Pacific Railroad and Morrill Land-Grant College Act, the tariff increases, the new excise and income taxes, and the creation of a national currency with the Legal Tender and National Banking Acts. While Curry carefully noted East/West divisions among Republicans on some of this program—especially bills involving federal land grants—he also showed that tax, currency, tariff, and especially antislavery legislation pitted the minority Democrats against the majority Republicans who passed those laws. And while he correctly faulted some Republican programs for "neo-Hamiltonianism: government for the benefit of the privileged few," his main argument remained that the Republicans' "passage of numerous pieces of sweeping legislation of novel character accustomed the American people (or at least, the numerically and politically dominant northern population) to think-ing of problems in national terms and looking to Congress and the President [not state and local governments] for solutions."[37]

In an even more detailed analysis of wartime banking and currency legislation, *Sovereignty and an Empty Purse: Banks and Politics during the Civil War* (1970), Bray Hammond also credited an explicitly national-istic desire of Republican lawmakers to subordinate state to national authority for passage of the National Banking Act that attempted to sub-stitute federally regulated national banks for state-chartered ones. According to his summary of a speech that Ohio senator John Sherman made on behalf of the act: A national banking system "took from the states and gave to the national government. It was aggressively national-ist."[38] Unbacked greenbacks authorized by the Legal Tender Acts, like national banknotes, represented another new national currency, yet, Hammond insisted in the most original and valuable part of his book, that legislation did not result from a nationalistic impulse. Instead it was a desperate response to Treasury Secretary Salmon P. Chase's utter incom-petence as a financier, a mistake-filled record that the former Federal Reserve official Hammond documented in withering and caustic detail.

Put briefly, Chase woefully underestimated the cost of the war and sought to avert taxation by relying on bond issues. He then undermined the ability of eastern banks to fund that debt by foolishly insisting that the government adhere to the hard money provisions of the 1846 Indepen-dent Treasury Act which required banks physically to transfer their gold reserves to government vaults when they bought bonds. By December 1861, banks were out of gold and had to suspend specie payments. To allow banks to repay their noteholders and depositors and to continue to buy bonds, eastern bankers demanded, and their congressional represen-tatives including Elbridge Spaulding and Samuel Hooper framed, the Legal Tender Acts, which Chase unsuccessfully opposed. The needs of bankers, not nationalism, produced greenbacks, a fact of delicious irony, since af-ter the war opponents of bankers and the National Banking System advocated unrestricted government printing of greenbacks to strip bank-ers of their control of currency.[39]

Despite Leonard Curry's claims that wartime legislation caused Ameri-cans to think "of problems in national terms" and to look to Washington for solutions, indeed, both the argument that the war induced a national consolidation of governmental power at the expense of the states and the corollary case that the northern war effort was more centralized than the Confederacy's have been revised, if not repudiated, by subsequent schol-arship. Historians, for example, have reconsidered some of the most ostensibly nationalistic northern policies. The Conscription Act of March 1863 clearly represented an unprecedented intrusion by the national government on individual rights, marked an attempt to transfer control of troop mobilization from the states to Washington, and unquestionably polarized Republicans against Democrats. Yet recent studies of the law and its implementation by Eugene C. Murdock and James Geary not only rehearse the well-known fact that the Confederacy resorted to a national draft eleven months before the North did. They also point out that this "semidraft," as Murdock calls it, yielded relatively few men, produced more money in commutation fees than troops, allowed the hiring of unfit substitutes, generated corrupt bounty brokers, and failed fully to nationalize control over the armies that fought the war. By stimulating additional volunteering to avoid the stigma of the draft, the law may have "worked" to help the North win the war, as Murdock asserts, but it hardly contributed to a permanent shift of power within the American federal system.[40]

What is more surprising, perhaps, is that the same conclusion has been reached by recent students of the evolution of federal policies for emancipation and black rights during the war, the questions on which partisan polarization between Republicans and Democrats was most complete. In this area the seminal works are two books by Herman Belz, a constitutional historian who is as concerned with policymakers' motives and conceptualizations about federal relations as he is with the substance of policies themselves. In *A New Birth of Freedom* (1976), Belz carefully explored the ad hoc, expedient process by which Republican policies aimed initially at depriving the Confederacy of black manpower forced Republicans to consider what basic rights freedom and citizenship entailed. At least through the end of 1862, he demonstrated, "Republicans in Congress did not conceive of emancipation as a matter of securing personal liberty and civil rights. Rather emancipation was intended to deprive the Confederacy of slave labor and to range black manpower on the side of the Union." By war's end, in contrast, they insisted that freedom entailed basic rights of citizenship and equality before the law. Those rights, however, entailed neither political nor social equality, but rather freedom from any governmental, but *not private,* restraint on physical mobility or the rights to own property, marry, make contracts, bring court suits, and keep what one earned. Equally important, Belz argued that this evolution, which culminated in the Civil Rights Act and Fourteenth Amendment in 1866, resulted in a federalization, a sharing of power between state and national governments but not a complete nationalization of civil liberty. Republicans during the war did give "the federal government power and responsibility over the liberty and rights of individuals which it had never possessed," but "without substantially depriving the states of similar power and responsibility." In other words, Republicans during the war sought a dual system of state and national citizenship with different rights accruing to each status. "In a relative sense," therefore, "state power was diminished by being made subject to restrictions that were previously unknown. Yet, in the absolute sense, the states lost little power." As late as early 1865, for example, the framers of the Thirteenth Amendment did *not* contend that it gave Congress a direct and plenary power to legislate on civil rights in general.[41]

Two years later, in *Emancipation and Equal Rights: Politics and Constitutionalism in the Civil War Era* (1978), Belz viewed the glass as half full rather than half empty by celebrating how the constitutional and legal changes the Republicans achieved, over strident Democratic resistance, produced a revolutionary commitment to the "national application of the principle of equality before the law in each state regardless of race." Nonetheless, he also demonstrated how two central constitutional principles cherished by Republicans—federalism or "state-rights' nationalism," as he called it, and the republican principle of government by consent of the governed even within the defeated southern states—prevented most Republican policymakers from condoning a total consolidation of authority over individual rights in the national government. As he concluded, "Republican defense of the Union in 1861 expressed a strong feeling of nationalism but not a desire to centralize American government. . . . Relative to antebellum times, wartime exigencies were to require a considerable degree of centralization, but Republicans' state-rights nationalism checked this tendency."[42]

While Belz concentrated on federal policies toward blacks, other constitutional and legal historians cast a broader net to dispute the argument about a unique centralization of power at the expense of the states in the North. Important studies by Harold Hyman and Morton Keller, for example, demonstrate that the authority and activism of Washington did not grow at the expense of state and local governments but in tandem with them. The Civil War years in the North, in sum, saw a surge of new kinds of governmental activism, financial obligations, and taxes to pay for them at all levels of the federal system. Moreover, as the political scientist Richard Franklin Bensel argued accurately, if ironically, in his important (and difficult) *Yankee Leviathan: The Origins of Central State Authority in America, 1859–1877* (1990), in terms of the mobilization of men and matériel necessary to fight the war, especially in managing the wartime economy, the Confederate central government actually exercised far more direct power than did Washington.[43]

Bensel's study is both accurate and ironic for another important reason. He wrote as part of an effort pioneered by fellow political scientists including Theda Skocpol and Stephen Skowronek to analyze the growth of the state—an administrative bureaucracy that is an independent variable in the political system, that acts from its own institutional imperatives, that creates politically influential clients through the programs it administers, and that thus can operate independently of political parties and partisan influences. Bensel identifies such a group of clients created by the wartime northern state—participants in the national banking system administered by the Treasury Department—just as Skocpol does in another study—veterans and soldiers' widows who benefited from pensions first enacted during the war.[44] But—and it's a *but* of enormous importance—Bensel confesses that the growth of central state power in the North was dependent upon and inextricable from Republican control of government.

New government power and activity, in sum, were products of partisan politics. The surge of governmental activism at all levels of the federal system identified by Hyman and Keller coincided with Republican capture of government at all levels, just as the retreat from activism they identified in the 1870s coincided with the return of Democrats to power in many places. To be sure, not all new uses of government—those in the area of public health, for example—generated partisan combat. Nonetheless, governmental activism, or positive use of state power, just like racial relations and Reconstruction, was a question that usually polarized Republicans against Democrats. At the very least, those parties disagreed about how governmental power should be used and over which level of government in the federal system should do the acting. Thus these new studies of the growth of the state might also be integrated into a synthesis stressing the dynamics, motives, and consequences of interparty interaction during the war.

To summarize with brutal brevity, literature about northern Civil War politics written since 1965 lacks coherence because political history as a field itself became fragmented during those years and, to a lesser extent, because political historians showed diminished interest in the problem of why the North won the war. Divergent approaches and attention to divergent subjects have yielded a number of important, often pathbreaking studies. Yet the sum of those parts falls short of an integrated whole. Were a brave soul to attempt a modern synthesis of that literature, it might usefully be structured around the *perceptions* and different values shaping interparty relations in both the electoral and policymaking arenas, the strategies that each party employed, and the impact that the parties achieved. To be a genuine synthesis, moreover, that hypothetical study should try to encompass and explain partisan combat and policy output at all levels of the federal system. It should link interparty combat to intraparty factionalism, which among Republicans at least, as Belz and others have demonstrated, had important ideological dimensions. It should examine both the genesis and the impact of public policy and relate that impact to the aspirations and experience of different social groups. And—to be perhaps utopian—it should be integrally related to the rhythms of the war itself, to the ebb and flow of military campaigns, and to the reason why the North ultimately prevailed. For if the exigencies of war required some of the policies Republican officeholders enacted, it was only northern victory that allowed others of them to endure.

# BEYOND STATE RIGHTS

## The Shadowy World
## of Confederate Politics

## GEORGE C. RABLE

"All eyes were turned to the army," recalled former governor Zebulon
Vance of North Carolina in an 1875 address to the Southern Historical
Society.[1] Perhaps because of his own wartime political experience, Vance
well understood both the contemporary, and what has become the historical, relationship between military and political affairs in the
Confederacy.[2] That the best talent had gone into the army was a widely
held maxim, and historians have reaffirmed this contemporary judgment.
Compare, for instance, the outpouring of books on Confederate military
history to the much smaller body of work on Confederate political history. But the differences are not merely quantitative. If many Confederate
citizens held the President, Congress, and other national and state politicians in low regard, so have students of the Civil War.[3] Not even the recent
controversies over the Confederate flag as a political and cultural symbol
have spurred much interest in the civic history of the South during the
war or prompted any historical rehabilitation of Confederate political
leaders. The reigning gods of the Confederate pantheon—Robert E. Lee,
Stonewall Jackson, and even Nathan Bedford Forrest—continue to dwarf
Jefferson Davis—not to mention the lesser politicians—in both historical
reputation and popular interest.

Yet modern commentators from Clausewitz on have acknowledged
the intimate and intricate connections between politics and war. Jefferson
Davis himself advanced one of the earliest political explanations for Confederate defeat. During the wrenching debate over the enlistment of slave
soldiers in the final months of the war, he waspishly remarked to a recalcitrant senator: "If the Confederacy falls, there should be written on its
tombstone, 'Died of a theory.'"[4] The theory was of course state rights.
Postwar southern writings, ironically including Davis's own memoirs, of-

ten contain elaborate and tedious expositions of this doctrine so central to the whole "Lost Cause" school of Confederate history.

Recent scholarship on southern politics during the war has paid some attention to hoary constitutional matters and has also posed some new questions. Over the past several decades, students of Confederate political culture have focused on three areas of inquiry: 1) The nature of the Confederacy and Confederate nationalism; 2) The formation of the Confederate state and public policy; 3) Political behavior and internal conflict.[5] Historians have advanced political explanations for Confederate defeat but have also studied Confederate political culture in its own right.[6]

Despite the sophistication of modern scholarship, Davis's bugaboo, state rights, still influences the study of Confederate politics and especially popular perceptions of Confederate weakness. Any consideration of recent works on wartime southern politics must begin with Frank Lawrence Owsley's classic, *State Rights in the Confederacy* (1925). For Owsley, the commitment to state rights was an inherent flaw that helped destroy the Confederacy. Governors withheld weapons, ammunition, and uniforms from the Confederate government, and too often directed their energies toward local rather than national defense. They shielded militia officers from conscription, raised technical objections to national draft laws, and interfered with the appointment of Confederate officers. In short, claims of state sovereignty hamstrung the Confederate war effort.[7]

But Owsley's presentation of a simple conflict between Confederate and state power obscured some complex problems. Although Jefferson Davis believed in the necessity of centralized power, he remained a strict constructionist who sometimes vetoed bills on the basis of niggling technicalities. As for governors and other politicians, Paul D. Escott cogently observed, their state rights rhetoric often masked localism, the protection of economic interests, political opportunism, and even defeatism.[8]

By the 1980s, historians appeared eager to move beyond debating the effect of state rights on Confederate politics. In their unfailingly provocative book, *Why the South Lost the Civil War,* Richard E. Beringer, Herman Hattaway, Archer Jones, and William N. Still, Jr., attempted to lay the issue to rest. They were too quick to minimize the importance of state rights appeals in Confederate political debate but more convincingly demonstrated that in any case the national government often prevailed on the most hotly disputed questions. To the extent that state rights ideology helped governors such as Vance to mediate disputes between the central government and disaffected citizens, it proved more an asset than a liability to the Confederate cause. According to Beringer and his colleagues, the debates over conscription and the suspension of habeas corpus did not hamper the army that much, and the governors more often than not cooperated with the Davis administration.[9]

Now over seventy years old and under increasingly sophisticated assault, the Owsley thesis has faded from historical (though hardly from popular) explanations for Confederate defeat. But its partial disappearance has also left something of a void in Confederate historiography. For if state rights ideology was neither central to understanding the Confederacy nor to explaining its demise, what was? Historians have had trouble specifying the distinguishing characteristics of Confederate nationalism, and some have raised doubts about its very existence. Part of the difficulty rests on shifting and conflicting contemporary descriptions of the Confederate experiment. Were the rebels merely fighting to be left alone, as Jefferson Davis once claimed, or did they sacrifice and die for something more positive and tangible?

Davis broadly asserted that the Confederacy embodied the last best hope of true republican liberty, and he worked to unite southerners on this basis. But, as Escott has pointed out, the adoption of conscription, the suspension of habeas corpus, and the resulting denunciations of executive despotism made such appeals problematic. Therefore Davis resorted to inflammatory rhetoric against cruel and barbarous Yankees; blaming the war on wicked northerners, he stressed the horrors of emancipation and reconstruction. Such a negative ideology, however, failed to prevent the spread of disaffection.[10]

Escott's perceptive analysis of these rhetorical twists and turns revealed the elusive quality of Confederate nationalism, but other historians have gone much further to argue that Confederate nationalism was a chimera at best. In an important though flawed essay, Kenneth M. Stampp asserted that, from the beginning of the war, many white southerners had doubts about secession because they were morally ambivalent about a slaveholders' republic. Beringer and his colleagues later expanded this seminal argument into a full-scale assault on the very notion of a vigorous Confederate nationalism. In *Why the South Lost the Civil War,* guilt over slavery is presented as the proverbial Achilles heel of the southern nation. Because the North and South were not separate cultures and slavery offered such a flimsy basis for sectional distinctiveness, the Confederacy never became a nation. A weak commitment to the cause and defeats on the battlefield produced a "cognitive dissonance" that forced many citizens to reconsider their decision to leave the Union even as they seemingly expressed renewed commitment to the cause. By the middle of the war, some Confederates were willing to sacrifice slavery for independence, worried that God had forsaken them, and in the end refused to fight a guerrilla war that would have likely brought victory.[11]

Other historians have agreed that Confederate leaders, especially Davis, played down the defense of slavery as a war aim. A few clergymen and politicians even considered reforming the institution, but whether many white southerners actually felt much guilt about slavery remains unproven. And whatever judgment is rendered on military strategy, Confederate casualty figures hardly suggest a lack of commitment.[12] Like the old arguments about state rights, this debate over the relative strength or weakness of Confederate nationalism has grown a bit stale.

Striking off in a new direction, Drew Gilpin Faust decided that Confederate nationalism deserved attention for its own sake and not merely as a means to explain the war's outcome. Faust's mining of neglected sources along with her cogent and provocative analysis brought a new level of sophistication to what many might have been considered an exhausted subject. In her view, Confederate ideology contained an unresolved tension between elite control and the need for popular support, but Davis and other leaders also appealed to Christianity as a source of political legitimacy. Although southern clergymen sometimes lamented that slaveholders had failed to live up to the ideals of the Christian master, they did not attack slavery itself, and their jeremiads more commonly focused on material sins such as greed and speculation. It was no accident that such sentiments seemed to echo from the past because Confederate leaders emphasized the historical foundations of their new nation. The Confederacy's founders, according to my recent book, portrayed themselves as defenders of classical republican values. This Confederate republicanism had strong religious overtones, fostered a general skepticism about politics, and was heavily buffeted by the war itself.[13]

Confederates used the word *revolution* gingerly, and in analyzing Confederate nationalism, historians have inevitably run up against the paradox of a "conservative revolution." Emory M. Thomas made the important observation that Confederates explicitly appealed to the spirit of 1776 to make their revolution appear safely conservative. In some respects the delegates who assembled at Montgomery, Alabama, in February 1861 sought not only to preserve the status quo antebellum but also to return to an eighteenth-century political culture. Throughout the war, however, Confederate propagandists adjusted their ideas about revolution to meet new crises.[14]

The formation of the Confederate state has not attracted the attention it deserves. William C. Davis's recent book, *"A Government of Our Own"* (1994), is by far the best account of the Montgomery convention.

With prodigious research and a deft style, Davis has written a fine narrative history in the tradition of Roy Nichols's *The Disruption of American Democracy* (1948). His account is replete with colorful personalities, political intrigue, and no small amount of petty bickering.[15] Davis discusses the provisional and permanent Confederate constitutions, but Charles R. Lee, Jr.'s long-standard account, *The Confederate Constitutions* (1963), remains helpful for its detailed delegate profiles and careful accounts of the drafting and ratification process.[16]

Historians have generally emphasized the similarities between the Confederate constitution and the original United States Constitution, paying only the briefest attention to the changes made at Montgomery. Largely ignoring the explicit references to slavery in the Confederate Constitution, Marshall L. DeRosa argued that the delegates at Montgomery simply reaffirmed a commitment to constitutional government circa 1787. Tracing the ideas of the Confederacy's founders back to the Anti-Federalists and John C. Calhoun, DeRosa concluded that this new constitution marked a return to eighteenth-century notions of state sovereignty. But his short study was more concerned with political theory than politics and had a curiously abstract quality that too easily dismissed the significance of wartime centralization.[17]

Despite their fundamental conservatism, the Montgomery delegates had their own agenda not only for protecting slavery but also for perfecting the work of the American founders. The Confederate constitution, as Don E. Fehrenbacher noted, did establish a slaveholders' republic. It paradoxically enshrined state rights principles but also set up a potentially powerful central government with substantial executive authority. Fehrenbacher's nicely balanced analysis interpreted the handiwork of the Montgomery convention as a well-crafted blend of conservatism and innovation. In a fine essay that questioned much conventional wisdom, Donald Nieman described the Confederate constitution as an embodiment of classical republicanism. Influenced by a general suspicion of power, antiparty attitudes, British parliamentary practice, and some hostility to democracy itself, the delegates at Montgomery acted as both preservers and reformers. Building on Fehrenbacher's and Nieman's insights, I emphasized a general hostility to traditional political practices, and especially to political parties, among the Confederacy's founders. The complexity of their task and the ambivalent results were apparent. The president's executive authority, for example, was expanded but his political power was curtailed.[18]

The delegates at Montgomery also selected a provisional president. The story of the election remains murky, but William C. Davis has recently shown through an ingenious marshaling of fragmentary evidence and no small amount of speculation how intrigue and bungling in the Georgia delegation helped Jefferson Davis capture the prize.[19] The choice has long been subject to controversy and second-guessing. Before a year was out, Davis had become a lightning rod for criticism, and even sympathetic historians have found his performance wanting. Bell I. Wiley faulted Davis for an inability to work with people and curry popular favor. Often obsessed with detail, sensitive to criticism, stubborn, and prone to argument, he lacked the capacity to grow in office. According to David M. Potter, Davis failed most of all as a revolutionary leader. The Mississippian was much happier poring over military plans and minute personnel matters than giving speeches or working with difficult political and military leaders. Compared to Lincoln, Allan Nevins added, Davis lacked the ability to inspire and move people. By the early 1960s, historians generally agreed that Davis may have been the wrong man for the job, but they had trouble suggesting who might have done any better. Clement Eaton's disappointingly thin and occasionally inaccurate biography of Davis failed to deviate from this orthodoxy. Escott and I treated Davis's political and rhetorical abilities more favorably but still critically.[20]

Yet the much abused president has not been without defenders. Frank E. Vandiver sympathetically assessed Davis's sometimes flinty personality while praising his political and military judgment. Ever the iconoclast, Ludwell Johnson even declared that Davis compared favorably to Abraham Lincoln in executive ability.[21] But the great obstacle in the way of any more favorable or even balanced assessment has been the absence of a good, modern biography. Therefore William C. Davis's *Jefferson Davis: The Man and His Hour* (1991) was especially welcome. This well-researched biography covered both the private and public man; Davis emerged from its pages as a deeply flawed but not unattractive human being. Often ill while struggling with enormous strategic, logistical, economic, and political problems, the prickly Mississippian overlooked glaring faults in his friends and failed to appreciate talent in his critics. William Davis offered an often sympathetic portrait of a man who possessed many ordinary character traits but to an "exaggerated degree," of an overworked and sometimes depressed leader who sacrificed much of himself for the Confederacy. A basic insecurity made decision making difficult but also meant that admitting error, once a decision had been made, was virtually impossible. Despite serious shortcomings, however, Jefferson Davis did about as well as anyone could have expected in a position fraught with difficulties and dangers.[22] As the publication of the Davis papers is completed and with new biographical studies soon to appear, a fuller picture of this fascinating and complex figure will emerge.[23]

If Davis has not fared well with students of Confederate politics neither has the Confederate Congress. Many contemporaries dismissed the body as a weak collection of mediocrities, and historians have followed suit.[24] In the first general treatment, W. Buck Yearns described the Confederate Congress as too subservient to the executive branch and not responsive enough to constituents. But congressional weakness was not built into the Confederate constitution; it only became apparent during course of the war. In a path-breaking quantitative analysis of voting patterns in the Confederate Congress, Thomas B. Alexander and Beringer showed that members from districts either under Federal occupation or threatened by invasion were most likely to support the president and favor tough war measures. Kenneth Martis's outstanding political atlas has demonstrated with maps and statistics how the admission of Kentucky and Missouri to representation in the Confederate Congress—a decision little discussed at the time—profoundly shaped the fate of important legislation. Members from these two states and other areas that fell under Federal control during the war constituted a core of support for the Davis administration in a Congress prone to internecine bickering and political fragmentation.[25]

The general neglect of the Confederate Congress is also apparent in the lack of biographical interest in representatives and senators. Aside from an indispensable collection of biographical sketches, few works bring these forgotten politicians to life. There are adequate biographies of Clement C. Clay, Jr., Robert Toombs, Louis Wigfall, and Howell Cobb, but William Lowndes Yancey, Benjamin Hill, William A. Graham, Laurence M. Keitt, and Robert M. T. Hunter all await modern biographers.[26]

Compared to the Congress, the Confederate state itself has received considerable attention; indeed, some of the best scholarship on the Confederacy has analyzed the growth of a centralized government in a political culture ostensibly committed to state rights. Emory Thomas took the lead in this revisionism. What was most remarkable about the Confederacy's brief political life, he argued cogently, was how rapidly its leaders abandoned the principles of limited government. The new nation adopted the first military conscription in American history, suspended the writ of habeas corpus, authorized impressment of commodities and slaves, and regulated railroads and manufacturing. Jefferson Davis has received credit for creating a powerful government that made great strides in promoting the manufacture of arms and ammunition to keep Confederate armies in the field much longer than anyone in 1861 might have predicted.[27]

Building on the fine work of Thomas and other scholars, Thomas Bensel presented an elaborate and impressive comparative analysis of how central state authority developed during the war. Although Confederates largely borrowed their administrative structure from their northern foes, much of the government expansion during the war was without precedent. Moreover, practices such as secret congressional sessions further enhanced centralized authority. Because Confederate conscription laws included more exemption categories than did the comparable Union statutes, Bensel saw the southern draft as more "statist." By the same token, the relative weakness of the Confederate Congress fostered greater government control over property and labor as members from occupied districts with shadow constituencies consistently supported more draconian measures. Bensel even concluded that Confederates were less divided than their Federal counterparts over the question of centralization.[28] This argument for the growth of the Confederate state has now reached its limits. Much of this scholarship rests on the close study of statutes, state papers, and legislative debates, but what historians now need to consider is whether laws that appeared to enlarge government authority actually did so. In other words, it is time to examine the gritty reality of day-to-day administration.

As centralization appeared at the national level, the state governments were not far behind. Because of conflicts between secession conventions and legislatures, some states experimented with executive councils and other forms of mixed authority and overlapping powers. Charles Edward Cauthen wrote a detailed account of the clash between the executive council and the governor in South Carolina. State legislatures, according to a careful study by May Spencer Ringold, began to hold annual sessions as they struggled with a rash of war-related problems. State lawmakers also became entangled in national politics as they both upheld and protested Confederate policies.[29]

The exigencies of war enhanced the power of state governors, and their biographers have struck another blow at the Owsley thesis. More often than not, the governors cooperated with the administration in Richmond and tended to subordinate their own doubts about conscription and other measures to the good of the Confederate cause. Like Jefferson Davis, they sparred with contentious legislators and were even accused of executive tyranny. Under their guidance, state governments expanded their power and increasingly intervened in the economic lives of many citizens.[30]

To assess the operations of both the Confederate and wartime state governments, it is necessary to move beyond constitutions, political theory, and structures to consider public policy. Studies of Confederate centralization have naturally cited conscription as a prime example of the war's revolutionary impact on state authority, but the politics of conscription were equally significant. Roll calls and geographical patterns of congressional voting on the question have received careful attention, though Memory F. Mitchell's 1965 study of the legal and judicial operations of the draft in North Carolina unfortunately stands alone. In the *Confederate Republic*, I briefly discussed the relationship between conscription and Confederate political values.[31] A comprehensive study of both the politics and administration of the Confederate draft is long overdue.

Historians have similarly slighted the habeas corpus question, perhaps because the contemporary discussion was often so abstract and arcane. In many ways, Owsley's account is still the most complete, but John B. Robbins has written a solid article. The reluctant and partial suspension of habeas corpus indicated how much Confederates cherished basic liberties, though few scholars have agreed with David Donald's claim that the Confederacy died of too much democracy. It was more politically advantageous and less dangerous to the Confederate cause for politicians to oppose the suspension of habeas corpus than to block the implementation of conscription. Despite much internal dissension and harsh attacks on the president and the Richmond government, the Confederate press remained remarkably free.[32]

Although the most heated legislative battles revolved around conscription and habeas corpus, economic questions were equally if not more important to most citizens. Students of the Confederate state, notably Thomas, Escott, and Bensel, have paid much attention to regulation, taxation, and government spending as examples of wartime centralization. In dealing with private property, the Confederates were more "statist" than their Union counterparts, Bensel has claimed. Government measures concerning cotton and impressment, as James L. Roark has pointed out, alienated some planters who also worried about slavery's future. More positively, Confederate economic policies stimulated the growth of industry and cities. Unfortunately, we know little about how states, local communities, or families fared in this increasingly complex economy, but there have been a few promising new works. Peter Wallenstein's excellent study of Georgia analyzed the changing incidence of state taxation, and Mary A. DeCredico carefully investigated the wartime growth of manufacturing in Georgia cities and the rise of a military-industrial sector in the state's economy.[33]

Beyond questions of centralization and economic change, historians have debated the impact of government fiscal policies on Confederate defeat. In what was long the standard work on Confederate finance, Richard Cecil Todd avoided evaluating or even interpreting various decisions and policies but presented valuable data for other scholars to make their own judgments. Several historians, including David Potter, have charged the Davis administration with serious errors in handling cotton and army supplies. Part of the problem, economist Stanley Lebergott maintained, was that planters insisted on growing cotton and that the Confederate government did little to stop the diversion of scarce resources into staple production. In the title of his book, *Financial Failure and Confederate Defeat,* and on nearly every page, Douglas B. Ball offered an even more searing indictment of the president and Secretary of the Treasury Christopher G. Memminger. The Confederacy's downfall occurred, according to Ball's blunt analysis, because of the "inadequate management of the . . . finances and economy" and especially the "flawed and inept administration of the . . . treasury." Davis and Memminger lacked the knowledge and imagination to handle the Confederacy's financial problems. The Confederate government, Ball maintained, should have taken control of the cotton crop, engaged in extensive blockade-running operations, imposed heavy taxes on property (including slaves), and forcefully explained to citizens the necessity for making real sacrifices. Such an argument implausibly suggests that Confederates were not already making considerable sacrifices both in the army and at home. This spirited and stimulating critique of the Davis administration and the frankly counterfactual treatment of wartime finance also ignored political realities and in effect asked Confederate leaders to transcend their historical experience and abandon some of their most cherished beliefs.[34]

Over the past two decades, historians have finally paid attention to the Confederacy's most apparently radical departure from southern orthodoxy: the proposed enrollment of slaves as soldiers. Michael Ballard and Raimondo Luraghi praised Davis for this bold effort to salvage Confederate independence. To Bensel, it "demonstrated the depth of southern nationalism and its new life independent of the slave culture that had originally given birth to the Confederacy." Beringer and his colleagues naturally disagreed, claiming that the entire discussion revealed confusion over Confederate war aims and the weakness of a national identity based on slavery. There has also been disagreement over precisely what was at stake in these discussions. Robert F. Durden subtitled his fine collection of documents *The Confederate Debate on Emancipation.*[35] But as Escott and Roark have pointed out, the final vote in Congress on enlisting slaves was very close, there was little public enthusiasm, and many planters remained adamantly opposed. Conspicuously missing from the discussion is a systematic consideration of soldier attitudes. The sheer desperation of the measure convinced Laurence Shore that it was not a turning point in southern history. Neither side in the debates (inside or outside Congress), I have argued, was willing to abandon the tenets of proslavery ideology.[36] These interpretative snarls illustrate the difficulties of analyzing public policy in the context of an evolving political culture sorely tested by war and internal conflict.

Such complexities have made studying Confederate political behavior both challenging and productive. For historians accustomed to tracking the give-and-take of party politics and elections, the Confederacy at first appears to be a nation without politics. With his usual knack for going to the heart of an issue, David Potter asserted that the most striking feature of the Confederate political system was the absence of political parties. Given the traditional American faith in the two-party system, it was not surprising when Potter concluded that organized opposition to the Davis administration would have strengthened the Confederate political system and produced wiser public policies. Building on this insight, Eric McKitrick argued that the absence of parties proved to be a serious weakness because the Confederate political system did not recruit talented leaders. The result was a mediocre cabinet and an ineffective Congress. Considerable friction developed between the executive and legislative branches, but there was no organized administration or opposition blocs in Congress to prevent policy differences from degenerating into petty and often personal squabbling. While Jefferson Davis suffered from harsh and not very constructive criticism, political parties strengthened the northern government.[37] McKitrick's brilliant and original essay has shaped a generation of scholarship. Whether explicitly or implicitly, his arguments have reappeared in one form or another in several major works on the Civil War.[38]

The few historians who have challenged this orthodoxy have taken two different tacks. One approach posited the existence of nascent political parties in the Confederacy. Despite the collapse of the second American party system in the 1850s, according to Alexander and Beringer, Democrat-Whig rivalries surfaced in the Confederate Congress and in some elections. In an especially thought-provoking article, Beringer hypothesized that these old party divisions along with lingering conflict between secessionists and Unionists and differences over how and when to conduct peace negotiations with the Federals might have eventually laid the groundwork for new political parties.[39]

Whatever might have developed had the war continued beyond 1865 or had the Confederacy won its independence, Alexander and Beringer found little evidence that pre-war party affiliation influenced voting in Congress. Did party sentiment then survive in the absence of party behavior? In his excellent study of North Carolina politics, Marc W. Kruman remarked on the great hostility to political parties at the end of the ante-bellum period. Antiparty attitudes cropped up in public discourse even if they sometimes masked partisan motives or merely reflected a drive for wartime unity. North Carolina politicians regularly accused their opponents of selfish partisanship but then ironically moved their state closer than any other to establishing a new party system. Whether the "Confederate" and "Conservative" factions qualified as organized parties is debatable, and the most important contests occurred within the "Conservative" ranks.[40]

Kruman's work formed a vital link between those historians who have emphasized the persistence of at least some vestige of partisanship and the most recent interpretations that have challenged the arguments advanced by both Potter/McKitrick and Alexander/Beringer. Bensel questioned whether more organized opposition would have strengthened Jefferson Davis and insisted that the absence of parties aided the expansion of centralized state authority. In a sweeping indictment of previous interpretations, I argued that Confederate political culture itself rested on a strong aversion to partisanship and even to politics itself. In practice of course, citizens and politicians deviated from their commitment to purified republicanism, but few even implicitly favored the formation of parties. Whether a two-party system was a source of strength in the North needs considerably more attention, and in any case, I concluded that it was unlikely that the Confederacy's fragmented and temporary coalitions would have coalesced into political parties.[41]

The debate over political parties in the Confederacy has for the most part focused on the strategies pursued by elites. The political behavior of Confederate citizens remains a badly neglected subject; opportunities for connecting ideology, public policy, and elections present considerable challenges. As I recently stated, "The Confederate voter is the forgotten man of Civil War history."[42] The literature on wartime elections is remarkably thin. In gathering valuable information and a few colorful anecdotes on the 1861 Confederate elections, Yearns emphasized the disruption of old party voting patterns, the impact of local issues, and general voter apathy. His treatment, however, was neither exhaustive, quantitative, nor systematic. Kruman examined the sometimes contentious congressional races in North Carolina, and Michael Dougan provided a solid account of the contests in Arkansas, but other states have been more or less ignored.[43]

Viewing the Confederacy as a whole, Alexander and Beringer determined that traditional party voting was not that significant in most congressional districts. But according to Martis, voter turnout was only about 40 percent, and therefore election results were difficult to interpret.

Some candidates ran on their military records, others focused on their support for disunion, but even the general triumph of secessionist Democrats may not have meant much. The obscurity of some House candidates, the influence of local issues, the interplay of political personalities, the complicated scramble for Senate seats, vague calls for national unity, and strongly expressed antiparty sentiments have all made the first Confederate elections confusing to contemporaries and scholars alike.[44] Even with Martis's excellent tables and maps, the dearth of extensive newspaper coverage and other primary materials will limit further study of these contests.

Historians have paid more attention to the 1863 Confederate elections, though primarily as barometers of public opinion on the war. Incumbents fared poorly as did some Davis administration stalwarts; voters tended to favor former Whigs and Unionists. But again turnout was low, many districts were occupied by Union armies, and given the often thin data, historians have naturally disagreed over the significance of the results. Yearns believed that these elections revealed strong opposition to the Davis administration and a general war weariness, but it is less clear whether they indicated growing support for peace negotiations. In North Carolina, for instance, Kruman discovered considerable factionalism among "Conservatives" and some reluctance to endorse a reconstructionist or peace program. I concluded that in both national and state elections frustrated and confused voters neither rallied to the President nor embraced peace candidates. Instead they searched for an ill-defined middle ground and remained hostile or at least indifferent to reviving old party squabbles or forming new political coalitions. Even some congressmen elected from disaffected districts supported Confederate war policies, and the anti-administration members never formed cohesive voting blocs in Congress.[45]

The course of the war itself, however, greatly complicated the study of political behavior, though historians have not properly integrated military events into the study of Confederate politics. Measuring the importance of party affiliation, stance on secession, wealth, and slaveholding, Alexander and Beringer found that none of these factors explained the results of congressional roll calls. Instead, geography had the largest influence on votes concerning conscription, habeas corpus, impressment, and other war measures. Congressmen and senators from occupied districts or states ("outsiders") were more likely to support legislation that expanded government control over manpower and the economy. Those representing areas still free of Federal troops ("insiders") were more responsive to constituent pressure and more reluctant to vote for unpopular measures. Martis's new maps have provided important visual evidence of how congressional roll calls followed the contours of military occupation.[46]

But political behavior involves human beings, and it seldom falls into neatly defined patterns that can be quantified, graphed, or mapped. Some historians have crunched numbers while others have recounted telling anecdotes, but policy and personality cannot be so easily separated. Whatever their method, scholars have tried to understand the divisions among Confederates. Wiley noted the importance of southern individualism and habits of contentiousness cultivated during decades of sectional controversy but also blamed the secrecy often practiced by Davis and other government officials for fostering distrust, cynicism, and conflict. Many writers have pointed out the extraordinary pettiness, pride, and arrogance that characterized all too many southern politicians. Both the president and his critics, William C. Davis has rightly remarked, tended to be quarrelsome, jealous, and stubborn. Constant bickering prevented compromise while encouraging public apathy. Attacks on the administration by fanatics such as Robert Barnwell Rhett and other South Carolinians contained approximately equal measures of principle, vitriol, and frustrated ambition. On this score, many historians have quoted a statement made by James Henry Hammond even before the first shots had been fired: "*Big-man-me-ism* reigns supreme & every one thinks every other a jealous fool or an aspiring knave."[47] Even the old states rights interpretation paid more attention to constitutional technicalities, legal obstructionism, and political infighting than to the possibility that some politicians and their constituents acted out of strongly held views about the role of government.

However, egotistic fulminations and political posturing were only part of the story. Ambition and obstinacy coexisted with a deep commitment to certain core values. Disaffection from the Confederate government, Kruman asserted, stemmed from genuine fears that administration policies threatened fundamental liberties. Warnings about military despotism carried the force of unswerving conviction. Many opposition politicians, as J. William Harris recognized, spoke in a language of republicanism. I maintained that strong attachments to eighteenth-century political principles, and especially antiparty ideology, eventually produced two distinct political cultures in the Confederacy. Jefferson Davis and other leaders labored to build a nation grounded in political unity and class harmony. As the war dragged on and a political stalemate developed in Richmond, opposition politicians increasingly appealed to traditional defenses of individual, community, and state liberty. Emphasizing Yankee barbarism while still invoking the spirit of 1776, Davis tried to rally citizens to the Confederate cause. Yet in language equally steeped in eighteenth-century ideas, his opponents warned the people never to surrender their rights to a ravenous, centralized, and potentially tyrannical government. These themes appeared not only in speeches and editorials but also in sermons and textbooks throughout the Confederacy's brief history.[48]

Biographies of key Confederate leaders are windows into this collective and individual world of politics, revealing the interplay of principles and practice, of conviction and maneuver. No one extolled libertarian values more passionately than the diminutive but talented Alexander H. Stephens. Opposed to immediate secession but then elected Confederate vice president, the veteran Georgia politician has generally been dismissed as an impractical obstructionist. In Thomas E. Schott's well-written biography, however, a much more complex and fuller picture emerges from the author's skillful interweaving of private and public events. Schott presented the often sickly vice president as a determined and consistent defender of constitutional liberty. Seldom bending to pleas of necessity, Stephens eventually lost confidence in Davis and in the Confederate cause itself. Quick to recognize faults in others, Stephens himself was vain, subject to bouts of melancholy, and susceptible to flattery—especially from the crafty Joseph E. Brown. Extracting valuable material from several large collections of correspondence, Schott offered an empathetic but balanced portrait of a fascinating figure; in some ways, the tragedy of Stephens's Confederate career and his anguished personal life became an archetype for the story of the southern revolution.[49]

There are no comparable studies of other important opposition politicians, in part because the manuscript materials on wartime politics are sparse. Joseph H. Parks's detailed biography of Joseph E. Brown eschews interpretation and fails to assess Brown's important and often misunderstood role in Confederate politics.[50] Fortunately, other historians have contributed brief but important analyses of the wily governor. Curtis Arthur Amlund was one of the first scholars to suggest that Brown could be cooperative as well as cantankerous in his dealings with the Confederate government. The governor had a knack for keeping abreast of public opinion and riding out political storms. Escott has well summarized Brown's political skills: "Blessed with the ability to appeal both to planters and to yeomen, Brown was a puzzling figure, as principled as he was unscrupulous, and as hostile toward the Davis administration as he was toward the United States." A political battler, and sometimes disingenuous hypocrite, Brown astutely supported relief measures for suffering Georgians. Petty and obstructive, he nevertheless promoted public welfare measures that made him politically unassailable in state politics.[51] Brown's career typified the paradoxes of principle and ambition so often found in successful politicians.

Historians have usually treated Brown and Governor Zebulon Vance of North Carolina primarily as opponents of the Davis administration. Like the Georgian, Vance awaits a biographer. Glenn Tucker's readable but now badly dated, *Zeb Vance: Champion of Personal Freedom* (1965), presented the Tarheel governor as a simple defender of individual liberty without taking into account his often striking flexibility. Similarly, Richard S. Yates's solid but brief study of Vance during the war was conventional in both style and interpretation.[52]

More recently, Vance's career has been reexamined as part of a larger reinterpretation of Confederate political history. To Beringer and his colleagues, Vance represented a classic example of cognitive dissonance—an original Unionist but brave soldier, a politician who had given up on Confederate nationalism but who also urged his people to fight on. In further downplaying the importance of state rights, David D. Scarboro recounted several instances of cooperation between Vance and the Confederate government.[53] Historians have often underestimated Vance's political skills. Frequent controversies with the Davis administration and a bitter election contest against William W. Holden and the peace faction of the Conservative Party required great adroitness and calm leadership. At the heart of Kruman's perceptive account of North Carolina politics is Vance, first as a subordinate and somewhat shadowy figure, and later as a colossus who comes to dominate state politics. I categorized Vance as a political centrist who mediated between the demands for national unity and the preservation of liberty. The governor's often brilliant maneuvering through the treacherous factionalism of North Carolina politics and his triumphant reelection in 1864 seriously weakened the peace movement and ironically strengthened the Confederate government.[54] Because Vance received so many letters and petitions from such a wide range of people, his correspondence shows how historians can move beyond the study of maneuvering by political leaders to incorporate military, economic, and social history into the study of wartime politics.

With the demise of state rights interpretations and the general neglect of traditional biography, some historians have turned to the study of political economy—a development that would not have surprised Brown or Vance. Originating partly from the larger Marxist analysis of southern life and the decline of race as an all-purpose explanatory tool, a generation of scholars have made class conflict a major theme in Confederate historiography. James L. Roark observed that racial fears often bound nonslaveholding whites to the slavery regime but planters nevertheless worried about the loyalty of yeomen and poor whites. Exploiting a rich body of petitions and letters sent to Confederate officials by all sorts of men and women, Escott made the strongest case for the centrality of class conflict to understanding Confederate history. Signs of yeomen discontent appeared early in the war as resentment over conscription, opposition to impressment, the denunciations of wealthy speculators for taking advantage of shortages and inflation steadily mounted. Confederate welfare policies could not stem this tide of disaffection, but governors such as Brown and Vance were attuned to the anxieties of the rich and the disgruntlement of the poor.[55]

The analysis of the relationship between class conflict and public policy went beyond simple divisions among privileged planters, suffering yeomen, and a rootless underclass. In southern history, notions of class were rooted in family and geography. Elizabeth Fox-Genovese, Eugene Genovese, and Steven Hahn have all emphasized the importance of localism in explaining yeomen responses to secession and war. Rural isolation and sporadic contacts with markets all shaped political attitudes and behavior.[56]

Despite much creative scholarship, it remains difficult to recapture the voices of the disheartened and the resentful, though the study of individual states and communities has shown considerable promise. The larger framework of class analysis has probably predetermined some of the conclusions because historians searching for conflicts between planters and yeomen naturally found them. Such scholarship also tends to ignore how many men of yeoman background fought hard and long for the Confederacy. Based on a close reading of Tennessee veterans' questionnaires Fred Arthur Bailey asserted that the simmering and complex class tensions of the antebellum period erupted during the war, inducing men of humble background to desert from the Confederate army, but he pushed his interpretations considerably beyond the available evidence.[57] Students of North Carolina history have explored how political strife affected often fragile social arrangements. The wealthy could wangle draft exemptions or secure safe staff appointments; inequality of sacrifice sparked grumbling and some disloyalty. According to Wayne K. Durrill, yeoman-planter tensions produced a virtual guerrilla war in Washington County. His forcefully argued case study, based largely on one important collection of manuscripts, carried the class conflict thesis too far, but most historians have conceded that the Confederacy never quite embodied the social harmony so fondly described by rebel propagandists. From the North Carolina mountains to northern Texas, Confederate sympathizers persecuted and sometimes assaulted suspected Unionists. James Marten examined the ethnic tensions and variety of dissent in Confederate Texas; Phillip Shaw Paludan and Richard B. McCaslin wrote well-crafted local studies of political terrorism.[58]

Historians have only begun to study the peace movement that sprang to life during the summer of 1863, but here too class conflict has become a dominant theme. Peace societies in Arkansas and North Carolina recruited members among nonslaveholders and generally failed to attract support from established political leaders. How much these groups encouraged desertion from the Confederate armies remains debatable. Equally unclear, despite some attention given to debates in the state legislatures, is the political base of support for the peace movement.[59]

In the best brief analysis of the peace question as a political issue, Escott described how Davis and Vance dealt with calls for negotiations with the Lincoln government. The resulting conflict created some odd and temporary alliances that paradoxically weakened both the peace movement and the Confederate government. A central problem of definition bedeviled efforts to locate the political support for the peace movement. No coherent, organized bloc supported peace resolutions in the Confederate Congress; nor could peace advocates paper over their own differences about the future of slavery. But most of all, the goals of the peace movement remained fuzzy. Were those who pressed for negotiations with the Lincoln government defeatists or did some, notably Alexander H. Stephens, truly believe that Confederate independence could be won through a diplomatic deus ex machina? Proposals for a convention of the states begged the question: to what end? For a time, as Larry E. Nelson has shown, hopes for peace rested on the prevention of Lincoln's reelection. Confederates of various stripes saw a victory for George B. McClellan on a peace platform as critical for winning southern independence.[60]

Many peace supporters—in Congress and out—were relatively obscure men about whom little is known. An exception was William Woods Holden. An ardent Democrat, Unionist, and critic of the Davis administration, the influential editor of the *Raleigh Standard* has attracted considerable historical attention. Horace W. Raper and William C. Harris have each published substantial biographies, but Raper's treatment of Holden's Civil War career is brief and superficial. In Harris's well-researched account, Holden's slashing journalistic style and penchant for controversy received detailed attention. The Tarheel editor defended libertarian political values in his often blistering attacks on both North Carolina and Confederate leaders. Harris has skillfully described how Holden created the Conservative Party and recruited Vance to run for governor. By the second half of 1863, however, Holden and Vance had a falling out over the peace question, and their gubernatorial contest the following year brought a crushing defeat for Holden. Kruman has questioned whether Holden was truly a reconstructionist, but there is no doubt that the Confederate government considered him a dangerous man and that Davis encouraged Vance to move against both Holden and the peace movement.[61] Despite the already extensive literature available on Holden and North Carolina politics, a large body of primary materials, both state and local, await closer study.

On February 28, 1864, in a sermon preached to a North Carolina brigade, shortly before twenty-two deserters were to be executed, John Paris blamed peace meetings, class envy, and political demagoguery for causing these unfortunate souls to abandon the Confederate cause.[62] This remarkable document suggests future directions for scholars interested in southern politics during the Civil War. Although historians need to pay more attention to elections, to political rhetoric, and to newspaper coverage of wartime politics, they also should broaden their definition of politics itself. Civil religion, the role of households in public life, the social world of Confederate politics, the political socialization of Confederate soldiers all can be integrated with more traditional topics such as state rights, Confederate nationalism, libertarian dissent, and political leadership. To study the men and women of the wartime South in as broad a context as possible might make the categories established for the essays in this volume seem artificial and outmoded within the next several decades, but this is the great promise of Civil War history.

# A CONSTITUTIONAL CRISIS

## MICHAEL LES BENEDICT

In a classic essay published some thirty years ago, Arthur E. Bestor pointed out that the Civil War was, at heart, a constitutional crisis.[1] The United States has a long and still powerful heritage of constitutionalizing conflicts over interests and beliefs. When that happens, as Bestor explained, "Questions of policy give place to questions of power; questions of wisdom to questions of legality."[2] The conflict over slavery was powerfully shaped by the United States Constitution. The issue of federal power to bar slavery in the territories became crucial because this was one of the few points where the Constitution seemed to give the federal government authority to deal with slavery; hardly anyone suggested that Congress had constitutional authority to interfere with slavery within the southern states.

The Civil War raised important constitutional issues. What was the nature of the war? Was it a rebellion of individuals? A war between states? Did the federal government have war powers that transcended the peacetime limits of federalism? How far could the government go in restricting civil liberties? Did the Constitution permit the confiscation of property as a war measure? Did it permit emancipation? Which branch of government was chiefly responsible for waging the war and establishing war measures? What determined United States citizenship? What rights did citizenship entail? Would emancipated African Americans be entitled to them? What did the nature of the war imply for the restoration of the Union once the conflict ended? To which branch of government did the Constitution entrust to do the job of restoration?

The centrality of these questions to the history of the Civil War has made constitutional history an important component of Civil War history in general. However, changes in historians' attitudes toward the field of constitutional history, as well as changes in the nature of the field itself, have affected how and how much historians have attended to constitutional aspects of the struggle. In the nineteenth-century United States, constitutional questions tended to center on where the power lay to resolve a disputed issue—that is, Americans argued over which government, state or federal, or which branch of government—legislative, executive, or judicial—was authorized to make the decision. The issue of federal power over slavery in the territories was a quintessential example. Issues of federalism and separation-of-powers have persisted through the twentieth century, but usually with less salience. Now the question tends to be, is government, state or federal, authorized to take certain kinds of actions at all? Can it ban abortions? Can it educate young men and women, black children and white children separately? Can it treat men and women differently? As a leading scholar put it, Americans have moved to "a constitutionalism of rights in a polity previously dominated by a constitutionalism of powers."[3] This change is reflected in American constitutional historiography, which likewise has moved from a concentration on the history of constitutional controversies over the distribution of governmental power to a concentration on the development of civil rights and liberties.

The Civil War began during the great era of what we now call "Whig history"—the idea that the history of the Anglo-American people was the story of the progress of human liberty. This concern with liberty placed constitutional history at the center of the historical discipline in Great Britain and the United States. British and American histories attended carefully to the growth of governmental institutions and to the struggle between tyranny and liberty.[4]

In the years immediately following Appomattox, both northern and southern historians viewed the Civil War from this perspective. Ex-Confederates, who wrote the first southern histories of the conflict, agreed with Bestor that constitutional issues were central. Confederate president Jefferson Davis, vice president Alexander H. Stephens, and journalist Edward A. Pollard all agreed that those naive enough to think that slavery caused the war were, in Stephens's words, "but superficial observers." The real origins of the war lay in "*opposing principles.*" It was the culmination of a struggle between those who believed that the government of the United States was "thoroughly National" and those who believed it "strictly Federal." Only a "strictly federal" union was consistent with liberty, the southerners insisted. A "thoroughly national" government was a tyrannical government. "Slavery . . . was but *the question* on which these antagonistic principles . . . were finally brought into actual and active collision with each other on the field of battle," Stephens explained.[5]

Thus the first sections of the southern histories were devoted to exegesis on the nature of the Union, followed by a chronicle of the events leading to the war, discussed entirely in terms of the constitutional conflict. The Confederate historians all defended secession as a constitutional right. Thus Southerners had not engaged in rebellion. The war was between belligerent, independent states, not between the federal government and rebellious citizens. Other constitutional issues paled in comparison to the fundamental one of the nature of the federal union. In his history, Stephens paid scant attention to the differences between himself and Jefferson Davis over state rights within the Confederacy, for example. Davis lambasted Abraham Lincoln's wartime interferences with civil liberties but hardly attended at all to similar charges that had been levied against himself.

The outcome of the Civil War shook southern faith in Whig teleology. Implicit in their histories was a metanarrative that hearkened back to the more pessimistic republican view of the history of liberty that Whig history had replaced. Liberty was fragile, always under threat. In the United States, as elsewhere in history, liberty had degenerated into license, civic virtue had given way to faction, constitutional government was lost to tyranny. For the Confederate historians, the logical culmination was Reconstruction. In their view, it marked the final collapse of constitutional government, completely erasing the line between state and federal authority and with it the last remnants of American liberty. Ultimately, southerners would devise a tale of Reconstruction in which they recovered their freedom by driving despotic carpetbaggers and scalawags and their black minions from power. This construction allowed southern history to reconnect to the metanarrative of Whig historiography.

Postwar Republican historians fit their tale to the contours of Whig historiography more easily. While the southern histories of the antislavery conflict stressed issues of federalism, histories by Republican participants stressed issues of civil liberty. Slaveholders' devotion to "state rights" was a mere subterfuge. For Horace Greeley, the Radical Republican editor of the *New York Tribune*, and Massachusetts senator Henry Wilson, vice president during the second Grant administration, the heart of the slavery conflict lay in the "slave power's" assault on civil liberty, black and white.[6] Slavery was more than a labor system exploiting slave labor; it was supported by a network of laws that deprived nonslaveholding southern whites of the power to challenge it. Even worse, the slave power extended its oppressive hand into the North and the territories as well. Greeley's chapter "The Pro-Slavery Reaction" was a forerunner of modern studies, describing the fight over the gag rule on antislavery petitions in Congress, southern interference with the delivery of antislavery material by the federal postal service, the attempt by the South's northern allies to pass laws to suppress abolition societies, and antiabolitionist violence fomented and condoned by dough-faced northern politicians.[7]

The Republican historians perceived the triumph of the North and the abolition of slavery to be another of the great milestones in the history of liberty. Neither saw wartime infringements of civil rights as threats. For Wilson, who continued his history through Reconstruction, Republican restoration policy had been necessary to secure the great victory. The laws and constitutional amendments securing civil and political equality for black Americans provided a triumphant coda to the war.

Northern Democrats saw matters differently. The eminent lawyer George Ticknor Curtis represented their views in the second volume of his *Constitutional History of the United States*.[8] The celebrated author of an optimistic constitutional history in 1854, Curtis had waited over thirty years to carry his study through the war and Reconstruction years. Curtis offered a sophisticated explanation of how the Constitution shaped the struggle, prefiguring modern-day understandings. Conflict focused on those areas where differing interpretations of the fundamental law were plausible, with the issue of congressional power over slavery in the territories becoming critical.[9] To settle such a conflict peacefully required restraint; the fanaticism of the abolitionists, "with a disregard of constitutional obligations . . . and utterly discarding the duties of citizenship," drove southerners to a reciprocal fury that ambiguous provisions of the Constitution could not contain.[10] Himself one of the attorneys for Dred Scott, Curtis was the first constitutional historian to dissect the opinion carefully, the first to argue that its crucial ruling that the Missouri Compromise was unconstitutional was merely dictum, because three of the six justices taking that position had held that Dred Scott was not a citizen entitled to bring suit in federal court.[11]

For Curtis the Civil War era had posed a profound threat to constitutional government. The emotions raised by the slavery issue had overwhelmed the constitutional provisions that were designed to contain and resolve even the deepest political disputes. No state could secede, he insisted, and thus the war had been waged against individual insurgents.[12] Committed to the preservation of constitutional limitations, he barely mentioned wartime issues, instead blasting Republican Reconstruction, which by treating southern states as out of the Union, "was inconsistent with the doctrine which had been all along maintained in the official action of the Federal Government."[13]

Constitutional issues continued to play a big role in the first scholarly histories of the Civil War era written by nonparticipants. Inspired by German models of "scientific" history, turn-of-the-twentieth-century American historians eschewed the romanticism of Whig history. Yet constitutional history retained its honored place. Historians, sociologists, and political scientists all conceived institutions to be the highest forms of social organization. Recounting their development was the historian's most important function. Constitutional history, with its interest in government institutions and with its sources consisting largely of public documents, lent itself to this approach. Those who were engaged in other historical research took seriously the role of the Constitution and constitutional principles in American history. The classic multivolume histories of the United States that appeared in the 1880 and 1890s, by James Schouler, James Ford Rhodes, John W. Burgess, and Edward Channing, paid close attention to the constitutional controversies that seemed to have played an integral part in the nation's history. Indeed, Burgess titled two volumes of his five-volume history of the United States *The Civil War and the Constitution* and *Reconstruction and the Constitution*.[14] However, the institutional and political focus tended to narrow the definition of constitutional history, confining it to the development of constitutional doctrines about governmental institutions, as discerned through the study of public documents.[15]

Burgess encouraged one of his best young graduate students, William Archibald Dunning, to write a dissertation on the Constitution in the Civil War, versions of which Dunning published in journals and then, with a companion essay on the Constitution during Reconstruction, in his influential book *Essays on the Civil War and Reconstruction,* which appeared in 1897.[16] Other young historians and political scientists wrote histories of constitutional doctrines regarding the territories, and studies of the Dred Scott case, Lincoln's policy of Reconstruction, and the impeachment of President Andrew Johnson.[17]

Although the great, multivolume histories recognized slavery was crucial to the struggle that led to war, they tended to describe North and South as divergent civilizations.[18] The sections argued over the Constitution, but this was only one aspect of the conflict, not the central one, as the southern apologists had insisted. Stressing the fight over slavery in the territories, historians paid little attention to other points of constitutional conflict. The main constitutional issue became the right of the federal government to exclude slavery from the territories, which turned on the nature of American federalism. By emphasizing the territorial issue, historians portrayed the North as the aggressors, however morally justified, on the slavery issue. Southern state-rights and state-sovereignty arguments appeared essentially defensive—a futile effort to erect a constitutional barrier against the increasing power of the free states.

The German-influenced American historians writing in the late-nineteenth and early-twentieth centuries were uniformly hostile to the southern view of the American federal system. Echoing Kant and Hegel, the German-trained Burgess described the state as "the realization of the universal in man, . . . the product of the progressive revelation of the human reason through history."[19] The Civil War was part of "the plan of universal history" to shake off localism; the historical purpose of secession was "to provoke the Nation to . . . free itself, and assert its supremacy, forevermore." The constitutional argument for secession was "from every point of view, a mere jugglery with words, . . . sophistries based upon . . . confused premises."[20] Rhodes was less philosophical but no less impatient with southern incantations of state rights and state sovereignty.[21] For Channing, too, the main theme of American history was the growth of the nation, especially "the victory of the forces of union over those of particularism."[22] On this central question, northerners were right, and southerners were wrong.

The late-nineteenth-century historians also established our common understanding that Lincoln only slowly came to the policy of emancipation, his caution frustrating more-radical Republicans. They treated emancipation primarily as a question between governmental power and white people's property rights. The nationalist Burgess did not doubt Lincoln's power to promulgate the Emancipation Proclamation under his war powers as commander-in-chief, but its effect could not, he opined, survive the war. Only the Thirteenth Amendment finally secured freedom.[23]

Dunning likewise did not distinguish emancipation from other wartime denials of civil liberty to southerners. More carefully than his contemporaries, Dunning analyzed how Union leaders justified emancipation, confiscation, and martial law in the South. He was the first historian to stress that the federal government treated southerners both as insurgents and as belligerents. Dunning conceded that "war is the negation of civil rights." Insurgents "become . . . enemies," and from that moment "the constitutional guarantees of civil liberty lose their effect as against the executive. It becomes authorized to enforce submission to the laws by bullets, not by indictments." But in an age when conservative intellectuals were committed to protecting property rights, Dunning could not condone confiscation. The modern laws of war did not countenance it. The confiscation procedures, moreover, were "wholly contrary to the spirit of the bill of rights" and grossly violated due process of law.[24]

For Dunning, the Civil War indicated that constitutional provisions could not constrain popular demands at a time of crisis. He was probably the first scholar to refer to Lincoln's presidential "dictatorship."[25] Lincoln disregarded constitutional limitations when he suspended the privilege of habeas corpus in the North, instituted a system of arbitrary arrests, and suppressed the publication of opposition newspapers. Lincoln had created "a perfect platform for a military despotism," and Congress's legislation on the subject ratified it.[26] Rhodes reached conclusions that were, if anything, more critical. Lincoln's infringements on civil liberty "revolt the spirit born to freedom," he opined.[27] Lincoln tempered his actions with kindness and mercy, but those very manifestations of Lincoln's humaneness prevented Americans "from appreciating the enormity of the acts done under his authority."[28]

Burgess, too, referred to Lincoln's temporary "military dictatorship,"[29] but he accepted as "the precedent of the Constitution in civil war that the President may suspend all of the safeguards of the Constitution in behalf of personal liberty anywhere in the country." It was Congress's job to hold him accountable if he abused the awesome power.[30] Burgess acknowledged that the 1866 Supreme Court decision *Ex parte Milligan*[31] denied the government's power to institute military trials where the courts were open and functioning. But he flatly denied its authority. He was sure that no matter what the Court said, "the practice of the Administration would be repeated under like circumstances."[32]

Sharing the widespread racism of their era, the turn-of-the-century constitutional historians denounced the enfranchisement of the freedmen during Reconstruction as, in Burgess's words, "a monstrous thing . . . a great wrong to civilization."[33] But as nationalists they agreed that Congress had the constitutional authority to set the terms for restoring the southern states to the Union. Thus Burgess rejected the Confederate historians' argument that the states were coordinate, preexisting sovereignties that retained sovereign powers not delegated to the national government. The nation existed separately from the Constitution, which divided and limited the powers of government, not the sovereignty of the nation. A state in a federal system was merely "a local self-government, under the supremacy of the general constitution."[34] It had no legal existence outside the nation. Thus, Burgess endorsed Radical Republican senator Charles Sumner's view that a state organization ceased to exist as a legal entity—committed suicide in Sumner's phrase—when it attempted to secede from the Union.[35]

In his essay "The Constitution of the United States During Reconstruction," Dunning categorized the various arguments about the status of the Confederate states at war's end and the nature of federal authority over them. Historians have generally followed his categorization ever since. According to Dunning, congressional Republicans correctly justified their

Reconstruction program by citing the obligation the Constitution imposed upon the United States to guarantee republican forms of government in the states. But if the Constitution authorized Congress to restore the states to normal relations in the Union, Burgess and Dunning agreed that the Reconstruction Act itself was patently unconstitutional. "[H]ardly a line in the entire bill . . . would withstand the test of the Constitution," Burgess intoned.[36] It imposed martial law in time of peace; it usurped the president's powers as commander-in-chief; it suspended the privilege of the writ of habeas corpus without the justification of a public danger. It was "the most brutal proposition ever introduced into the Congress of the United States by a responsible committee."[37] Burgess, Dunning, and Rhodes, and, by the turn of the century, most Americans, accepted the Confederate constitutional history of Reconstruction after the war. It was not the story of African Americans' search for freedom and civil and political rights, but of white southerners' desperate struggle for liberty against a corrupt despotism sustained by black votes.[38]

The attention nineteenth-century historians paid to constitutional issues was based on the idea that constitutional law and constitutional argument mattered—that human beings are basically rational creatures who respond to reason and are persuaded by argument. But the late-nineteenth century witnessed the beginnings of a revolution in our understanding of human motivation and behavior. The new science of psychology seemed to demonstrate that people were driven by subconscious instincts, which intellect merely rationalized. New techniques of analysis suggested that human behavior could be associated statistically with social and economic characteristics. These discoveries undermined the belief that autonomous individuals make decisions based on the reasoned application of principles; they implied that human behavior could be explained only by understanding deeper causes than the superficial determinations of individuals. In the words of Thomas L. Haskell, "[W]hat once had been accepted as an adequate explanation was . . . seen as superficial, merely formalistic."[39]

The impact of this new understanding of social causation upon both law and history was staggering. Ultimately, it led legal scholars to what became known as "legal realism." "Legal realism" repudiated the idea that law was designed to promote a neutral system of justice; rather law reflected the realities of power in society and itself reflected the competition among interest groups.[40] Such concepts destroyed the foundations upon which the older generation of constitutional historians had constructed their work. To the modern historians of the early twentieth century, it seemed fatuous to speak of the founding fathers, or judges, or statesmen, as being devoted to abstract principles of liberty separate from the interests and perceptions of the social and economic groups to which they belonged. To the Progressive historians Charles A. Beard, Frederick Jackson Turner, Arthur M. Schlesinger, Sr., and Vernon L. Parrington, constitutional arguments were merely superficial manifestations of deeper economic conflicts—or worse, mere weapons picked up one day and cynically discarded the next. Schlesinger put it bluntly: "[E]conomic or some other local advantage has usually determined the attitude of states and parties towards questions of constitutional construction."[41]

Constitutional history ceased to interest most historians. Why study the manifestation when you can analyze the deeper social and economic causes? In 1922 Schlesinger published a series of essays designed to introduce the results of recent historical research to the popular audience. Aptly entitled *New Viewpoints in American History,* it contained only two essays touching on constitutional history, and the titles were instructive. One was "Economic Aspects of the Movement for the Constitution" and the other was called "The State Rights Fetish."[42]

Constitutional historians were affected by the new understandings. Andrew C. McLaughlin, the dean of the field in the 1930s, knew that "institutions and principles do not develop or move in a vacuum." To comprehend constitutional history, he wrote in his 1935 Pulitzer Prize-winning *Constitutional History of the United States,* "one must have in mind social and industrial change and movement." But this meant that constitutional history "when viewed in its entirety is of almost limitless extent."[43] Unable to establish boundaries, constitutional historians stuck primarily to the narrow account of constitutional development and conflict gleaned from the legislative and judicial record.

McLaughlin's constitutional history, Homer C. Hockett's 1939 constitutional history, and James G. Randall's *Constitutional Problems under Lincoln* were outstanding studies of this type.[44] But they would be among the last constitutional histories written by historians for some time. Into the vacuum rushed political scientists and lawyers. Following the examples of the great Edward S. Corwin and Charles Warren, they treated constitutional history as the history of constitutional law. More and more they focused on the Supreme Court. For historians, constitutional history seemed ever remote from the mainstream of the field.[45] As late as 1986, when the *Journal of American History* was planning its number celebrating the bicentennial of the Constitution, editor David Thelen explained that he avoided asking specialist constitutional historians to contribute, because they focused entirely on the Constitution itself and were "not . . . much concerned with the consequences of the Constitution or of the courts' changing interpretations of its meanings."[46]

Both McLaughlin and Hockett devoted several hundred pages to the constitutional issues of the slavery, Civil War, and Reconstruction conflict. Each presented balanced and thorough accounts of the rise of southern state-sovereignty constitutional theories, and both fully described the constitutional arguments in Congress about federal power over slavery in the territories.[47] Both made abortive starts to recovering the antislavery constitutional argument, dealing with efforts to suppress antislavery agitation through the mail and through petitions to Congress, although McLaughlin was far more sensitive than Hockett to the way race lay at the core of the slavery issue.[48]

Randall's *Constitutional Problems under Lincoln* became the standard work on Civil War constitutional issues for more than a generation, informing both McLaughlin's and Hockett's work, and it probably still remains a starting point for further research and analysis. Echoing McLaughlin, Randall conceded, "Whether any great question is primarily 'constitutional' is doubtful." "True historical insight," he wrote, "must penetrate through the statements, writings, and arguments of political leaders to the broad human purposes which they were seeking to accomplish. Viewed in this light, constitutional history becomes a part . . . of social history."[49] Yet Randall too kept his focus narrow. Although he used unpublished materials, they were the official correspondence of government officials, closely connected to the public record, which still provided most of his documentation. Like Beard, Randall left constitutional history to work in other fields.

Randall's is still the fullest discussion existing of the specific constitutional issues raised by the war—the legal nature of the struggle, the contemporary law of treason, the suspension of the privilege of the writ of habeas corpus and martial law, freedom of the press, the power of the government over occupied southern territory, the draft, confiscation, and emancipation. In his view court decisions had endorsed the Lincoln administration's position that the Constitution sanctioned the exercise of extraordinary powers during the war.[50] Nonetheless, like preceding historians and his contemporaries, Randall was struck by the "irregular and extra-legal characteristics" of the government under Lincoln. "It is indeed a striking fact that Lincoln, who stands forth in popular conception as a great democrat, . . . was driven by circumstances to the use of more arbitrary power than perhaps any other President." The constitutional arguments utilized to justify the excesses "often smacked of sophistry," and the usual constitutional checks generally failed."[51] As against this, however, Randall stressed "factors which at least partly redeemed the situation"—"the legal-mindedness of the American people" and the character of their great leader. Lincoln's "humane sympathy, his humor, his lawyer-like caution, his common sense, his fairness toward opponents, his dislike of arbitrary rule, his willingness to take the people into his confidence . . . operated to modify and soften the acts of overzealous subordinates and to lessen the effect of harsh measures."[52] Randall made the point in more detail in a seminal article "Lincoln in the Role of Dictator," republished in his tellingly titled *Lincoln the Liberal Statesman,* and he incorporated it into his 1937 textbook, *The Civil War and Reconstruction,* which as revised by David Donald in 1961, remained the standard for fifty years.[53]

No historian of the Confederacy published an overview of constitutional issues in the Confederacy to complement Randall's study. The closest analog was Curtis Arthur Amlund's concise *Federalism in the Southern Confederacy,* a slim volume which covered a broader range of constitutional issues than its title suggested.[54] Although they produced no magisterial volume like Randall's, historians did look closely at a variety of constitutional issues in the South. Albert Burton Moore published a seminal study of the Confederate draft, concluding that the conflict between the Confederate states and the central government over conscription showed "the utter impossibility . . . of maintaining a permanent and effective national government based upon states with unlimited potency."[55] Studying similar struggles over the suspension of the writ of habeas corpus, control and supply of military forces, and the taking of private property for military use, Frank L. Owsley echoed Moore's conclusion. "[T]he seeds of death are sown at our birth," Owsley wrote, and in the case of the Confederate States of America, the seed was the South's constitutional ideology. It sustained state governors who treated Confederate forces as state militias, who insisted on retaining units for home defense and on limiting the supplies they furnished to the use of their own state units. It enabled local officials to challenge various Confederate government efforts to centralize authority. Owsley concluded: "If a monument is ever erected as a symbolical gravestone over the 'lost cause' it should have engraved upon it these words: 'Died of State Rights.'"[56] Amlund published his study of Confederate federalism to counteract these claims. "Despite their firmly held states' rights beliefs, southerners were compelled by wartime exigencies to increase the powers of the central government far beyond what was intended originally," he wrote. The result was that, by the end of the war, the Confederate government "bore a striking resemblance to the one from which the South had withdrawn."[57]

In somewhat filiopietistic analyses, southern historians described the Confederate Constitution as a significant advance upon that of the United States.[58] Designed to cure the shortcomings of its predecessor—its encouragement of centralization, political corruption, and profligate

spending—the Confederate Constitution was, William M. Robinson en-
thused, "the peak contribution of America to political science."[59] Robinson
and Albert N. Fitts stressed how the new Constitution reflected southerners'
commitment to state rights, noting the reduced powers of the central government and the increased influence of the states. Both pointed to the
innovations designed to encourage economy and honesty in administration—the Confederate president's line-item veto, its requirement of a
two-thirds majority for spending bills that originated in Congress rather
than in a request from the president, the establishment of a professional
civil service removable only for cause, the provision for a single, six-year
presidential term.

Fitts pointed to reservations many of the framers had about democracy, as adherents of an "aristocratic republicanism" founded on agrarian
rather than industrial values. He also detailed fights over constitutional
provisions dealing with slavery, between proslavery extremists and
"reconstructionists," who hoped to attract the free states of the old northwest into the new confederacy. Both Robinson and Fitts stressed that the
Constitution incorporated aspects of British government into the Confederate system—"the best in the European parliamentary system without
breaking down the distinctive American separation between the executive
and legislative functions."[60] In 1963 Charles Robert Lee wrote the fullest
description of the framing and ratification of the Confederate provisional
and permanent Constitutions up to that time, but while he added a good
deal of detail, he concentrated most of his analysis in a brief conclusion
that added little to that of his predecessors.[61]

In one area, historians of the Confederacy outstripped constitutional
historians of the Union. William M. Robinson prepared a thorough study
of the courts of the Confederacy that surpassed anything available on
mid-nineteenth century United States courts.[62] The Confederate Constitution provided for a Supreme Court but left the details to the Confederate
Congress. Robinson attended closely to the debate over the question in
Congress.[63] In the end, Congress deadlocked over whether to give a Supreme Court the power to hear appeals on federal questions from the
state courts—an issue that had wracked American constitutional politics
since 1789—and the Confederate Supreme Court was never organized.
However, the Confederacy had district courts, courts martial, and a Department of Justice ten years before one was established in the United
States. Robinson described the organization and operation of all of these,
as well as the state courts, the Confederate patent office, and the printing
office's publication of court reports.

A substantial tome, Robinson's study of the Confederate courts paid surprisingly little attention to their decisions and the legal principles they articulated, a shortcoming that a contemporaneous article by the prolific southern historian J. G. deRoulhac Hamilton only partially remedied.[64] Despite Don E. Fehrenbacher's excellent essay surveying the topic, it still needs full explication.[65]

Recent scholarship on the Confederate Constitution has built upon the observations of the first analysts. Like them, Donald G. Nieman and George C. Rable have stressed the Constitution's antiparty, anticorruption, and antidemocratic nature. Rable concluded that the whole Confederate enterprise was a "revolution against politics," which became a central element of developing southern national identity.[66] Nieman pointed out that antipartyism and fear of corruption were characteristic of a longstanding strain of classical republicanism in American ideology. Contrary to the conclusions of Hamilton, Fitts, and Rable, therefore, the Confederate Constitution was "well within the mainstream of the American constitutional tradition."[67] Like Amlund, Fehrenbacher challenged earlier historians' conclusions about the degree to which the Constitution incorporated state-rights ideology. Despite the specific limitations the new fundamental law placed upon federal power and the increased influence it gave states in the constitutional structure, Fehrenbacher observed, "the truly striking feature of this constitution . . . is not the extent to which it incorporated state-rights doctrines, but rather the extent to which it transcended those principles in order to build a nation."[68] These views are challenged by Marshall L. DeRosa in a close analysis of the Confederate Constitution. Sympathetic to state rights and modern conservative constitutionalism, DeRosa provides the fullest demonstration offered of how the terminology of the Constitution challenged the constitutional nationalism that came to predominate in the United States.[69]

When Randall published his influential textbook *The Civil War and Reconstruction* in 1937, it reflected not only the historiography of the Civil War and the Constitution at that time but also the position of constitutional history in general. Remarkably, given his constitutional history origins, Randall barely noticed the constitutional arguments surrounding slavery in the territories; he did not mention antislavery constitutional theory at all. His chapter "The Government and the Citizen" condensed his book on wartime constitutional problems into twenty-two pages. He approached Emancipation almost entirely as a political question; as a constitutional issue he treated it from the perspective of federal power over white men's property. He perceived Reconstruction to be an assault on liberty by "Vindictives" and "Jacobins." The Republican Reconstruction

Acts inaugurated a "corrupt and abusive era of carpetbag rule," replacing "native white governments genuinely supported and put in power by the southern people."[70] His language made clear that Randall did not consider black southerners part of "the southern people." Randall conceded that the Black Codes imposed by those native white governments "in some respects . . . treated [Negroes] as inferior." But they were "a social and economic necessity" that failed to engage Randall's concern for liberty and democracy.[71]

Only McLaughlin seemed to question the nearly monolithic historiographical condemnation of Republican Reconstruction policy as oppressive and unconstitutional.[72] He recognized that the desire to protect black rights played a large role in Reconstruction. But his reservations about the dominant historiography had no immediate impact on the constitutional history of the Civil War era.

Revulsion at the perceived tyranny of Republican government in the South, reinforced by Progressive hostility to the business-allied Republican party of the 1920s and 1930s, led historians to rethink the origins of Reconstruction. Repudiating the conclusions of nationalist historians like Rhodes and Burgess, they sympathized with Andrew Johnson's position that Reconstruction was within the president's jurisdiction. Johnson had attempted to carry forward Lincoln's mild Reconstruction program, and he was opposed and ultimately impeached by the same vindictive radicals who had assailed the great martyr. In waging their struggle, Radical Republicans tried to establish congressional supremacy, not only attacking the Executive but the Judiciary.[73] The impeachment of Johnson, always viewed with alarm by conservative historians, was now viewed as the final step in an effort to destroy the constitutional system of checks and balances. Its failure saved the presidency.[74] Even the judicious McLaughlin agreed that "the government was in the hands of an 'irresponsible directory.'"[75]

Although disregard of constitutional limitations remained a key charge leveled against postwar Republican Reconstruction policy, it seemed obvious to historians that the real issue of Reconstruction was political and economic. As in the crisis that precipitated the war, the constitutional issues surrounding its resolution were but superficial reflections of deeper causes. "Revisionists" portrayed Reconstruction as a struggle for economic supremacy rather than a constitutional one between president and Congress over federalism and competing visions of civil liberty. As Howard K. Beale put it, one must separate "claptrap" from "issues."[76] With even constitutional scholars like Randall minimizing the salience of constitutional issues, historians could no longer fathom why Americans were unable to settle the slavery controversy peaceably, especially when they also were blind to its moral dimension. For a southern-born historian like the prolific Avery Craven, the war was an eminently "repressible conflict," the fault of "politicians and pious cranks!"[77] Randall himself condemned the "blundering generation" that failed to find a solution short of war.[78] As interest in constitutional history declined, historians of the Civil War era paid only slight attention to the constitutional aspects of their subjects.[79] Randall's great *Constitutional Problems* seemed to foreclose new research on constitutional aspects of the war itself. When David Donald revised Randall's textbook, he changed barely a word of Randall's chapter on the subject.[80]

For historians of the antislavery movement, however, constitutional issues remained central. Like the postwar Republican chroniclers, they stressed the civil-liberty rather than governmental-structure aspects of the conflict. Gilbert Hobbs Barnes articulated the importance of the antislavery petition movement, which inundated Congress with antislavery resolutions, and the challenge to political freedom posed by the "Gag Rule" against considering such petitions that Congress established in response.[81] Implicitly protesting the stress his contemporaries were placing on economic causes of the Civil War, Dwight L. Dumond published a classic study of its antislavery origins, paying serious attention to antislavery constitutional arguments.[82] But American constitutional historians failed to connect these works to their field. The first editions of Alfred H. Kelly and Winfred A. Harbison's constitutional textbook, *The American Constitution,* maintained the narrow focus of its predecessors.[83]

World War II and the events of the following decades reversed both the decline in American constitutional history and historians' understanding of the issues that precipitated the Civil War and Reconstruction. The war not only sensitized Americans to the evils of racism and intolerance, but it seemed to prove that moral issues could be worth fighting for. It was in the immediate aftermath of the war that Bernard DeVoto issued his famous challenge to revisionist historians to explain *why* antebellum Americans could be so exercised by the apparently trivial issue of the expansion of slavery into the territories. That paradox "cannot be impatiently shrugged away or dismissed with a denunciation of some agitators," he insisted.[84] A few years later, Arthur M. Schlesinger, Jr., issued a similarly trenchant and seminal challenge, arguing that moral questions have their own salience and need not merely reflect deeper, material interests.[85]

The struggle against totalitarian fascism and communism on the one hand, and against anticommunist threats to civil liberties on the other, revived scholarly interest in liberal democracy in general and constitutionalism in particular. One of the most vocal combatants, historian Henry

Steele Commager, set his student Harold M. Hyman on to the history of loyalty oaths, which contemporary anticommunist demagogues were championing over the resistance of civil libertarians. Exercised by the contemporary use of such oaths to suppress dissent, Hyman was critical of their abuse during the Civil War and Reconstruction.[86] His perspective fit comfortably with the traditional hostility to Radical Republican policies. But the Civil Rights Movement of the 1950s and 1960s reeducated Hyman and other civil libertarians. With some southern exceptions, American historians, like most American intellectuals, enlisted in the cause. The Civil War was no longer primarily a battle to save the Union; it was, as indicated by the title of the book that would synthesize the historical work of the following decades, the *Battle Cry of Freedom*.[87]

At the same time, American constitutional history became more than the history of government institutions; it once more became the history of liberty and, more than that, the history of American *constitutionalism*—the popular commitment to the principles that made constitutional government possible. The sources of constitutional history were no longer limited to public records and materials closely associated with them. Newspaper articles, books and pamphlets, controversial writings of all types, private correspondence, diaries, even visual arts, material culture, and fiction—any source that elucidated thought about fundamental law and liberty, that described how social and political conflicts became constitutional conflicts, was grist for the constitutional historian's mill. This expanded definition of subjects and materials brought into the canon of constitutional history the range of works on abolitionism, southern thought, African American history, and other topics that had before been identified as remotely rather than directly relevant to the field.

Historians' revived interest in constitutional history, was reinforced by the celebration of the bicentennial of the American Revolution and the framing and ratification of the Constitution. Seminal works stressed the salience of constitutional ideas and rhetoric, which were now perceived as having an independent historical force of their own.[88] This perception was related to the poststructural "linguistic turn" in humanistic research in general, which stressed the role of language in ordering human perception.[89] Rather than an epiphenomenal reflection of the material world, constitutional rhetoric shaped the way people understood that world. The explanatory power of constitutional rhetoric in understanding the causes of the Civil War was made clear by Bestor's influential 1964 article "The American Civil War as a Constitutional Crisis," which introduced this essay. Much reprinted, it was a potent rejoinder to the revisionist criticism of the "blundering generation."

Hyman, Bestor, Paul Murphy, and other constitutional historians produced a large number of prolific students. Eminent intellectual and political historians turned to constitutional history subjects or attended closely to constitutional issues in more general works.[90] The number of the *Journal of American History* celebrating the bicentennial of the Constitution illustrated the crossfertilization. The contributors included more specialists from other subfields than it did constitutional historians, all writing cogently and insightfully on constitutional aspects of their own interests.[91] At the same time a large number of legal scholars developed strong historical skills, many of them complementing their legal training with advanced degrees in history.[92]

The result of this ferment was an outpouring of work on constitutional aspects of the Civil War era by historians and legal scholars. Inspired by legal challenges to school segregation in the courts, lawyers reinvestigated the origins of the Thirteenth and Fourteenth Amendments to the Constitution. They rediscovered the vibrant antislavery constitutional arguments propounded by abolitionists and more moderate opponents of slavery in the years before the Civil War. Antislavery constitutionalism informed the meaning of the Thirteenth Amendment and was explicitly incorporated into the Fourteenth.[93] William M. Wiecek researched the origins of antislavery constitutional thought, identifying several lines of development that ultimately informed the constitutional theories of the Republican party, while Eric Foner recovered the crucial role of Salmon P. Chase, later chief justice of the Supreme Court, played in the process.[94]

Sensitized to civil liberties and civil rights issues in the mid-twentieth century, historians investigated civil liberty and rights in the antebellum North. Their discoveries made sense of the antislavery charge that slavery threatened the liberty of all Americans, white and black. They detailed legal and extralegal efforts to suppress antislavery agitation in the antebellum North.[95] They described the antiabolitionist violence of the 1830s and the fight over the "gag rule" in Congress.[96] Closely linked have been studies of black rights before the war, with special attention to the Fugitive Slave Acts, which extended the spirit of the southern slave codes into the North, virtually licensing the kidnaping of African Americans there.[97]

Bestor's great article signaled renewed interest in the constitutional controversy over slavery in the territories. Careful analyses, including another influential essay by Bestor, culminated in Don E. Fehrenbacher's monumental, Pulitzer Prize-winning work on the Dred Scott case and its background.[98] Paul Finkelman studied how the slavery issue—especially the rendition of fugitive slaves and the status of slaves brought to the

North temporarily by their owners—affected the formal interrelations between states, or "comity."[99] Wiecek limned the emergence and elements of a distinctive southern constitutional experience, founded upon slavery and designed to project southern power through control of the national government.[100] These analyses demonstrated the degree to which southerners had succeeded in converting the Constitution into a proslavery document by the 1850s, a process that culminated in the *Dred Scott* decision, the deeply flawed work of determinedly proslavery jurists. As Fehrenbacher explained in a 1989 essay, "Those who control the operations of the federal government shape the applicative meaning of the Constitution. By 1860, southern influence had made the document more of a bulwark for slavery than its framers ever intended."[101] No longer were southerners perceived to be the victims of northern disregard of constitutional limitations; Fehrenbacher's judgment instead echoed antislavery Republican charges that slaveholders had perverted the Constitution. Indeed, some constitutional historians echoed the more extreme view of the abolitionists: the Constitution *had* been intended to strengthen the protections for slavery; it had been, as William Lloyd Garrison had charged, a "covenant with death and an agreement with hell," acquiesced in by the ostensibly antislavery Americans of the revolutionary generation.[102]

In the view of modern constitutional historians, the Republican victory of 1860, and especially the inspired constitutional politics of Abraham Lincoln, set the United States back on the course of constitutional liberty. Hyman's student Phillip Shaw Paludan portrayed Lincoln as the Hercules who led Americans through the "crisis in constitutional integrity" that proslavery constitutionalism had precipitated.[103] Garry Wills's evocative *Lincoln at Gettysburg* conveyed to a popular audience how Lincoln reshaped Americans' understanding of the federal system, hallowing the nationalism of Hamilton, Marshall, and Webster with the power of his words.[104] Historians continued to dismiss the notion, popularized among political scientists by Clinton L. Rossiter, that Lincoln exercised a "constitutional dictatorship."[105] Indeed, Mark E. Neely found that the Lincoln administration's arbitrary arrests were not nearly so draconian as earlier historians had believed.[106] Hyman, whose distaste for wartime infringements on civil rights had been apparent in his earlier work on loyalty oaths, got a look at southern and Copperhead demands for civil liberty from a shockingly different perspective as he prepared a biography of Secretary of War Edwin M. Stanton. Acts indemnifying federal officers for wartime actions did not seem so despotic when he found state judges encouraging punitive lawsuits against Union officers trying to carry out their duties. Trial by military commission seemed appropriate for men who murdered African Americans and unionists without fear of state prosecution. Loyalty oaths did not seem so unreasonable when they were aimed at keeping local government out of the hands of real traitors rather than imaginary communists.[107]

Nothing could better illustrate the difference between new approaches to American constitutional history and the old, than a comparison between Randall's *Constitutional Problems under Lincoln* and Hyman's monumental *A More Perfect Union,* which joined the older work as the standard account of the Civil War and the Constitution.[108] While Randall stuck close to the public record and focused on narrowly legal issues, Hyman ransacked private correspondence, obscure pamphlets, and crumbling newspapers to offer a wide-ranging account of constitutional controversy and change. The demand for constitutional change, he demonstrated, emanated not from politicians in Washington but from a broad range of activists with a thousand projects. He dealt not only with the traditional issues upon which Randall had focused, but with constitutional development in the states, changing theories of municipal government, the impact of reforming elites on bureaucracy and administration, and the pressure for more active government at every level of the federal system. Leonard P. Curry and political scientist Richard Franklin Bensel also transcended traditional approaches to the exercise of federal power during the war, pointing to the permanent, radical changes inherent in financial, commercial, educational, and transportation legislation.[109]

For the new generation of constitutional historians, emancipation was no longer an issue of wartime power over property rights. It was a milestone in the effort of African Americans to secure racial justice in the United States and part of a long process of defining American citizenship.[110] Nor were African Americans the passive subjects of the conflict. As Mary F. Berry made clear, African Americans won their own freedom and established their claim to equal rights by successfully demanding inclusion in the Union armed forces.[111] Eric Foner and Donald G. Nieman showed that they were just as active in the struggle to define the rights of American citizenship in the wake of emancipation.[112]

The most radical change occurred in the constitutional historiography of Reconstruction. Nearly unanimous in their support for equal rights in the "second Reconstruction" of the 1960s, historians reversed their understanding of the first. Rather than Lincoln's mortal enemies, the Radical Republicans were "Lincoln's Vanguard for Racial Justice."[113] The tragedy of Reconstruction was not that Republicans subjected white southerners to oppressive regimes, but that white southerners were able to thwart the efforts of Republicans and African Americans to secure racial justice. Reconstruction remained, as Foner subtitled his standard synthetic account, "America's Unfinished Revolution."[114]

Hyman and his students saw Reconstruction as constitutionally conservative rather than radical, attributing Republicans' failure to take more-radical action to northern commitment to preserving the essentials of the federal system.[115] In contrast, legal scholar Robert J. Kaczorowski insisted that Republicans intended a constitutional revolution that was tragically undermined by a conservative judiciary.[116] Inspired by an activist Supreme Court, other legal scholars attended closely to the debates over civil rights legislation, hoping to divine the original understanding of the Fourteenth Amendment.[117]

Historians absolved postwar Republicans of trying to establish congressional supremacy. Far from undermining the judiciary, Republicans expanded its authority, attempting to make it the frontline weapon for the protection of civil rights. Nor did the Supreme Court supinely retreat in the face of congressional attacks.[118] In the new view of constitutional historians, it was President Johnson rather than the Republican Congress who was the aggressor in the Reconstruction controversy. Sympathetic to Republican efforts to promote racial justice and hostile to the "imperial presidency" that had developed in their own time, historians even revised their understanding of impeachment, arguing that Congress undertook the proceeding reluctantly to defend its program against Johnson's assault.[119]

In 1982 Hyman and Wiecek published a synthesis of American constitutional history during the Civil War era that incorporated the revisions in interpretation since the civil rights revolution. Reflecting the new thrust of the field, they called it *Equal Justice under Law*.[120] Far more sophisticated in approach and analysis than its early predecessors, it marked the distance that constitutional history in general had come from its narrow origins in the study of the public record. It also marked the triumph in historiography of antislavery constitutionalism.

No series of events more clearly demonstrates the power of constitutional rhetoric to shape disputes than those that led to the Civil War. Southerners had devised a theory of constitutional law that provided no forum where constitutional disputes could be resolved in a way that bound all the parties. The result was secession and war. Constitutional principles and law not only structured the terms of the debate over slavery; they powerfully influenced Civil War politics and played a crucial role in the struggle over Reconstruction as well. Understanding the constitutional conflicts of the Civil War era remains essential to understanding the subject as a whole.

# WHAT DID
# THE WINNERS WIN?

*The Social and Economic History
of the North during the Civil War*

PHILLIP SHAW PALUDAN

No war, and arguably no combination of all other wars in American history, has had such an abiding impact as the Civil War.[1] It spawned three constitutional amendments, led to the election of at least five presidents, destroyed the major social and economic institution of half the nation, freed over 4,000,000 people from slavery, swept 3,000,000 men into military service, killed 620,000 of those men, destroyed an ideology that threatened to shatter the country. It has proven to be the most fertile ground ever for writing about the history of the nation. But the vast majority of that writing has targeted generals and presidents, congressmen and judges, people who set the war in motion. It has described the actions of leaders who shaped day-to-day events. What has not been discussed very much is the social and economic history of the conflict.

This is a very significant omission, for only by assessing the impact of the war on the economy and society of the nation can we evaluate what was achieved in compensation for the loss of 620,000 on Civil War battle-fields, the destruction of resources, and the reshaping of lives. We need to know what the war did to families, to mothers and fathers and children, to workers, to employers, to economic growth, to the distribution of wealth. We need to know how, or if, war changed the way people connected with their communities and their friends and their kin, what their opportunities were, what their farms and towns and cities provided for ordinary people trying to live in the world the Civil War made. Yes the battles determined the result, the laws unleashed or withheld resources, presidents and generals made decisions that set armies in motion, and the soldiers became casualties or heroes for their triumphs or their endurance. And all these things matter, but we cannot assess whether this vast expenditure of life and resource was worth it after all unless we know what kind of society and economy the war created and what kind of lives were led after the killing stopped.

We have been getting some answers. There has been productive work describing the impact of the war on women and on African Americans. The South has attracted a range of fruitful research. Yet the North as a society remains a relatively unexplored land. Seventy-eight years passed between the first and the second single-volume study of northern society and its economy at war. Studies of the northern economy have been subsumed in a debate over the magnitude and speed of that economy's wartime growth, while studies of northern society have been very few indeed. We have glimpses into the nature, the worth, and the costliness of wartime changes, but there are miles to go in this inquiry.

The economic history of the North in the war era has had some serious study. The controlling paradigm of this study has been that of the "Second American Revolution." Essentially the foundation for this paradigm was the publication in 1927 of Charles A. Beard and Mary R. Beard's *The Rise of American Civilization*. The Civil War, the Beards wrote, "was a social war, ending in the unquestioned establishment of a new power in the government, making vast changes in the arrangement of classes, in the accumulation and distribution of wealth, in the course of industrial development. . . . [The war was a] social cataclysm in which the capitalists, laborers and farmers of the North and West drove from power in the national government the planting aristocracy of the South." While battles were important, "the core of the vortex lay elsewhere. It was in the flowing substance of things limned by statistical reports of finance, commerce, capital, industry, railways and agriculture . . . prosaic muniments which show that the so-called civil war was, in reality, a Second American Revolution and, in a strict sense, the First." The Beards' description was reinforced in 1940 when Louis M. Hacker, in *The Triumph of American Capitalism*, described the war as the victory of the "spokesmen for industrial capitalism" over the agrarian ideals of the South. "The war furnished them with the opportunity to round out the *economic* program of the class which they represented. Industrial capitalism was now in control of the state."[2]

The Beard-Hacker thesis appealed to a range of perspectives in its age. In the first place it simply sounded right—the greatest war in the nation's history naturally could be expected to have revolutionary consequences. Perhaps in light of the huge loss of life it was comforting to believe that great changes had resulted. Various groups in the society could also draw on the thesis to sustain their vision of the modern world. Proponents of the modern industrial age could be satisfied that their success corresponded with the most heroic of the nation's wars. Critics of industrial society could share the distaste that the Beards and Hacker had for the triumph of the age of shoddy and gilt. Southern critics could find nostalgic pleasure in the story of how Grant the butcher, the stub of cigar in his mouth, soon to preside over the Gilded Age, backed by the relentless and well-supplied Union army, overcame gentleman Robert E. Lee and his shoeless legions and how mad Sherman's brutal rampaging bummers destroyed the glory that was Tara.

The Beard-Hacker thesis was sufficiently persuasive that several historians, popular and professional, applied it to Reconstruction as well. Economic motivation and the triumph of northern industrialism became the major theme for a string of popular studies of the post–Civil War years: 1929 saw Claude Bowers's *The Tragic Era;* the next year witnessed George Fort Milton's *The Age of Hate,* and Howard K. Beale's *The Critical Year.* These works, especially Beale's, depicted the victory of "Big Business" over the agrarian South. Depression-era readers, scholars and the general public, were easily persuaded that the Beards and Hacker had things just right.[3]

But by the late-1950s and mid-1960s historians of Reconstruction were beginning to doubt the validity of a simple picture of northern industrialists taking over the nation. While Bowers, Milton, and Beale had emphasized economic motives to challenge arguments that slavery and race drove war-era events, more modern historians brought race and slavery back into the story. Influenced by civil rights struggles of those years, they began increasingly to emphasize the importance of racial egalitarianism as the driving force of northern reform. And as racial reform emerged as the motivation for Reconstruction, the image of single-minded northern industrial advocates came apart. Several authors demonstrated that the Republican party was divided over tariffs, greenbacks, the rights of labor. Radical congressman Thaddeus Stevens supported greenbacks, his associate William Fessenden feared them. Stevens wanted a high tariff, Radical senator Charles Sumner opposed it. Radical George Julian favored legislation to mandate an eight-hour-day for federal workers; Sumner opposed that. Ben Wade was so "unsound" on the money question (he favored greenbacks) that some of his colleagues voted against impeaching Andrew Johnson for fear that Wade (next in line for the presidency as president pro tem of the Senate) would threaten economic stability. In 1988 Eric Foner could still point out the importance of free-labor economics in weakening the commitment of northerners to helping freedmen, but the Beard-Hacker idea had been eroded. Historians had shown the complexity of the economic motives of Reconstruction lawmakers. [4]

But to historians of the war years the core concept of the war as economic and social revolution, with northern economic visions triumphant, had staying power. That power was suggested when Barrington Moore adapted it to the growing understanding by historians and the general public that the fundamental change wrought by the war took place when slavery died and the struggle for equality began. Changing views about the glory of Tara (made glorious on the backs of slaves) and the world that "Marse (short for master) Robert" and his tattered rednecks fought to preserve produced modifications in the Beard-Hacker major claim.[5]

Writing in 1966, Moore took the thesis and reconsidered the importance of slavery in defining the meaning of the war. The Civil War was, as Moore put it, "The Last Capitalist Revolution," but slavery was at the core of that revolution. The Beards had argued that "the institution of slavery was not the fundamental issue during the epoch preceding the bombardment of Fort Sumter"; the clash of different economic cultures over the reins of power was. But Moore insisted that slavery was fundamental to southern culture and economics. Moore also differed in how slavery fit into the national economy. The Beards had pictured southern agrarian ideals as an obstacle to modernization. Moore argued that slavery was not a direct economic threat to industrialization; in fact profits from slavery helped fund national economic development. What slavery did create was a society fearful of change and thus in competition with the free-labor ideals of the North. Political and social democracy were more endangered by the South than was northern industrialization. As Moore put it "the institutional requirements for operating a plantation economy based on slavery clashed with . . . the corresponding requirements for operating a capitalist industrial system." When war came northern industrialists joined with western farmers and more successful urban workers to defeat the political power of slavery's supporters and gain control of the government. The government then advanced the wide ranging northern economic program as well as ideals of democratic free labor.

They did this by force and violence. That made the Civil War a revolution. Moore compared an 1860 world with its "federal enforcement of slavery, no high protective tariffs, no subsidies nor expensive tax creating internal improvements, no national banking and currency system" to Republican reversals in all these areas. Those reversals made, Moore said, a "very persuasive" case for terming the war a revolution. And when the end of slavery that bound 4,000,000 people (nearly 13 percent of the country's population) was given its due attention, the case looked overwhelming. By adopting the Beards' claim that the war produced a revolution over who would rule the nation and paying proper attention to emancipation, Moore made the thesis acceptable to the egalitarian sensibility of the 1960s and after, which put race and slavery at the center of that revolution.[6]

Few historians in the last thirty years have been more energetic in describing the meaning of that egalitarian sensibility in the war era than James M. McPherson. In two major works on egalitarian crusades from the 1830s to the 1920s, McPherson had shown the vitality of the struggle for equality.[7] Thus when he wrote, as late as 1990, about "The Second American Revolution" it is not surprising that he defined that revolution in a way that supported Moore's variations on the Beard-Hacker theme. McPherson agreed with Moore and with Hacker and the Beards that when the South seceded and then lost the war the national government was taken over by lawmakers who supported the industrializing of the nation. What he elaborated was how much a revolution the end of slavery had brought to the South. Basing much of his argument on work by economic historians Roger Ransom and Richard Sutch, McPherson pointed out that slaveowners lost at least 3 billion dollars in property when emancipation came. Former slaves got back a third more from their labor than they had under slavery (a return that rose from 22 to 56 percent). Black literacy jumped by 400 percent from 1865 to 1900; black farmers who owned land in Dixie jumped from practically zero in 1865 to about 25 percent of the black population by 1915. Utilizing Foner's work on Reconstruction (Foner subtitled his work, *America's Unfinished Revolution*), McPherson also pointed to involvement of hundreds of thousands of black men in southern politics in the postwar years again to argue for revolution. Although he recognized that many black gains fell to a white counterrevolution by the 1880s, McPherson still believed that the war produced revolution. It was a position that historians and the general public committed to ongoing battles for racial justice found easy to accept.[8]

But while the Beard-Hacker thesis, as it applied to the war, gained the support of the egalitarian perspective, and while its story of the victory of an industrializing society over an agrarian one seemed secure, another challenge was being mounted from a different direction. The Beards had said more than that the war brought a new industrial leadership to the nation, a new alliance between industrial growth and national authority. Perhaps carried away by their own elegant rhetoric, they declared that when power changed hands the results were "vast changes in the arrangement of classes, in the accumulation and distribution of wealth, in the course of industrial development." The breathless rhetoric of swift and rapid transformation—the war a "vortex," industry marching in "seven-league boots," the "hastening" of inevitable economic transitions, of men "caught up and whirled in a blast too powerful for their wills, too swift for their mental operations"—all gave the sense of seismic shifts in the pace and direction of the economy and the nation. It was at this vision of earthquakes and 180-degree changes that the economic historians targeted their attack.[9]

In September 1961 Thomas Cochran turned the Beard-Hacker assertion on its head and asked, "Did the Civil War Retard Industrialization?" His answer: "It sure did." Relying on the 1949 edition of *Historical Statistics of the United States* as well as on statistical series generated by Robert Gallman in 1960, Cochran noted that several key indicators showed a decline in the growth rate of the economy in the decade between 1860 and 1870. Total commodity output slowed in those years from high rates of the decade before. In fact the average annual increase in total commodity output of those years was, at 2 percent, the slowest of the nineteenth century. Value added by manufacturing grew 76 percent from 1849 to 1859 but only 25 percent from 1859 to 1869. The next decade saw a growth of 82 percent. Pig iron production slowed; so did miles of railroad track laid. Immigration and, hence, the numbers of workers went down, and farm mechanization led by the sale of reapers, also slowed; so did building construction. The war years advanced the industrial revolution of the nineteenth century but did so at the slowest rate of the midcentury.[10]

Cochran's data clearly contradicted the Beard-Hacker story, challenging the intuitive idea that a great war produced a great change. Yet once presented, Cochran's data also made intuitive sense—war destroys property, kills large parts of the labor force, draws workers away from farm and factory, disrupts commerce between warring parties and foreign trading partners. As a 1994 summary put it, "The war placed enormous stress on an economy already going full tilt. With the withdrawal of the services of perhaps one-fifth of the labor force, the disruption of normal channels of supply, and the weakening of foreign exchange earnings by loss of raw cotton exports, it would, in fact, have been very surprising if the war had not disrupted industrial growth."[11]

By 1966 Cochran's overall position was endorsed from several directions. Stanley Engerman, perhaps the most widely respected economic historian of the war era, essentially adopted Cochran's view. Then two conferences inspired by Cochran's article almost unanimously agreed with his conclusions. A 1979 study concluded that the war did not even accelerate growth in the manufacturing of iron and steel, watches, boots and shoes, agricultural machinery, paper, or even *explosives*. The earthquake had become a tremor, the turn a speed bump; the "vortex" of change had lost its momentum, it seemed, when the guns began firing.[12]

There was still some support for seeing the war as generating major economic change. Some few economists emphasized that it was not so much the size of the economic changes that mattered, it was their strategic location—the few miles of track laid which linked up huge expanses; wealth gained in war, held conservatively in the conflict, used later to invest profligately. These scholars suggested that the focus of the Cochran school—the war itself, the years 1860–1865, was too narrow a gauge to judge the impact of the war on economic growth. If one took a longer view, then it was possible to argue that the war years were imperative in laying ground for postwar growth. Some statistics pointed this way. The average annual increase in commodity output of the years 1840 to 1860 was 4.6 percent per annum. While the war years reduced that figure to a mere 2 percent, between 1870 and 1900 the nation experienced an average growth in commodity output of 4.4 percent. In terms of per capita income growth the North grew at a rate of 1.7 percent between 1860 and 1879, up from a 1.3 percent rate for the period 1840–1860. These numbers made it possible to argue that in the long run the war hardly retarded the industrialization of the nation. The revolution from agrarian to industrialized America simply took longer than four years to occur. The war, after all, was part of the Industrial Revolution; comparisons to the first American Revolution obscured that fact.[13]

Research on that long-term transformation showed the inappropriateness of the comparison. A large body of scholarship beginning as early as the 1960s demonstrated that the economic growth that the Beards said was the product of Civil War had been under way for at least three decades before the war began. Some historians spoke of a "take off" in the 1820s and 1830s. Yearly per capita income began to grow at about 1.6 percent per year—a large step up from earlier figures of 1 percent per year. GNP went from $1.62 billion in 1839 to $2.43 billion in 1849 to $4.10 billion in 1859. While agriculture was still the main business of the nation, the economic output provided by manufacturing was growing more rapidly than was the farm economy. A transportation and market revolution took place after the War of 1812 that also accelerated the economy. Nine thousand miles of railroad in 1850 had become 21,000 in 1860—more track than all other railroads in the world at the time. To be fair to the Beards, they did note that the economic momentum of the nineteenth century, even before the war, was clearly in the industrialists' direction. But they underestimated how much change in the industrial sector was under way before the war came. They did so, probably, because, despite the talk of "the flowing substance of things limned by statistical reports," the Beards used precious few statistics and had access to little of the data that later critics would acquire and generate.[14]

But when the statistics came in they eroded the Beard-Hacker story of wartime acceleration. In so doing they raised wider questions about the Beard-Hacker story of the war. Given substantial prewar northern growth, was it possible to accept even that part of the thesis which argued that the war freed the northern economy from a inhibiting hand of southern lawmakers? If the North was already such a burgeoning economic giant, how plausible was the claim that the South was holding it back and that a war was needed to free northern industrialization from southern shackles? Indeed, how strongly could one hold on to the most elemental of the Beard-Hacker claims that it was the war that tore the reins of leadership from southern agrarians and handed them to northern industrialists? Wasn't the South losing that war before a battle was fought? Wasn't secession a recognition by the South that it stood on the brink of defeat? Modern historians have yet to confront these questions.

The questions have tragic overtones. The Beard-Hacker thesis suggests that the war was fought, or that northerners were ready to fight, to secure northern economic success. Richard Franklin Bensel endorses this view by showing that the areas of the North most interested in industrial development were most ready to support coercion of the seceding South.[15] But was a war really necessary for the industrializing northern economy to prevail? And what were the costs of not awaiting that ultimate triumph?

Economists Claudia Golden and Frank Lewis have estimated the price of the war. Looking at the cost of lives lost and of wounds that reduced productivity, as well as at property destroyed, and adding in government expenditures to fight the war, Golden and Lewis concluded that the overall cost of the war was over $6.5 billion. That amount would have allowed the government to purchase and free all the 4,000,000 slaves (at 1860 market prices), give each family 40 acres and a mule, and still have provided $3.5 billion for reparations to former slaves for a century of lost wages.[16] And a growing economy, without a war to retard its progress, would have continued to boom, arguably advancing the industrial economy of the North, increasing its capacity to pay the South to end slavery, without taking the life of a single soldier.

Of course the war came for more than economic reasons. And there is little reason to believe that the South in 1860, or within a decade, maybe more, would have put slavery up for sale. Certainly in the midst of the war, even the border states (those least committed to slavery) turned Lincoln down when he offered gradual compensated emancipation. Yet Lincoln still had some faith that compensated emancipation was viable. His December 1862 annual message was about twenty pages long; he spent almost five pages comparing the costs of war with the cost of compensated emancipation. This suggests that economic calculations about the costs of war and the end of slavery deserve some consideration. And even if white southerners had refused to sell, is it possible that the $6.5 billion could have built such a dynamic free-labor North that southern slave states would have been drawn into free labor's orbit and gradually abandoned slavery?[17]

Although they did not directly confront the question of whether the war was worth the cost, two books of the early 1990s built the evidence for raising that question, even as they confronted other elements of the Second American Revolution paradigm.[18] Roger Ransom and Richard Bensel both looked at the war and essentially accepted the Beard-Hacker ideas. Ransom agreed with the Beards that the war was "A Second American Revolution." "The war," he said, "unleashed (or at least greatly accelerated) political and economic forces that fundamentally altered the economic structure of the United States after 1860." But Ransom was much surer about the revolution in the South, where slavery had been destroyed and a new economic structure needed building, than he was about the North. There, he observed, the effects of the war "were more diffuse."[19]

When he looked north Ransom began to talk less like a Beardian. He agreed with the Cochran-Engerman thesis that the war slowed down the growth of the economy, pointing to a decline in GNP per capita during the 1860s. Only agriculture expanded with some speed, but even that sector's growth could not overcome the general decline in the growth of the economy in the North and especially the South.

Ransom recognized that people who lived through the war believed that they were living in a time of huge economic change. He knew that supporters of the war-as-revolution thesis quoted newspapers, letters, and diaries to that point.[20] But Ransom argued that they were deceived by the fact that prices went up rapidly during the war; in the aftermath of a business recession in the late 1850s the war economy seemed burgeoning indeed. But in fact the real GNP grew very little—inflation accounted for the illusion of economic revolution. Furthermore the exertions for the war effort, longer hours for men, and particularly the increased participation by women and children, also gave the illusion of a greater economic activity.[21]

Adding to the vision of economic change and growth were laws passed in wartime to stimulate economic growth and to consolidate economic power in the North. During the conflict Congress increased the tariff, chartered a company to build a transcontinental railroad, established land grant universities, created the Department of Agriculture, gave land to anyone willing to farm it, and began to shape a centralized banking system for the nation. The Beards had pointed to these laws as the major evidence of the revolution that placed industrial capitalism at the controls of the nation's economy.

But after looking carefully at banking and tariff laws, railroad legislation, and the Homestead Act, Ransom doubted that the war had generated a revolution or that the forces of industry alone benefitted. Tariffs may have brought more money for investments to northern industrialists, though even here, according to Patrick O'Brien in one summary of the recent literature, "The case for tariffs [as increasing the rate of development] remains unproven."[22] But the agrarian sector of the North, and frequently of the South, gained from homestead laws, from a railroad system that helped them market their crops, from a currency system that let them pay off debts with cheaper money, from a banking system that made borrowing and lending more stable, from colleges and universities that trained students in scientific farming as well as in industrial arts. Farmers, in a nation that was still over 75 percent rural, provided strong political support for these measures. Indeed, looking only at the war years, it was the farmers of the North who experienced the best years of their lives.[23]

Furthermore, even after the war farmers did not initially protest going back to the gold standard or the early growth of corporations. "Capitalist farmers," Ransom notes, "as well as capitalist entrepreneurs of commerce and industry—were the forces that shaped . . . postwar economic development." Ransom agreed that the war had put industrial capitalists ultimately in the driver's seat, but they had some encouragement even from the former drivers. The Beards had, of course, seen that war brought victory to the whole northern economy, but Ransom brought a useful reminder that an industrializing society was a diverse society and that descriptions of the war era that spoke of victory for an industrializing North needed to be presented with some subtlety.[24]

Richard Franklin Bensel also saw a war that pitted a less modernized agrarian South against a modernizing and industrializing North. He agreed with the Beardian view that industrialists gained control of the national government and advanced their own interests. But Bensel noted that even before the war the North was an economic giant. The section was so strong that it could utilize the strengths of its market economy to finance the conflict without the massive state economic interference that the South had to employ. Here again arose the nagging and potentially tragic question of whether war was necessary to bring about those changes.

Bensel added an element to the Beard story by noting that the Union war effort not only gave victory to existing industrial sectors; it also created new forces in the victorious North. It brought into being a new class of finance capitalists who organized the economy to pay for the war. These men benefitted greatly from the creation of national power that the Union generated. Furthermore, Bensel differed from the implicit Beardian view that war helped modernize the South. In fact, Bensel believed the war set back southern modernization, devastating it for decades, creating a colonial economy, losing resources to a northern economic elite through the new banking, currency, railroad and tariff laws that advanced the North. He offered the intriguing suggestion that if the South had achieved independence it might have modernized much faster than it did, and that, free of the costs and destruction of war, both regions might also have modernized faster. But Bensel essentially agreed with the main Beard-Hacker thesis that two cultures, one industrializing the other agrarian, clashed in the war and the industrializers triumphed. "[T]he war had transformed the American state into the coordinating agent of northern development," Bensel proclaimed. "Over the longer term, the operation of the tariff, military pensions disbursements, Treasury debts and money policies, transportation subsidies and the concentration of federal services and employees in the North all contributed to a massive redistribution of wealth out of the South and into northern industrial and westward expansion. . . . [T]he American Civil War significantly accelerated the modernization of the northern political economy." Charles and Mary could hardly have said it better.[25]

Ransom and Bensel thus disagree about the extent to which war produced *revolution*. Ransom thinks that for the overall national economy the term fits, but its applicability to the North is doubtful. Bensel is more willing to follow the Beardian view. The debate goes on. Looking at the national economy seems to produce more scholarship but few answers. But that result may arise from the fact that the subject under study, "the national economy," lacks a certain reality. For all the apparent persuasiveness of macroeconomic statistics, of "overall commodity output" and "value added by manufacturing" and "per capita income growth rates," it is well to remember that people don't live in statistical universes. They live in places, at specific times, and in a large nation with a diverse economy stretching from a two-hundred-year-old metropolis serving international and domestic needs, such as Philadelphia, to infant cities on the prairie, such as Chicago. The true testing of the Second American Revolution thesis ought to be in these places, where industrial America was born and lived.

But even here the diversity of the economy produces conflicting views. Some scholars find wartime cities where changes were obvious and dramatic. Chicago, Theodore Karamanski says in *Rally Round the Flag: Chicago and the Civil War* (1993), was "forever transformed by the war." While industrialization and market growth were building economic strength for the city, war accelerated growth in meat packing, iron rolling, railroad cars. Industrialists such the McCormicks of reaper fame, accumulated millions of dollars which they invested in land in the city's downtown area to keep up with wartime inflation. They prospered as the city grew.[26]

Stuart Sprague argues that the war profoundly energized the Cincinnati economy. Railroads that were near bankruptcy before the war were, by 1863, paying off mortgages and loans and acquiring other lines. Track mileage in the region went up from 3,200 in 1860 to 5,000 in 1862. Military contracts for soap and candles built wartime fortunes for a company like Proctor and Gamble. Large firms especially benefitted because only they could bid successfully to meet the huge military orders. The Union's western campaigns helped almost every manufacturer in the "Queen City." Wartime profits built the Southern railroad and the Roebling suspension bridge, further increasing the city's prosperity. "Clearly Cincinnati benefitted from the war," Sprague concludes.[27]

What explains the contrast between the Cochran-Engerman view that the war retarded economic growth and the evidence from Chicago and Cincinnati? Sprague suggests that Cochran-Engerman relies too much on eastern state census figures—especially figures from Massachusetts and New York in 1865. But some eastern cities also seem to have grown economically because of war. Clearly such was the case when Alan Lessof studied Washington, D.C. The nation's capital had been dramatically changed by the rise in federal workers, its economic growth benefitted from the cooperation of business and government that had worked successfully in the war. And Boston, according to Howard Mumford Jones, saw a rapid postwar expansion based on the increase in financial activity and industrialization. Smaller cities also grew. In his study of the changes in shoe making in Lynn, Mass., Alan Dawley suggested that the war years set the stage for vigorous growth. Factory owners accumulated funds from wartime orders which they invested in expansion. At the local level several cities and towns seemed to be participating in the revolution the Beards described.[28]

But Matthew Gallman, whose father had provided the statistics for much of the Cochran-Engerman argument, challenged the picture of war as a major agent of change. He studied Philadelphia and insisted that the Beard-Hacker view was wrong. Except for textiles and building trades, Gallman argued, Philadelphia experienced a wartime slowdown. Prewar trends which saw the rise of machine making and the manufacture of drugs and medical supplies continued throughout the war without any huge leap forward. Depending on which business they were in, ordinary citizens saw their fortunes fall, then rise, and then fall again as prices rose and fell during the conflict. But the war did not accelerate economic growth in the city or change its structure. Gallman also claimed that New York City as well as the state of Massachusetts shared these trends. In contrast, Philip Scranton found that Philadelphia textile manufacturers accumulated profits during the war which they later used to expand their fortunes and influence.[29]

Clearly the evidence from local and from national analysis is conflicting as to what the war did to urban economies. Perhaps western cities grew more rapidly than eastern ones did. Perhaps students of those western cities are too much taken by qualitative evidence—newspaper reports, personal recollections; maybe they ignore the power of inflation to distort growth statistics. Perhaps students of the national economy are too eager to draw arbitrary lines that divide the wartime North from the postwar North. Some reconciliation and restudy may be necessary. Until that work is done, and maybe after it is done, both the Beard-Hacker and the Cochran-Engerman theses will remain viable—not an unacceptable result in such a diverse nation, in such a complex time.

Yet some outlines of the picture seem clear. For the economy as a whole, in the short run the war slowed down the rapid economic growth of the North. This conclusion is not surprising given the general disruptions of war—and this war absorbed a greater percentage of men and treasure and attention than any other American conflict. During the war wealth was drawn from building businesses and infrastructure and used to destroy the enemy and to feed and equip an army and navy. Overall the Cochran-Engerman position seems right. The impact of the war, *during the war*, was to retard economic growth. Summarizing the results of economic historians' investigations by 1994, Jeremy Atack and Peter Passell assert in a leading textbook in economic history: "We are suspi-

cious of the grand scheme . . . that the Civil War spurred American industrialization and the hegemony of urban-industrial interests over
rural-agricultural interests." The war "did not eliminate fundamental
impediments to industrial growth since it is hard to find many impediments to be eliminated. Rather the war . . . [set back] the process of
industrialization and retard[ed] the rate of economic growth during the
years of struggle."[30]

But in the longer run the Beard-Hacker position seems right. Clearly,
laws passed during the war helped forge the infrastructure of the economy,
chartering railroad, establishing financial institutions, providing a more
educated workforce, opening up western lands for development, allowing
investment funds to be accumulated, protecting growing industries. After
the war was over, the statistics, as we have seen, show a continued growth
of the economy at almost the same rate as before the war started. And it
seems likely that the crucible of the war years helped to generate the continued acceleration of the nation's economy in the nineteenth century. But
while the war played a major role in this change, the question of whether
it was indispensable to it remains unproven, and the question of costs and
benefits remains unresolved.

While economic historians have produced much literature on the general economy, they have been comparatively silent about the impact of the
war on American workers. In this they are not alone. In a war widely
described, both in the 1860s and in modern historiography, as a struggle
between a free-labor and a slave-labor society, few historians have paid
much attention in recent years to what the war meant for the labor movement or for workers.[31] Historians have been more interested in the growth
of wealth than in its distribution, perhaps a predictable attitude given the
generally favorable view of the war that currently dominates Civil War
writing. Barrington Moore's argument that the war saw a victory for "competitive democratic capitalism" may have been persuasive to modern
writers.[32]

Perhaps historians have been distracted from the condition of northern white workers by the undoubted advances made by southern black
workers. There is much to emphasize in an emancipation which, according to Ransom and Sutch, raised black returns on their labor from 22 to
56 percent. But while black bondsmen in the South clearly stepped up
from slavery, white laborers in the North may have stepped down. In the
inflation of the war years real wages dropped, helping to generate hundreds, perhaps thousands, of strikes and the organization of many more
labor unions than had existed before the firing on Fort Sumter. War con-
solidated the wealth and power of organized business and industry (a

fundamental part of the Beard-Hacker story), increasing the relative power of management over labor in any conflict between them, and the army was used in behalf of owners to put down several of the strikes. Furthermore the war seems not to have affected the income distribution in the North or in the nation. Lee Soltow measured the degree of inequality in 1860 and 1870 and concluded that *"the distribution of wealth in the North remained essentially the same during the Civil War decade"* (his italics). The top 20 percent of the northern population owned 84 percent of the region's wealth in 1860 and the same 84 percent in 1870. While the war reduced drastically the proportion of national wealth owned in the South, it hardly transferred much of that wealth into the pockets of northern workers.[33] But few historians have paid much attention to those pockets or those workers.

Richard Bensel did so. He challenged Barrington Moore's idea that social democracy benefitted by the war. Given the power of economic elites in the North that war had fostered, lower-class workers hardly gained much. Furthermore Bensel hypothesizes that economic democracy was undercut by the results of the war. After the war the northern Democratic party was tied to the state-rights, small-government policies of its southern wing. Had it been free of that incubus it might have "embraced a state centered program of social welfare expansion and marketplace regulation that might have competed successfully with Republican developmental policies." It is one of those counterfactual hypotheses that economists delight in, but, given Frank Klement's work in 1960 that linked Democratic copperheadism with the early Granger movement, it may point to a serious subject for historical inquiry.[34]

Bensel's questions about the impact of the war on workers find significant answers in two books that stand out for their thoughtful integration of social and economic history with the more traditional focus on the war years. Grace Palladino and Iver Bernstein take traditional topics of Civil War study—violent protests in the 1860s by miners and workers against conscription—and place them within the larger story of the rise of industrialization in the United States.

Palladino describes a conflict beginning in the 1840s between Pennsylvania miners and owners over who should control the workplace and wages. Both miners and owners saw the war as an opportunity. Miners thought that the need for coal would give their organizations leverage. Owners saw a chance to stabilize an unstable business through the profits of wartime. When a combination of real-wage losses and conscription produced murder, riots, and strikes between 1862 and 1865, the army was on the side of the owners, accepting the argument that miners were disloyal, that their protest helped the Confederacy. What workers saw as an economic question—a conflict about their right to protection from the power of the owners, Republican owners saw as a political issue—Democrats were stirring up ignorant Irish workers to protect the party's power, and, intentionally or otherwise, these protests empowered disunion. Army provost marshals (some holding stock in the mines) and federal soldiers came in to suppress worker protests. This wartime alliance between owners and the army had postwar consequences. When violence against the still oppressive working conditions broke out in the 1870s the memories of "copperhead disloyalty" were revived to discredit the miners' cause. Civil War stories, as written by mine owners and their allies, thus strengthened the power of capital at the expense of labor in industrializing America.[35]

Iver Bernstein's *New York City Draft Riots* begins in the 1850s with a clash of interest between workers and merchants and shop and factory owners. When war broke out and the draft began New York workers shared the vision of Pennsylvania miners: "As they watched a centralizing national government become increasingly identified with the prerogatives of a local elite they associated with exploitation and interventionist authority, rioters of all persuasions sought to reclaim the polity in the name of the community." Workers fought back. The most deadly urban riot in U.S. history ensued, put down in part by regiments of New York Irish Americans, men fresh from the Gettysburg battlefield. While workers did gain some relief from the draft, after Appomattox their wartime riots came back to haunt them. When they struck again in the 1868 and especially in 1872 owners and merchants resurrected the image of bloodthirsty traitors to smother protests against economic inequality. I had argued that the war allowed industrialists to wrap their burgeoning power in the bunting of patriotism. Bernstein and Palladino revealed that they also gained power by tarring opponents with treason.[36]

Bernstein's and Palladino's work thus endorsed the Beard-Hacker argument that the war empowered the forces of industrialization. But their work provided a much more subtle description of how that was done—by undercutting the economic protests of workers even as economic power grew in the hands of owners and capitalists. The Beards and Hacker agreed with Moore that "The Civil War . . . cut short the drift to radicalism." The Beards especially emphasized that the industrial leaders of the Republican party had "flung" the national domain "to the hungry proletariate as a free gift more significant than bread and circuses." Bernstein and Palladino showed that workers were not only bought off by land; they were also weakened by the ability of industrial leaders to label their labor protests as abiding acts of disloyalty.[37]

Work by Palladino and Bernstein shows the benefits of having social historians analyze the Civil War. Considering the conflict in the larger context of labor protest against industrial change, they have shown that the question "Was the Civil War a Second American Revolution?" needs to be answered, in part, by asking, "For whom?" While the answer for Black Americans is a strong yes, for industrial workers the answer is much less positive.

The significant contribution of Palladino and Bernstein to the discussion of economic change in the Civil War, however, throws into sharp contrast how little social historians have done in analyzing the Civil War. While economic historians were having a rich debate over the meaning of the Civil War, most social historians were strangely silent about the nation's most significant conflict.

What makes the silence strange is that for almost three decades social history has been perhaps the most active branch of the profession. Emerging in the 1960s, the "new" social history used race, class, and gender as fundamental elements of historical analysis to describe the lives of the "inarticulate"—farmers and urban workers, ordinary men, women, and children. The goal was to provide "a people's history" of the nation. In terms of numbers of studies and numbers of historians at work, this "new" history was a great success. By 1978 there were more dissertations on social history than there were on political history. By the 1980s close to 35 percent of all historians in the United States called themselves social historians.[38] Some attention to the Civil War might have been expected from such a crowd.

Furthermore, the social history of the war had an early forerunner whose work might have been built upon. In 1910 Emerson Fite published *Social and Industrial Conditions in the North during the Civil War,* describing the impact of the war on agriculture, mining, transportation, commercial life, capital, labor, public improvements, education, "luxuries and amusements," and charity. The book provided a cornucopia of government and private industry reports and statistics, newspaper analyses and journal investigations of how an industrializing North experienced and fought the war. Here was a foundation to build a social history of the war upon.[39] But that history did not emerge.

Perhaps potential scholars were put off by the fact that builders on Fite's foundation would have to supply their own analytical cement. Fite provided statistics about almost everything; he interpreted and contextualized nothing. The book was exactly and only what the dusty title said—a description of life in the North during the war that ignored politics and military experience. Fite never mentioned the large economic and social changes that the nation was undergoing in the mid-nineteenth century. He lifted the war out of the larger history and described life behind northern lines for four years of struggle and then dropped the discussion, leaving the impression that the war had no abiding effect. The book was an excellent compendium of events and experiences, but it related hardly at all to ongoing history. It is not surprising that if writing the history of society at war meant revisiting this historical antique shop, historians demurred. Yet here was a field awaiting interpreters, a promising ground for ambitious scholars. To some extent the Beards would supply that interpretive framework, but few social historians in the last three decades have followed their lead.

Other invitations to launch investigations of the war and society also produced meager results. As far back as the 1890s Frederick Jackson Turner was calling for a history which recognized that institutions and constitutions were the products of social and economic forces. At Columbia University a group calling themselves "New Historians" began to insist that history be broadened beyond politics to study these forces. Furthermore, they held, there was a social purpose behind the new study. It would teach ordinary Americans the important role they had played in history and let them see the origins of the world in which they worked and lived. In the context of the progressive historians' critique of industrial society, such writing implied that objective historical inquiry would be energized by the imperatives of social criticism. By the 1920s Arthur Schlesinger and Dixon Ryan Fox were putting together a twelve-volume series called *The History of American Life*. Volumes by Allan Nevins covering 1865 to 1878 and especially by Arthur Cole on 1850 to 1865 were excellent presentations of the impact of war on society—although Cole spent only four of the book's fifteen chapters on the post-Sumter period and Nevins's interpretation of the meaning of the war itself was never directly presented. Still these works pointed out the topics that social historians might explore. But for several decades no serious work followed these pointers. Indeed despite the frequent urgent calls by leaders in the profession for more work on social history generally, covering topics such as cities, women, and immigrants, very little of it was done.[40]

Some critics attributed the lack of interest to the failure of the *American Life* volumes to confront serious political questions such as who exercised the most power and where. The volumes thus became, like Fite's work, more eclectic gatherings of facts than compelling syntheses of important trends and directions. There was no driving theme and no revelation about what forces and which people had organized and controlled society and who had benefitted by their control.[41]

Whatever the reason for what Richard Hofstadter called the "still birth" of early social history, Civil War studies shared in the silences that reigned over social analysis of the nation's past. But the silence lasted much longer for Civil War studies than it did for social history of the nation in general. While social historians crashed onto the scene in the 1960s and 1970s, exploring and condemning inequalities of class, race, and gender, major works in the new social history such as Stephan Thernstrom's, *Poverty and Progress* (1964) and Merle Curti's *Making of an American Community* (1959) hardly mentioned the Civil War. In a long string of community studies, works by Michael Frisch, Alan Dawley, and Don Doyle, studying urbanizing communities, were lonely exceptions that targeted prewar social and economic changes.[42]

As late as 1985, after a least two decades of fruitful, stimulating, and occasionally contentious work in social history, Olivier Zunz lamented that "an analysis of the greatest conflict and major crisis of identity experienced by the United States, . . . the Civil War, still eludes social historians." "Only the social history of the conflict itself," Zunz added, "the identification of the roles social groups played in it—will permit us to balance the search for causes with the search for consequences, and to assess the impact of the war on social change and on the formation of a more unified nation." Four years later Maris Vinovskis was still noting that social historians had on the whole "lost" the Civil War, and often didn't know where to find it.[43]

But Zunz's and Vinovskis's calls have produced little attention by social historians to the North and the war. Vinovskis edited a fine collection of essays containing work on enlistments, support for the war in two New Hampshire towns, soldiers and the values of their communities, relief work in Philadelphia, Chicago politics, membership in the GAR, and the impact of the war on widows. But that volume has still not inspired much further work. The fact remains that except for work on race and gender, social historians have shown an abiding lack of interest in finding the war.[44]

One sign of that lack of interest appeared when Peter Stearns, editor of the 1994 *Encyclopedia of Social History* (New York and London: Garland), chose a graduate student to write the entry on the social history of the Civil War. Two of the four books that Timothy Haggerty cited at the end of his article were works in traditional history: James M. McPherson's narrative history of the war, *Battle Cry of Freedom*, and Daniel Sutherland's, *Expansion of Every Day Life*. Only two were clearly what modern scholars would consider social history: Gerald Linderman, *Embattled Courage: The Experience of Combat in the American Civil War* and Maris Vinovskis's fine selection of essays. Iver Bernstein, Grace Palladino, and Matthew Gallman were conspicuous by their absence; so was *Divided Houses,* the excellent collection of essays edited by Catherine Clinton and Nina Silber on gender in the Civil War; so was the most recent study of northern society at war.[45]

Citation of Linderman and Vinovskis did reflect, to some extent, the state of the field, however. For there is one area in which social historians have provided a substantial body of work on the North at war. They have tried to answer the question, "who fought?" Work by Maris Vinovskis, Gerald Linderman, Reid Mitchell, Earl Hess, James Robertson, Randall Jimerson, and James McPherson has given us invaluable information about why soldiers fought and who they were.[46] While this work is the subject of Reid Mitchell's essay in the present volume, it needs also to be discussed here for two reasons: first, to illustrate just how protean analysis of traditional topics using social history questions can be; and second, to show, by contrast, how much is lost when social historians lose the war.

The basic question raised in determining who fought has been, "Was the Civil War 'a rich man's war and a poor man's fight?'" The question has been part of every traditional history of the war. When Maris Vinovskis took a careful statistical look at Newburyport, Massachusetts, to see who fought, he concluded, as had William Rohrbaugh and James McPherson, that the charge was not true. Vinovskis showed that skilled workers were more likely to enlist than were unskilled workers and that native-born men enlisted more than did foreign-born. And yet the data Vinovskis analyzed could also support the opposite view. While skilled workers served more often than unskilled, young men from the wealthiest ranks in the town were much less likely to be taken in the draft or to volunteer. Furthermore, as Vinovskis says, "Foreign born and second generation American soldiers and sailors were more likely to die or be wounded than servicemen with native born parents." Here was evidence about who was paying the highest price of war that the people of the 1860s would have found much more striking than distinctions between skilled and unskilled labor relied on by Vinovskis. And this possibility is confirmed by William Marvel's study of Conway, New Hampshire. He found that in Conway many more poor rural men than wealthier men served and died in the war.[47] In this instance social history analysis has nurtured fruitful debate about a significant issue.

In contrast, there has been little interweaving of social and traditional history on the question of the postwar impact of the war on Union soldiers. Taking a long-range view of soldiers' experiences (perhaps inspired by the longer-range views of social history), Larry Logue has recently

argued that, despite fears by soldiers and civilians, war did not make soldiers unfit for peace. Crime rates actually went down after the war, although
they rose in 1870 for some unexplained reason. There was some increase
in drinking, helping to inspire the creation of the WCTU. War service
seems not to have given any advantage to workers in competing for most
jobs—veterans and men who did not serve seem to have held the same
jobs. In fact, in large cities postwar economic difficulties sent ex-soldiers
into the streets with signs that said "Looking for Bread and Work." The
war created families even as it destroyed them, for the marriage rate  rose
after the war. These findings provide challenging subjects for wider study.
Logue's work, however, was an undocumented survey aimed at a popular
audience. There still has been no analysis by social historians of these
issues.[48]

Stuart McConnell's 1992 study of the Grand Army of the Republic is
also a work of traditional history—paying little attention to race, class,
and gender and showing little interest in the fate of workers facing the
changes of industrialization. But McConnell is sensitive, as most social
historians are, to long-range trends and change, and he provides a framework for studying the impact of the war that social historians need to
confront. It would have been "very clear to a Victorian American,"
McConnell writes, that "the late nineteenth century was a post war era."
McConnell knows of the great chasm in soldiers' minds between peace
and war. During the war "violence had been justified, social distinctions
leveled, individual preferences submerged in discipline and order, death
experienced as a daily occurrence." Veterans returned to the dramatically
different environment of peacetime. But McConnell also suggests that
veterans saw the war as a unique event, as something they put behind
them. Although McConnell does not discuss the point at length, it should
be observed that if most of the soldiers had their way, there would be no
changes at all. The America they rejoined would not be a society transformed. They would walk back into their memories. During the battles
and around the campfires the soldiers talked and dreamed of home. They
wanted their families to preserve "home," to write to them about its abiding stability, to relive with them memories of the way things had been
before they went to war.[49]

But while suggesting that the war did not create major transitions,
McConnell does demonstrate the need of the soldiers to accommodate
themselves to Civil War changes. Focusing on the GAR, he studies such
issues as the place of war memories in peacetime, new relationships between the nation and the individual, society's obligation to the poor and
the injured. He also adds to our understanding of assimilation by noting

that the GAR, although it did encourage class distinctions in some of its posts, was open to veterans of all faiths. Even Catholics who found the Masons anathema joined the organization and other foreign-born veterans also joined up. In cities Germans joined German posts and Irishmen joined Irish posts, but in less urban places men of all nationalities were assimilated into the rituals and memories, the brotherhood of the war. McConnell thus examines fraternalism, the organization of private groups and their role in responding to the growing industrial and social changes of the era. To its members the organization was a political club, a patriotic organization, a special-interest lobby, as well as a charity and a lodge. And the GAR was only one of hundreds of new orders formed after the war. McConnell thus suggests that the war created brotherhood, even as it was a brothers' war.

McConnell's approach is that of the traditional historian, looking at a particular organization in a particular time and place. Aware of social issues, he nonetheless looks at his subject whole, cognizant that time and place matter. By contrast, two works by devout social historians show the possibilities of social analysis while also revealing the failure of social history to attend to the nation's greatest crisis. Mary Ann Clawson's *Constructing Brotherhood: Class, Gender and Fraternalism,* published in 1989, contains no reference to the Civil War and no discussion of that cataclysm's connection to the strength and nature of Freemasonry. Clawson is interested in the Masons' "social and cultural significance in the articulation of class and gender relations in the nineteenth century United States." Yet the significance she seeks has no connection in her book to a war that created hundreds of Masonic-like groups such as the GAR. Despite excellent work that has recently appeared about how war shaped gender roles, Clawson writes as though the years 1861–1865 were indistinguishable from other years of that century. Class and gender categories become real in and of themselves, unrelated to the major events that actually help define how men and women, rich, poor, and middle-class, lived out their lives.[50]

Mark Carnes's 1989 book *Secret Ritual and Manhood in America* is similarly innocent of the relevance of the Civil War. Carnes studies the rituals of fraternal orders and asks what those rituals meant for defining ideas of manhood in the postwar world. He does not consider the relationship between war and manhood and that postwar search. He even takes time to explain how the idea of death fit into the ritual processes of Masons, Odd Fellows, and Knights of Pythias. But it does not occur to him to consider whether there was a connection between the parts of the rituals focusing on death and symbolic mutilation and the 620,000 deaths and thousands of mutilations in the Civil War. His one moment of interest in the war itself is seen in his discussion the postwar debate over admitting amputees to the Masons, which required initiates to be "upright in body, not deformed or dismembered, but of whole and entire limbs, as a man ought to be."[51]

After that glance the war passes from Carnes's view. Yet his evidence almost shouts the relevance of the Civil War. He emphasizes that initiation ceremonies replicated the act of fathers passing manhood on to their sons, and notes that the need for such rituals may be attributed to absent fathers. But the impact of the Civil War, which put millions of men into armies away from home, does not occur to him. Someone needs to consider these fraternal societies with the Civil War in mind. One might do so by considering the late-nineteenth-century division between those who had been "touched with fire" in Oliver Wendell Holmes's phrase, and the postwar generation who had not yet proven their manhood and who sought ways to achieve the "moral equivalent of war." Maybe the lodges, with ritual symbols of death and mutilation, assured younger men that their "battle-hardened" fathers took them through the horrors of battle before accepting them. All these questions about veterans and their children might be explored if social historians tried to find the Civil War.

But so far they have shown little interest in doing so, failing not only to consider men's social groups but also almost ignoring families and children.[52] Tamara Haraven, the maven of family history, surveys recent writings on history of the family and, in almost thirty pages, makes no mention of the Civil War, or even of war itself.[53] Were no fathers, no children, no mothers, no grandparents, and no extended families affected when fathers left home for months and years and came back home in wooden boxes or without arms and legs?

Four years of slaughter, 620,000 deaths, a half a million wounded, tens of thousands of amputations surely meant something significant to family life. The scores of wartime songs written to and about mothers surely suggest the deep feelings about family and home. But there is very little writing by historians to tell us exactly what. Some historians have written about the relationships between fathers and sons, but the number is very small.[54] If historians of World War I talk about the loss of a generation of young men in Europe, why isn't there more interest in similar losses in the United States?[55] A war that killed 620,000 young men produced thousands of orphans and raised many issues about adoption. But since Robert Bremner's survey of philanthropy and welfare in the war era there has been very little work on the subject. Bremner focused on public charities in large cities; what happened in the smaller cities and towns? Is there a way for Civil War historians to learn what the war meant to children, to replicate in some way William Tuttle's fine work on World War II children?[56] James Marten and Peter Stearns and Timothy Haggarty have made an interesting beginning by analyzing children's magazines during and after the war. Peter Bardaglio is stimulating in his comments on slave children, but the impact of the war on children is an almost entirely open field for study.[57]

No work has discussed in any general sense the nature and meaning of the new status of children after the war or the impact of the war on families. Has anyone sampled census records to explore family structures before and after the war? Has anyone even counted the number of orphans and orphanages in the major cities during and after the war? There is a growing body of significant work on the impact on family life of the Civil War pension system. By 1890 over 40 percent of the federal budget was spent on pensions to wounded and elderly soldiers and widows and orphans of the conflict. During the war the existence of a pension system that would compensate families for the loss of a father and husband helped encourage men to enlist in Union regiments.[58] Social historians could serve all historians by investigating more thoroughly the many interactions between the nation's greatest war and the family members who stayed at home. Lori Ginzberg has explored the impact of the war on women in charity causes, but as Ginzberg's focus is on public activities, there is more to be said about how war shaped essentially private family life. Reid Mitchell has shown what soldiers thought about the homes they were fighting for, but we need more work on what war did to those homes.[59]

Yet there is reason to hope that social historians will find the war. Recent changes in social history reflect a desire to bridge the distance between social and traditional history. Social historians have claimed for years, at least since Frederick Jackson Turner and the "New History," that their field ideally was "total history"; it covered the entire range of human activity. That was because politics and law rested on social and economic foundations. The move "from social history to the history of society," as Eric Hobsbawm, one of the most significant of the founders of modern social history, said, would require not narrow study but the most inclusive perspectives.[60] Some twenty years ago, in 1976, Herbert Gutman warned against the new social history's drift toward "over specialization"—its tendency to vivisect lives lived into disconnected subcategories. "Something is learned from such specialized studies, but in themselves such works often substitute classification for meaning and wash out the wholeness that is essential to understanding human behavior." While many social historians have ignored these pronouncements from their patriarchs, the words still stand as admirable ideals and ones that we may be closer to realizing.[61]

Social historians have recently been debating approaches that suggest integration with more traditional genres. Even as social history has taken a cultural turn social historians have been warned to look at concrete realities and not just cultural constructs. Recent issues of the *Journal of Social History* have seen a debate over the dangers of overemphasizing the ways in which people culturally construct the world in which they live and struggle. Reminders are issued that while identities may be culturally constructed, they still have a basis in material interests, economic relations, and institutional dynamics.

In this vein, Patrick Joyce, writing in January 1995 in the journal *Social History,* challenged fellow social historians to emphasize structure less and human agency more—a call for writing that looks very much like traditional narratives in which people shape their own fate. Joyce's call may have been inspired by James M. McPherson's *Battle Cry of Freedom,* the most widely read modern book on the Civil War. *Battle Cry of Freedom* provided an implicit challenge to the idea that social and economic forces created and drove the war. McPherson emphasized human agency— decisions made, battles won at crucial junctures that determined which social visions would control the nation for the nineteenth and twentieth centuries. In his narrative, action accounts for social change more than social change accounts for action. Joyce's admonition was clearly needed. Between 1989 and 1996 only two articles in thirty-two issues of the *Journal of Social History* focused on civil war and society. But now the challenge has been issued.[62]

Other social history directions may bring scholars to attend to the significance of events such as the Civil War. The longstanding insistence by anthropologist Clifford Geertz that societies can be understood by deep reading and "thick descriptions" of particular customs has caused social historians to learn about the meaning of storytelling within cultures. This interest seems to have led to fascination with narrative strategy and technique. The journey of social historians toward narrative can been seen in the fact that early social history was described as "social science history," using the title of one of the leading journals in the field. And the field almost defined itself as an enemy of narrative. As William H. Sewell, Jr., noted, "Narrative history represented everything that social science history was not; it was soft rather than hard, impressionistic rather than rigorous, and literary rather than scientific. It delighted in presenting the sentiments and personal stories of the few rather than seeking out the social structures that determined the lives and fortunes of the many." By fall 1992 one entire issue of *Social Science History* and half of another consisted of articles advocating narrative and illustrating its uses in social history.[63] From here it may be a short jump to interest in narrating events within the Civil War, as Bernstein and Palladino have done. Perhaps the war itself may find social history narration.

Still another new direction in social history may help social historians to find the war. New studies in urban history have highlighted the importance of politics and political culture in shaping the lives of ordinary citizens. Until the Civil War era, Philip Ethington argues in studying San Francisco, class issues did not shape politics so much as politics shaped class issues. San Francisco politicians of the 1860s thought that "social relations were the result of political institutions and policies." Different interests in the city would be subsumed by a political process which would operate to define and advance the city toward a common good. But after the war a world emerged in which social differences defined the operation of politics. The wedge for this change was the Civil War, which, by emphasizing race as a defining difference between parties, allowed politicians to claim that their opponents were simply interested in favors for special groups, not benefits for the whole society. Both blacks and the thousands of Chinese immigrants that the railroads had brought into the state were clearly marked and seen as the pliant masses controlled by big-business Republicans.[64]

Belief in a single common community interest was being replaced by belief that society was a clash of interests that could not be reconciled by virtuous participation in the public sphere. Politics could no longer control social differences. Just as Bernstein and Palladino saw the war as shaping the results of class conflict, so Ethington saw the war as changing the relative importance of class and political culture in defining the nature of society. By emphasizing politics over class he suggested the importance of comparatively short-term political events rather than more long-term class relations in defining experience. Perhaps in that context the Civil War itself will be seen by social historians to be a defining and important event.

Ethington's work epitomizes a larger trend in scholarship. Led by Theda Skocpol, political scientists have been "bringing the state back in" to studies of politics and society. Rather than describing how class, race, and gender ideas drove politics, Skocpol and other scholars emphasize the significance of decisions by governments in determining class relationships and influences. Skocpol focuses on Civil War pensions in providing opportunities for millions of widows and families. Millions of federal dollars had a significant impact on the lives and families of the recipients.

Once again the war is seen a shaping event in the history of class, race, and gender relationships.[65]

Perhaps "bringing the state back in," a growing concern for the public sphere, and the resurgent interest in narrative and in the power of people to shape rather than to respond to the forces of their society will combine to produce a social history of the Civil War that will live up to the hopes of Gutman and Hobsbawm. Maybe then the answer to Vinovskis's question, "Have social historians lost the Civil War?," will be, "For a time they did but they are now finding a more diverse and complex and integrated conflict than anyone had imagined. They have found and are learning to describe the human significance of the nation's most pivotal and awe-inspiring event. As they look at northern society they are preparing to join economic historians in answering the question, 'What did the winners win and at what cost?'"

# BEHIND THE LINES

## Confederate Economy and Society

### JAMES L. ROARK

The artillery had barely cooled in 1865 when southern generals and statesmen launched a literary war over responsibility for the Confederacy's defeat. Striding fearlessly into the thickets of military strategy, battlefield tactics, and political leadership, each participant proved conclusively that he was not responsible for Appomattox. On the heels of the apologias of the officers and politicians came the Lost Cause myth-histories, works that sought to sanctify the southern nation. Conveniently forgetting much of what they knew about Confederate history, defenders of the noble experiment etched a scene of social harmony and political unity. Tears welled up as they described Confederate soldiers standing shoulder to shoulder in selfless sacrifice. Despite the soldiers' heroism, however, southern virtue succumbed to Yankee might.[1]

In 1937, Charles W. Ramsdell offered the inaugural Walter Lynwood Fleming Lectures in Southern History (published posthumously in 1944 as *Behind the Lines in the Southern Confederacy*), in which he attempted to shift the locus of the debate about Confederate failure from the battlefields and political arenas to the home front. He argued that it was upon "civilians that the strength of the armies in the last analysis depended." Although he approached his subject sympathetically, generously concluding that the Confederate raft was so crowded with internal problems that its sinking was probably inevitable, he described life behind the lines as a crazy quilt of ill-advised fiscal policy, primitive transportation, constricted agriculture, puny industry, inefficient bureaucracy, callous governmental agencies, muddled legislation, and maddening shortages. The accumulating economic and administrative catastrophe provoked class friction, social disintegration, and eventually the collapse of civilian morale. Confederate authorities had jettisoned notions of laissez-faire and limited government, he observed, but they failed to solve the problems of the home front. That failure proved fatal to the new nation.[2]

For three decades after Ramsdell's Fleming lectures, historians remained resistant to social explanations of Confederate failure, in part no doubt because of the war's conspicuous military and political nature but also because the focus on armies and politics fit the historical discipline's traditional definition of proper subject matter. In 1965, Allan Nevins, the dean of Civil War historians, observed that "military and political aspects of the far-felt convulsion have received an attention disproportionate to that given the social, the economic, the ideological, the cultural, and the administrative aspects of the era."[3] But since the 1960s transformations in the discipline of history—in the questions historians ask, the approaches they employ, and the perspectives they bring—have galvanized behind-the-lines analysis of Confederate defeat.

The arrival of social history directed scholarly attention away from the elite few and toward people traditionally overlooked by political and military accounts. The civil rights and feminist movements encouraged fresh appreciation of the unexpected historical agency and potency of groups whose voices had been ignored or silenced. New Left political analysis emphasized the ways labor systems and hegemonic power left deep marks not only on economies but also upon social relations, ideological beliefs, and cultural values. More recently, the postmodernist turn stimulated distrust of master narratives that mirrored contemporary hierarchies and structures of power. By emphasizing plurality over unity and by noting exceptions to oft-repeated generalizations, historians have made room for local landscapes, personal stories, and diverse experiences. These varied intellectual developments have not led in the same direction (nor have they proven equally valuable to historians), but students of the Confederacy have increasingly adopted one or more of these new perspectives. Confederate history, consequently, is once again aligned with the central thrusts of the discipline.[4]

Historians have disassembled the simple, uncomplicated, and monolithic Confederacy and replaced it with a Confederacy of multiple and sometimes clashing experiences. War, as Stephen Hahn observes, "tests the fabric of a social order as does nothing else, taxing social and political ties as much as human and material resources."[5] While there is no consensus about the home front's role in the outcome of the war, historians increasingly argue that the slave-labor Confederacy suffered grave deficiencies and proved significantly less able socially, economically, and ideologically than the free-labor North to fight and win a modern war. Under intense pressure, according to this argument, the South's antebellum accommodations gave way along the seams of race, class, gender, and ideology. As agents of this disintegration, slaves, nonslaveholding whites, women, unionists, and contrarians of every stripe have taken on major roles in the Confederate drama. As antebellum fault lines became fissures, Confederate society failed to cohere, and an internally divided Confederacy came apart from within. While concerned with more than assigning blame, recent literature on the Confederate home front remains for the most part deeply invested in the question of responsibility for Confederate defeat.

Behind-the-lines explanations of Confederate defeat have by no means driven military explanations from the field. Indeed, Confederate studies today enjoys a lively debate between the "internal" school that emphasizes economic and social realities of the southern home front and the "external" school that argues the centrality of what happened when Confederates met Yankees on the battlefields. But tidy categories have blurred. Scholars increasingly focus on the interplay of home front and battlefield. Two-way traffic runs between them, and the debate often concerns the direction of the heaviest influence. Another question taken up by the new literature is often more implied than explicit. It concerns the relationship of the Confederate government and the people. Older studies tended to assume a good fit and saw the government as the natural outgrowth and realization of the Old South. Newer scholarship is more likely to query the relationship and what it meant for the war. But few Civil War historians today ignore Charles Ramsdell's injunction to remember the home front.

The economic history of the Civil War era has emerged in recent years as a particularly robust field. This vital scholarship, however, is often framed in ways that limit its usefulness for understanding the Confederate economy. One subfield, for example, asks broad questions about the war's overall economic consequences, particularly its impact on the speed and direction of the nation's development. Although this literature professes to be national in scope, it usually focuses on the North and industrial capitalism.[6]

Even economic studies that concentrate on the South give short shrift to the war years. One such body of work seeks to measure the results of the war by comparing and contrasting the antebellum and postbellum southern economies. Within this debate, economists tend to seek the roots of the South's economic backwardness, while historians probe continuity and change, asking whether there really was an Old and a New South.[7] A fine example of a longitudinal study is Robert Tracy McKenzie's *One South or Many?*, an analysis of Tennessee agriculture that exploits the decennial censuses for 1850 through 1880 to explore a broad range of topics, including geographic and economic mobility, wealth distribution, patterns of landholding and tenure, and farm size and income.[8] Works like this are invaluable for understanding change and persistence over time, but subsuming the war years in larger chronologies obscures the Confederate economic experience. That vast and often brilliant recent literature that hones in on the South's transformation from slavery to free-labor agriculture also offers less leverage on the Confederate economy than one might expect. These studies often begin where the Confederacy ended, with emancipation. They tend to view the war as prologue to a decidedly post-Confederate story—the evolution of a regional economy without slavery.[9]

Unlike social historians who have aggressively established beachheads in Confederate studies, economic historians have been more tentative, and perhaps for understandable reasons. Emory Thomas, the historian who has most carefully charted the transformation of the Confederate economy, admits that much of the change, particularly the modernization, "did not survive the total defeat and destruction of the Confederate state."[10] In the wartime North, on the other hand, the Republican Party devised a blueprint that guided the nation's postbellum economic development.[11] Not only did defeat make the Confederate economic program a dead end, but it also destroyed the Old South's economic system. And as Harold Woodman observes, the war "was but a part, the destructive half, of the revolution in the South." Southerners completed the economic revolution war instigated when they rebuilt their economy on free labor.[12] No wonder, then, that economic historians have resisted the Confederate years. Who wants to tell merely half a story? This relative neglect helps explain the staying power of several classic economic studies, including those by John C. Schwab, Robert Cecil Todd, and Paul W. Gates, works that appeared decades ago but remain useful today.[13]

Economic historians who have approached the Confederacy as a distinct epoch usually have a specific purpose: to assess the role of the Confederate economy in the outcome of the war. Had the war been as short as most southerners expected, the balance sheet of economic resources between North and South would have been inconsequential. But in the war that came, a modern industrial war of attrition, economic resources and their mobilization counted a great deal. Recent work runs the gamut from studies that emphasize the Confederacy's economic adaptability and achievement to those that stress its limits and failure. No scholar has argued the case for economic departure more cogently than Emory Thomas. In a nation founded by planters to preserve plantation agriculture, Thomas argues, capital swelled, cities mushroomed, and war industries burgeoned. The "Confederate South underwent nothing short of an economic revolution."[14] William Freehling, on the other hand, portrays a Confederate economy more continuous with the Old South and in the end mortally wounded by slavery. The magnitude of the Confederacy's "internal problem" would have "baffled the greatest statesmen," he argues. Only a miracle could have transformed the southern economy into a "sophisticated military-industrial complex."[15]

Although our understanding of aspects of the Confederate economy remains more impressionistic than systematic and sketches of veterans returning to wasted farmsteads still outweigh serious analyses of the devastation, scholars have in recent years sought to chart the course of the Confederate economy by taking on a wide range of topics: agriculture; manufacturing; economic and fiscal policy; urban growth; slave labor; railroads and transportation; blockade and trade; economic privation and public relief, and more. Richmond's task of mobilizing the region's resources for total war required that it intrude into society more and more and in increasingly unprecedented ways. The Confederate government sought to make the home front more and more Confederate.

An irony of the Confederate South is that in one of the world's most powerful agricultural economies, people went hungry. The starting place for an answer to the conundrum remains Paul Gates's *Agriculture and the Civil War* (1962), the first five chapters of which map the radical and far-reaching changes in the farming operations of the Confederacy. Gates portrays a productive but vulnerable agricultural economy dependent on slavery and the export of staple crops. When war and the Union blockade ended the South's hugely profitable relationship with the Atlantic market, staple crops metamorphosed from a major strength to a significant weakness. With broad strokes, Gates sketches the massive shift from staples to grain, forage, and livestock and explores the factors that inhibited the transformation.

As Gates explains, most whites believed that not only would independence guard slavery but that it would also free their slave economy from the North's colonial exploitation. In reality, secession threw an economy that had known prosperity for a decade into an immediate tailspin. The assembly of large armies drew upwards of a half-million white men from agriculture, seriously reducing productivity, especially on yeoman farms where routines were disrupted earlier and more severely than on plantations. But war also disrupted the labor power of plantations, as slaves were pressed into Confederate service, ran away, and resisted field work. Invading Yankees captured and occupied vast territory, including the rich agricultural areas of Tennessee and the Mississippi Valley. Like locusts, marching armies devoured the fruits of the earth. Fighting scorched the land. Gates suggests that class hostility over slavery and exemptions might also have undercut production. He faults the Confederate government for failing to construct a unified agricultural policy and comprehensive logistical system for supplying armies and civilians. He levels withering fire at the policy of impressment. Almost from the beginning, he argues, the Confederacy resorted to impressment of horses, mules, forage, grain, tools, slaves, and many other commodities. Although he admits the lack of data on impressment's effect on agricultural production, he suggests that it caused controversy, resistance, avoidance, evasion, maldistribution, and inflation. In addition to problems of production, poor transportation made shipping of provisions difficult or impossible. The inability of the seceding states to produce and distribute enough food to sustain both their military and civilians, Gates concludes, was a major cause of Confederate defeat.[16]

In 1994, John Solomon Otto published *Southern Agriculture during the Civil War Era,* the first comprehensive treatment of Confederate agriculture since Gates. While lacking its predecessor's literary grace, it rests on better economic data, which Otto skillfully integrates with the scholarship of the last three decades. Like Gates, Otto wrestles with the question of hunger in a land of plenty, but he concludes that the answer lies more with a crisis of trade and transportation than with production. "In order to survive as a nation," Otto declares, "the Confederacy had to continue exporting agricultural commodities and importing consumer goods." Early on, however, the government's self-imposed embargo on cotton exports, which severely limited the Confederacy's ability to import foreign supplies, signaled Richmond's ineptness. By the end of 1861, "the Confederate transportation system lacked the resources to trade with foreign nations, maintain river commerce, or replace deteriorating railroads." By 1864, farm families and town dwellers were going hungry, while "Confederate soldiers possessed first-class ordnance but had second-class accouterments and ate third-class rations." Farmers were not to blame. Although a majority of the Confederacy's farm laborers were missing from the fields by 1864, the workers who remained had managed to increase dramatically the acreage devoted to food. Hunger, Otto concludes, was "self-inflicted." Richmond had botched agricultural mobilization.[17]

The South's staple crops have also received considerable attention, and the wartime portrait is one of grim similarity. The early invasion and occupation of Louisiana's "sugar bowl" by Union troops brought the sugar industry to the edge of extinction. By war's end, only 15 percent of the state's 1,291 sugar estates were still operating. Production fell from 264,000 tons in 1861 to only 9,950 tons in 1865.[18] John Rodrigue analyzes the triangle of the U.S. Army, sugar planters, and slaves to provide the most thorough analysis of disintegration of southern Louisiana's sugar economy.[19] Tobacco flourished in the upper South, which became a battle-ground between armies. Marching soldiers, resisting slaves, and state prohibition left the tobacco industry in shambles.[20] South Carolina's rice industry, as Peter Coclanis demonstrates, was in trouble before the war because of increasingly stiff foreign competition, but severe wartime destruction significantly accelerated rice's demise.[21]

The fate of cotton, the South's premier cash crop, resembled that of the other staples. A combination of developments—including the Confederate embargo, Union blockade, state restrictions, labor shortages and resistance, military destruction and disruption, and refugeeing—caused production to plummet from a record crop of more than 5 million bales in 1861 to a quarter of a million bales in 1865.[22] Stanley Lebergott, however, challenges the notion that cotton growers largely abandoned the crop during the war. He points out that the Confederate Congress neither restricted cotton planting nor prohibited the export of cotton and argues that state limitations proved ineffectual. Consequently, planters, who "insisted on their right to grow unlimited amounts of cotton, to retain it for sale whenever they chose, and to sell it whenever, and to whomever, they chose"—produced nearly 7 million bales during the war. Planters' commitment to their own short-term interests proved deadly for the Confederacy, Lebbergot concludes, for it meant, among other things, that an army of slaves grew cotton for private profit instead of serving the needs of Confederate independence.[23]

Uncomfortable with exaggerated regional uniformities, scholars have recently been at pains to demonstrate that the war did not have the same economic consequences everywhere. Several state studies provide fine-grained portraits of southern agriculture that illustrate that not all areas suffered equally. Robert Tracy McKenzie's analysis of Tennessee, perhaps the state with the greatest agricultural diversity, makes clear the danger in conflating plantation and nonplantation areas, for upcountry and Black Belt fared very differently.[24] Carl Moneyhon found that in Arkansas severe food shortages arrived in first year of the war, in part because planters continued to grow cotton for illegal trade with Yankees.[25] As Paul Escott has shown, war made North Carolina "a world upside down." It plunged tens of thousands of proud and formerly self-reliant farmers into extreme want and near starvation.[26] But two states—Texas and Florida—avoided widespread devastation. Secession denied Texas cattlemen their northern markets, but southern demand increased so dramatically that some ranchers actually fattened off the war. As Confederate veteran and fabled cattle-man Charles Goodnight observed: "The stay-at-home fellows had the cattle and we poor-devils had the experience."[27] The value of agriculture in the lower South, Robert Taylor observes, grew with each Union advance into the upper South. Relatively untouched by Union armies, Florida increas-ingly became the Confederacy's "granary and butcher shop."[28] Several important studies have taken on smaller geographies. Michael Wayne has analyzed the consequences of the federal invasion of the lower Mississippi Valley for the fabulously wealthy cotton planters of the Natchez area.[29] Stephen Ash vividly portrays life in middle Tennessee, where Union inva-sion and occupation came early and where advancing and retreating armies ravaged, smashed, and burned, leaving enormous physical devastation and utter economic derangement in their wake.[30]

The path of the fighting, of course, had a great deal to do with the severity of the disruption of agriculture. But as Stephen Ash's important new study demonstrates, so too did patterns of Yankee occupation. *When the Yankees Came* adds spatial and temporal dimensions to our under-standing of the economic and social consequences of federal invasion. Ash argues that invasion established three zones, which he labels garri-soned towns, the Confederate frontier, and no-man's-land. Their boundaries were constantly in flux, but they each had sharply defined experiences. Towns under federal control often throbbed with economic life, and federal authorities sometimes stepped in to relieve whatever suf-fering there was. The Confederate frontier experienced serious disruption, but the Confederate presence, even if sporadic, preserved enough order and safety to make economic activity possible. But in the twilight zone of no-man's-land, which neither side controlled, chaos and economic devas-tation ruled. Without labor, work animals, fencing, trade, mobility, or safety, this economic desert could not support agriculture or any other productive activity. Ash makes clear that the great interior of the Confed-eracy, where Union soldiers failed to penetrate until near the end of the war or even after, enjoyed immunity to the worst consequences of Yankee invasion.[31]

The fate of Confederate agriculture was also integrally linked to the fortunes of slavery. While an enormous literature exists on the emancipa-tion experiences of blacks and whites, especially the unraveling of paternalism and other complex human relationships, the wartime opera-tions of the slave economy—farm production and productivity, coercion and incentives, labor routines and organization, impressment of slaves, use in nonagricultural activities, slave leasing and sales—have received much less attention. John Inscoe correctly observes that scholars have given little attention to the impact of war on the economies of slavery in areas not in the path of fighting, except as slave labor fed directly into the Confederate war effort.[32] War changed the slave labor system even in the most isolated parts of the Confederacy, but we know much more about the birth of free labor in Union-occupied territory than the last days of slavery in the Confederacy.[33]

On one level, slavery proved a strength to the Confederacy, on another, more important level, it became a major liability. Each slave who worked in the fields released a white man for immediate military service. But slaves did not prove to be dependable laborers. They ran away to the Yankees, where they worked for the enemy or even put on his uniform. When they stayed home, they toiled less, undercutting agricultural efficiency, and resisted more, forcing Confederate officials to shift troops to the home front or fashion policies such as the 20-Negro law that provoked class friction among whites. But local circumstances and the exigencies of war still had influence. In certain areas of the lower and mountain South, for example, slavery remained stable and profitable throughout the war. In western North Carolina, labor shortages presented fresh opportunities for refugeeing planters to lease slaves to private entrepreneurs for war-generated work in agriculture, mining, railroads, and industry.[34] Elsewhere, planters in proximity to federal lines sometimes traded cotton for substantial profits. Cotton's substitute—provisions— also meant cash to planters in proximity to booming cities.[35] But time and again slaves undermined the planters' economic dreams by declaring their freedom, and whites were forced to make new accommodations in order to get blacks to work.

Despite occasional oases of prosperity, the dominant story is the deterioration of the plantation as an economic and social unit. Slavery unraveled differently in different times and places, but eventually all planters confronted emancipation and the destruction of their principal form of wealth. Before then, typically long before then, production had slowed and profits shriveled. Yeoman farms, worked by women and children who cultivated without draft animals, sometimes could not produce enough food to feed a single family. Some historians argue, however, that even at the very end of the war the Confederacy had enough food. What Confederates lacked were transportation with which to ship it and cash with which to purchase it.[36]

Another irony of the Confederate economy is that industry outperformed agriculture. When the war began, industry was the slave South's stepchild. The familiar figures of the census of 1860 enumerate both agriculture's dominance in the South and the vast superiority of northern industry over southern industry. To make the lopsidedness worse, most Confederate manufactures were flour mills, sawmills, tobacco factories, tanneries, and textile mills. Few Confederate factories produced machines, firearms, ships, railroad locomotives, cars, or rails, the sinews of modern warfare.[37] Secession thrust the Confederate South into an enormous industrial war and forced the rebels to create an industrial economy of their own and to do so almost overnight. The authors of *Why the South Lost the Civil War* comment that no one has ever fully told the story of the rise of Confederate industry, but in recent years a number of scholars have examined important aspects of the story.[38] With varying degrees of enthusiasm, they agree with the proposition that wartime industrialization succeeded. Even Roger Ransom, who argues strongly that slavery doomed the Confederacy's efforts to mobilize its resources, admits that "the Confederacy was actually rather successful in creating a military-industrial complex that was able to provide reasonably ample supplies of munitions to its armies throughout the war."[39] An awed Ramondo Luraghi concludes: "What the South accomplished is astounding."[40]

Although the Confederate constitution contained provisions to blunt government intrusion into the economy and to whittle back state authority in general, Richmond responded pragmatically to the industrial challenge. Unable to purchase sufficient quantities of war matériel abroad because of a shortage of specie and the blockade, the government set about increasing industrial production at home.[41] Frank Vandiver tells the remarkable tale of Josiah Gorgas, an organizational genius who as chief of the Confederate Ordnance Bureau built the shops, powder mills, arsenals, foundries, gunworks, and laboratories that armed the Confederacy.[42] William N. Still, Jr., describes the Confederacy's success in converting, contracting for, or laying down 150 ships, including some 50 ironclads.[43] The government also entered into thousands of contracts with civilian manufacturers, stimulating an explosion in private production. Charles B. Dew recounts the extraordinary growth of Richmond's Tredegar Iron Works, which before the war was already one of the nation's largest ironworks and during the war proved so successful in expanding its capacity to produce guns, armor, and rails that it out paced the supply of raw materials.[44]

Industry in Georgia, like that in most other states, received a high-voltage stimulus. Mary DeCredico examines the aggressive entrepreneurs who flocked to Georgia's cities to build war-related businesses on antebellum industrial foundations, textiles in Augusta and Columbus, metals fabrication in Atlanta, and shipping in Savannah. By serving the needs of civilians and the government, these robust capitalists prospered, at least until the Yankee whirlwind arrived to destroy rebel manufacturing.[45] Clarence Mohr has demonstrated in telling detail the crucial role of slave labor in Georgia's industrial transformation. Plantation masters eagerly leased thousands of surplus field hands to the state's private entrepreneurs who needed labor to replace white workers who had joined the army or to increase production of war-related matériel. Slaves labored in leather works, shoe factories, weapons and munitions plants, gunpowder factories, iron works, mines and mineral processing, salt making, lumbering, and textile production. Slave men were fairly evenly distributed across Georgia's industries, while slave women were hired primarily for cooking and washing. Thousands of blacks crowded into cities to work in factories that were vital to the Confederate war effort.[46]

Shrewd small fry found hundreds of ways to prosper in war-related manufacturing. William Weaver, owner of Buffalo Forge, an iron-making enterprise in the Valley of Virginia, understood that money could be made by supplying articles that were in great demand. When Tredegar Iron Works announced that it needed iron, Weaver charged all the market would bear. His slave-operated blast furnace rode the price of iron from $40 a ton in 1861 to $672 in early 1863. But like Tredegar, Buffalo Forge experienced shortages—in iron ore, charcoal fuel, and provisions for slave workers—that cut into its operations. The days of the highly profitable open market were numbered in any case, for Buffalo Forge fell increasingly under government control. In 1864, it signed a contract with the Nitre and Mining Bureau for 60 tons of horseshoe iron, but by war's end shortages of materials and labor defections meant that Buffalo Forge had virtually stopped making iron for the Confederacy.[47]

The Confederate government whipped its industrial problem by direct government production, targeted contracts with private manufacturers, and manipulation of conscription and labor exemptions to channel scarce manpower into strategic war industries. Centralized control of production was not a feasible way of encouraging farm production, however, and, as Roger Ransom explains, the structure of the South's slave economy made it difficult to rely, as the North had done, on market arrangements to mobilize resources for the war effort.[48] Moreover, the northern government paid for supplies with funds raised by taxes or bonds. The Confederate government had far fewer funds, in part because it mishandled its finances.

The Confederate fiscal program has long been a bull's-eye for scholars, and recent work emphasizes Richmond's culpability in the financial disaster. From the beginning, the government proved ineffective. Convinced of a short-war scenario, it failed to prepare for the economic dislocations that followed. Loans and a modest tariff for revenue proved inadequate early on.[49] It was not until April 1863 that Richmond enacted a comprehensive tax law. Even then, in four years the Confederate government derived from taxes only 7 percent of its total revenue. Borrowing, or the sale of bonds, accounted for another quarter of its funds. Impressment to obtain provisions and other supplies for the military accounted for 17 percent of total Confederate receipts. And fully half of its revenue came from treasury notes.[50] Furiously printing paper money not backed by specie, taxing at ridiculously low levels, and never creating an adequate means of collecting revenue exploded the Confederate debt and propelled inflation into the wild blue yonder.

The most important full-scale study of Confederate finance is Douglas B. Ball's impressively researched and sharply argued *Financial Failure and Confederate Defeat,* which offers a devastating critique of Confederate fiscal policies. Ball flatly denies that the Confederacy's financial problems were intractable. Instead, "willful and negligent" money management bankrupted the war effort. Secretary of the Treasury Christopher Gustavus Memminger and President Jefferson Davis were both "innocent" in matters of financial theory and proceeded without a plan, a strategy, or an adequate understanding the South's predicament. They irritated Europe with the cotton embargo, squandered money by refusing to establish a centralized purchasing system overseas, failed to take control of the banks' limited supply of specie, missed an early opportunity to float bonds in Europe and buy local cotton, neglected to control private blockade-runners, and generally pursued ill-advised policies long after it became clear that the war would be neither short nor easy. A "bankrupt treasury," Ball concludes, "played a significant role in Confederate defeat."[51]

While no one doubts that Richmond's efforts to finance the war failed, blame remains an issue. Before Ball, the standard study, Richard Cecil Todd's *Confederate Finance,* indicted the Confederate Congress.[52] Rather than make villains of the politicians, Stanley Lebergott targets Confederate citizens, who may have voted for secession but who proved reluctant to pay taxes to support the war. He notes especially large slaveholders' selfish and shortsighted refusal to pay their fair share.[53] Roger Ransom identifies the rigid structural realities of a slave society. He argues that the rural South's severe shortage of cash made it difficult for the government to raise revenues through either taxation or bond sales. As a consequence, the government had to rely on taxes-in-kind, usually provisions and feed, which was not only inefficient but also generated enormous bitterness as agents literally carted away families' food.[54] Whether the causes were structural or human, financial problems undercut the government's war effort.[55]

The Union naval blockade of the Confederacy has also become a hotbed of historiographical debate. Scholars divide sharply on the blockade's effectiveness, its impact on the Confederate economy, and its consequences for the Confederacy's ability and willingness to make war.[56] Painstaking research in stubborn sources has resulted in vastly improved evidence about the number of ships involved as blockade-runners and blockaders, the frequency of Confederate sailings and ratios of capture by Union ships, and the cargoes and their value, but better evidence has not quieted controversy.

By far the most thorough analysis of the blockade is Stephen R. Wise's *Lifeline of the Confederacy*. As the title suggests, Wise challenges the view that a gradually constricting blockade eventually choked off the export of cotton and the arrival of vital war matériel. Employing a mountain of statistics, Wise argues that blockade-running succeeded spectacularly. The task of sealing off the coastline was simply beyond the Union navy, and blockade-runners brought in a large fraction of the Confederacy's arms, lead, ingredients for powder, paper for cartridges, and cloth and leather for uniforms. Blockade-running would have been even more successful, he argues, if the government had incorporated it into its plan of supply from the beginning. Only in February 1864 did Richmond achieve partial control by banning the importation of luxuries and requiring that blockade-runners reserve half their cargo for government shipments.[57] Rather than emphasize the porousness of the blockade, the authors of *Why the South Lost the Civil War* argue that the roaring success of the Confederacy's industrial revolution largely negated whatever impact the blockade had. The Confederacy, they conclude, "did not lose the Civil War because of the blockade."[58]

But James McPherson has proposed another way to calculate the blockade's effectiveness. He admits that five out of six runners got through (declining from nine out of ten in 1861 to one out of two in 1865) and that they carried valuable cargoes of cotton abroad and shoes, rifles, gunpowder, and cannon back. But he asks, do these figures make for a "paper blockade"? Rather than seeking the answer in the number of ships that got through, McPherson suggests that we consider "how many ships carrying how much freight *would have* entered southern ports if there had been no blockade." Viewed from that perspective, the blockade "reduced the South's seaborne trade to less than a third of normal" at a time when "the Confederacy's needs for all kinds of supplies were much greater than the peacetime norm." The half-million bales of cotton shipped through the blockade during the last three years of war is dwarfed by the ten million bales exported in the three years before the war. Blockade-induced shortages had many consequences, he argues, including fueling ruinous inflation. Thus, McPherson concludes, the blockade "did play an important role in Union victory."[59]

Although scholars disagree about the impact of the blockade on the Confederate economy, no one doubts that economic welfare within the Confederacy declined with each year of the war. Disruption and destruction pushed hundreds of thousands of southerners, particularly white farm families whose men were in the army, into extreme privation. The traditional interpretation has emphasized the unresponsiveness of government and the cold disregard of the planter elite to the plight of the poor. It holds that Richmond officials stubbornly insisted that supply and demand would have to determine prices for scarce commodities and did little to halt speculation and inflation. Slaveholders selfishly calculated their private gain and demonstrated little sympathy for their poor neighbors.[60] But scholars have begun reevaluating what Paul Escott calls "the welfare problem" and have found government officials and private citizens more responsive than previously understood.

Recent studies of welfare measures in Georgia, Virginia, and North Carolina portray government officials and local planters making extraordinary efforts. In Georgia, Peter Wallenstein explains, Governor Joseph E. Brown recognized that because small farmers outnumbered planters it had to be a poor man's fight, but he was determined that fiscally it should also be a rich man's war. Georgia regulated crop production, raised taxes to fund an ambitious welfare program, and spent more on civilian needs than on the military. Rather than balk at their escalating tax bills, Wallenstein argues, planters recognized what was at stake and supported the "Robin Hood pattern of taking from the rich to give to the poor."[61] In Virginia, according to William A. Blair, planters responded generously to the needy, largely because they understood that feeding poor families would dampen discontent on the home front and keep men in the ranks.[62] In North Carolina, Paul Escott finds, county governments distributed $20 million, while the state government nearly spent itself into bankruptcy trying to alleviate suffering.[63] By 1863, seceding states had provided debtor relief, welfare programs, and economic regulations intended to increase production of scarce commodities. These massive efforts helped, but they were not enough. Swamped by the task, states demanded that Richmond join the relief effort.[64]

Contrary to traditional opinion, recent studies argue, the Davis government entered the relief business, compelled by the need to maintain loyalty. The April 1863 tax-in-kind legislation raised great quantities of food for the armies, but some of it went to county officials desperately trying to feed the poor. The exemption law of February 1864 required planters who stayed at home or sought an exemption for overseers to grow food for the needy. A large fraction of Virginia's population could buy food at below market prices. Still, the Confederate government failed to solve the problems of poverty and hunger, in large part because it held to its belief that its primary purpose was to feed soldiers, not civilians. Sometimes Confederate policies actually negated state efforts at poor relief. In Georgia, Confederate impressment stripped farmers of food and other necessities, effectively countering the "Robin Hood pattern that prevailed in state and local finance." Hungry farm families and urban mechanics pushed for Richmond to make food more available and affordable, but with limited success.[65]

In December 1864 Abraham Lincoln declared that the Union was "*gaining* strength, and may, if need be, maintain the contest indefinitely. . . . Material resources are now more complete and abundant than ever. . . . The national resources, then, are unexhausted, and, as we believe, inexhaustible."[66] Despite the Confederacy's considerable success in mobilizing its human and material resources and redirecting the antebellum economy, no one in Richmond made a similar claim. Indeed, the North's "hard war" policy had taken dead aim at the South's economic resources and war-making capability.[67] Richard Current was so taken with the disparity between the northern and southern economies that he concluded that "it would have taken a miracle. . . to enable the South to win."[68] More recently, others have denied that either initial economic weakness or eroding industrial capacity doomed Confederate armies. As a trump card for their argument, they assert: "No Confederate army lost a crucial battle or campaign because of a lack of ammunition, guns, or even shoes and food, scarce though these latter items became."[69] But there is no doubt that the South's economic troubles and the government's efforts to make the home front more Confederate profoundly affected life behind the lines. How developments on the home front in turn influenced Confederate fortunes is a question that in recent years has generated both scholarly heat and light.

While historians generally agree that slavery was the antebellum South's distinguishing social fact, they disagree about whether slavery promoted cohesion or division among the various classes of whites.[70] Secession, consequently, has been portrayed as both a common effort among white southerners to defend a valued society and as a coup by planters that hoodwinked yeomen into "a rich man's war and poor man's fight." Differences in interpretations of the antebellum South and secession naturally help shape understandings of the fate of the Confederacy. War meant disruption, destruction, and eventually defeat, but scholars disagree about whether the Confederacy came apart first on the home front—ripping along its weak antebellum seams—or succumbed on the battlefields, a victim of the North's unrelenting military power. On the eve of the war, the southern elite claimed that slavery united whites across class and gender lines and also bound whites and blacks, weaving masters and slaves into a sturdy tapestry of rights and obligations. However, war tested the loyalty of yeomen, made women reevaluate their commitments, and exposed the flimsy nature of planter paternalism and slave contentment.[71]

At the outset, the Confederacy's appeal to turn back the Yankee invaders and protect southern liberty stirred a majority of whites to defend the new flag. Confirmed unionists stood as the great exception. Carl N. Degler's *The Other South* situates southern unionism in the broad sweep of whites' struggle with conflicting identities and loyalties.[72] Degler observes that union sentiment sprang from diverse motivations and took a variety of forms. During the secession crisis, for example, a large fraction of white southerners, perhaps a majority, expressed antisecession unionism. Unionism of this stripe could be found throughout the South but was strongest in those areas where slavery was weakest. Daniel Crofts's *Reluctant Confederates* offers a valuable political analysis of antisecession unionism in the Upper South. Reluctant Confederates made strenuous efforts to beat back secession, he argues, but Abraham Lincoln's resort to military coercion to put down the rebellion stampeded most unionists into the Confederacy. While "conditional unionists" caved in, "consistent unionists," individuals who maintained their loyalty beyond secession, began a brutal four-year ordeal, a story that falls beyond the scope of Crofts's study.[73]

With rare exceptions, consistent unionism has been addressed as a category within the larger rubric of dissent and disaffection.[74] The trend began in 1934 with Georgia Lee Tatum's pathbreaking *Disloyalty in the Confederacy*, one of the first studies to take unionism seriously.[75] Later studies have also understood unionists primarily as part of the larger mass of dissenters that plagued the Confederate government. Paul Escott portrays unionism more as an outgrowth of antebellum class and political hostilities and of wartime suffering and discontent than a positive identification with the United States.[76] Like Escott, Marc Kruman has situated unionism within the broad spectrum of discontent with Confederate rule, especially Richmond's efforts at centralization, which some viewed as tyranny.[77] In *Lincoln's Loyalists,* Richard Current focuses on those white southerners who expressed their unionism by joining the invading army. More than 100,000 whites from seceding states fought for the Union; if black soldiers are added to that total, then some southern states supplied more federal troops than some northern states.[78]

When scholars have isolated unionism from the larger phenomenon of dissent within the Confederacy, they have usually worked on a small scale, concentrating on local studies of particular groups, families, or individuals. Studies range from Phillip Paludan's *Victims*, which examines the brutal recriminations experienced by unionists in western North Carolina, to William Auman's investigations of Quaker abolitionists in North Carolina, to Auman and David D. Scarboro's study of the militant, anti-Confederate secret organization known as the Heroes of America, to Richard McCaslin's chilling retelling of the great hanging of unionists in Gainesville, Texas, in 1862.[79] Local studies range beyond the *Official Records* and exploit the correspondence of neighborhood officials, newspapers, private manuscript collections, family histories, applications to the Southern Claims Commission, court records, and more, and they reveal in vivid detail the trouble unionists caused the Confederacy and the heavy price they themselves paid. The sources that reveal the day-to-day trials of unionists so dramatically, however, threaten to limit unionist history to the microcosm of a crime, a family, or a town and require that historians make special efforts to connect the local with the larger sweep of Confederate and Civil War history.

By 1863, certainly, discontent within the Confederacy had spread far beyond the ranks of die-hard unionists. The North had adopted the strategy of "hard war," and invading armies targeted the Confederate home front in an effort to destroy the rebels' social cohesion and will to fight. According to some accounts, the Yankees succeeded. These historians argue that as the costs of war mounted, old animosities flared and new ones erupted. The fissure along class lines grew particularly dangerous. The antebellum social structure had managed to absorb class tensions, but the pressures of a long war of attrition caused yeomen to kick over the traces and denounce the government in Richmond as little more than a vehicle for illegitimate planter power. Nonslaveholders condemned the government for intruding into their lives and making unequal demands on citizens. They pointed to conscription, impressment, taxes-in-kind, the suspension of habeas corpus, runaway inflation, and debilitating shortages. Poor people found the class bias in the 20-Negro law and in the provision in the conscription law that allowed for substitutes particularly galling. Closer to home, desperately needy families sometimes received nothing more from their wealthy neighbors than a cold shoulder. Planter selfishness, unjust legislation, and inequitable sacrifice, then, bred bitterness and resistance among the common people. Draft dodgers, deserters, and resisters of all kinds multiplied. Class hostility sometimes boiled over into violence. In Washington County, North Carolina, Wayne K. Durrill argues, neighbor attacked neighbor in a "property war" that pitted the landless against the landed. According to this general perspective, therefore, friction across class lines frayed the ties that bound whites together, and eventually class animosity undermined the Confederate war effort.[80]

While a heightened sense of class consciousness and increased social friction were apparent, they did not necessarily equal disloyalty or disaffection. The most subtle rejoinder to the argument that animosity among whites on the home front caused defeat is found in William A. Blair's recent dissertation on Virginia. The vast majority of common people, Blair argues, remained loyal to the Confederacy even when they grew dissatisfied with the government and their rich neighbors. Fighting Yankees on home ground, he found, spurred them to resist and provided concrete evidence that they were fighting for their liberty. Having the enemy so near also helped create a common identity. And rather than criticizing the Confederate government for intruding in their lives, common people often welcomed the intrusion. Intervention often came as a response to pleas from the home front for government to address specific local needs, such as economic relief, order, and equitable sacrifice. By providing more generously for the poor, instituting martial law, and conscripting free people of color into labor battalions, Richmond demonstrated its responsiveness to community wishes. By rescinding class-based exemptions from military service, it proved that it was trying to make the war more of a rich man's fight. Blair also found that planters showed more concern for the needs of the poor than is commonly portrayed. Not all of the efforts of government and the elite helped, but the gestures themselves eased the outrage poor people felt toward officials and the rich. As a result, Virginians viewed Union soldiers as the real enemy and gave everything they had to defeat the invaders.[81]

Had the Confederacy, then, been betrayed from within or overwhelmed from without? Had internal or external enemies proved more deadly? One perspective emphasizes internal strife along class lines as the key to Union victory. In William Freehling's view, planters pursued their ideology and social mastery beyond the limits of the South's fragile social structure. Nonslaveholders, as well as blacks and women, refused to play the roles assigned by those "overreaching men." When the South's social system failed to meet the challenge of war, the Confederacy suffered "internal collapse."[82] Another perspective insists that even in wartime centripetal social forces continued to overcome the centrifugal. While recognizing that war shook the white southern social order to its roots, Stephen Ash concludes that in most of the South "as an entity it remained intact."[83] Emory Thomas admits profound dislocation and disruption but denies that planters lost control. He finds pivotal the fact that the hundreds of thousands of whites who fought in rebel armies were of the same class as those who dissented. "The Confederate quest for home rule," he concludes, "never became a contest over who should rule at home."[84]

Of the many ties that bound people together in the Old South, religion—specifically evangelical Christianity—constituted one of the strongest. Religious faith and the church gave meaning and purpose to millions of lives. Christine Leigh Heyrman's elegant *Southern Cross* explains how Baptists and Methodists transformed themselves from outcasts to insiders by gradually accepting the conventional southern understandings of patriarchal authority, racial privilege, regional patriotism, and masculine honor.[85] As churches grew into vital cultural institutions, clergy wielded secular as well as sacred influence. Protestant ministers helped fashion powerful defenses of both slavery and the southern social order and by the 1850s claimed that their region was the nation's most virtuous, most Christian.[86] In *Masters of Small Worlds,* Stephanie McCurry deftly analyzes the critical role that evangelicalism played in yeomen's decision to join planters in embracing disunion and the Confederacy.[87] Ministers lent God's blessing to the new nation, promising that God would watch over the men and women who were doing his work. Confederate legislators echoed the sentiment when they selected "Deo Vindice"—"Defended by God"—as their country's motto.[88]

Given both the centrality of religion to Confederate identity and what John Boles in the mid-1980s called "the discovery of southern religious history," it is surprising that scholars have devoted so little attention to religion in the Confederacy. Thick bibliographies for the antebellum and postbellum eras dwarf the scholarship for the war years.[89] Still, several valuable works sketch the lineaments of Confederate religious developments. The recent flood of interest in women's wartime experiences has provided one avenue into the subject. For women confronting heartbreaking losses, religion assumed profound personal importance. Women's wartime organizations, such as sewing circles and aid societies, often operated within the confines of the church, as had prewar organizations. In addition, war made the institutional church more female than ever. Short of men, ministers, and money, and with travel difficult and dangerous, some churches were forced to shut their doors and others to curtail services. As a consequence, worship tended to move from church to home, where women took primary responsibility for prayer and Bible study. In contrast to churches' hard times on the home front, religious revivals swept the army, easing young soldiers into the distressing world of strangers, harsh discipline, rigid hierarchy, and death.[90]

Southern clergy had promised that God was on the Confederacy's side, and early victories on the battlefield seemed to confirm God's favor. But what were citizens to make of accumulating defeat? One answer was that they lacked proper faith and piety, and ministers and government officials prescribed days of fasting, prayer, and humiliation. Some clergy also wondered if defeat was not God's judgment on southern slavery, and they mounted a reform effort "to humanize the institution, and to bring it up to 'Bible standards.'"[91] Continuing slaughter, however, suggested that God did not wear gray. After first sustaining morale, the authors of *Why the South Lost the Civil War* argue, religion in time had the effect of undermining it, for if God were not on your side, why continue to fight?[92] But not all Confederates concluded that God was against them. While they found their abandonment distressing, ministers discovered theological explanation. They concluded that God was testing the new nation, Job-like, and out of suffering would come strength and redemption. Even defeat did not necessarily prove the lack of God's esteem, for some argued that northern might, not virtue, had won the war. A majority of white southerners, Charles Reagan Wilson explains, came in time to understand defeat as an exile in the wilderness, a fiery furnace, a "baptism in blood," that foretold moral victory.[93]

To understand fully how civilians experienced the Civil War, historians have turned increasingly to local studies.[94] In Edgefield, South Carolina, observes Orville Vernon Burton in one of the most thorough analyses of a southern community, individuals "interpreted the meaning of the conflict and reacted to its demands from the perspective of their own families, relatives, friends, and the local community."[95] In fact, everywhere on the home front, war was a local affair. Structured by similar racial, gender, and social hierarchies, antebellum southern communities brought together white and black, male and female, and rich and poor in complex webs of domination and subordination. A variety of factors muted conflict among whites—devotion to slavery, white supremacy, the sanctity of property, honor, republican values, Protestant Christianity, kinship ties—and in recent years scholars' favorite, patriarchy. As Stephanie McCurry and others have explained, households organized a majority of the population under a male head, either yeoman or planter. Similar domestic authority linked slaveholder and hardscrabble farmer not as social equals but as patriarchs who commanded the dependent members of their households. Shared patriarchal prerogatives helped knit white men together across the chasm of inequality and gave them another reason to defend the existing social order. While scholars disagree about the stability of such accommodations, it is clear that southern communities on the eve of the war enjoyed considerable coherence.[96]

One of the home front's earliest casualties was the family.[97] Families were torn apart when patriarchs marched off to fight. Secessionists had promised that independence would secure the southern household from abolitionist attack, but disunion destroyed domestic security and introduced radical change. Patriarchs intended to protect their families by leaving but instead endangered them. At first, LeeAnn Whites argues, war reinforced gender roles—men joined the army and women did not. But war quickly dissolved traditional boundaries between men's work and women's work, authority and subordination, and protector and protected. As society's rigid definitions of woman's place gave way, farm women plowed fields and plantation mistresses assumed awesome new responsibilities for managing slaves.[98] Drew Gilpin Faust, George Rable, and others argue that southern white women were unprepared for their new roles and resented their unprecedented burdens. They resisted the transformation and hugged prerogatives of race and class, as well the privileges of gender. But the real threat to a woman's patriotism lay in her recognition that the war was killing, not protecting, what was dearest to her. Because modern wars require broad civilian support and women deserted the ranks, Faust argues that women bore heavy responsibility for the war's outcome.[99]

When the war ended, women welcomed home their men, at least those who survived. With slaves free and refusing any longer to wear masks of servility, men were determined to restore proper authority within their households. But scholarship on the reconstruction of southern families remains scanty. George Rable argues that traditional notions about femininity survived and LeeAnn Whites that there was a general retreat to family life, but it remains unclear how much energy men had to expend reconstructing patriarchal authority or how eager women were to return to gender subordination.[100] In 1989 in a much discussed article, "Have Social Historians Lost the Civil War?," Maris Vinovskis argued that despite the prodigious outpouring of literature, scholars had neglected fundamental social history questions.[101] A good example is the demographic and social consequences of the war for the southern family. Approximately 260,000 white southern men of fighting age (17–45) died, and a larger number returned home permanently maimed and perhaps less likely to marry or, if already married, perhaps less likely to resume a traditional role within the family. Analysis of the impact of the war on southern family relationships and behavior, including marriage patterns, child rearing, economic responsibilities, and the distribution of power within the household remains in its infancy.[102] Peter Bardaglio perceptively analyzes changes in laws regulating domestic relations, especially the way the war undercut patriarchal power and curbed men's sexual authority.[103] Mary Margaret Johnston-Miller examines the search of elite white women for a substitute for slavery and how women's desires for obedient house servants clashed with their planter husbands' need for field labor.[104] But much work remains.

The disruption of family life on an unprecedented scale tore holes in the social fabric, but southern communities suffered other losses. The exodus of white men and the unrest of slaves conjured up the old nightmare of slave insurrections. White unity was founded on black slavery, but during the war that foundation crumbled.[105] Moreover, in areas where the fighting was most vicious, war smashed community by attacking the institutions through which rural culture made itself felt: churches, schools, courthouses, taverns, country stores, communal patterns of work, and more.[106] Poverty could also have enormous social impact. A number of local studies conclude that hardship and unequal sacrifice threatened to rip the Confederacy apart. To gentry, traditional principles of hierarchy seemed endangered, while to poor whites, planters had abandoned their paternal obligations and thus forfeited deference and respect.[107] In some areas community authority collapsed entirely, and citizens were quite literally at one another's throats.[108] "By the end of the war," J. William Harris concludes in his study of the hinterlands of Augusta, Georgia, "the bonds of community had so far dissolved that Confederate victory was impossible."[109] Rebels battled rebels within. Civil strife replaced civil life.

Yet other community studies tell a different story. Few communities "hosted more soldiers or witnessed more combat" than Culpepper County, Virginia, asserts Daniel E. Sutherland in *Seasons of War*. Culpepper also suffered the loss of its male population, increased banditry, surges of refugees, and confiscation of scarce food when blue- and gray-coated armies came and went. Uncertainty and hardship wore people down. They grew tired and depressed. But Culpepper maintained its equilibrium. Its white people did not split into hostile groups, much less warring factions.[110] War also challenged community in Orange County, North Carolina, the subject of Robert C. Kenzer's *Kinship and Neighborhood in a Southern Community*. At least 70 percent of the men left, the remaining relatives and neighbors could no longer take care of the needy, and the influx of refugeeing slaves raised the specter of rebellion. But dense networks of kinship among whites promoted stability and social cohesion and prevented class division.[111] In these communities class tensions never spilled over into social anarchy.[112]

Still, when the war ended, rural communities bore little resemblance to the prosperous and relatively harmonious places that whites remembered. Many communities bore the physical scars of the fighting, and almost all reflected the war's terrible wear and tear on human psyches and relationships. Nearly every community experienced catastrophic military casualties, a crisis of gender, and economic prostration. Most profoundly, southerners experienced the revolution of emancipation, which blacks and whites alike in 1865 recognized had shattered the keystone of the old social order. Masters had become landlords, and slaves, free laborers. Traditions of paternalism, deference, and personalism lay in the dust. The trajectory of white and black emotions headed in different directions, and neither whites nor blacks knew what the new world held for them.

Although nearly nine of every ten southerners lived in rural areas on the eve of the war, the South was not without towns and cities. Not every historian portrays the southern city as the tail of the plantation dog, but most place cities on the social and economic, as well as the geographic, periphery, where they served as ports and financial centers for the agricultural economy. A manufacturing center like Richmond was an anomaly. More diverse than the countryside, the urban South sheltered immigrants and native born, free blacks and slaves, and industrial workers, artisans, and professionals. During the war most urban populations grew rapidly as whites and blacks converged to work in war industries, hospitals, and supply depots, or refugee, or serve in the army. Traditional urban aggravations—robbery, prostitution, inadequate services, disease, assertive slaves—increased and affected all whites. New problems—prices that badly outpaced wages—punished working families and bred frustration and resentment.[113]

After years of neglect, historians have discovered Confederate cities. Although no one has yet attempted a synthesis of the urban Confederacy, historians have taken on individual towns and cities. Some authors situate their studies within the historiography of southern urban history and engage established questions, such as the impact of the Civil War on urban growth, on urban leadership, and on southern urban distinctiveness.[114] More configure their work as community studies. A blinkered focus does not necessary mean narrowness, however, for the best of these microhistories wrestle with the Confederacy's big issues. Chester G. Hearn's study of Harpers Ferry, Virginia, and Ernest B. Furgurson's examination of Richmond offer well-written narratives of resistance and disintegration.[115] Studies by Harriet Amos and by Arthur W. Bergeron, Jr., of Mobile, Alabama, by Michael Shirley of Winston-Salem, North Carolina, by Kenneth Coleman of Athens, Georgia, and by Mary DeCredico of four other Georgia towns and cities analyze economic transformation as well as social change.[116] Occupied cities often had very different experiences, as studies of New Orleans and Nashville make clear.[117] Urban black Confederates are also gaining attention. As portrayed in John Blassingame's study of New Orleans, Robert Francis Engs's Hampton, Virginia, Bernard E. Powers, Jr.'s Charleston, and Whittington B. Johnson's Savannah, blacks carved out greater independence for themselves and thereby added to the chaos of southern cities in wartime.[118]

One of the best new urban studies, Steven Elliott Tripp's *Yankee Town, Southern City*, examines all levels of society in Lynchburg, Virginia, just before, during, and just after the Civil War. Tripp advances our understanding along the broad front of race, class, and gender, but he achieves his greatest triumph in his portrait of Lynchburg's white artisans and semi-skilled workers. Investigating "life in the grogshop, at the military encampment, and on the street corner and the shop floor," he re-creates the white workingmen's culture and the complicated dynamic of their class and race relations. Although white workers could be viciously racist, they could not easily be deflected from their own class interests by race-baiting aristocrats. Although they hated conscription and elite privilege, white workers hated Yankees more and devoted themselves to the Confederate cause. Tripp's honest admission of ambiguity and countervailing impulses does not dull his argument; it sharpens its analytical edge.[119] Cities were hardly typical southern communities, but Lynchburg demonstrates that the inhabitants of city and countryside shared fundamental assumptions and faced the same fiery trial.

For four years, white southerners fought to establish an independent nation. Historians disagree about whether slavery had created a distinctiveness powerful enough to give rise to a separate southern culture and identity. Nearly a half century ago, Avery O. Craven concluded in his oddly named volume, *The Growth of Southern Nationalism, 1848–1861*, that southern nationalism did not exist.[120] More recently, John McCardell, although denying that southerners and northerners were separate people, finds that southerners believed that they constituted a separate nation.[121] Incipient or something more, southern nationalism required concerted attention to become a fully realized ideology. After secession, Confederate slaveholders "moved rapidly to shape this discussion in their own interest," Drew Gilpin Faust explains, "for nationhood was itself a creation of this interest." Offering republican, evangelical, and proslavery arguments, as well as nationalist doctrines, slaveholders sought to create a sense of transcendent national purpose that would produce the widest possible support for the war for southern independence.[122] The very effort, of course, spoke to planters' worries about the distance between the Confederate government and the southern people upon whom national independence depended.

Some historians find Confederate nationalism feeble and fraudulent and pin defeat squarely on its failure to attach the various segments of southern society to the new nation. If Confederates, particularly yeomen, had believed deeply enough in independence, they argue, they would have sacrificed and given their all. Instead, they lost the will to win and gave up. "Confederate morale . . . evaporated before any final fight to the death," William Freehling asserts.[123] Critics respond that this line of reasoning comes close to requiring as proof of nationalism victory in the war, or annihilation. As it was, half of the 900,000 Confederate soldiers were killed or wounded. How many men had to die to demonstrate commitment? Other historians link weak morale to deficiencies in the Confederacy's central value. Kenneth Stampp argues that southerners felt guilty about slavery and that defeat offered escape from slavery's "moral burden."[124] Clarence Mohr asserts that the moral crisis led first to the reform of slavery, then to "Confederate emancipation," the measure passed by the government in March 1865 to arm and presumably free some slaves.[125] Critics have found little evidence of guilt and almost no evidence outside of Richmond that civilians supported emancipation. While the government was willing to consider limited emancipation, most whites agreed with the *Charleston Mercury*'s January 1865 declaration that without slavery the South would become a *"most magnificent jungle."*[126]

If not internal division, doubt, and disloyalty on the home front, what explains the defeat of the Confederacy? When someone asked George Pickett who was responsible for the Confederate loss at Gettysburg, he replied: "I've always thought the Yankees had something to do with it."[127] Yankees in one's back yard had stimulated resistance and Confederate identity, but eventually the Union military juggernaut undermined resistance on the home front. Especially after the fall of 1864, news from the battlefields made it difficult not to conclude that the Yankees had beaten them. "The people of Culpepper [County, Virginia] gradually turned away from rebellion," Daniel Sutherland concludes, "not so much because they lost faith in their cause but because they became intimidated by the destructive power and demoralizing forces of war."[128]

But other populations have been pummeled and fought on, resorting to guerrilla war if necessary. In the Algerian war against France and the

Vietnamese war against France and the United States, militarily weaker people eventually triumphed. Some scholars suggest that southerners' rejection of guerrilla war in 1865 signaled a lack of devotion to slavery and the cause of southern independence.[129] To gain leverage on the southern decision in 1865, George Fredrickson analyzes the guerrilla campaign undertaken by the Boers in 1900 against the British in South Africa. He concludes that bushwhacking would have put the planter elite at risk. With their authority already weakened, southern planters resisted following a path that promised to undermine their status and power even more.[130] Planters probably understood, moreover, that a guerrilla campaign could not achieve what four years of conventional warfare had not—that is, the preservation of slavery. Guerrilla war promised instead racial conflagration and total social collapse.

In recent years, the Confederate home front has come into its own. Historians have taken up the challenge that Charles W. Ramsdell issued some six decades ago.[131] The home front that has emerged from modern scholarship is even more fractured, divided, and conflicted than Ramsdell's. Slaves and women, as well as yeomen and unionists, have found their voices. But we continue to wrestle with the old question: Did deterioration of the home front destroy the army's capacity to fight, or did defeat on the battle front undermine and eventually destroy the people's willingness to continue? We are uncomfortable with the dichotomy, for we know that the answer is both, but we nevertheless feel compelled to stake out positions in one camp or the other. And recently home-front interpretations seem to have gained the high ground in the historical debate. Complex analyses of the deficiencies a slave economy and society at war have rightfully gained adherents.

But in a curious way, recent literature sometimes still concludes on a note that Ramsdell himself struck in the final remarks in his Fleming lectures. He did not want to end "croaking the word 'failure,'" and instead paid tribute to the legions of "ragged, hungry men who fought on after they knew their cause was hopeless" and to those women who "endured privations and subdued their fears while they struggled against every sort of adversity to provide for their children and other dependents while their men were at the front."[132] Shorn of Ramsdell's sentimentality and despite the mountains of evidence of discontent and friction within the Confederacy, modern scholars can also stand in awe of the stubborn endurance of Confederates. George Rable is representative when he reflects on the war: "Indeed, what remains most remarkable about the Confederacy was not its internal weaknesses—political, social, or economic—but its staying power and especially the ability of so many men and women to endure and make sacrifices."[133] We still do not fully understand that astounding stubbornness, that commitment to a nation that was in the beginning so distant and abstract. But no one should be accused of celebrating the Lost Cause because he or she recognizes that white southerners—and because of them, many others—paid a horrendous price attempting to establish an independent republic. We are still calculating the costs and consequences, especially on the home front.

# "Ours as Well as That of the Men"

## Women and Gender in the Civil War

### DREW GILPIN FAUST

Efforts to record women's Civil War experiences preceded the emergence of women's history as an academic field by more than a century. From the outbreak of conflict itself, northerners and southerners alike struggled to define the place of women in a war that proved as central to personal as to national definition and identity. As Confederate nurse Kate Cumming insisted, the war was "certainly ours as well as that of the men."[1]

The appearance of celebratory accounts of women's wartime contributions even before the silencing of the guns at Appomattox suggests that these early paeans were as much prescriptive as descriptive; they were rhetorical weapons in an ongoing war. Manpower shortages in the Confederacy may have rendered the South even more desperate than the North to mobilize female energies and thus even more effusive in its public flattery. Southern state legislatures passed resolutions of appreciation; Henry Timrod, the Confederate poet laureate, wrote tellingly of "Two Armies," one "facing battle, blight and blast,"

The other with a narrower scope,
Yet led by not less grand a hope,
Hath won, perhaps, as proud a place,
And wears its fame with meeker grace.
Wives march beneath its glittering sign,
Fond mothers swell the lovely line,
And many a sweetheart hides her blush
In the young patriot's generous flush.[2]

In the North, L. P. Brockett and Mary C. Vaughan had begun by 1863 the volume that would appear four years later as the revealingly titled *Women's Work in the Civil War: A Record of Heroism, Patriotism and Patience*. In the introduction to her own recent study of northern women, historian Elizabeth Leonard has argued persuasively for the tendentious nature of this volume—and of most treatments of women published during the first postwar decades. After the end of the conflict, she contends, the purposes of chronicling women's achievements changed— from encouraging departures from traditional female behavior to reversing the changes in gender roles the war had inaugurated. Brockett and Vaughan seemed well aware of the larger political context in which they wrote, explaining that their discussion of women's part in war bore significant implications for "a sex whose rights, duties and capacities are now under serious discussion." But their conclusions, Leonard finds, were essentially reactionary, for these writers struggled to contain woman's wartime activities within the traditional framework of her nurturing role.[3]

Focusing on benevolent women at work in hospitals, relief organizations, freedmen's schools, and soldiers' homes, Brockett and Vaughan dismissed women who dressed as men in order to join the ranks as not really women at all. Postwar authors such as Brockett and Vaughan, or Frank Moore, who published *Women of the War: Their Heroism and Self-Sacrifice* in 1866, were, Leonard asserts, working "furiously to construct an image . . . that would encourage women's silent retreat to their homes."[4]

But at least some late-nineteenth-century chroniclers told a rather different story. In their two-volume *History of Woman Suffrage,* published in 1882, Elizabeth Cady Stanton, Susan B. Anthony, and Matilda J. Gage hailed the war as transformative. "The social and political condition of women was largely changed by our civil war,"—in considerable measure, they explained, because war "created a revolution in woman herself."[5]

Appomattox was not yet two decades past and already a growing literature on women and the war flowed from the pens of participants and observers. Women's wartime diaries, their postwar memoirs, compilations of their reminiscences and writings echoed Kate Cumming's wartime demand for recognition of women's centrality to the war experience. These volumes presaged questions that would remain crucial to future generations of writers on women and the war; the framework of the early debate would persist into our own time. How important were women's contributions to the war effort in both North and South? How significantly, in turn, did war affect women and their perceptions of themselves? How, in short, did women change the war and how did the war change women?[6]

Women's contributions, writers of the early-twentieth century seemed to agree, were invaluable; their sacrifices extraordinary; their achievements inspirational. Titles of volumes on Confederate women continued to hail their "heroism" and their "ultimate triumph over adversity." One of the first efforts based in the kind of systematic research associated with modern historical scholarship, Francis Butler Simkins and James Welch Patton's *Women of the Confederacy* (1936) continued this celebratory—and essentially patronizing—legacy in a study that focused on the lives of the South's privileged white women. The chapters in Simkins and Patton's book represented the categories of investigation that had become fundamental to studies of women and the war. Their approach documented women's wartime contributions and honored women's sacrifices by describing their participation in voluntary organizations and in new kinds of work such as teaching, nursing, and government employment and recounting their tribulations with shortages of clothing and food and their sufferings as refugees.[7]

Despite the persistence of these categories of analysis, however, a new interpretive emphasis emerged by midcentury as women's history began to serve as a vehicle for a growing awareness of women's rights and women's progress. Scholars increasingly shifted their focus from what women did for the war to what the war did for women. In the tradition of Stanton, Anthony, and Gage, such female writers as Agatha Young in *The Women and The Crisis: Women of the North in the Civil War* (1959) and Mary Elizabeth Massey in *Bonnet Brigades: American Women and the Civil War* (1966) not only described women's war efforts but also argued that the years between 1861 and 1865 constituted a period of significant change. In a study that encompassed North and South, Massey concluded that the Civil War compelled women to become more active, self-reliant and resourceful, and this ultimately contributed to their "economic, social, and intellectual advancement." Agatha Young's investigation of northern women similarly emphasized the emancipatory force of the war for women, but she saw women already eager in the 1850s to move into the "new and larger world" war would open for them. "There were . . . revolutionary results of the Civil War," Young concluded, "less conspicuous than the freeing of the slaves, and one of the more important was the greater freedom of women."[8]

Stressing a new war-born "opportunity to work" as the most substantial component of this newly achieved freedom, Young revealed the most profound limitation of her study, as well as that of almost every general treatment of women and the war into the 1970s and even beyond. The category *woman* in the hands of these writers actually, though implicitly, designated white middle- and upper-class females. Agatha Young mentioned Harriet Tubman and Sojourner Truth in passing, but no other author sought even to address black women's lives in North or South. And Young's remarks about the liberatory power of work indicated her entire neglect of white women from classes that regarded women's agricultural or industrial labor as essential to survival, as long-endured necessity rather than war-born opportunity. Perhaps the most significant shift in the historiography of women and the Civil War in recent years has been its dedication to complicating the category *woman,* to recognizing the significance of differences of class, race, region, and even age in shaping women's experience of war.[9]

Anne Scott's enormously influential study, *The Southern Lady: From Pedestal to Politics* (1970), marked an initial step in this transition. Scott's book, like so many of those that came before it, was celebratory. But her work was less concerned with women's contributions to the war effort than with what the war did for women. In Scott's hands, the war became a watershed that "speeded social change" and led southern women directly to the political activism of the Progressive era. The war served as a vehicle to carry the southern lady from pedestal to politics. At the moment of its publication in 1970, the links between Scott's work and the emerging feminist movement were clear. Yet in embracing the war as a foundation for modern feminism, Scott was essentially just taking one step further along a path Massey, Young, and others had forged. The most striking innovation in Scott's work lay elsewhere: she made the limitations of her study explicit; her book dealt with the "lady," with the female members of a white elite. In specifically identifying the segment of the southern population her study encompassed, she opened the possibility that other southern women might have experienced the war differently.[10]

Five years after Scott's work appeared, Bell Irvin Wiley published *Confederate Women.* Three initial chapters explored the lives of members of the southern elite, Mary Chesnut, Virginia Tunstall Clay, and Varina Howell Davis, but an intriguing fourth chapter drew on Wiley's lifetime of research on the plain people of the South to introduce the issue of class into a broader consideration of women's wartime experiences. Although Wiley, who had earlier published on African Americans in the war as well, acknowledged a need for work on black women, he cited a "scarcity of pertinent records" as limiting his ability to do more than offer evidence of their "yearning for freedom." But his treatment of poor white women opened an important subject that has only recently begun to receive sustained attention. "Failure of the Confederacy to alleviate the suffering of soldiers' families," Wiley suggested, "may have contributed more to Southern defeat than any other single factor." Wiley's emphasis upon the suffering and discontent of the women of the South's lower orders and upon the social unrest it produced is echoed in Victoria Bynum's 1987 article "'War within a War': Women's Participation in the Revolt of the North Carolina Piedmont," as well as in her 1992 book *Unruly Women: The Politics of Social and Sexual Control in the Old South*. The female bread riots that broke out in towns and cities across the South in 1863 have become a particular focus for explorations of yeomen women's discontent and subversion. But the Civil War experience of lower-class white women of either region still remains largely unstudied, and Wiley's 1975 invitation to further research still only partially answered.[11]

In fact, the Civil War, seemingly the era of statesmen and generals, received little attention of any sort from women's historians of North or South during the late 1970s and early 1980s. Yet at the same time, the war-born process of emancipation was bringing new social historical perspectives to bear that would eventually generate not only a revolution in Civil War historiography but a new interest in the war experiences of black women as well. In 1985 Jacqueline Jones published *Labor of Love, Labor of Sorrow: Black Women, Work and the Family from Slavery to the Present*, a survey of black women's history that devoted a chapter to the lives of freedwomen in the Civil War and Reconstruction. Jones described an experience that differed markedly from that either of white women or black men. "To provide for the safety of those dependent on her while she tested the limits of a newfound freedom," Jones wrote, "formed the core of a slave-becoming-freedwoman's dilemma."[12]

The new perspective Jones offered was made possible in considerable part by the ongoing work of the Freedom and Southern Society project. Housed at the University of Maryland under the direction of Ira Berlin, this effort aimed to provide a documentary history of emancipation by publishing a significant proportion of the rich material housed in the Freedman's Bureau Papers and other collections in the National Archives. Although no volume in the series is explicitly devoted to women, all are filled with invaluable evidence of their wartime experiences.[13]

Yet in the more than a decade since Jones published, few scholars have devoted attention to black women and the war. Catherine Clinton's *Tara Revisited: Women and the Plantation Legend* is intended to explore the lives of black and white plantation women, but Clinton concludes that it is "exceptionally difficult for us to know the concrete details of black women's roles during the war." Unpublished work by Noralee Frankel and Nancy Bercaw on Mississippi, Leslie Schwalm and Marli

Frances Weiner on South Carolina, and Tera Hunter on Atlanta, Georgia represents a significant commitment to this effort, and recent writing by Thavolia Glymph, who served as a co-editor on the University of Maryland project, promises rich yields suggested by her brief essay "This Species of Property: Female Slave Contrabandists in the Civil War." "Although contraband women have not been entirely ignored within the scholarship on the Civil War," she notes, "they have nevertheless too often seemed like passive participants." Glymph is committed to transforming this representation, insisting that even though they could not don Union uniforms, black women "fought for freedom no less than their black male counterparts." The particulars of that story, however, remain largely unexplored, an important opportunity awaiting further scholarly consideration.[14]

Increasing attentiveness to the presence and significance of African American women has contributed to revisions in one of the elements central to traditional historiography of women and the war. For more than a century, portraits of Civil War nursing celebrated white women's sacrifice and achievement and often embraced their efforts as dramatic and lasting new departures in female lives. However, recent studies by Jane Schultz and Clarence Mohr, as well as a chapter on women's work in my 1996 book *Mothers of Invention: Women of the Slaveholding South in the American Civil War,* have suggested that attention to matters of class and race in Civil War hospitals reveals a somewhat different picture. An overwhelming percentage of the women who cared for patients on the wards were regarded as menial laborers of low class—or caste. But these slaves, freedpeople, and common whites did not win the attention and accolades of contemporary observers nor of later historians chronicling women's hospital work. The emphasis of almost all historical treatments of Civil War nursing has been—and remains—upon the middle- and upper-class white women who were more likely to act in the capacity of matrons or ward managers than as actual caretakers. Jane Schultz is currently in the midst of a study that will for the first time make full use of the extensive records on Union nursing in the National Archives, enabling her to offer statistically accurate data about who nurses were and the kinds of work they performed. While comparable data is not available for Confederate nursing, scattered surviving hospital records may make parallel understanding possible. Clarence Mohr's use of such materials in his study of Georgia were pathbreaking in their revelation that the great preponderance of hospital workers were not the much lauded Confederate women but in fact African American slaves.[15]

Scholars have differed about the transformative nature of women's hospital work. Certainly it seems that northern nurses were more likely to use their wartime experiences as a foundation for a new sense of self and vocation, and in the North, the war provided a catalyst for women's advancement into both professional nursing and medicine. In the South, a higher percentage of women were erstwhile volunteers or visitors, rather than long-term, salaried hospital workers, and their labors were more likely to prove a temporary extension of the domain of nurturant domesticity than a lasting transgression of conventional gender boundaries. The lives of Clara Barton and Dorothea Dix exemplify this northern pattern, one which leads Elizabeth Leonard to conclude that northern nurses "trespassed en masse into the 'public sphere'" and became "wielders of a kind of institutional power previously hoarded by men."[16]

Despite these underlying contrasts, many females working in both northern and southern hospitals found themselves inevitably engaged in conflict with male physicians and officials about women's appropriate responsibilities. These "gender wars" cannot but have exerted a profound influence on women's recognition of themselves as females facing common challenges, however their responses to this new awareness may have differed, North and South.

The contrasts between women's lives in prewar northern and southern societies were reflected in women's wartime experiences and, logically, have been evident in differing emphases of historical inquiry in the two regions. Much of the most important early work done in the field of women's history as it began to emerge in the 1970s explored northern women's reform and philanthropic efforts. White southern women were engaged in less extensive, more limited sorts of benevolence, eschewing abolition and other of the more radical "isms" which absorbed much of northern reform, although recent studies have begun to consider white southern women's interest and engagement in politics. The historical literature on northern women and the Civil War, by contrast, directs considerable attention to women's political activism and to wartime extensions or embodiments of the much studied antebellum reform impulse. Like the historiography out of which they grew, these works regard reform as a critical site for the emergence of feminist consciousness. Wendy Hammond Venet's *Neither Ballots nor Bullets: Women Abolitionists and the Civil War* (1991) describes northern women's wartime political activism operating on a variety of fronts and for a variety of goals: abolition, first and foremost, but also such ends as Lincoln's reelection, female suffrage, equal pay for women nurses. Venet embraces these women's experiences as transformative and liberatory. "The petitioning, public speaking and political organizing that Northern women performed during the war," she concludes, "helped to gain new acceptance for women in the public sphere after the war." Lori Ginzberg, however, has her doubts about the extent to which Civil War activism ultimately empowered northern women. Her study of northern wartime benevolence invokes the image of gender wars to describe male and female reformers' conflicting styles, but finds that the legacy of the Sanitary Commission's success was not an advance in female power and opportunity but an "elitist repudiation of an older style of female benevolence." Efficiency replaced the traditional values of sacrifice and the power of "virtuous femininity," enshrining a new class-based philanthropy of order and control.[17]

Like Ginzberg, Jeanie Attie places women's wartime charitable work within a larger context of emerging capitalism and identifies an essential conservatism at the heart of female benevolent efforts. In an essay based in extensive research on the U.S. Sanitary Commission, Attie argues that the ideology surrounding women's wartime work "provided a place for women in public life while at the same time safeguarding the gender hierarchy of northern society." But Attie discovers as well numbers of female activists who challenged this conceptualization of their efforts by moving beyond legitimations based in ideas of "women's natural moral superiority" to embrace new social theories based in assumptions of equality of the sexes.[18]

An emphasis on the mixed legacy of the Civil War experience for transformation or improvement in women's position has emerged as a central theme in recent historical writing. Elizabeth Leonard's study of the lives of three prominent northerners, nurse Sophronia Bucklin, soldiers' relief worker Annie Wittenmyer, and physician Mary Walker, in her *Yankee Women: Gender Battles in the Civil War* (1994), shares the half empty/half full perspective of Ginzberg and Attie. Leonard concludes that the "gender system in the end demonstrated remarkable rigidity at its core." War expanded, she argues, but did not eliminate gender limits.[19]

Recent studies of white southern women reach similar conclusions, all but abandoning the triumphal tone of much earlier historiography. Two treatments of southern women published in the mid-1980s treated the Civil War only in passing, but both concluded that it was marked more by continuity than change. Suzanne Lebsock's *Free Women of Petersburg: Status and Culture in a Southern Town, 1784–1860* suggested that the war and its aftermath largely confirmed women's subordination, in no small measure because of the economic and racial pressures it generated. Jean Friedman's consideration of southern women and evangelical community concluded that women continued to focus their lives on religion and domesticity and did not for the most part move into a more public sphere. For the South, this emphasis on the persistence of tradition seems especially fitting. George Rable's *Civil Wars: Women and the Crisis of Southern Nationalism* (1989) uses extensive manuscript research to conclude that by the end of the war, Confederate women had become "Janus-faced," looking both forward and backward amid "Change without change." Postwar reaction brought an era of diminishing expectations for all southerners, reversing or limiting the impact of shifts in women's behavior that war had inaugurated.[20]

Although Rable's study addresses the experience of all white southern women, he acknowledges that the nature of his sources inevitably introduces something of an "elite bias." In *Mothers of Invention* I endeavored to confront that bias head-on in a study explicitly focused on white women of the South's slaveholding families. When white men left for war, women took on unaccustomed and unwanted responsibilities for managing slaves and households across the South. Their struggles with these new roles, I suggest, may have weakened the home front and certainly contributed to the disintegration of slavery. Exploring how white women's privileges of class and race affected their response to the conflict, I find them by war's end eager to reverse the changes that had undermined their power and status in southern society. By 1865 white women were unable any longer to believe in the competence and reliability of their defeated men and thus unwilling to trust the paternalist contract that had supposedly ensured both their subordination and their protection. After Appomattox dependence seemed dangerous, yet the burdens of independence appeared frightening. *Mothers of Invention* shows how gender identity emerged as negotiable for privileged southern women of the Civil War era.[21]

Although I approach my subject through the analytical perspective of gender, I focus my study on women's lives and self-perceptions. Other recent efforts more fully embrace the history of gender by including men. This approach was heralded by a collection of essays edited by Catherine Clinton and Nina Silber in 1992, *Divided Houses: Gender and the Civil War*. A number of the contributions to the volume were precursors for books that have since appeared. Dealing with both men and women, North and South, with the war and with Reconstruction, *Divided Houses* offered a valuable representation of the shape of things to come. Reid Mitchell's essay on "Soldiering, Manhood, and Coming of Age," for example, introduced the focus on the meaning of wartime masculinity that would serve as the central theme of his 1993 book *The Vacant Chair: The Northern Soldier Leaves Home,* an exploration of how ideologies of gender molded the Union soldier's experience. The masculine world of the military, Mitchell argues, was grounded in a "feminine, domestic sphere." The home was critical to the soldier's motivation to fight and to his understanding of himself; just before the battle he thought not of politics or of God or of death, but of mother. Gender in Mitchell's rendering becomes indispensable to explaining the battlefront, as well as life behind the lines.[22]

LeeAnn Whites entirely recasts the essence of the Civil War, redefining it as a "crisis in gender." Her 1995 study of Augusta, Georgia, between 1860 and 1890 is, she explains, "a consideration of the ways in which white manhood and womanhood . . . were transformed in the context of war and its aftermath." Whites sees gender issues playing a critical role in the outbreak, course, conduct, and outcome of the conflict. The Confederacy was dedicated, she believes, to a notion of manhood as founded in "largely autonomous and self directing household heads." Yet the experience of war brought almost immediate challenges to this very definition of its purposes. White women found themselves moving into more public roles at the same time that black men's struggle to achieve masculinity further destabilized the secure foundations of white male identity. This wartime disruption of class, race and gender identities compelled a postwar "reconstruction" of southern white manhood, with the critical contributions of women to this rehabilitation ensuring them a newly empowered place within postbellum southern society's gender system. But at the same time, "Confederate men looked to the domestic arena as the one remaining location of legitimate domination" and thus valued their mastery over the women of their households all the more emphatically. Ultimately, Whites concludes, "southern white manliness did indeed have the victory."[23]

The centrality of gender to the postwar period lies at the heart of Nina Silber's study of the ideologies of reunion. Her exploration of how northerners interpreted their triumph argues that the language of gender was central to explaining the meaning of the war. Her book *The Romance of Reunion* thus underlines and enhances the significance of works addressing these issues within the context of the war years themselves.[24]

Approaching the experience of women through the lens of gender emphasizes the constructedness of identity. Such a perspective has given renewed importance to the study of women as writers, as inventors of stories and creators of narratives in which they imagine and fashion a self. Writing was one arena in which a respectable mid-nineteenth-century woman might aspire to distinguish herself, and the very process of authorship itself nurtured growing female self consciousness. Scholars have in recent years turned a fresh eye on well-known writers such as Harriet Beecher Stowe, Louisa May Alcott, Lydia Maria Child, and Augusta Jane Evans, situating them more firmly in their cultural and historical context. But scholars have also begun to use tools of literary analysis on diaries and letters of less prominent Civil War women, investigating the cultural work their writing was intended to accomplish, exploring the intersections of reading, writing, and changing female identity.[25]

A growing recognition of the centrality of gender to the Civil War has led even historians distant from the field of women's history to look more closely at the negotiability of identity and at the significant sites of male-female interaction during the war years. The expansion of interest in the social history of the war that has paralleled and encouraged the burgeoning of women's Civil War history has yielded a number of community studies, chiefly southern in focus, that necessarily devote considerable attention to women's actions and interactions. Contemporary directions in women's and gender history have also resulted in serious attention to an aspect of women's wartime experience that heretofore has been ignored or marginalized. Union nurse Mary Livermore estimated that at least 400 northern and southern women disguised themselves as men in order to serve in the military.[26] Even though such action was far from commonplace or representative, it has attracted growing scholarly interest because it exemplifies the notion of gender negotiability, of the wartime breakdown in fixed gender categories. The recent publication of letters of a northern female soldier named Sarah Rosetta Wakeman is likely to be but the first of many efforts more fully to explore the meaning of this admittedly atypical choice, as perhaps one end of a spectrum of options for changed identity opened to women by the war. Female soldiers now appear to historians not so much a curiosity as an interpretive opportunity.[27]

Questions about gender roles and identities merge naturally with another new focus of current interest: that of sex and sexuality. Martha Hodes's essay, "Wartime Dialogues of Illicit Sex: White Women and Black Men," suggests that considerable sexual activity took place between white women left behind on plantations and their male slaves and indicates that women were often the initiators of these encounters. The absence of white men would seem logically to have encouraged sexual contacts between women on the southern home front as well, but few scholars have yet explored this question. Thomas Lowry's recent popular history of sex and the Civil War raises important questions about rape and prostitution, issues that invite further systematic study in Union military records. The conclusion that the Civil War was a comparatively "low-rape war" is

likely to stand, but this general characterization has led scholars to neglect the sexual victimization of African American women by both Union
and Confederate soldiers. The apparently low incidence of sexual assaults
reported against white women may be in some sense a result of the numbers of unreported and unprosecuted rapes of blacks. The study of sex
and sexuality in the Civil War seems likely to be an important focus of
future research.[28]

Scholarly work on women and gender in the Civil War has in the last
decade complicated not only our understanding of the war but also of
women themselves. Battlefront, home front, and the process of emancipation have all become gendered. At the same time, we are much
more aware of the diversities within the category *women,* of females
whose Civil War experiences differed in accordance with differences
of race and class and age and region. Curiously, a recent outpouring
of work on southern women has created something of a regional imbalance, with, for perhaps the first time since the field of women's
history was born, the study of northern women comparatively neglected. Because southern women lived in invaded territory, in a society
pressed to its limits by the demands of military and economic mobilization, the impact of war on them was far more all-encompassing
than upon the women of the North. The Civil War was central to the
experience of black and white women of the South in a way it was not
for many northern women. One result of this discrepancy is that it is
harder to frame a historical study of northern women, harder to devise an analytical approach that disentangles the effects of a distant
war from all the other forces operating in northern society during these
years. In the South, even for women removed from the front lines, high
conscription levels, the impact of the blockade, economic hardships, and
the disintegration of slavery all meant that war *was* what was happening.
This regional contrast has made the southern woman's war story both a
more compelling one and, in many ways, an easier one to approach, define and tell.[29]

Nearly a century has failed to resolve debate about the war's impact on women, but the centrality of this question to the concerns of
contemporary feminism suggest that it is unlikely to be abandoned as
a framework for viewing women's experiences between 1861 and 1865.
Nevertheless, most recent historical work paints a far more nuanced
picture that balances change and continuity and characterizes white
Civil War women as achieving at best mixed success in their progress
toward the emancipatory goals of today's woman's movement. Black
women demonstrated less ambivalence about changes in roles and status,

but despite the end of slavery, their progress toward full equality was of course inhibited by the reaction that followed Reconstruction. The Civil War women of today's historical literature are not the uncomplicated heroines of an older historiography, but in their diversity, their ambivalence, their uncertainty, their confusion about their goals and identities, they are arguably a great deal more interesting. Yet we remain only at the beginning of an explosion of scholarship that promises at last to achieve what Kate Cumming called for more than a century ago: to make the war "ours as well as that of the men."[30]

# SLAVERY AND FREEDOM IN THE CIVIL WAR SOUTH

## PETER KOLCHIN

### I

During the first half of the twentieth century, few historians of the Civil War paid much attention to slavery or black Americans. Writing in an era of pervasive racist assumptions among white Americans, "revisionist" scholars such as Charles W. Ramsdell, Avery O. Craven, and James G. Randall rebutted the notion that there were fundamental differences between the slave South and the free North and portrayed the conflict as a "needless war" brought on by a "blundering generation."[1] Adherents of Charles and Mary Beard's thesis that the war was a "Second American Revolution," in which the masters of capital wrested control of the country from planter aristocrats, played down the significance of disagreements over the status of African-Americans and insisted that professed concern for equal rights was a smoke screen designed to promote—and obscure—the *real* goal of Republican politicians: advancing the economic interests of northeastern capital.[2] There were exceptions, of course, especially among a tiny number of black and Marxist scholars,[3] but before World War II they had little impact on the mainstream of historical scholarship. Whether regarding the Civil War as a tragic and unnecessary conflict between Americans with few substantive differences or as an unavoidable showdown between divergent economies or civilizations, historians of the war typically gave short shrift to the thralldom of four million African Americans.[4]

One can hardly say the same about Civil War scholars during the second half of the twentieth century. The needless-war interpretation, which had seemed almost self-evident to many in the wake of postwar disillusionment with World War I, quickly lost its appeal following America's very different experience in World War II.[5] The narrow economic interpretation of Republican policy as driven by the selfish goals of northeast-ern business interests disintegrated as scholars demonstrated that both businessmen and Republicans were sharply divided among themselves on the leading issues of the day and that the most Radical policies found little support among business spokesmen.[6] In an era of renewed interest in civil rights, the notion that some Civil War–era northerners really cared about the fate of black southerners no longer seemed so ludicrous. Rather than looking for hidden motives, historians were now more willing to take seriously the professed goals of Civil War participants, goals that preemi-nently included both preserving and overthrowing slavery.[7]

In short, unlike most of their predecessors, recent historians have usu-ally agreed that slavery and the fate of black Americans lay at the heart of the struggle between North and South. This essay is designed to explore the ways they have dealt with this subject. Although I will make occa-sional references to earlier interpretations, my focus will be on scholarship that has appeared since the 1960s. In part because of limitations of space, I will confine my attention primarily to the South during the Civil War years, and will have little to say about Civil War causation, postwar Re-construction policies, or free blacks in the North; broadly conceived, a consideration of the coming and consequences of the war would encom-pass most of nineteenth-century American history (and more), a scope well beyond the confines of this essay. My goal is not to mention all (or even most) relevant historical works—there have been far too many to include in any but the most cursory manner—but to raise a number of interrelated historical issues and consider how historians have approached these issues. As is usually the case, the most interesting issues continue to provoke sharp historiographical debate.

II

The most salient feature of recent studies of slavery and African Americans during the Civil War is their emphasis on black agency. Like historians of antebellum slavery and Reconstruction, Civil War historians have increasingly seen blacks not as passive objects of white action but as subjects helping to make their own history. In doing so, these historians have also cast in a new light the entire history of the United States in the Civil War era.

Brief examination of an early study, Bell Irvin Wiley's *Southern Ne-groes, 1861–1865* (1938), serves to highlight many of the subsequent themes. "The first professional historian to wade into this difficult field," Wiley authored a transitional book, one whose very existence testified to recognition of the need to challenge established myths but whose interpretation was in many ways quite traditional. Showing strong interest in whether slaves behaved themselves, he laced his study with terms such as "good conduct" and "misconduct" and concluded that "the work of Negroes during the early years of the free-labor regime was most unsatisfactory." Noting the disruption of traditional agricultural relations in areas of Yankee presence, he argued that "except in invaded regions, and in areas near the Federal lines, the war seems not to have wrought any great changes in the life to which the slave was accustomed." In short, although outside agitators riled blacks up, "unfaithfulness and disorder" were "rare in the interior."[8]

In an era of renewed interest in civil rights and black power, such an approach quickly lost its appeal and came to seem a dated relic of the distant past. Two books published during the 1950s decisively rebuffed the notion that most slaves were passive spectators of the war and set the tone for future scholarship. In a lively, anecdotal survey, *The Negro in the Civil War*, Benjamin Quarles told of the "grapevine" that kept slaves informed of wartime developments, of mass migrations of slaves to Union positions, of slaves who acted as spies for the Yankees, and of those who worked for and served in the Union military. "The Negro's tale was not merely a passive one; he did not tarry in the wings, hands folded," Quarles insisted. ". . . To him, freedom was a two-way street; indeed, he gave prior to receiving."[9] Dudley Taylor Cornish made much the same argument in *The Sable Arm*, a thorough, scholarly account of blacks in the Union army. Noting the courage required of black soldiers, who had to contend not only with threat of execution if captured by southerners but also with daily discrimination at the hands of northerners, Cornish stressed that in contributing to Union victory, "the American Negro proved his manhood and established a strong claim to equality of treatment and opportunity."[10] Many of the themes set forth by Quarles and Cornish received cogent enunciation in James M. McPherson's 1965 documentary collection *The Negro's Civil War*, which significantly bore the subtitle *How American Negroes Felt and Acted during the War for the Union*. "The Negro was not merely a passive recipient of the benefits conferred upon him by the war," McPherson explained in his foreword. "Negro orators and writers provided leadership in the struggle for emancipation and equal rights. Colored people were active in the movements to bring education, suffrage, and land to southern freedmen. And perhaps most important of all, the contribution of Negro soldiers helped the North win the war and convinced many Northern people that the Negro deserved to be treated as a man and an equal."[11]

During the next thirty years, this central theme of black assertion received extensive elaboration. In rebutting the notion of black passivity, a few scholars focused on black actions on behalf of the Confederacy, especially in Virginia. In a carefully researched study entitled *The Confederate Negro,* James Brewer argued that blacks "contributed a sustaining effort to the War for Southern Independence," although he refrained from exploring what circumstances might have led slaves to work on behalf of a slaveholders' rebellion. Ervin L. Jordan, Jr., pushed this argument even further in his highly idiosyncratic book *Black Confederates and Afro-Yankees in Civil War Virginia.* Maintaining that "Black Confederate loyalty was more widespread than American history has acknowledged," he concluded that "Afro-Virginians of the Civil War era are shining examples for present and future generations. They were heroic in every sense of the word as warriors, musicians, farmers, craftsmen, revolutionaries, and survivors."[12]

Far more extensive, however, has been work detailing the ways in which—and the extent to which—southern blacks helped the Union war effort and thereby helped win their own freedom. Most direct and obvious was service in the Federal armed forces. Of the approximately 180,000 blacks who served in the Union army during the war, well over half came from the Confederate states and more than three quarters came from slave states (including those that remained loyal); the vast majority of these had been slaves. On one level, these soldiers made a crucial contribution to Union victory; as Joseph T. Glatthaar has recently argued, their presence relieved an acute and growing shortage of manpower during the last two years of the war, and "their absence would have foiled Grant's strategy," which depended on overwhelming numerical superiority. On another equally important level, historians stressed the way in which military service gave the lie to the Sambo stereotype, thus at once providing blacks a "sense of manhood" and convincing white northerners that they were deserving of freedom—and perhaps even equality.[13]

Historians also probed with increasing sophistication the behavior of slaves who did *not* serve in the military.[14] They looked at the flight of slaves to Union lines, where their reception varied dramatically according to time, place, and the whim of individual officers and soldiers; they detailed the varied experiences of blacks in Union-occupied areas; they studied the changing fortunes of those who remained on farms and plantations within the ever-shrinking Confederacy; and they examined the "moment of freedom" as a prism through which previously murky relationships could be illuminated, often with surprising results. They did not always agree either on what they found or on its significance; below, I will explore some of the interpretive controversies that have ensued. With virtual unanimity, however, they rejected the notion that southern blacks were passive spectators in a contest that pitted white northerners against white southerners and agreed that those blacks played an important role in helping to shape their changing world. An essential, shared conviction thus underlies the numerous historical debates that have raged during the past generation, and serves to set that generation off in basic respects from previous generations of historians.[15]

## III

Interrelated with black agency was the theme of slavery's disintegration under the relentless pressure of changed wartime conditions. This theme first received widespread currency in the 1970s, and in one version or another quickly became part of the accepted orthodoxy, as historians focusing on the white Confederacy, such as Emory M. Thomas and James L. Roark, joined those writing on southern blacks to challenge the once-prevalent view that nothing much changed behind the lines, that slavery remained more or less intact until its death at the hands of the Yankee conquerors. "Slavery eroded, plantation by plantation, often slave by slave, like slabs of earth slipping into a Southern stream," wrote Roark in an important work that helped shape subsequent historical interpretation. ". . . Military defeat finally ended slavery, but vital relationships—that of master to slave and of slave to plantation—were everywhere strained, and sometimes snapped, by the time Federal troops arrived to compel emancipation."[16]

In the new version, slaveowners used to exercising patriarchal sway over their "people" lost much of their traditional authority as the Confederate government told them not to grow cotton and commandeered their slaves to perform military labor, as it became necessary to "refugee" slaves to safer terrain, as shortages and hardship dispelled the masters' aura of invincibility and control, and as Yankee troops neared. Slaves became increasingly recalcitrant—"uppity" in slaveowner parlance—as masters turned over farms and plantations to women and overseers, and as relations that had once seemed immutable now appeared threatened. They worked less, questioned more, and increasingly took to running away, not only singly and in pairs, as had been common before the war, but in large groups as well. As we will see, historians often differed on the particulars, but just as they reached a common consensus on black agency, so too did they generally agree that slavery gradually disintegrated as the war progressed and that the slaves themselves played a major role in this process.[17]

In the most recent years, a new attention to gender relations has both confirmed and accentuated the degree to which slavery changed during the war. Although previous historians had noted in passing the strains produced by the wartime absence of masters called to military service, it was left to Drew Gilpin Faust to show just how destructive female "mastery" was of traditional patriarchal relations. Unused to exercising the kind of firm authority that slavery demanded, increasingly afraid of their slaves, resentful at their inability to command unquestioned obedience from either slaves or overseers, and alarmed over the potential loss of their domestic servants, plantation mistresses constituted a weak link in slavery's chain of command: in Faust's words, "the authority of their class and race could not overcome the dependence they had learned to identify as the essence of their womanhood."[18] Meanwhile, other scholars turned new attention to the way the war affected the lives of black women and children,[19] previously largely ignored by those who saw in the war confirmation of black "manhood."

As slavery disintegrated, an increasing number of white southerners put forth proposals to reform it, proposals that varied from promoting slave literacy to providing legal recognition of slave marriage and protection of slave families. Although historians have agreed that such proposals can be viewed as an index of the war's impact on the peculiar institution, they have differed sharply on their significance. Whereas some have seen the wartime movement to "humanize" slavery as a sign of slavery's rapid erosion, and suggested that even a Confederate victory might not have saved the institution,[20] others have noted the continuity between such reform and similar efforts in the late antebellum period that were designed not to overturn but to strengthen slavery. "The ideology of Confederate reform might well have worked toward the perpetuation of southern slavery," not its abolition, suggested Drew Gilpin Faust.[21] In any case, the ultimate, ironic, evidence of the extent to which the war undermined slavery lay in the dying Confederacy's willingness to consider the massive use of black soldiers, who would be freed after victory. "The fact was that the Confederacy was prepared to let slavery perish and to fight on!" declared Emory Thomas. ". . . In four years the Southern nation had given up that which called it into being. . . . Born in revolution the Confederacy herself became revolutionized." Whether or not the Confederacy was in fact prepared to let slavery perish—as George Rable has recently noted, most Confederate officials saw in the proposal to free slaves as a reward for military service an unacceptable admission of moral bankruptcy—the war to preserve slavery had indeed killed it.[22]

The death of slavery and the transformation of slaves into freedpeople came at different times, from early in the war for those on the sea islands or in southern Louisiana to "Juneteenth" (June 19, 1865), when word of emancipation penetrated the distant reaches of Texas; for many, however, it came well before the war's end. Historians have explored a dizzying variety of responses to this "moment of truth" when those held in bondage realized that they were no longer slaves, from ecstatic celebration of the "great jubilee" to caution in the face of an uncertain future; the diversity of slaveowner responses was equally great. If violence against people and property was rare in most of the South, historians have described the fury with which lowcountry Carolina slaves assaulted property abandoned by their fleeing masters, property that, in the words of Julie Saville, was "smeared with excrement, smashed, shredded, and otherwise dismantled beyond use" in "a contemptuous effacement and destruction." Despite the variety of responses, however, recent historians have in at least two ways shared judgments that differed radically from the stereotypical assertion of humble darkies standing loyally by their loving masters. They found widespread desertion by slaves typically assumed to be the most loyal—trusted house servants—and they saw in this desertion telling evidence concerning the wider nature of slave relations in the antebellum South. The intense feelings of betrayal expressed by many masters indicated both how little they had in fact known their "people" and how much the war had laid bare the brutal reality that underlay their paternalistic pretensions.[23]

## IV

If historians have agreed on both black agency and the wartime unraveling of slavery, they have differed over precisely how the two were related. Taking the notion of black agency to its ultimate conclusion, some scholars have recently put forth the thesis that the slaves themselves were the prime actors in bringing about emancipation. Others, while accepting the active role played by slaves and free blacks, have rejected the notion of "self-liberation," insisting that freedom came out of the barrel of a Yankee gun—and Yankee legislation. Because this controversy encapsules fundamental issues concerning slave behavior, Federal policy, and historical causation, it is worth examining in some detail.

The clearest assertion of the "self-liberation" thesis has come from the editors of *Freedom,* a massive, ongoing documentary history of emancipation in the United States South.[24] In their lengthy and informative introductory essays, later published as a separate volume, they played down the importance of federal action in bringing about the end of slavery and stressed instead the actions of the slaves. "Once the evolution of emancipation replaces the absolutism of the Emancipation Proclamation and the Thirteenth Amendment as the focus of study, the story of slavery's demise shifts from the presidential mansion and the halls of Congress to the farms and plantations that became wartime battlefields," they proclaimed. "And slaves—whose persistence forced federal soldiers, Union and Confederate policy makers, and even their own masters onto terrain they never intended to occupy—become the prime movers in securing their own liberty." A more extreme version of this argument appeared in a separate article by Barbara J. Fields, one of the *Freedom* editors. Charging that "Lincoln did his best to evade the whole question" of black freedom, she noted that "at the moment of its issuance, the final Emancipation Proclamation freed not a single slave who was not already entitled to freedom by act of Congress" and insisted that the slaves forced a reluctant president to embrace emancipation. It was not the government but the slaves themselves who deserved the credit, for "by the time Lincoln issued his Emancipation Proclamation, no human being alive could have held back the tide that swept toward freedom."[25]

A direct response came from James M. McPherson, who had previously been instrumental in recognizing black agency but now concluded that the argument was being pushed too far. Praising Lincoln as a "principled opponent of slavery on moral grounds," McPherson insisted that, although some slaves managed to escape slavery on their own, only Union victory brought the peculiar institution to an end. The "crucial point," he continued, was that the "slaves did not emancipate themselves; they were liberated by the Union army." Ultimately, therefore, the "traditional answer to the question 'Who Freed the Slaves?'" was more accurate than "the new and currently more fashionable answer": in short, "Abraham Lincoln freed the slaves."[26]

This response, in turn, drew a reply from *Freedom* project editor Ira Berlin. Terming McPherson's depiction of the editors' position "more in the nature of a caricature than a characterization," Berlin once again challenged the notion that emancipation came from above: "the [Emancipation] Proclamation's flat prose, ridiculed as having the moral grandeur of a bill of lading, suggests that the true authorship of African-American freedom lies elsewhere—not at the top of American society but at the bottom." At the same time, however, Berlin seemed to retreat somewhat from an uncompromising assertion of emancipation from below. Pointing out that the editors had never used the term "self-emancipation," he conceded that "the Emancipation Proclamation transformed the war in ways only the President could" and that "both Lincoln and the slaves played their appointed parts in the drama of emancipation." In short, "slaves were the prime movers in the emancipation drama, not the sole movers."[27]

Making sense of the debate over who freed the slaves ultimately involves grappling with a series of interrelated issues, including the character and goals of President Lincoln and his government, the behavior and impact of southern slaves, and the relationship between national politics and local practice. It involves making both moral and causal judgments and distinguishing between the two. And it involves coming to grips with a variety of historical interpretations and pronouncements, few of which are so clearly expressed as either Fields's or McPherson's, and most of which combine at least some elements of both.

Although historians have properly rejected a model of slave behavior during the war characterized by docility, passivity, and loyalty to masters, they have not in general replaced it with one of constant resistance and rebelliousness. Slaves took advantage of wartime disruption in numerous ways: they obeyed orders with less alacrity, they challenged weakened authority more readily, they followed the progress of Yankee forces and aided that progress in a variety of ways from providing valuable military intelligence to enlisting in the Union army, and they fled in increasing numbers, especially when Federal troops neared. Despite heightened fears on the part of the white population, however, they did not engage in the kind of massive uprising that occurred in Saint Domingue during the French Revolution and that remained the constant bugaboo of the white South; "whenever possible, black people avoided the deadly prospects of massive, sustained confrontation," observed Vincent Harding, "for their ultimate objective was freedom, not martyrdom." Perhaps Leon F. Litwack put it best in stressing the varied, ambiguous, and cautious behavior of slaves in the Confederacy. Most, he wrote, "were neither 'rebellious' nor 'faithful' in the fullest sense of those terms, but rather ambivalent and observant, some of them frankly opportunistic, many of them anxious to preserve their anonymity, biding their time, searching for opportunities to break the dependency that bound them to their white families."[28]

Clearly, such actions would not have produced the overthrow of slavery were it not for the war and Union victory. But one can also say the same thing about Abraham Lincoln's actions. Recent historians have generally agreed in stressing the president's principled opposition to slavery, but most have also recognized the caution, pragmatism, devotion to the Constitution, and commitment to the Union that prevented him from advocating immediate abolition before 1861 and restrained him from moving decisively against slavery even during the early months of the war. As late as August 22, 1862, Lincoln somewhat disingenuously insisted to antislavery editor Horace Greeley that slavery was a peripheral issue: "My paramount object in this struggle *is* to save the Union, and is *not* either to save or to destroy slavery," he asserted. "If I could save the Union without freeing *any* slave I would do it, and if I could save it by freeing *all* the slaves I would do it, and if I could save it by freeing some and leaving others alone I would also do that. What I do about slavery, and the colored race, I do because I believe it helps to save the Union."[29]

In short, emancipation would not have come either from above or from below had it not been for the Civil War; it was the war that provided the opportunity both for the slaves to chip away at slavery by refusing to act like slaves and for the Federal government to move against slavery as it could not do before. The Emancipation Proclamation was important, as scholars from John Hope Franklin to Eric Foner have recognized, not because it immediately ended slavery (it didn't), but because it marked a crucial change in the nature of the Civil War, from a war for Union to a war for freedom. A balanced appraisal, I believe, recognizes the ways in which slaves prodded the Federal government to take decisive action against slavery, but also recognizes the centrality of this action to the overthrow of slavery—in other words, sees the slaves both as subjects helping to make their own history *and* as objects of historical action. From such a perspective, it is necessary to understand what occurred both on the plantations *and* in the halls of Congress in order to explain the end of slavery. Perhaps the dispute over "who freed the slaves" is not in fact so intractable as it appears, because most historians—and even some of the original protagonists—seem to be inching toward this position. Although differences of nuance and emphasis remain, almost all would agree that the *war* provided the opportunity for the destruction of slavery, but that this destruction would not have occurred without the actions of both the slaves and the federal government.[30]

## V

One's ultimate judgment of the war's impact on black Americans depends on one's evaluation of what came after slavery. In this regard, two central, interrelated questions continue to arouse intense debate among historians: first, what was the nature of the new freedom, and second, to what extent—and how—did conditions change after emancipation? The remaking of the slave South into a free-labor South did not await the surrender at Appomattox or the Thirteenth Amendment to the Constitution but began during the war itself.

Beginning in 1964, with the publication of Willie Lee Rose's pathbreaking *Rehearsal for Reconstruction,* an increasing number of scholars probed the wartime experiments in free labor that were undertaken in areas of the South occupied by Federal forces. On the sea islands off the coast of South Carolina and Georgia, in southern Louisiana, in northern Virginia, in the lower Mississippi Valley, and then elsewhere, ex-slaves worked for a variety of employers—former owners, white southern and northern lessees, and less often themselves—under a variety of arrangements predicated on their "freedom" and therefore encompassing some form of compensation. At the same time, northern missionaries representing benevolent organizations such as the American Missionary Association undertook to educate the freedpeople and thereby prepare them for their new role as citizens in a republican society. Historians reached diverse conclusions about these wartime efforts at reconstruction.[31]

Rose's account of the Port Royal Experiment was a remarkably even-handed study that displayed sensitivity to diverse perspectives while identifying fully with none. Carefully distinguishing among the various northern players, she presented a sympathetic if occasionally critical portrait of the teacher-missionaries, whose chief motivation was "the desire to strike a blow for freedom," noted that "the army gave at least grudging cooperation" to the reform experiments, but found the Treasury Department's cotton agents totally uninterested in what they considered schemes of bleeding-heart philanthropy. Blacks made the same distinctions: "where the superintendents met stubborn and passive resistance, the teachers were joyfully accepted everywhere." As for the former slaves, they were unhappy working in dependent relationships, which seemed curiously similar to slavery, and showed "strong opposition to planting the old staple" (cotton). Although Rose generally avoided imposing judgment on the characters in her drama, she could not resist noting that "the pronouncements of the laissez-faire evangels ring a harsh and stupid note in the middle of the twentieth century."[32]

Few other historians showed such detachment. Indeed, by the 1970s, a widespread consensus had emerged that the reform effort was woefully inadequate. Federal officials frequently displayed a racist contempt for black southerners and typically seemed more interested in insuring that former slaves worked hard than in defending their freedom. As a consequence, the "free labor" sequel to slavery was characterized by coercive management, limited compensation, and even more limited rights; rather than bringing freedom to southern blacks, military officers and Freedmen's Bureau officials practiced widespread collusion with planters to maintain a subservient labor force that was free in name but at best semifree in fact. Blaming adherence to the "free-labor ideology of the day which, however well suited for the exploitation of the nation's natural resources, prom-

PETER KOLCHIN

ised very little of an economic nature for the black plantation workers of the South," William F. Messner lambasted the army for instituting a form of quasi slavery in southern Louisiana, with former slaves "once again firmly tied to the land as plantation laborers working under the direction, and largely for the profit, of white landowners." This repressive wartime labor policy, in turn, set the stage for future setbacks after the war: "the economic history of black people during Reconstruction," Messner concluded, "would serve only to reaffirm a previously determined conclusion."[33]

Although historians have generally given higher marks to the educational efforts than to the labor policies of Yankee reformers,[34] some have linked the two as part of a common program characterized by paternalism, racism, and self-interest. Robert Francis Engs, for example, although conceding the reformers' "spectacular success in educating freedmen" in Hampton, Virginia, lamented that "they could not connect the right to be free with the right to be different. They too proved guilty of that arrogance from which blacks sought freedom." Even more critical was Jacqueline Jones's portrait of condescending and self-righteous Yankee schoolmarms who went to Georgia, women who were so preoccupied with the bourgeois virtues of punctuality, cleanliness, sobriety, and order that they could not see the irony of trying "to instill the Protestant work ethic in persons who had literally slaved their whole lives for other people." In short, the proffered aid was not what it seemed, because it "came with strings attached."[35]

A few historians directly responded to such criticisms with defenses of the wartime and postwar efforts on behalf of the freedpeople. Rather than criticizing the effort "to return the freedmen to their accustomed labors," for example, Joel Williamson suggested that "quite properly, officials viewed this as the real solution to the problem of relief." Herman Belz stressed the differences between the various wartime free-labor experiments and slavery, suggested that criticizing the limitations of Republican policies was present-minded, and praised the architects of those policies, who "insisted on civil equality for blacks in spite of pervasive social prejudice." Barry A. Crouch, in a careful study that focused on the actions of lower-level Freedmen's Bureau agents in Texas, also detected "generational chauvinism" (that is, present-mindedness) in negative judgments of the Bureau and concluded that these "agents, at least in Texas, acquitted themselves rather remarkably." And James M. McPherson emphasized the idealism of former abolitionists, who during the Civil War, Reconstruction, and post-Reconstruction periods continued to struggle for racial justice.[36]

Although these harsh judgments (and occasional defenses) have not entirely vanished in the 1980s and 1990s, they have increasingly given way to an effort to understand the goals of the contending parties on their own terms as they engaged in an intense struggle over the meaning—and nature—of freedom. In this scheme, which allowed for more diversity, ambivalence, and complexity, the bipolarity between free and unfree, pro-freedperson and pro-planter, yielded to a world of conflicting views of what freedom and "free labor" were all about. If freedpeople typically struggled to maximize their autonomy and independence, planters strove to secure a docile and dependent labor force, and Federal reformers took an immense variety of positions in between, sometimes appearing to support the aspirations of the freedpeople and sometimes appearing to favor planter interests but rarely identifying entirely with either.[37]

Even while accepting this framework, however, historians have differed over its character. Some have continued to stress the coercive nature of Federal policy, insisting that whatever gains blacks made were entirely the results of their own efforts. Noting the degree to which the Freedmen's Bureau in Virginia "colluded with planters in the apprenticeship system," for example, Lynda J. Morgan generalized that despite the benevolent actions of individual agents, "the bureau became preeminently an agency that helped deliver emancipated labor back into the hands of the planters." James L. Roark, however, maintained that "it would be wrong to assume that the Union army and the planters were allies, that their differences were insignificant, and that the planters were content with the army's substitute for slavery." Similarly, suggesting that the Freedmen's Bureau "can best be understood as the agent of the northern free labor ideology itself," Eric Foner portrayed the Bureau—and Federal policy in general—as one that fully satisfied neither freedpeople nor planters. In striving to put "freedmen back to work on plantations, the Bureau's interests coincided with those of the planters." On the other hand, "to the extent that the Bureau demanded for the freedmen the rights to which northern laborers were accustomed, it meant an alliance with the blacks." Such a view was by no means incompatible with making strong moral judgments about the past, but it typically went hand in hand with an effort to understand the behavior of Civil War–era protagonists in terms of what was feasible at the time rather than arguing that they "should" have acted according to the values of a subsequent age.[38]

In probing different understandings of *freedom*, historians have widely agreed that most former slaves strove to maximize their autonomy and independence, to get as far as they could from slavelike dependence. Thus, they strove to acquire their own land and resisted labor relations that appeared subservient, including gang labor and direction by overseers; similarly, they placed a high value on the security of their families, the independence of their churches, the education of their children (and often of adults as well), and the right to move without restrictions.[39] But scholars have continued to differ on precisely how freedpeople struggled for freedom. If almost everyone has recognized their desire for land, for example, some have seen the freedpeople as striving to take part in the commercial economy; but others—especially in studying the South Carolina and Georgia lowcountry—have argued that former slaves typically shunned growing staples for market in favor of a limited autarky based on communal rather than individual patterns of landholding.[40] In part, these differences represent interpretive disagreements among historians, but it is likely that they also reflect variations that existed among different regions of the South—and perhaps within regions as well. As I will suggest below, the existence of such variations provides scholars with an ideal opportunity to apply a comparative approach to the Civil War and emancipation, even while keeping the focus squarely on the United States.

## VI

Intertwined with the question of what freedom was all about is that of how much things actually changed as a result of the war and emancipation. Of course, the proverbial question of change versus continuity can be applied to all of the past, but it is especially pertinent—and has been an item of especially hot contention—with respect to the war and emancipation, because they seem to mark such a sharp demarcation in American history. If these two occurrences did not produce fundamental change, one might well question what could.

Nevertheless, many scholars have stressed the basic continuity of the Civil War era, and in the extreme version argued that when all is said and done, the changes that occurred were largely cosmetic. Such a position has most often (although not always) been associated with the view that not "enough" was done on behalf of former slaves, and that the effort to remake the South—and therefore the Civil War itself—must be regarded as a "failure." Of course, the view of Reconstruction as a failure has been widely held among historians committed to the goals of racial equality and social justice, and some scholars have managed at the same time to emphasize both failure and the existence of fundamental change. Carried to its logical extreme, however, the failure paradigm is clearly most consistent with assertion of continuity.[41]

It is not surprising, then, that as historians came to believe that the North should have done more to transform the South and uplift the freedpeople, many of them also emphasized the consequent insufficiency of change. In some versions, social continuity resulted from a failure to institute land reform;[42] in others, it stemmed from lack of commitment to racial equality or from outright racism;[43] still others pointed to various institutional shortcomings that hobbled the southern economy.[44] Whatever the cause, however, these scholars stressed the continued poverty, exploitation, and hierarchical social structure that plagued the South in the postwar years. "The social structure remained essentially unchanged," asserted Crandall A. Shifflett in detailing the continued "class rule" and grinding poverty that prevailed in Louisa County, Virginia. "The story of Louisa is one of a missing revolution."[45]

In 1969, in an article that led to a pointed exchange with Phillip S. Paludan, John S. Rosenberg explicitly linked Civil War–era continuity to the war itself, arguing that because the war did not produce fundamental change, it was not worth its "cost" of 620,000 dead Americans. Suggesting that each generation reinterprets the Civil War to meet its own needs, Rosenberg called for a new, Vietnam-era revisionism based on realization that "the limited improvement in the status of the Negro in this country was not worth the expenditure in lives required to make that improvement possible." Because the war did not produce any major improvements in American society, those who died in the conflict "did die in vain." Suggesting that "Rosenberg's humanity overwhelmed his professional judgment," Paludan countered that the young scholar had underestimated the improvement in black lives that stemmed from the overthrow of slavery and concluded that "as a result of the Civil War a 'new birth of freedom' did occur," but Rosenberg was not persuaded. Reiterating his previous judgment about the lack of progress among blacks, he shifted the main focus of his argument, maintaining that given the sorry state of modern America, the war to preserve the integrity of the United States represented a colossal waste. Paludan responded one more time, criticizing Rosenberg's present-minded approach and again insisting that the positive results very much justified the war-imposed sacrifices.[46]

Although they have rarely used such cost-accounting arguments, an increasing number of historians came during the 1980s and 1990s to agree with Paludan that the Civil War produced major changes—changes that were so extensive that they justified use of terms such as "revolution" and "transformation." Disputing the prevalent view of continuity between the Old South and the New, Harold D. Woodman pointed to "a fundamental and revolutionary transformation of the South." Terming the "image of continuity" "illusory," James L. Roark explained that "almost overnight, Southern planters crossed from the world of slave labor to that of compensated labor, from substantial wealth and ease to relative poverty and drudgery, from political dominance to crippled influence. Continuity in their practice of racism and rural exploitation could not mask the revolution in their lives." Eric Foner concurred, asserting that "like a massive earthquake, the Civil War and the destruction of slavery permanently altered the landscape of Southern life."[47] Although the Reconstruction effort to remake the South constituted part of the "revolution," its essential feature for most scholars was the abolition of slavery and the institution of "free labor," which stemmed directly from the Civil War. If in some respects this interpretation seems to resemble the Beardian "Second American Revolution," it is important to remember, as Eric Foner pointed out, that "unlike the Beards, . . . who all but ignored the black experience, modern scholars tend to view emancipation itself as among the most revolutionary aspects of the period."[48]

Agreement on the existence of revolutionary changes by no means resulted in agreement on the nature, significance, and extent of those changes. If some historians wrote of "an unambiguous and substantial improvement in [the] economic well-being" of black Americans,[49] others stressed the sharply exploitative nature of the "free labor" system, and suggested that the shift from slavery to market capitalism, although revolutionary, was hardly salutary for the black laborers on whom both systems depended: the discipline of the market could be as merciless as that of the lash. In this context, the notion of a "failed" or "unfinished" revolution could serve to reconcile assertion of fundamental change with continued poverty, exploitation, and degradation.[50] But other scholars found substantial long-term changes—including benefits—that raised questions about the extent of the revolution's "failure": Claude F. Oubre and Loren Schweninger, for example, demonstrated that black landownership continued to expand rapidly in the post-Reconstruction years, especially in the upper South, where the proportion of farmowners among blacks engaged in agriculture increased from 2.2 percent in 1870 to 44 percent in 1910. And William Cohen, who had previously argued that many blacks became trapped in "involuntary servitude," found that "in the years from 1865 to 1915, blacks in the South had considerable freedom of movement," a freedom that they exercised extensively "in a continuing quest for better wages and fair treatment."[51]

In making sense of change versus continuity in the Civil War–era South, the question of perspective becomes crucial. Clearly, much changed and much did not; just as one can accurately describe a glass as half full or half empty, so too one can emphasize what changed or what remained the same in the Civil War South.[52] But the significance of these developments depends on one's point of reference. Unfulfilled expectation of or desire for radical change is likely to produce perception of substantial continuity, whereas even small changes will seem momentous to someone seeking to preserve existing ways.[53] Similarly, the nature of developments elsewhere can help put those in a particular location in perspective. In short, the character of change assumes meaning only in the comparative context, "compared to what?"

Viewed in this light, the particular vehicle for emancipation in the southern United States—civil war—takes on new significance. Because slavery ended in the South by force of arms, its demise was unusually sudden and the changes that ensued were unusually far-reaching. Elsewhere, the end of slavery was frequently a gradual process and slaveowners frequently won compensation for their lost property. As traitors to the Union, however, southern masters received little of the consideration that landholding elites did elsewhere, and played a far smaller role in shaping the new order that replaced slavery. Emancipation was sudden and uncompensated, and slavery was followed by an unusually vigorous effort—Reconstruction—to transform the South into a free-labor society. A comparative perspective, in other words, reinforces perception of change in the post-emancipation South: if emancipation everywhere involved a shift from slavery to some form of "free labor," that shift appears *particularly* revolutionary for the southern United States, in light of the way that it occurred elsewhere.[54]

## VII

A survey of past approaches to slavery and freedom in the Civil War inevitably suggests some future directions as well. Although predictions are always hazardous, it seems likely that scholars will continue to explore many of the new lines of research discussed above. Because the Civil War represented both a beginning and an end, Civil War scholarship will continue to shed light on both what went before and what came after. As scholars continue to probe these issues, a number of specific subjects and approaches seem especially promising. Some of these, such as reactions to the "moment of truth," have already received considerable attention but deserve even more, because they are so revealing of fundamental relationships and values. In other cases, new technology promises to facilitate the accumulation of important historical information. The National Park Service, for example, has just developed an internet database of all United States Colored Troops who served in the Civil War.[55] In still other areas, such as the study of gender relations, families, women, and children, Civil War scholarship remains in its infancy, despite the existence of exciting new work, and represents a field with extensive opportunities for enter-prising researchers. In all of these areas, however, the war should continue to serve as a prism shedding valuable light on the old order, the new order, and the transition from one to the other.

In considering new directions of research, I would like to make a special pitch for the utility of comparative analysis. Although comparison has been a major tool of historians of slavery, relatively few scholars have taken advantage of the unusual way that slavery ended in the United States South, to apply a comparative approach to the Civil War and emancipa-tion. The implications are Janus-faced. Looking forward, southern slavery's violent end created a more decisive break with the past than that typical in other countries, and thereby paved the way for a more radical effort to remake the social order; in international context, the South's sudden, un-compensated emancipation—together with the far-reaching if incomplete Reconstruction effort that followed—was highly unusual.[56] Looking back-ward, the willingness of southern slaveholders to go to war for slavery, rather than yield as slaveholders did elsewhere (however reluctantly) to government-sponsored emancipation, points to their extraordinary com-mitment to the peculiar institution; in C. Vann Woodward's felicitous formulation, "the end of slavery in the South can be described as the death of a society, though elsewhere it could more reasonably be charac-terized as the liquidation of an investment."[57] So far, however, whether using the Civil War to look backward or forward, or to examine the war itself in the light of civil wars elsewhere, historians have barely scratched the surface of potential comparative scholarship.[58]

A somewhat different kind of comparative perspective holds out the prospect of other unrealized insights. The impact of the war on slavery, and the wartime experiences of black Americans, varied considerably: if fighting raged almost incessantly in Tennessee and Virginia, for example, most of Alabama and Texas saw little action until the last days of the war; meanwhile, both whites and blacks reacted to events in diverse ways that reflected the variety of human personality and behavior, a variety height-ened by pressure of wartime conditions. On one level, historians have not only been aware of this diversity, but have often emphasized it in their historical accounts. The varied responses of both blacks and whites to their changing relations is the most persistent theme in Leon F. Litwack's monumental *Been in the Storm So Long* and clearly emerges as well in the publications of the *Freedom* project; project editors stressed the sharp variations in northern white attitudes toward southern blacks, major dif-ferences in northern understandings of free labor, and remarkably diverse paths of southern blacks to freedom, the subsequent recounting of which produced "as many tales as tellers."[59]

Historians have barely begun to take advantage, however, of the opportunities for comparative analysis presented by the internal variations in wartime slavery. Frequently, what appear to be differences of interpretation stem at least in part from differences in experience, but we lack the kind of comparative research that would permit us to determine to what extent. For example, Randolph B. Campbell has argued that "slaves in Texas . . . did relatively little to hinder the Confederate military effort or contribute to Union victory" and that slave flight "did not increase dramatically" during the war; it is unclear, however, whether this argument represents a challenge to prevailing interpretations or is based on Texas's geographic remoteness and military isolation. Similarly, some historians have argued that former slaves strongly preferred cultivating food crops to staples such as cotton and rice, and often opted for a condition of quasi-peasant autarky and cooperative agriculture over individual involvement in the commercial economy, but their most extensive evidence has come from the Carolina and Georgia lowcountry, where slave conditions had long been atypical of those in the South as a whole.[60] Because there were many "slaveries" rather than one and many wartime experiences rather than one, more rigorous comparative study—across state and regional lines, for example, but also within particular states and regions—should be especially useful in helping scholars weigh the impact of geographic and historical conditions, distinguish specific developments from general trends, and explore the full complexity of how slavery ended.

## VIII

Although much remains to be done, recent historians have made enormous progress in studying slavery, freedom, and African-Americans in the Civil War. Once barely visible in Civil War historiography and marked by stereotypical generalizations unsupported by serious research, these subjects are now at the heart of Civil War scholarship, as historians continue to explore the ways in which the war undermined slavery and led to emancipation and the social transformation of the South. In this development, slavery's impact on the war is in some ways as important as the war's impact on slavery. If it was the war that killed slavery, more than anything else it was slavery that gave meaning to the war—both to contemporaries and to current historians—transforming senseless slaughter into a struggle over the nature of American society. As James M. McPherson has suggested in explaining Americans' continuing fascination with the Civil War, "great issues were at stake, . . . issues whose resolution profoundly transformed and redefined the United States but at the same time are still alive and contested today."[61] Today, we cannot examine the Civil War without considering these fundamental issues—systems of labor, meaning of freedom, nature of American democracy—that underlay the conflict between North and South. In recognizing the centrality of these issues, recent historians have helped to expand the study of the Civil War from the preserve of military historians and war buffs into a preoccupation of those who would understand the character of the country—and especially the South—in the nineteenth century.

# NOTES

## INTRODUCTION

1. Lonnie R. Speer, *Portals to Hell: Military Prisons of the Civil War* (Mechanicsburg, Penn.: Stackpole Books, 1997).

2. Emory M. Thomas, *Robert E. Lee: A Biography* (New York: W. W. Norton, 1995); Steven E. Woodworth, *Davis and Lee at War* (Lawrence: University Press of Kansas, 1995).

3. Paddy Griffith, *Battle Tactics of the Civil War* (New Haven: Yale University Press, 1989).

4. David M. Potter, "Jefferson Davis and the Political Factors in Confederate Defeat," in *Why the North Won the Civil War,* ed. David Herbert Donald (Baton Rouge: Louisiana State University Press, 1960), 91–114.

5. Maris Vinovskis, "Have Social Historians Lost the Civil War? Some Preliminary Demographic Speculations," *Journal of American History,* 76 (June 1989), 34–58.

6. Thomas C. Cochran, "Did the Civil War Retard Industrialization?" *Mississippi Valley Historical Review,* 48 (September 1961), 197–210.

## BLUEPRINT FOR VICTORY:
## NORTHERN STRATEGY AND MILITARY POLICY

1. "Men at War: An Interview with Shelby Foote," in Geoffrey C. Ward, *The Civil War: An Illustrated History* (New York: Knopf, 1990), 272.

2. George Wythe Randolph to Molly Randolph, October 10, 1861, quoted in Herman Hattaway and Archer Jones, *How the North Won: A Military History of the Civil War* (Urbana: University of Illinois Press, 1983), 18. Former Confederate army commander P. G. T. Beauregard similarly remarked after the conflict that "[n]o people ever warred for independence with more relative advantages than the Confederates," among which he listed a determined populace and geography well suited to frustrating northern invaders. "[I]f, as a military question, they [the Confederate people] must have failed," Beauregard concluded, "then no country must aim at freedom by means of war." G. T. Beauregard, "The First Battle of Bull Run," in *Battles and Leaders of the Civil War,* 4 vols., ed. Robert Underwood Johnson and Clarence Clough Buel (New York: Century, 1887–88), 1:222.

3. Two excellent brief discussions of the definitions of strategy are James M. McPherson, "Lincoln and the Strategy of Unconditional Surrender," in *Lincoln, the War President: The Gettysburg Lectures,* ed. Gabor S. Boritt (New York: Oxford University Press, 1992), 35–37, and Alan T. Nolan, *Lee Considered: General Robert E. Lee and Civil War History* (Chapel Hill: University of North Carolina Press, 1991), 61–63.

4. For a perceptive treatment of the connections between politics and military planning, see Archer Jones, "Military Means, Political Ends: Strategy," in *Why the Confederacy Lost,* ed. Gabor S. Boritt (New York: Oxford University Press, 1992), 45-77. Jones wrote that "military strategy has such a close relation to the war's political objectives and concerns that any intelligible treatment must show its links to politics. Further, it is convenient to distinguish between military and political strategy by defining the former as military action designed to deplete the hostile military force and the latter as military action intended to produce a political result directly. Yet military and political strategy rarely have such clear-cut boundaries because most military actions have political effects" (45–46). Interestingly, the debate over the allocation of strategic resources between the eastern and western theaters, which has occupied many able historians of Confederate military affairs, has no counterpart in the literature on northern strategy.

5. Abraham Lincoln, Message to Congress, December 3, 1861, in Abraham Lincoln, *The Collected Works of Abraham Lincoln,* 9 vols., ed. Roy P. Basler (New Brunswick, N.J.: Rutgers University Press, 1953–1955), 5:48–49.

6. W. E. B. DuBois, *Black Reconstruction: An Essay Toward a History of the Part Which Black Folk Played in the Attempt to Reconstruct Democracy in America, 1860–1880* (New York: Harcourt, Brace, 1935), 57, 81, 84. On August 9, 1863, Lincoln urged U. S. Grant to push recruitment of black troops along the Mississippi River: "I believe it is a resource which, if vigorously applied now, will soon close the contest. It works doubly, weakening the enemy and strengthening us." Almost exactly one year later, the president wrote disgruntled Democratic editor Charles D. Robinson about emancipation and the enrollment of black men in the army. "The way these measures were to help the cause," he explained, "was . . . by inducing the colored people to come bodily over from the rebel side to ours." Lincoln, *Collected Works,* 6:374, 7:500.

7. Leon F. Litwack, *Been in the Storm So Long: The Aftermath of Slavery* (New York: Knopf, 1979), xi; Ira Berlin, Barbara J. Fields, Thavolia Glymph, Joseph P. Reidy, and Leslie S. Rowland, eds., *Freedom: A Documentary History of Emancipation, 1861–1867, Series 1, Volume 1: The Destruction of Slavery* (Cambridge: Cambridge University Press, 1985), 3. See also Ira Berlin, Barbara J. Fields, Steven F. Miller, Joseph P. Reidy, and Leslie S. Rowland, *Slaves No More: Three Essays on Emancipation and the Civil War* (Cambridge: Cambridge University Press, 1992), and *Free at Last: A Documentary History of Slavery, Freedom, and the Civil War* (New York: New Press, 1992), edited by the same five scholars, for the argument that slaves were the principal agents in achieving their freedom.

8. Barbara J. Fields, "Who Freed the Slaves?," in Ward, *The Civil War,* 181, 178. Fields's dramatic conclusion about an irresistible tide overlooks the fact that Confederate arms very nearly prevailed at more than one point after January 1863; only millions of northerners who did believe the Union worth the sacrifice of thousands of lives ensured that the war would continue—and that the tide for emancipation would roll on toward Appomattox.

9. Mark E. Neely, Jr., "Lincoln and the Theory of Self-Emancipation," in *The Continuing Civil War: Essays in Honor of the Civil War Round Table of Chicago,* ed. John Y. Simon and Barbara Hughett (Dayton, Ohio: Morningside,

1992), 46, 47–50, 56, 58. In *The Emancipation Proclamation* (Garden City, N.Y.: Doubleday, 1963), 140, John Hope Franklin observed that "Slavery, in or out of the Confederacy, could not possibly have survived the Emancipation Proclamation. Slaves themselves, already restive under their yoke and walking off the plantation in many places, were greatly encouraged upon learning that Lincoln wanted them to be free. They proceeded to oblige him."

10. McPherson, "Lincoln and the Strategy of Unconditional Surrender," 54, 61. In *The American Way of War: A History of United States Military Strategy and Policy* (New York: Macmillan, 1973), 138, Russell F. Weigley took a slightly different view of Lincoln's proclamation: "Certainly the Emancipation Proclamation issued on September 22 involved strategy as well as national policy."

11. Joseph T. Glatthaar, *Partners in Command: The Relationships between Leaders in the Civil War* (New York: Free Press, 1994), 230.

12. Charles Sumner spoke for many radicals when he observed in early June 1861 that "[n]othing could be more painful to me than this conflict, except that I feel that it was inevitable, & that its result will be the extinction of Slavery. . . . This is the expectation of all the more earnest and thoughtful." Charles Sumner to the Duchess of Argyll, June 4, 1861, in Charles Sumner, *The Selected Letters of Charles Sumner*, 2 vols., ed. Beverly Wilson Palmer (Boston: Northeastern University Press, 1990), 2:70. Outside the political mainstream, abolitionists also saw the war as a potential struggle for black freedom from the outset. In *The Struggle for Equality: Abolitionists and the Negro in the Civil War and Reconstruction* (Princeton: Princeton University Press, 1964), 52, James M. McPherson summed up the abolitionists' expectations: "The coming of a war which they hoped would destroy slavery posed a serious moral dilemma for pacifist abolitionists. Only a small number of abolitionists were actual non-resistants, but nearly all nineteenth-century reformers professed peace sentiments to some degree. . . . When confronted by a choice between a (potentially) antislavery war and a proslavery peace, however, most abolitionists did not hesitate to choose war."

13. T. Harry Williams, *Lincoln and the Radicals* (Madison: University of Wisconsin Press, 1941), 9–10, 14, 18.

14. Hans L. Trefousse, *The Radical Republicans: Lincoln's Vanguard for Racial Justice* (New York: Knopf, 1969), 169, 231, 265.

15. Charles Sumner's published letters provide a convenient window on Radical Republican and abolitionist attitudes. Sumner wrote hopefully in the wake of Union defeat at First Bull Run: "Never did I feel so sure of the result. The battle & defeat have done much for the slave. . . . I told the Presdt that our defeat was the worst event & the best event in our history; the worst, as it was the greatest present calamity & shame,—the best, as it made the extinction of Slavery inevitable." Charles Sumner to Wendell Phillips, August 3, 1861, in Sumner, *Selected Letters*, 2:74.

16. Joel H. Silbey, *A Respectable Minority: The Democratic Party in the Civil War Era, 1860–1868* (New York: Norton, 1977), ix; Christopher Dell, *Lincoln and the War Democrats: The Grand Erosion of Conservative Tradition* (Rutherford, N.J.: Fairleigh Dickinson University Press, 1975), 9–10, 144–45, 210–11.

17. T. Harry Williams, *Lincoln and His Generals* (New York: Knopf, 1952), 3; Williams, "The Military Leadership of North and South," in *Why the North Won the Civil War*, ed. David Herbert Donald (Baton Rouge: Louisiana State University Press, 1960), 35–36; Bruce Catton, "The Generalship of Ulysses S. Grant," in *Grant, Lee, Lincoln, and the Radicals*, ed. Grady McWhiney (Evanston, Ill.: Northwestern University Press, 1964), 8–9; McPherson, "Lincoln and the Strategy of Unconditional Surrender," 47–48; Robert A. Daughty, Ira D. Gruber, et al., *The American Civil War: The Emergence of Total Warfare* (Lexington, Mass.: D. C. Heath, 1996), 106–7, 129, 159. See also Daniel E. Sutherland, *The Emergence of Total War* (Fort Worth: Ryan Place Publishers, 1996), which describes John Pope's Virginia campaign of 1862 as the outgrowth of Lincoln's "new military strategy" that sought to defeat "both Confederate civilians and soldiers" (13, 15).

18. Mark E. Neely, Jr., "Was the Civil War a Total War?," *Civil War History* 37 (1991): 25, 27, 11.

19. Charles Royster, *The Destructive War: William Tecumseh Sherman, Stonewall Jackson, and the Americans* (New York: Knopf, 1991), 358, 79–82, 89.

20. On December 24, 1864, Sherman wrote to Union Chief of Staff Henry W. Halleck that the North was "not only fighting hostile armies, but a hostile people, and must make old and young, rich and poor, feel the hard hand of war, as well as their organized armies." U.S. War Department, *The War of the Rebellion: A Compilation of the Official Records of the Union and Confederate Armies*, 127 vols., index, and atlas (Washington: GPO, 1880–1901), series 1, 44:799. Grimsley also acknowledged that Bruce Catton and James M. McPherson previously had used the phrase "hard war." Mark Grimsley, *The Hard Hand of War: Union Military Policy Toward Southern Civilians, 1861–1865* (Cambridge: Cambridge University Press, 1995), 5 n.4.

21. Grimsley, *Hard Hand of War*, 3–4. Grimsley's identification of a "pragmatic" phase during which northern commanders pursued battlefield victories echoed in some ways Weigley's analysis in *The American Way of War*. "For almost a year after McClellan's departure," wrote Weigley with evident disapproval, "his successors in the eastern Federal command gave themselves over to the Napoleonic mania for the climactic battle" (135).

22. Grimsley, *Hard Hand of War*, 4.

23. Joseph T. Glatthaar, *The March to the Sea and Beyond: Sherman's Troops in the Savannah and Carolinas Campaigns* (New York: New York University Press, 1985), xii, 135, 146.

24. Archer Jones, *Civil War Command and Strategy: The Process of Victory and Defeat* (New York: Free Press, 1992), 242–43. Jones also offers an excellent discussion of the degree to which the Civil War was a "modern" conflict.

25. Mauriel Phillips Joslyn, ed., *Charlotte's Boys: Civil War Letters of the Branch Family of Savannah* (Berryville, Va.: Rockbridge Publishing Company, 1996), 310.

26. Williams, *Lincoln and His Generals*, vii, 7–8, 62.

27. Williams, "Military Leadership of North and South," 30–32, 35–37. In

*Our Masters the Rebels: A Speculation on Union Military Failure in the East, 1861–1865* (Cambridge, Mass.: Harvard University Press, 1978), Michael C. C. Adams accepted Williams's assessment of McClellan and other Union generals as ardent Jominians wedded to the concept of limited war. He went further in asserting that for many northern soldiers, "as for Jomini, the concept of limited war was part of a larger view of the world" in which Ulysses S. Grant, who pursued a strategy that harmed civilians as well as enemy soldiers, "had no place" (172–73). Other scholars, among them Herman Hattaway and Archer Jones in *How the North Won*, have taken issue with Williams's interpretation of Jomini's writings.

28. Williams, *Lincoln and His Generals*, 18, 27, 134–36; Williams, *McClellan, Sherman, and Grant* (New Brunswick, N.J.: Rutgers University Press, 1962), 32; Williams, "Military Leadership of North and South," 41–42.

29. Williams, *Lincoln and His Generals*, 312–14, 295, 306–7; Williams, *McClellan, Sherman, and Grant*, 101–2, 105.

30. Williams, "Military Leadership of North and South," 45; Williams, *McClellan, Sherman, and Grant*, 77.

31. Williams, "Military Leadership of North and South," 45. Although Williams never made it clear to his readers, neither Grant nor Sherman derived his strategic ideas from reading Clausewitz.

32. J. F. C. Fuller, *Grant & Lee: A Study in Personality and Generalship* (1933; rpt. Bloomington: Indiana University Press, 1957), 256–58; J. F. C. Fuller, *The Generalship of Ulysses S. Grant* (1929; rpt. Bloomington: Indiana University Press, 1958), 210, 362, 375, 380.

33. Alfred H. Burne, *Lee, Grant and Sherman: A Study in Leadership in the 1864–65 Campaign* (Aldershot: Gale & Polden, 1938 [American edition, New York: Charles Scribner's Sons, 1939]), 201–3, 198.

34. Colin R. Ballard, *The Military Genius of Abraham Lincoln* (Cleveland: World, 1952), 2, 138–39, 145, 239. The British edition was published in London by Oxford University Press.

35. Kenneth P. Williams, *Lincoln Finds a General: A Military Study of the Civil War*, 5 vols. (New York: Macmillan, 1949–59), 1:ix–x. Volume 5 takes the war through the battle of Chickamauga in the fall of 1863.

36. Catton, "Generalship of Ulysses S. Grant," 29, 20, 4–5. For an extensive narrative of Grant's Civil War career that expands on these arguments, see Catton's *Grant Moves South* (Boston: Little, Brown, 1960) and *Grant Takes Command* (Boston: Little, Brown, 1968), which carry forward the biography begun by Lloyd Lewis in *Captain Sam Grant* (Boston: Little, Brown, 1950). For a more compact narrative, see Catton, *U. S. Grant and the American Military Tradition* (Boston: Little, Brown, 1954).

37. Weigley, *American Way of War*, 141, 143–45, 149, 151–52.

38. John Keegan, *The Mask of Command* (New York: Viking, 1987), 191–92, 219–20, 232–33, 207–8.

39. John Y. Simon, "Grant, Lincoln, and Unconditional Surrender," in *Lincoln's Generals*, ed. Gabor S. Boritt (New York: Oxford University Press, 1994), 198.

40. Williams, *McClellan, Sherman, and Grant,* 101–2; Michael Fellman, "Lincoln and Sherman," in *Lincoln's Generals,* ed. Boritt, 140–41, 159.

41. Brooks D. Simpson, *Let Us Have Peace: Ulysses S. Grant and the Politics of War and Reconstruction, 1861–1868* (Chapel Hill: University of North Carolina Press, 1991), 96, xv.

42. Glatthaar, *Partners in Command,* 195, 231, 200–201, 205, 219.

43. Williams, *Lincoln and His Generals,* 18; Keegan, *Mask of Command,* 191–92; Winfield Scott, *Memoirs of Lieut.-General Scott, LL.D.,* 2 vols. (1864; rpt. Freeport, N.Y.: Books for Libraries, 1970), 2:626–27.

44. See, for example, Williams, *Lincoln and His Generals,* 11–12, 16–17, and Stephen W. Sears, "Lincoln and McClellan," in *Lincoln's Generals,* 50. The quotation is from Williams, *Lincoln Finds a General,* 2:479.

45. Catton, "Generalship of Ulysses S. Grant," 20; Stephen W. Sears, *George B. McClellan: The Young Napoleon* (New York: Ticknor & Fields, 1988), 166. For an excellent example of McClellan's attitude toward the emancipation dimension of Lincoln's strategy, see McClellan to William H. Aspinwall, September 26, 1862, wherein he blasted the Emancipation Proclamation as "inaugurating servile war, emancipating the slaves, & at one stroke of the pen changing our free institutions into a despotism." George B. McClellan, *The Civil War Papers of George B. McClellan: Selected Correspondence, 1860–1865,* ed. Stephen W. Sears (New York: Ticknor & Fields, 1989), 482. McClellan's comprehensive strategic blueprint is set forth in *Letter of the Secretary of War, Transmitting Report on the Organization of the Army of the Potomac, and of Its Campaigns in Virginia and Maryland, under the Command of Maj. Gen. George B. McClellan, from July 26, 1861, to November 7, 1862* (Washington: GPO, 1864).

46. Edward Hagerman, *The American Civil War and the Origins of Modern Warfare* (Bloomington: Indiana University Press, 1988), 65–66; Warren W. Hassler, Jr., *George B. McClellan: Shield of the Union* (Baton Rouge: Louisiana State University Press, 1957), 40, 44, 318–20, 322, 330.

47. Catton, "Generalship of Ulysses S. Grant," 20–21; Glatthaar, *Partners in Command,* 231; Stephen E. Ambrose, *Halleck: Lincoln's Chief of Staff* (Baton Rouge: Louisiana State University Press, 1962), 159–60, 207; Keegan, *Mask of Command,* 192; Williams, "Military Leadership of North and South," 41–42.

48. Hattaway and Jones, *How the North Won,* x, 35.

49. Ibid., 683–84.

50. Ibid., 685–87.

51. Ibid., 143–44, 687.

52. Ibid., 701. For a fuller development of Hattaway and Jones's argument that the Confederacy lost the war because of weak popular will and an absence of strong nationalism among its citizenry, see Richard E. Beringer, Herman Hattaway, Archer Jones, and William N. Still, Jr., *Why the South Lost the Civil War* (Athens: University of Georgia Press, 1986). For the counterargument that Union armies played the decisive role, see Gary W. Gallagher, *The Confederate War* (Cambridge, Mass.: Harvard University Press, 1997), especially chapter 4.

53. Hattaway and Jones, *How the North Won,* 696, 701.

54. In *How the North Won,* x, Hattaway and Jones paid tribute to Williams, stating that their approach stood "in a reciprocal relationship to his." They strove to revise his findings but at the same time meant "to honor and revere him." Jones presented the principal arguments of *How the North Won* in his much shorter, undocumented *Civil War.* For an even more compact expression of many of the same points, see Jones's "Military Means, Political Ends: Strategy."

55. Bruce Tap, *Over Lincoln's Shoulder: The Committee on the Conduct of the War* (Lawrence: University Press of Kansas, 1998), 6, 257–58. For examples of congressional studies that shied away from the strategy-related questions T. Harry Williams and Tap addressed, see Allan G. Bogue's *The Earnest Men: Republicans of the Civil War Senate* (Ithaca, N.Y.: Cornell University Press, 1981) and *The Congressman's Civil War* (Cambridge: Cambridge University Press, 1989).

56. John J. Hennessy, "I Dread the Spring: The Army of the Potomac Prepares for the Overland Campaign," in *The Wilderness Campaign,* ed. Gary W. Gallagher (Chapel Hill: University of North Carolina Press, 1997), 70–71. Most campaign studies virtually ignore the political context within which the armies maneuvered and fought. Two exceptions are John J. Hennessy's *Return to Bull Run: The Campaign and Battle of Second Manassas* (New York: Simon & Schuster, 1993) and Ludwell H. Johnson's *Red River Campaign: Politics and Cotton in the Civil War* (Baltimore: Johns Hopkins University Press, 1958).

57. John J. Hennessy, "We Shall Make Richmond Howl: The Army of the Potomac on the Eve of Chancellorsville," in *Chancellorsville: The Battle and Its Aftermath,* ed. Gary W. Gallagher (Chapel Hill: University of North Carolina Press, 1996), 4–5.

58. Eric T. Dean, Jr., "'We Live under a Government of Men and Morning Newspapers': Image, Expectation, and the Peninsula Campaign of 1862," *Virginia Magazine of History and Biography* 103 (January 1995): 26–27; Brooks D. Simpson, "Great Expectations: Ulysses S. Grant, the Northern Press, and the Opening of the Wilderness Campaign," in *The Wilderness Campaign,* 9–10, 32–33.

59. Richard S. West's *Mr. Lincoln's Navy* (New York: Longmans, Green, 1957), an uncritical and lightly documented work, is the best of a very weak group of modern titles specifically devoted to the Union navy. The leading general study of the naval war remains Bern Anderson's *By Sea and by River: The Naval History of the Civil War* (New York: Knopf, 1962), and Raimondo Luraghi's *A History of the Confederate Navy* (Annapolis: Naval Institute Press, 1996) sets a standard for research and analysis to which students of northern naval operations should aspire. Among the many popular narratives, Virgil Carrington Jones's *The Civil War at Sea,* 3 vols. (New York: Holt, Rinehart and Winston, 1960–1962) combines broad coverage and sprightly prose.

60. Rowena Reed, *Combined Operations in the Civil War* (Annapolis: Naval Institute Press, 1978), 188–89, 260.

61. Ibid., 263, 382.

62. John D. Milligan, *Gunboats Down the Mississippi* (Annapolis: United States Naval Institute, 1965), 178–79; Glatthaar, *Partners in Command,* 176–77,

186–87. In *Guns on the Western Waters: The Story of River Gunboats in the Civil War* (Baton Rouge: Louisiana State University Press, 1949), H. Allen Gosnell also stressed the United States Navy's role in western military campaigns. Undocumented and sometimes breathlessly written, Gosnell's narrative focused on the "unique thrills" and "adventures" of the "little men-of-war on the bayous" (272).

63. Robert M. Browning, Jr., *From Cape Charles to Cape Fear: The North Atlantic Blockading Squadron during the Civil War* (Tuscaloosa: University of Alabama Press, 1993), x, 59–60, 82, 301–2, 304, 307, 309.

64. The debate over whether Grant or Sherman was the more important strategic figure probably does not require much more attention. Indeed, this really amounts to a nonissue. Grant and Sherman would have agreed that Grant was the crucial actor and Sherman his talented but clearly subordinate lieutenant.

## REBELLION AND CONVENTIONAL WARFARE: CONFEDERATE STRATEGY AND MILITARY POLICY

1. General Orders No. 9, in *The Wartime Papers of R. E. Lee*, ed. Clifford Dowdey and Louis H. Manarin (Boston: Little, Brown, 1961), 934–35; Richard N. Current, "God and the Strongest Battalions," in *Why the North Won the Civil War*, ed. David Herbert Donald (Baton Rouge: Louisiana State University Press, 1960), 22.

2. On this point, see Gary W. Gallagher, *The Confederate War: How Popular Will, Nationalism, and Military Strategy Could Not Stave Off Defeat* (Cambridge, Mass.: Harvard University Press, 1997).

3. Edward A. Pollard, *The Lost Cause: A New Southern History of the War of the Confederates* (New York: E. B. Treat, 1866), 727–29.

4. See James M. McPherson, "American Victory, American Defeat," in *Why the Confederacy Lost*, ed. Gabor S. Boritt (New York: Oxford University Press, 1992), 15–42. McPherson posits a dichotomy similar to that presented here between "overwhelming numbers and resources" and Confederate flaws. He labels these themes "external" and "internal" causes of defeat.

5. Frank Lawrence Owsley, *State Rights in the Confederacy* (Chicago: University of Chicago Press, 1925), 277.

6. Andrew N. Lytle, *Bedford Forrest and His Critter Company* (New York: Minton, Balch, 1931); Allen Tate, *Jefferson Davis, His Rise and Fall* (New York: Minton, Balch, 1929); and *Stonewall Jackson: The Good Soldier* (New York: Minton, Balch, 1928). Quotations from *The Lytle-Tate Letters: The Correspondence of Andrew Lytle and Allen Tate,* ed. Thomas Daniel Young and Elizabeth Sarcone (Jackson: University Press of Mississippi, 1987), 20–21. Allen Tate's "Ode to the Confederate Dead" is in Allen Tate, *Poems, 1922–1947* (New York: Charles Scribner's, 1948).

7. Bell Irvin Wiley, *Southern Negroes, 1861–1865* (New Haven: Yale University Press, 1938); *The Life of Johnny Reb: The Common Soldier of the Confederacy* (Indianapolis: Bobbs-Merrill, 1943); *The Life of Billy Yank: The Common Soldier of the Union* (Indianapolis: Bobbs-Merrill, 1952); and *The Road to Appomattox* (1956; College Edition, New York: Atheneum, 1968), 119–21.

8. Douglas Southall Freeman, *R. E. Lee: A Biography,* 4 vols. (New York: Charles Scribner's Sons, 1934–1935); and *Lee's Lieutenants: A Study in Command,* 3 vols. (New York: Charles Scribner's Sons, 1942–1944), xxv–xxvii.

9. Charles W. Ramsdell, *Behind the Lines in the Southern Confederacy* (Baton Rouge: Louisiana State University Press, 1944), 85; Albert B. Moore, *Conscription and Conflict in the Confederacy* (New York: Macmillan, 1924); Ella Lonn, *Desertion during the Civil War* (New York: Century, 1928); Georgia L. Tatum, *Disloyalty in the Confederacy* (Chapel Hill: University of North Carolina Press, 1934). See also Douglas B. Ball, *Financial Failure and Confederate Defeat* (Urbana: University of Illinois Press, 1991).

10. Raimondo Luraghi, *The Rise and Fall of the Plantation South* (New York: New Viewpoints, 1978), 5.

11. See Raimondo Luraghi, *Gli Stati Uniti* (Torino: Unione Tipografice–Editrice Torinese, 1974) and *Storia della guerra civile americana,* 4th ed. (Torino: Einaudi, 1966). Quotations from Luraghi, *Rise and Fall,* 150–52.

12. Frank E. Vandiver, *Ploughshares into Swords: Josiah Gorgas and Confederate Ordnance* (Austin: University of Texas Press, 1952) and *Rebel Brass: The Confederate Command System* (Baton Rouge: Louisiana State University Press, 1956).

13. Frank E. Vandiver, *Their Tattered Flags: The Epic of the Confederacy* (New York: Harper's Magazine Press, 1970) and *Basic History of the Confederacy* (Princeton: Van Norstrand, 1962), 96.

14. Vandiver, *Basic History,* 65; see also *Tattered Flags,* 156–57.

15. Vandiver, *Tattered Flags,* 121. See also 94. And see Vandiver's essay "Jefferson Davis and Confederate Strategy" in Avery O. Craven and Vandiver, *The American Tragedy: The Civil War in Retrospect* (Hampden-Sydney, Va.: Hampden-Sydney College, 1959), 19–32, and his "Jefferson Davis and Unified Army Command," *Louisiana Historical Quarterly* 38 (1955), 26-38.

16. William C. Davis, *Jefferson Davis: The Man and His Hour* (New York: HarperCollins, 1991), 700–701.

17. Emory M. Thomas, *The Confederacy as a Revolutionary Experience* (Englewood Cliffs, N.J: Prentice-Hall, 1971; rpt. Columbia: University of South Carolina Press, 1991), 52.

18. Emory M. Thomas, *The Confederate Nation, 1861–1865* (New York: Harper & Row, 1979), 248–49, 304–5.

19. Ibid., 297–99; the quotation is from my "Reckoning with Rebels," in *The Old South in the Crucible of War,* ed. Harry P. Owens and James J. Cooke (Jackson: University Press of Mississippi, 1983), 10–11.

20. Paul D. Escott, *After Secession: Jefferson Davis and the Failure of Confederate Nationalism* (Baton Rouge: Louisiana State University Press, 1978). See also Escott's essay "The Failure of Confederate Nationalism: The Old South's Class System in the Crucible of War," in *Old South in the Crucible,* 15–28.

21. Drew Gilpin Faust, *The Creation of Confederate Nationalism: Ideology and Identity in the Civil War South* (Baton Rouge: Louisiana State University Press, 1988).

22. David Herbert Donald, "Died of Democracy," in *Why the North Won,* 77–90. The quotation is from p. 90.

23. David M. Potter, "Jefferson Davis and the Political Factors in Confederate Defeat," in *Why the North Won,* 91–114; quotations from pp. 111, 112.

24. T. Harry Williams, "The Military Leadership of North and South," in *Why the North Won,* 23–47; quotations from pp. 40, 46. See J. F. C. Fuller, *Grant & Lee: A Study in Personality and Generalship* (1933; rpt. Bloomington: Indiana University Press, 1957).

25. Herman Hattaway and Archer Jones, *How the North Won: A Military History of the Civil War* (Urbana: University of Illinois Press, 1983); see especially the final chapter. Archer Jones, *Confederate Strategy, from Shiloh to Vicksburg* (Baton Rouge: Louisiana State University Press, 1961).

26. Thomas Lawrence Connelly and Archer Jones, *The Politics of Command: Factions and Ideas in Confederate Strategy* (Baton Rouge: Louisiana State University Press, 1973), 200.

27. Ibid., 170–200.

28. Thomas Lawrence Connelly, *Army of the Heartland: The Army of Tennessee, 1861–1862* (Baton Rouge: Louisiana State University Press, 1967) and *Autumn of Glory: The Army of Tennessee, 1862–1865* (Baton Rouge: Louisiana State University Press, 1971).

29. Thomas Lawrence Connelly, *The Marble Man: Robert E. Lee and His Image in American Society* (New York: Knopf, 1977).

30. Ibid., xiv.

31. Thomas Lawrence Connelly and Barbara L. Bellows, *God and General Longstreet: The Lost Cause and the Southern Mind* (Baton Rouge: Louisiana State University Press, 1982), 106.

32. Connelly, *Marble Man,* 195–208.

33. Russell F. Weigley, *The American Way of War: A History of United States Military Strategy and Policy* (New York: Macmillan, 1973), 126–27.

34. Grady McWhiney and Perry D. Jamieson, *Attack and Die: Civil War Military Tactics and the Southern Heritage* (University, Ala.: University of Alabama Press, 1982), 180, xv.

35. Richard E. Beringer, Herman Hattaway, Archer Jones, and William N. Still, Jr., *Why the South Lost the Civil War* (Athens: University of Georgia Press, 1986).

36. Ibid., 39–52, especially.

37. Ibid., 53–63; William N. Still, Jr., *Iron Afloat: The Story of the Confederate Armorclads* (1971; rpt. Columbia: University of South Carolina Press, 1985); *Confederate Shipbuilding* (1969; rpt. Columbia: University of South Carolina Press, 1987); Raimondo Luraghi, *A History of the Confederate Navy* (Annapolis: Naval Institute Press, 1996); Stephen R. Wise, *Lifeline of the Confederacy: Blockade Running during the Civil War* (Columbia: University of South Carolina Press, 1988), 226.

38. Beringer et al., *Why the South Lost,* 439.

39. Ibid., 351–67; E. Merton Coulter, *The Confederate States of America, 1861–1865* (Baton Rouge: Louisiana State University Press, 1950), 566; Kenneth M. Stampp, "The Southern Road to Appomattox," in Stampp's *The Imperiled Union: Essays on the Background of the Civil War* (New York: Oxford University Press, 1980), 269; the epitaph is from Beringer et al., *Why the South Lost,* 34.

40. Beringer et al., *Why the South Lost,* 440.

41. Archer Jones, *Civil War Command and Strategy: The Process of Victory and Defeat* (New York: Free Press, 1992), 222.

42. Edward Hagerman, *The American Civil War and the Origins of Modern Warfare* (Bloomington: Indiana University Press, 1988), xvii.

43. Ibid., 143, 44.

44. See reviews of *The American Civil War* by Earl J. Hess in *Journal of Southern History* 56 (1990): 357–58 and by Albert Castel in *Civil War History* 35 (1989):172–76.

45. Charles Royster, *The Destructive War: William Tecumseh Sherman, Stonewall Jackson, and the Americans* (New York: Knopf, 1991), xii. On the topic of "total war," Mark E. Neely, Jr.'s "Was the Civil War a Total War?," *Civil War History* 37 (1991): 5–28, is important in this context.

46. Phillip Shaw Paludan, *Victims: A True Story of the Civil War* (Knoxville: University of Tennessee Press, 1981); Lesley J. Gordon, "The Seeds of Disaster: The Generalship of George E. Pickett After Gettysburg," in *Leadership and Command in the American Civil War,* ed. Steven E. Woodworth (Campbell, Calif.: Savas Woodbury, 1995), 147–94; Brian Steel Wills, *A Battle from the Start: The Life of Nathan Bedford Forrest* (New York: HarperCollins, 1992), 177–96. See also Michael Fellman, *Inside War: The Guerrilla Conflict in Missouri during the American Civil War* (New York: Oxford University Press, 1989).

47. George M. Fredrickson, "Why the Confederacy Did Not Fight a Guerrilla War after the Fall of Richmond: A Comparative View" (Gettysburg, Pa.: Gettysburg College, 1996); quotations from pp. 27, 29.

48. Gabor S. Boritt, ed., *Why the Confederacy Lost* (New York: Oxford University Press, 1992). Other books in this series include: *Lincoln: The War President* (New York: Oxford University Press, 1992); *Lincoln's Generals* (New York: Oxford University Press, 1994); and *Why the Civil War Came* (New York: Oxford University Press, 1996). Borritt edited all three.

49. James M. McPherson, "American Victory, American Defeat," in *Why the Confederacy Lost,* 18–42.

50. Gary W. Gallagher, "'Upon Their Success Hang Momentous Interests': Generals," in *Why the Confederacy Lost,* ed. Boritt, 79–108, quotation, 85. This essay anticipates Gallagher's *The Confederate War.*

51. Ibid., 107–8. Gallagher himself has convened a conference each year at the Mont Alto campus of Pennsylvania State University, and from these gatherings have come six collections of essays to date. These books,

all edited by Gallagher, include: *Antietam: Essays on the 1862 Maryland Campaign* (Kent, Ohio: Kent State University Press, 1989); *Struggle for the Shenandoah: Essays on the 1864 Valley Campaign* (Kent, Ohio: Kent State University Press,1991); *The First Day of Gettysburg: Essays on Confederate and Union Leadership* (Kent, Ohio: Kent State University Press, 1992); *The Second Day of Gettysburg: Essays on Confederate and Union Leadership* (Kent, Ohio: Kent State University Press, 1993); *The Third Day at Gettysburg and Beyond* (Chapel Hill: University of North Carolina Press, 1994); and *Chancellorsville: The Battle and Its Aftermath* (Chapel Hill: University of North Carolina Press, 1996). Each of these works includes work by well-known scholars intended for scholars and general readers at once.

52. Richard M. McMurry, *Two Great Rebel Armies: An Essay in Confederate Military History* (Chapel Hill: University of North Carolina Press, 1989).

53. Alan T. Nolan, *Lee Considered: General Robert E. Lee and Civil War History* (Chapel Hill: University of North Carolina Press, 1991).

54. Charles P. Roland, *Reflections on Lee: A Historian's Assessment* (Mechanicsburg, Pa.: Stackpole Books, 1995), 102.

55. I first put forth this thesis in a paper delivered in November 1993 at a meeting of the Southern Historical Association and subsequently published in the *Douglas Southall Freeman Historical Review* (Spring 1994). This journal is a publication of the Beta Mu chapter of Phi Alpha Theta at the University of Richmond. The emphasis on Lee's search for a decisive battle and his unresolved conflict with Davis is found in my *Robert E. Lee: A Biography* (New York: Norton, 1995), 255–57, 288–93, 301–3.

56. Steven E. Woodworth, *Jefferson Davis and His Generals: The Failure of Confederate Command in the West* (Lawrence: University Press of Kansas, 1990), 316.

57. Steven E. Woodworth, *Davis and Lee at War* (Lawrence: University Press of Kansas, 1995), xii. "I endeavor to show that although Lee did pursue a largely offensive grand strategy, his policy was in fact one of two possible ways in which the South could conceivably have obtained its independence. The other, the thoroughly defensive, survival-oriented grand strategy so much praised by many modern scholars, was the strategy of Jefferson Davis, and the tension between Davis's ideas and Lee's offensive quest for early victory is the central feature of the climactic stages of Davis's war for Virginia and the Confederacy."

58. Archer Jones, "Military Means, Political Ends: Strategy," in *Why the Confederacy Lost*, 43–77. For an enlightened critique of Clausewitz's dictum in the present, see John Keegan, *A History of Warfare* (New York: Knopf, 1993), 390–92, in which Keegan concludes, "Politics must continue; war cannot."

59. Reid Mitchell, "The Perseverance of the Soldiers," in *Why the Confederacy Lost*, 109–32; *Civil War Soldiers* (New York: Viking, 1988); *The Vacant Chair: The Northern Soldier Leaves Home* (New York: Oxford University Press, 1993).

60. Mitchell, *Vacant Chair*, 155; Mitchell, "The Perseverance of Soldiers," 122–32.

61. Drew Gilpin Faust, "Altars of Sacrifice: Confederate Women and the Narratives of the War," first published in the *Journal of American History* (1990) but more readily available in *Divided Houses: Gender and the Civil War*, ed. Catherine Clinton and Nina Silber (New York: Oxford University Press, 1992), 171–99; quotations from pp. 197–98, 199.

62. Joseph T. Glatthaar, "Black Glory: The African-American Role in Union Victory," in *Why the Confederacy Lost*, 133–62; *The March to the Sea and Beyond: Sherman's Troops in the Savannah and Carolinas Campaigns* (New York: New York University Press, 1985); *Forged in Battle: The Civil War Alliance of Black Soldiers and White Officers* (New York: Free Press, 1990); *Partners in Command: The Relationships Between Leaders in the Civil War* (New York: Free Press, 1994). The quotation is from "Black Glory," 161.

63. One of the best exhibitions of the enlightenment available in the expansive literature of Confederate war making is Michael C. C. Adams, *Our Masters the Rebels: A Speculation on Union Military Failure in the East, 1861–1865* (Cambridge, Mass.: Harvard University Press, 1978). Adams offers intellectual history to sustain his thesis that many northern people, including numerous general officers, perceived "the Southerner as a superior martial figure" (vii). This perception fed insecurities among northern soldiers and generals and so limited the performance of Federal armies. Here is insightful military history grounded in the works of Harriet Martineau, James Silk Buckingham, Frances Anne Kemble, Frederick Law Olmsted, and others equally unacquainted with small unit tactics.

64. A recent discussion of this issue is James M. McPherson, "What's the Matter with History?" in his splendid collection of essays *Drawn with the Sword: Reflections on the American Civil War* (New York: Oxford University Press, 1996), 231–53.

## BATTLEFIELD TACTICS

1. Quoted in John Esten Cooke, *A Life of Gen. Robert E. Lee* (New York: Appleton, 1871), 184.

2. See "Considerations on the Government of Poland," in *Rousseau: Political Writings*, ed. Frederick Watkins (London: Thomas Nelson, 1953), 236–45.

3. See Carl L. Davis, *Arming the Union: Small Arms in the Civil War* (Port Washington, N.Y.: Kennikat Press, 1973).

4. U. S. Grant, *Personal Memoirs*, Vol. 1 (New York: Charles L. Webster, 1885), 95; Jac Weller, "Civil War Minie Rifles Prove Quite Accurate," *American Rifleman* (July 1971): 36–40.

5. Numerous scholars, including Weller, state that soldiers preferred the Enfield. Bell Wiley's and my own research in soldiers' letters and diaries indicates otherwise. See Bell Irvin Wiley, *The Life of Billy Yank: The Common Soldier of the Union* (Indianapolis: Bobbs-Merrill, 1952), 62–63.

6. Robert V. Bruce, *Lincoln and the Tools of War* (Indianapolis: Bobbs-Merrill, 1956).

7. See Fred Albert Shannon, *The Organization and Administration of the Union Army, 1861–1865*. 2 vols. (Cleveland: Arthur H. Clark, 1928). Theodore Frelinghuysen Upson, *With Sherman to the Sea: The Civil War Letters, Diaries, and Reminiscences of Theodore F. Upson*, ed. Oscar Osburn Winther (Baton Rouge: Louisiana State University Press, 1943).

8. L. Van Loan Naisawald, *Grape and Canister: The Story of the Field Artillery of the Army of the Potomac* (New York: Oxford University Press, 1960). Naisawald reduces the effective range of Napoleons to 1,200 yards, but Edward Porter Alexander, perhaps the brightest artillerist on either side in the war, employed them well at three-quarters of a mile. See Gary W. Gallagher, ed., *Fighting for the Confederacy: The Personal Recollections of General Edward Porter Alexander* (Chapel Hill: University of North Carolina Press, 1989).

9. In the Civil War, a large number of different artillery guns served the armies. The Napoleon, the Ordnance Gun, and the Parrot were the most common. With rifled guns, the Union also used percussion shells, which exploded on impact.

10. Edward Hagerman, *The American Civil War and the Origins of Modern War: Ideas, Organization, and Field Command* (Bloomington: Indiana University Press, 1988).

11. Grady McWhiney and Perry D. Jamieson, *Attack and Die: Civil War Military Tactics and the Southern Heritage* (University, Ala.: University of Alabama Press, 1982).

12. Herman Hattaway and Archer Jones, *How the North Won: A Military History of the Civil War* (Urbana: University of Illinois Press, 1983); Richard E. Beringer, Herman Hattaway, Archer Jones, and William N. Still, Jr., *Why the South Lost the Civil War* (Athens: University of Georgia Press, 1986).

13. Albert Castel, "Mars and the Reverend Longstreet; or, Attacking and Dying in the Civil War," *Civil War History* 33, no. 2 (1987):103–14; rpt. in Castel, *Winning and Losing in the Civil War: Essays and Stories* (Columbia: University of South Carolina Press, 1996), 119–32.

14. Paddy Griffith, *Battle Tactics of the Civil War* (New Haven: Yale University Press, 1989). Earl J. Hess, *The Union Soldier in Battle: Enduring the Ordeal of Combat* (Lawrence, Kans.: University Press of Kansas, 1997).

15. For Griffith's statistics, see p. 147. Seventeen of his 113 distances (nearly 15 percent) came from the Battle of Seven Pines, which according to his sources had an average range of 68 yards. He has more ranges from Seven Pines than for all the battles of 1863.

16. James M. McPherson, *For Cause and Comrades: Why Men Fought the Civil War* (New York: Oxford University Press, 1997).

17. See James M. McPherson, *Battle Cry of Freedom: The Civil War Era* (New York: Oxford University Press, 1988). Also see D. Scott Hartwig, "No Troops on the Field Had Done Better: John C. Caldwell's Division in the Wheatfield, July 2, 1863," in *The Second Day at Gettysburg*, ed. Gary W. Gallagher (Kent, Ohio: Kent State University Press, 1993), 136–71.

18. Gary W. Gallagher, ed., *Fighting for the Confederacy: The Personal Recollections of General Edward Porter Alexander* (Chapel Hill: University of North Carolina Press, 1989).

19. Naisawald, *Grape and Canister,* viii; Jennings Cropper Wise, *The Long Arm of Lee: The History of the Artillery of the Army of Northern Virginia,* 2 vols. (Lynchburg, Va.: J. P. Bell, 1915), 1:268.

20. Larry J. Daniel, *Cannoneers in Gray: The Field Artillery of the Army of Tennessee, 1861–1865* (University, Ala.: University of Alabama Press, 1984).

21. Stephen Z. Starr, *The Union Cavalry in the Civil War,* 3 vols. (Baton Rouge: Louisiana State University Press, 1979–1985).

22. Brian Steel Wills, *A Battle from the Start: The Life of Nathan Bedford Forrest* (New York: HarperCollins, 1992).

23. James Pickett Jones, *Yankee Blitzkrieg: Wilson's Raid through Alabama and Georgia* (Athens: University of Georgia Press, 1976). Wilson's cavalry also demonstrated effectiveness in pursuit after the Battle of Nashville, although scholars may have overstated the case. Many of Wilson's prisoners were likely wounded from Franklin and Nashville and would have fallen captive to any sort of infantry pursuit. Also see Robert K. Krick, "'The Cause of All My Disasters': Jubal A. Early and the Undisciplined Valley Cavalry," in *Struggle for the Shenandoah: Essays on the 1864 Valley Campaign,* Gary W. Gallagher (Kent, Ohio: Kent State University Press, 1991), 77–106.

24. Gerald F. Linderman, *Embattled Courage: The Experience of Combat in the American Civil War* (New York: Free Press, 1987).

25. Charles Royster, *The Destructive War: William Tecumseh Sherman, Stonewall Jackson, and the Americans* (New York: Knopf, 1991).

26. Gary W. Gallagher, *The Confederate War: How Popular Will, Nationalism, and Military Strategy Could Not Stave Off Defeat* (Cambridge, Mass.: Harvard University Press, 1997).

27. Mark Grimsley, *The Hard Hand of War: Union Military Policy Toward Southern Civilians, 1861–1865* (Cambridge: Cambridge University Press, 1995); Joseph T. Glatthaar, *The March to the Sea and Beyond: Sherman's Troops in the Savannah and Carolinas Campaigns* (New York: New York University Press, 1985). By petty thievery, I refer to jewelry, money, and so on. Foodstuffs and animals were legitimate objects for confiscation as contraband of war.

28. Reid Mitchell, *Civil War Soldiers* (New York: Viking, 1988); Reid Mitchell, *The Vacant Chair: The Northern Soldier Leaves Home* (New York: Oxford University Press, 1993).

29. William A. Blair, *Virginia's Private War: Feeding Belly and Soul in the Confederacy* (New York: Oxford University Press, 1998). Also see Earl J. Hess, *Liberty, Virtue, and Progress: Northerners and Their War for the Union* (New York: New York University Press, 1988). Hess perceives an ideological consensus formed in the North, based on individualism, egalitarianism, self-government, and self-control.

30. Perry D. Jamieson, *Crossing the Deadly Ground: United States Army Tactics, 1865–1899* (Tuscaloosa: University of Alabama Press, 1994).

31. Jay Luvaas, *The Military Legacy of the Civil War: The European Inheritance* (Chicago: University of Chicago Press, 1959).

32. William L. Shea and Earl J. Hess, *Pea Ridge: Civil War Campaign in the West* (Chapel Hill: University of North Carolina Press, 1992). A few other quality battle and campaign studies, but by no means all, published in the last ten years are: Mark L. Bradley, *The Last Stand in the Carolinas: The Battle of Bentonville* (Campbell, Calif.: Savas Woodbury, 1996); Albert Castel, *Decision in the West: The Atlanta Campaign of 1864* (Lawrence: University Press of Kansas, 1992); William D. Matter, *If It Takes All Summer: The Battle of Spotsylvania* (Chapel Hill: University of North Carolina Press, 1988); Gordon C. Rhea, *The Battle of the Wilderness, May 5–6, 1864* (Baton Rouge: Louisiana State University Press, 1994); Noah Andre Trudeau, *Bloody Roads South: The Wilderness to Cold Harbor, May–June 1864* (Boston: Little, Brown, 1989).

33. See Robert K. Krick, *Stonewall Jackson at Cedar Mountain* (Chapel Hill: University of North Carolina Press, 1990); Robert K. Krick, *Conquering the Valley: Stonewall Jackson at Port Republic* (New York: William Morrow, 1996); Harry W. Pfanz, *Gettysburg: The Second Day* (Chapel Hill: University of North Carolina Press, 1987); Harry W. Pfanz, *Gettysburg—Culp's Hill and Cemetery Hill* (Chapel Hill: University of North Carolina Press, 1993); John J. Hennessy, *Return to Bull Run: The Campaign and Battle of Second Manassas* (New York: Simon & Schuster, 1993); John Bigelow, *The Campaign of Chancellorsville* (New Haven: Yale University Press, 1910); Richard J. Sommers, *Richmond Redeemed: The Siege of Petersburg* (Garden City, N.Y.: Doubleday, 1981).

34. John Keegan, *The Face of Battle: A Study of Agincourt, Waterloo, and the Somme* (New York: Viking Press, 1976).

35. Dean Thomas, an expert on Civil War small arms and ammunition and author of *Round Ball to Rimfire: A History of Civil War Small Arms Ammunition* (Gettysburg: Thomas Publications, 1997), has been extremely helpful in providing information on the Williams cleaners. The War Department first ordered them in December 1861. Capt. A. B. Dyer in his report on "Williams" improved bullet, 18 June 1862, RG 156, National Archives, touted the performance of the Williams cleaner, although he fired cleaners exclusively. Union soldiers usually had two per ten rounds of ammunition. According to Thomas, the cleaners helped a little, but not dramatically, perhaps increasing the number of rounds one could fire before cleaning to twenty or so. Complaints about them from Sherman's army led to the termination of the contract. Some officers believed that they damaged the rifling grooves, although Thomas doubts that was the case.

## "NOT THE GENERAL BUT THE SOLDIER"

1. Lloyd Lewis, *Sherman: Fighting Prophet* (New York: Harcourt, Brace, 1932); Bruce Catton, *A Stillness at Appomattox* (Garden City, N.Y.: Doubleday, 1953).

2. Bell Irvin Wiley, *The Life of Johnny Reb: The Common Soldier of the Confederacy* (Indianapolis: Bobbs-Merrill, 1943); *The Life of Billy Yank: The Common Soldier of the Union* (Indianapolis: Bobbs-Merrill, 1952).

3. Wiley, *Billy Yank,* 12.

4. Ibid., 13.

5. Bell Irvin Wiley, *The Plain People of the Confederacy* (Baton Rouge: Louisiana State University Press, 1944), 69.

6. Wiley, *Plain People,* 29–30

7. Michael Barton, *Goodmen: The Character of Civil War Soldiers* (University Park: Pennsylvania State University Press, 1981).

8. Joseph T. Glatthaar, *The March to the Sea and Beyond: Sherman's Troops in the Savannah and Carolinas Campaigns* (New York: New York University Press, 1985).

9. Gerald F. Linderman, *Embattled Courage: The Experience of Combat in the American Civil War* (New York: Free Press, 1987).

10. Ibid., 1, 8.

11. James I. Robertson, Jr., *Soldiers Blue and Gray* (Columbia: University of South Carolina Press, 1988); quotations from pp. ix–x.

12. Randall C. Jimerson, *The Private Civil War: Popular Thought during the Sectional Conflict* (Baton Rouge: Louisiana State University Press, 1988); Earl J. Hess, *Liberty, Virtue, and Progress: Northerners and Their War for the Union* (New York: New York University Press, 1988); Reid Mitchell, *Civil War Soldiers* (New York: Viking, 1988).

13. Hess, *Liberty,* 1, 103.

14. Joseph Allan Frank and George A. Reaves, *"Seeing the Elephant": Raw Recruits at the Battle of Shiloh* (New York: Greenwood Press, 1989).

15. Joseph T. Glatthaar, "The 'New Civil War' History: An Overview," *Pennsylvania Magazine of History and Biography* 115 (July 1991): 355.

16. Larry J. Daniel, *Soldiering in the Army of Tennessee: A Portrait of Life in a Confederate Army* (Chapel Hill: University of North Carolina Press, 1991); James M. McPherson, *What They Fought For, 1861–1865* (Baton Rouge: Louisiana State University Press, 1994).

17. Daniel, *Soldiering,* xii.

18. Ibid., 147.

19. McPherson, *What They Fought For,* 16, 36, 42–43.

20. Joseph T. Glatthaar, *Forged in Battle: The Civil War Alliance of Black Soldiers and White Officers* (New York: Free Press, 1990); Stuart McConnell, *Glorious Contentment: The Grand Army of the Republic, 1865–1900* (Chapel Hill: University of North Carolina Press, 1992); Michael Fellman, *Inside War: The Guerrilla Conflict in Missouri during the American Civil War* (New York: Oxford University Press, 1989); Reid Mitchell, *The Vacant Chair: The Northern Soldier Leaves Home* (New York: Oxford University Press, 1993).

21. McConnell, xiv. Rank-and-file Confederate veterans have not received equivalent treatment, but Gaines M. Foster, *Ghosts of the Confederacy: Defeat, the Lost Cause, and the Emergence of the New South, 1865 to 1913* (New York: Oxford University Press, 1987), and Charles Reagan Wilson, *Baptized in Blood: The Religion of the Lost Cause, 1865–1920* (Athens: University of Georgia Press, 1980) both treat veterans' organizations.

22. Fellman, v–vi.

23. Mark Grimsley, *The Hard Hand of War: Union Military Policy toward Southern Civilians, 1861–1865* (Cambridge: Cambridge University Press, 1995), 4.

24. Charles Royster, *The Destructive War: William Tecumseh Sherman, Stonewall Jackson, and the Americans* (New York: Knopf, 1991); John J. Hennessy, *Return to Bull Run: The Campaign and Battle of Second Manassas* (New York: Simon & Schuster, 1993); Stephen W. Sears, *To the Gates of Richmond: The Peninsula Campaign* (New York: Ticknor & Fields, 1992); and Harry W. Pfanz, *Gettysburg: The Second Day* (Chapel Hill: University of North Carolina Press, 1987).

25. I have attempted to address some of these issues in "The GI in Europe and the American Tradition," in *Time to Kill: The Soldiers Experience of War in the West 1939–1945,* ed. Paul Addison and Angus Calder (1997), 304–16.

26. James M. McPherson, *For Cause and Comrades* (New York: Oxford University Press, 1997); Earl J. Hess, *The Union Soldier in Battle: Enduring the Ordeal of Combat* (Lawrence: University Press of Kansas, 1997).

27. Hess, *Union Soldier,* ix.

28. Reid Mitchell, "Foreword," in *Letters Home: Henry Matrau of the Iron Brigade,* ed. Marcia Reid-Green (Lincoln: University of Nebraska Press, 1993), vii–xiv.

29. Two recent articles apply twentieth-century ideas about Posttraumatic Stress Disorder to Civil War soldiers. See Eric Dean, "We Will All Be Lost and Destroyed: Posttraumatic Stress Disorder and the Civil War," *Civil War History* 38 (June 1991): 138–53, and John E. Talbott, "Combat Trauma in the American Civil War," *History Today* 46 (March 1996). Both Dean and Talbott are writing books considering Civil War combat trauma in a comparative setting.

## ABRAHAM LINCOLN VS. JEFFERSON DAVIS

1. Professor Robert Bonner of the University of Southern Maine generously read this essay and offered much sound advice.

2. David Herbert Donald, ed., *Why the North Won the Civil War* (Baton Rouge: Louisiana State University Press, 1960), 112.

3. Frank J. Williams et al., eds., *Abraham Lincoln: Sources and Style of Leadership* (Westport, Conn.: Greenwood, 1994).

4. Ludwell H. Johnson, "Jefferson Davis and Abraham Lincoln as War Presidents: Nothing Succeeds Like Success," *Civil War History* 27 (March 1981): 49–63. On page 53 Johnson points out the exaggerated influence of the Confederate diarists, two of them mere war department clerks, and one of those, often quoted, a relative of George W. Randolph. When Davis caused Randolph's resignation as secretary of war, he removed diarist R. G. H. Kean's uncle and thus likely tainted Kean's testimony on Davis's abilities. See also Johnson's note 20. Though more concerned with international comparisons, Carl Degler does make Lincoln out to be more like Bismarck than Davis as a nation-builder in Degler, "One Among Many: The United States and National Unification," in Gabor S.

Boritt, ed., *Lincoln, the War President* (New York: Oxford University Press, 1992), 89–119.

5. For a forward-looking reappraisal of Davis's leadership in strategic matters, see William J. Cooper, "A Reassessment of Jefferson Davis as a War Leader: The Case from Atlanta to Nashville," *Journal of Southern History* 36 (May 1970): 189–204.

6. James G. Randall, *Lincoln the President: Springfield to Gettysburg, Volume I,* and *Lincoln the President: Bull Run to Gettysburg, Volume II* (New York: Dodd, Mead, 1945); *Lincoln the President: Midstream* (New York: Dodd, Mead, 1953); and Randall and Richard N. Current, *Lincoln the President: Last Full Measure* (New York: Dodd, Mead, 1955); John G. Nicolay and John Hay, *Abraham Lincoln: A History,* 10 vols. (New York: Century, 1890).

7. Robert McElroy, *Jefferson Davis: The Real and the Unreal,* 2 vols. (New York: Harper, 1937), 2:720. The most exhaustive assessment of Davis historiography is Herman Hattaway, "Jefferson Davis and the Historians," in *The Confederate High Command & Related Topics: The 1988 Deep Delta Civil War Symposium: Themes in Honor of T. Harry Williams,* ed. Roman J. Heleniak and Lawrence L. Hewitt (Washington, D.C.: White Mane, 1990), 142–71 (148–49 for Eckenrode). Changing racial assumptions made considerable difference in Lincoln scholarship, too.

8. See, for example, the "Critical Bibliography" in Robert McElroy, *Jefferson Davis: The Real and the Unreal,* 2 vols. (New York: Harper, 1937), 2:699–759. It is dominated by works on Davis's capture and by polemical works. Though obviously dated, Walter L. Fleming's "Jefferson Davis, the Negroes and the Negro Problem," *Sewanee Review* 16 (October 1908): 407–27, is useful.

9. I have relied heavily here on Stephenson's article and on his excellent biographical sketch of Davis in *The Dictionary of American Biography,* 21 vols. (New York: Charles Scribner's Sons, 1930), 5:123–31.

10. Nathaniel W. Stephenson, "A Theory of Jefferson Davis," *American Historical Review* 21 (October 1915): 73–90.

11. But see Richard E. Beringer, "Jefferson Davis's Pursuit of Ambition: The Attractive Features of Alternative Decisions," *Civil War History* 38 (March 1992): 5–39, which applied the theory of "cognitive dissonance" to Jefferson Davis's indecisiveness. It did not evaluate his personality as a whole or analyze his physical or psychosomatic symptoms.

12. John Mack Faragher, *Sugar Creek: Life on the Illinois Prairie* (New Haven: Yale University Press, 1986), 90–91. Grady McWhiney emphasized Davis's poor health and the similar condition of many around him in "Jefferson Davis and His Generals," in McWhiney's *Southerners and Other Americans* (New York: Basic Books, 1973), 86.

13. Clement Eaton, *Jefferson Davis* (New York: Free Press, 1977), 16, 20, 22–23, 49, 53, 109, 262; George C. Rable, *The Confederate Republic: A Revolution against Politics* (Chapel Hill: University of North Carolina Press, 1994), 209.

14. Edmund Wilson fused psychology and assessment of public life in *Patriotic Gore: Studies in the Literature of the American Civil War* (New York: Oxford

University Press, 1962), 96–130; the same path was followed by Dwight G. Anderson in *Abraham Lincoln: The Quest for Immortality* (New York: Knopf, 1982). George B. Forgie gave Wilson's theory cultural emphasis in *Patricide in the House Divided: A Psychological Interpretation of Lincoln and His Age* (New York: Norton, 1979). Taking Wilson's psychological emphasis toward intimate biography were Michael Burlingame, *The Inner World of Abraham Lincoln* (Urbana: University of Illinois Press, 1994); Charles B. Strozier, *Lincoln's Quest for Union: Public and Private Meanings* (New York: Basic Books, 1982); John Y. Simon, "Abraham Lincoln and Ann Rutledge," *Journal of the Abraham Lincoln Association* 2 (1990): 13–33; and Douglas Wilson, "Abraham Lincoln and the Evidence of Herndon's Informants," *Civil War History* 36 (December 1990): 301–24, among others. An exception is Phillip Shaw Paludan, *The Presidency of Abraham Lincoln* (Lawrence: University Press of Kansas, 1994), assessed later herein.

15. Frank E. Vandiver, *Jefferson Davis and the Confederate State* (Oxford: Clarendon Press, 1964), 21–22. Vandiver, "The Civil War as an Institutionalizing Force," in Vandiver, Martin Hardwick Hall, and Homer L. Kerr, *Essays on the American Civil War* (Austin: University of Texas Press, 1968), esp. 79–81. Vandiver likewise inspired revaluations of Davis's reputation as strategist and commander-in-chief; William J. Cooper, for example, notes his indebtedness to Vandiver in "A Reassessment of Jefferson Davis," 191. Cooper cites in particular Vandiver's "Jefferson Davis and Confederate Strategy," in Avery O. Craven and Vandiver, *The American Tragedy: The Civil War in Retrospect* (Hampden-Sydney, Va.: Hampden-Sydney College, 1959), 19–32.

16. Emory M. Thomas, *The Confederacy as a Revolutionary Experience* (Englewood Cliffs, N.J.: Prentice-Hall, 1971; rpt. Columbia: University of South Carolina Press, 1991), 58–59.

17. Ibid., 77.

18. Eaton, *Jefferson Davis*, 273.

19. William C. Davis, *Jefferson Davis: The Man and His Hour* (New York: HarperCollins, 1991), 704.

20. Ludwell Johnson's comparison of Lincoln and Davis relied heavily on this modernizing view, as expressed in particular by Raimondo Luraghi, whom Johnson quoted on the first page and invoked on the last page of his article "Jefferson Davis and Abraham Lincoln as War Presidents," 49, 63. See also Raimondo Luraghi, *The Rise and Fall of the Plantation South* (New York: New Viewpoints, 1978), esp. 151.

21. Paul D. Escott, *After Secession: Jefferson Davis and the Failure of Confederate Nationalism* (Baton Rouge: Louisiana State University Press, 1978), 190–91. Rable, considered later herein, deems this judgment on Davis's later ideology too harsh but admits that Davis's formulations of Confederate ideology declined in power.

22. Escott, *After Secession*, 137.

23. Ibid., 269.

24. No one could altogether ignore disaffection in the Confederacy. Thomas took note of it by putting the best face on it, saying, "The Confederacy spawned a

plural society" and pointing out that opportunities for advancement in military service and government bureaucracy increased (*The Confederacy as a Revolutionary Experience*, 101, 112–13). The emphasis on class conflict in the Confederacy was particularly pronounced in regional and area studies, which are chosen not for their local interest but for their manageability as case studies of the new social history, focusing on the history of the Confederacy from the bottom up. See, for example, Eric Foner, *Reconstruction: America's Unfinished Revolution, 1863–1877* (New York: Harper & Row, 1988), 11–18; Wayne K. Durrill, *War of Another Kind: A Southern Community in the Great Rebellion* (New York: Oxford University Press, 1990) (though the author denies it, this is a class interpretation); and Steven Hahn, *The Roots of Southern Populism: Yeoman Farmers and the Transformation of the Georgia Upcountry, 1850–1890* (New York: Oxford University Press, 1983).

25. Lynda Lasswell Crist, ed., *The Papers of Jefferson Davis*, vols. 7, 8, and 9 (Baton Rouge: Louisiana State University Press, 1992, 1995, 1997).

26. The most systematic assessment in recent years is William Gienapp, "Abraham and Presidential Leadership," in James M. McPherson, ed., *"We Cannot Escape History": Lincoln and the Last Best Hope of Earth* (Urbana: University of Illinois Press, 1995), 63–85.

27. T. Harry Williams, *Lincoln and the Radicals* (Madison: University of Wisconsin Press, 1941), 18.

28. Ibid., 170–71.

29. LaWanda Cox, *Lincoln and Black Freedom: A Study in Presidential Leadership* (Columbia: University of South Carolina Press, 1981).

30. Ibid., 6.

31. James MacGregor Burns, *Presidential Government: The Crucible of Leadership* (Boston: Houghton Mifflin, 1966), 42, 44. Burns said that "Lincoln became increasingly implicated in the popular commitment to emancipation and to equality for the Negro" during the war (37–38). He retained his critical view of Lincoln in his later *Leadership* (New York: Harper & Row, 1978), 391–92.

32. *Lincoln and Black Freedom*, 183.

33. Ibid., 172.

34. Ibid., 170–71.

35. Leon F. Litwack, *Been in the Storm So Long: The Aftermath of Slavery* (New York: Knopf); Ira Berlin, Joseph P. Reidy, and Leslie S. Rowland, eds., *Freedom: A Documentary History of Emancipation, 1861–1867, Series II: The Black Military Experience* (Cambridge: Cambridge University Press, 1982); Ira Berlin, Barbara J. Fields, Thavolia Glymph, Joseph P. Reidy, and Leslie S. Rowland, eds., *Freedom: A Documentary History of Emancipation, 1861–1867, Series I, Volume I: The Destruction of Slavery* (Cambridge: Cambridge University Press, 1985); Barbara J. Fields, *Slavery and Freedom on the Middle Ground: Maryland during the Nineteenth Century* (New Haven: Yale University Press), esp. 117. See also Vincent Harding, *There Is a River: The Black Struggle for Freedom in America* (New York: Harcourt Brace Jovanovich, 1981).

36. For an answer see James M. McPherson, "Who Freed the Slaves?" in his

*Drawn with the Sword: Reflections on the American Civil War* (New York: Oxford University Press, 1996), 192–207.

37. David Herbert Donald, *Lincoln Reconsidered: Essays on the Civil War Era (*1956; 2nd ed., enl., New York: Vintage Books, 1961).

38. Phillip Shaw Paludan, *The Presidency of Abraham Lincoln* (Lawrence: University Press of Kansas, 1994), xv, xvi, xvii; James M. McPherson, "How Lincoln Won the War with Metaphors," in his *Abraham Lincoln and the Second American Revolution* (New York: Oxford University Press, 1991), 93–112. William Gienapp's essay "Abraham Lincoln and Presidential Leadership" properly places emphasis on his role as party leader and, very closely related to party leader in the era before civil service reform, administration leader. But he perhaps puts too much weight on Lincoln's role as "leader of the American people"—this despite Gienapp's own clear-sighted recognition that "one of the most surprising aspects of Lincoln's tenure as president was his failure to make more speeches in order to rouse popular support for his policies." See Gienapp's essay in James M. McPherson, ed., *"We Cannot Escape History,"* 77.

39. Donald, ed., *Why the North Won the Civil War,* 112.

40. Ibid., 113.

41. William Nisbet Chambers and Walter Dean Burhham, eds., *The American Party Systems: Stages of Political Development* (New York: Oxford University Press, 1967), vii.

42. Ibid., 120.

43. Michael F. Holt, for one, praised McKitrick and then offered criticism in "Abraham Lincoln and the Politics of Union," in *Abraham Lincoln and the American Political Tradition,* ed. John L. Thomas (Amherst: University of Massachusetts Press, 1986), 111–12.

44. Rable, *The Confederate Republic,* esp. 252. See also Richard Bensel, "Southern Leviathan: The Development of Central State Authority in the Confederate States of America," in *Studies in American Political Development,* Vol. 2, ed. Karen Orren and Stephen Skowronek (New Haven: Yale University Press, 1987), 68–136, and Bensel, *Yankee Leviathan: The Origins of Central State Authority in America, 1859–1877* (Cambridge: Cambridge University Press, 1990), esp. 228–35.

45. See, for example, the essays in Gabor S. Boritt, ed., *Why the Confederacy Lost* (New York: Oxford University Press, 1992). James M. McPherson's essay there dedicates a couple of paragraphs to Lincoln-Davis comparison, granting Lincoln superior qualities but pointing elsewhere for complete answers: "Yet Lincoln made mistakes as a war leader. He went through a half-dozen failures as commanders in the eastern theater. . . . And as late as the summer of 1864, when the war seemed to be going badly for the North, when Grant's forces had suffered horrendous casualties to achieve a stalemate at Petersburg and Sherman seemed equally stalemated before Atlanta, Lincoln came under enormous pressure to negotiate peace with the Confederacy. . . . Lincoln resisted this pressure, but at what appeared to be the cost of his re-election. . . . If the election had been held in August 1864 instead of

November, Lincoln would have lost. He would thus have gone down in history as an also ran, a loser unequal to the challenge of the greatest crisis in the American experience. And Jefferson Davis might have gone down in history as the great leader of a war of independence, the architect of a new nation, the George Washington of the southern Confederacy" (39).

46. David Herbert Donald, *Lincoln* (New York: Simon & Schuster, 1995).

47. David Herbert Donald, *The Politics of Reconstruction, 1863–1865* (Baton Rouge: Louisiana State University Press, 1965), 17.

48. Arthur M. Schlesinger, Jr., *The Imperial Presidency* (Boston: Houghton, Mifflin, 1973); George E. Reedy, *The Twilight of the Presidency: From Johnson to Reagan* (rev. ed., New York: New American Library, 1987), 25–38, 141; Aaron Wildavsky, *The Beleaguered Presidency* (New Brunswick, N.J.: Transaction Publishers, 1991).

## AN ELUSIVE SYNTHESIS

1. Allan G. Bogue, *The Congressman's Civil War* (Cambridge: Cambridge University Press, 1989), xvii.

2. James A. Rawley, *The Politics of Union* (Hinsdale, Ill.: Dryden Press, 1974).

3. Some of the important contributions published during the 1960s that defended Democrats from charges of disloyalty are Frank L. Klement, *The Copperheads in the Middle West* (Chicago: University of Chicago Press, 1960); Leonard P. Curry, "Congressional Democrats, 1861–1863," *Civil War History* 12 (September 1966): 213–29; and Richard O. Curry, "The Union as It Was: A Critique of Recent Interpretations of the Copperheads," *Civil War History* 13 (September 1967): 25–39.

4. T. Harry Williams, *Lincoln and the Radicals* (Madison: University of Wisconsin Press, 1941); David Herbert Donald, "The Radicals and Lincoln," in his *Lincoln Reconsidered: Essays on the Civil War Era* (1956; 2nd ed., enl., New York: Vintage Books, 1961); Donald, "Devils Facing Zionward," and Williams, "Lincoln and the Radicals: An Essay in Civil War History and Historiography," in *Grant, Lee, Lincoln and the Radicals,* ed. Grady McWhiney (New York: Harper & Row, 1966), 72–91, 92–177.

5. See, for example, Gabor S. Boritt, ed., *Lincoln: The War President* (New York: Oxford University Press, 1992); Mark E. Neely, Jr., *The Last Best Hope of Earth: Abraham Lincoln and the Promise of America* (Cambridge, Mass.: Harvard University Press, 1993); Phillip Shaw Paludan, *The Presidency of Abraham Lincoln* (Lawrence: University Press of Kansas, 1994); and David Herbert Donald, *Lincoln* (New York: Simon & Schuster, 1995).

6. The standard monograph on the 1864 election is William F. Zornow, *Lincoln & the Party Divided* (Norman: University of Oklahoma Press, 1954), which stresses Radical Republicans' opposition to Lincoln's renomination, but see also David Long, *The Jewel of Liberty: Abraham Lincoln's Re-election and the End of Slavery* (Mechanicsburg, Pa.: Stackpole, 1994).

7. See, for example, J. Morgan Kousser, "Toward a 'Total Political History':

A Rational-Choice Research Program," *Journal of Interdisciplinary History* 20 (Spring 1990): 521–60; Sean Wilentz, "On Class and Politics in Jacksonian America," *Reviews in American History* 10 (December 1982): 45–63; and William W. Freehling, *The Reintegration of American History: Slavery and the American Civil War* (New York: Oxford University Press, 1993). I have sounded my own tocsins about the dangerous fragmentation of political history into compartmentalized subfields and suggested some remedies to it in my *Political Parties and American Political Development from the Age of Jackson to the Age of Lincoln* (Baton Rouge: Louisiana State University Press, 1992), 1–32, and my "Rethinking Nineteenth-Century American Political History," *Congress & The Presidency: A Journal of Capital Studies* 19 (Autumn 1992): 97–111.

8. Fermentation that led to new ways to approach political history actually began in the late 1940s and intensified throughout the 1950s, but almost all of the most influential published fruits of that fermentation appeared after 1960. Overviews of the origins and checkered career of the "new political history" abound, as do hostile critiques, but Allan Bogue has written two of the most balanced and valuable evaluations: "The New Political History in the 1970s," in *The Past Before Us: Contemporary Historical Writing in the United States,* ed. Michael Kammen (Ithaca, N.Y.: Cornell University Press, 1980), 231–51; and *Clio and the Bitch Goddess: Quantification in American Political History* (Beverly Hills: Sage Publications, 1983). Formulation of the realignment/party system model is usually credited to the political scientist Walter Dean Burnham in his "The Changing Face of the American Political Universe," *American Political Science Review* 59 (March 1965): 7–28; and Burnham, *Critical Elections and the Mainsprings of American Politics* (New York: Norton, 1970). See also, however, James L. Sundquist, *Dynamics of the Party System: Alignment and Realignment of Political Parties in the United States* (Washington, D.C.: Brookings Institution, 1973); and especially the seminal collection of essays by both historians and political scientists, *The American Party Systems: Stages of Political Development,* ed. William N. Chambers and Walter Dean Burnham (New York: Oxford University Press, 1967).

9. Virtually every historian influenced by these approaches implicitly accepted this tenet, but it is articulated with particular force by Cornell's Joel H. Silbey in *The Partisan Imperative: The Dynamics of American Politics before the Civil War* (New York: Oxford University Press, 1985) and *The American Political Nation, 1838–1893* (Stanford: Stanford University Press, 1991). See also Richard L. McCormick, *The Party Period and Public Policy from the Age of Jackson to the Progressive Era* (New York: Oxford University Press, 1986), which accepts the centrality of political parties for most of the nineteenth century even while cogently arguing that an emphasis upon them and their voters fails to account for changes in the contours of public policy.

10. Paul Kleppner, *The Third Electoral System, 1853-1892: Parties, Voters, and Political Cultures* (Chapel Hill: University of North Carolina Press, 1979); Stephen L. Hansen, *The Making of the Third Party System: Voters and Parties in Illinois, 1850–1876* (Ann Arbor: UMI Press, 1980); and Dale E. Baum, *The Civil*

*War Party System: The Case of Massachusetts, 1848–1876* (Chapel Hill: University of North Carolina Press, 1984).

11. Eric McKitrick, "Party Politics and the Union and Confederate War Efforts," in *The American Party Systems,* ed. William N. Chambers and Walter Dean Burnham, 117–51. The inclusion of McKitrick's piece in this seminal collection of essays is noteworthy, for this piece, along with Burnham's work and Richard P. McCormick's *The Second American Party System: Party Formation in the Jacksonian Era* (Chapel Hill: University of North Carolina Press, 1966), brought the party-system paradigm to the attention of other political historians in the 1960s.

12. See, for example, Michael F. Holt, "Abraham Lincoln and the Politics of Union," in *Abraham Lincoln and the American Political Tradition,* ed. John L. Thomas (Amherst: University of Massachusetts Press, 1986, 111–41; David Herbert Donald, *Liberty and Union* (Lexington, Mass.: D. C. Heath, 1978); and William Gillette, *Jersey Blue: Civil War Politics in New Jersey, 1854–1865* (New Brunswick, N.J.: Rutgers University Press, 1995). In sharp contrast, Mark Neely has argued very recently that political historians have too readily accepted the validity of McKitrick's argument and that the unusually rancorous and impassioned partisan conflict between Democrats and Republicans actually impeded the northern war effort while inflating Confederate hopes of ultimate victory. Mark E. Neely, Jr., "The Civil War and the Two-Party System," in *"We Cannot Escape History": Lincoln and the Last Best Hope of Earth,* ed. James M. McPherson (Urbana: University of Illinois Press, 1995), 86–104.

13. In a series of compelling essays, Richard L. McCormick has astutely criticized the chasm between popular voting behavior and policymaking left unbridged by the "new political history" and proponents of the realignment/party system model. Those essays are usefully collected in his *The Party Period and Public Policy.*

14. See especially Jerome M. Clubb, William H. Flanigan, and Nancy H. Zingale, *Partisan Realignment: Voters, Parties, and Government in American History* (Beverly Hills: Sage Publications, 1980).

15. Lex Renda, "The Polity and the Party System: Connecticut and New Hampshire, 1840–1876" (Ph. D. dissertation, University of Virginia, 1991); Renda, "Credit and Culpability: New Hampshire State Politics during the Civil War," *Historical New Hampshire* 48 (Spring 1993): 3–84. The sections of Renda's dissertation dealing with New Hampshire has been published as *Running on the Record: Civil War–Era Politics in New Hampshire* (Charlottesville: University Press of Virginia, 1997). John R. Kirn's University of Virginia dissertation on the Civil War party system in New York, which includes a statistical analysis of almost 30,000 roll-call votes in the state legislature, should be completed in 1998.

16. Jean H. Baker, "A Loyal Opposition: Northern Democrats in the Thirty-seventh Congress," *Civil War History* 25 (June 1979): 140–41.

17. Baker's book, published four years after the previously cited article, is *Affairs of Party: The Political Culture of Northern Democrats in the Mid-Nineteenth Century* (Ithaca, N.Y.: Cornell University Press, 1983). I discuss this dazzling

book below, for it marks a conscious rejection of the "new political history" and realignment/party system model. The political scientist David W. Brady in *Critical Elections and Congressional Policy Making* (Stanford: Stanford University Press, 1988) does attempt to demonstrate a heightening of statistical measures of partisan conflict in the 1860s, yet he measures that increase against indices during the 1850s, when party lines were manifestly inchoate, not against patterns during the stable phase of the second party system in the 1840s. It remains unclear, in sum, whether levels of interparty conflict actually jumped following the realignment of the 1850s as the theory posits they should have.

18. For the original debate between Williams and Donald, see the works cited in note 4 above.

19. David Herbert Donald, *The Politics of Reconstruction, 1863–1867* (Baton Rouge: Louisiana State University Press, 1965).

20. Hans L. Trefousse, *The Radical Republicans: Lincoln's Vanguard for Racial Justice* (New York: Knopf, 1969); LaWanda Cox, *Lincoln and Black Freedom: A Study in Presidential Leadership* (Columbia: University of South Carolina Press, 1981); for the debate among Lincoln's biographers about his priorities, compare Neely, *Last Best Hope of Earth*, with Paludan, *Presidency of Abraham Lincoln*.

21. Herman Belz, *Reconstructing the Union: Theory and Policy during the Civil War* (Ithaca: Cornell University Press, 1969); Belz, *Emancipation and Equal Rights: Politics and Constitutionalism in the Civil War Era* (New York: Norton, 1978); Michael Les Benedict, *A Compromise of Principle: Congressional Republicans and Reconstruction, 1863–1869* (New York: W.W. Norton, 1974); Allan Bogue, *The Earnest Men: Republicans of the Civil War Senate* (Ithaca: Cornell University Press, 1981), and Bogue, *The Congressman's Civil War*. Much of Bogue's research was originally presented in a series of important articles, as were the studies by Glen M. Linden of Radical voting patterns on economic policies in the House and Senate. Those articles and others about the wartime Congress have been conveniently collected in *The United States Congress in a Partisan Political Nation, 1841–1896*, vol. 2, ed. Joel H. Silbey (Brooklyn, N.Y.: Carlson Publishing, 1991). Readers should refer to that volume for individual titles.

22. Though focusing primarily on the implementation of Lincoln's own Reconstruction policies rather than on policy formation in Congress, Peyton McCrary, *Abraham Lincoln and Reconstruction: The Louisiana Experiment* (Princeton: Princeton University Press, 1978) also demonstrates considerable tension between Lincoln and congressional Republicans.

23. Bogue, *Congressman's Civil War*, 30.

24. Frank L. Klement, *Dark Lanterns: Secret Political Societies, Conspiracies, and Treason Trials in the Civil War* (Baton Rouge: Louisiana State University Press, 1984); Curry, "Congressional Democrats, 1861–63," and Baker, "A Loyal Opposition," 139–55. Democratic racism is also stressed in the two best books about the party published since 1965, Baker's *Affairs of Party* and Joel H. Silbey, *A Respectable Minority: The Democratic Party in the Civil War Era, 1860–1868* (New York: Norton, 1977), just as it is in more general studies of northern

Negrophobia during the war years, such as V. Jacque Voegeli, *Free but Not Equal: The Midwest and the Negro during the Civil War* (Chicago: University of Chicago Press, 1967) and Forrest Wood, *Black Scare: The Racist Response to Emancipation and Reconstruction* (Berkeley and Los Angeles: University of California Press, 1968).

If Democrats were virulently racist, however, some historians stress the less-than-egalitarian motives behind policies for southern blacks Republicans adopted during the war. See, for example, Louis S. Gerteis, *From Contraband to Freedman: Federal Policy Toward Southern Blacks, 1861–1865* (Westport, Conn.: Greenwood, 1973); and Herman Belz, "The Freedmen's Bureau Act and the Principle of No Discrimination According to Color," *Civil War History* 21 (September 1975): 197–217.

25. Renda, "The Polity and the Party System"; Renda, "Credit and Culpability: New Hampshire State Politics During the Civil War," 83; Thomas R. Kemp, "Community and War: The Civil War Experience of Two New Hampshire Towns," in *Toward a Social History of the American Civil War*, ed. Maris A. Vinovskis (Cambridge: Cambridge University Press, 1990), 31–77; Iver Bernstein, *The New York City Draft Riots: Their Significance for American Society and Politics in the Age of the Civil War* (New York: Oxford University Press, 1990).

26. See, for example, G. R. Tredway, *Democratic Opposition to the Lincoln Administration in Indiana* (Indianapolis: Indiana Historical Bureau, 1973); Christopher Dell, *Lincoln and the War Democrats: The Grand Erosion of Conservative Tradition* (Rutherford, N.J.: Farleigh Dickinson University Press, 1975); Silbey, *A Respectable Minority*; and Gillette, *Jersey Blue.*

27. Silbey, *A Respectable Minority*, xi.

28. Ibid., 157, 175.

29. Ibid., 40–61; Dell, *Lincoln and the War Democrats,* 9.

30. See my previously cited "Abraham Lincoln and the Politics of Union" which argues that divergent responses by Lincoln and congressional Republicans to the threat of a Democratic comeback were the primary cause of wartime disputes between the president and the party and that Lincoln infuriated Republicans by trying to convert their party into a Union party that could attract northern Democrats and southerners, whom Republicans despised.

31. Michael Perman, *The Road to Redemption: Southern Politics, 1869–1879* (Chapel Hill: University of North Carolina Press, 1984).

32. Baker, *Affairs of Party*; the quotation and Baker's rejection of quantitative approaches are found on 11–12; Earl J. Hess, *Liberty, Virtue, and Progress: Northerners and Their War for the Union* (New York: New York University Press, 1988).

33. Grace Palladino, *Another Civil War: Labor, Capital, and the State in the Anthracite Regions of Pennsylvania, 1840–1868* (Urbana: University of Illinois Press, 1990).

34. For full citation, see above, note 25.

35. See, for example, David Herbert Donald and James G. Randall, *The Civil War and Reconstruction*, (2nd rev. ed., Lexington, Mass.: D. C. Heath, 1969),

346; Carl N. Degler, *Out of Our Past: The Forces That Shaped Modern America* (New York: Harper & Row, 1959), 199–207 (quotation, p. 206); and especially Leonard P. Curry, *Blueprint for Modern America: Non-Military Legislation of the First Civil War Congress* (Nashville: Vanderbilt University Press, 1968).

36. William B. Hesseltine, *Lincoln and the War Governors* (New York: Knopf, 1948), 389.

37. Curry, *Blueprint for Modern America;* quotations from pp. 148, 250.

38. Bray Hammond, *Sovereignty and an Empty Purse: Banks and Politics during the Civil War* (Princeton: Princeton University Press, 1970); quotation is from p. 300.

39. To be fair, Curry in his earlier *Blueprint for Modern America* also noted Chase's mistakes and the role of specie suspension in requiring the Legal Tender Acts, but he presented them primarily as creating "a truly national currency" ( 248), and his critique of Chase lacks the unabashed ferocity of Hammond's.

40. Eugene C. Murdock, *One Million Men: The Civil War Draft in the North* (Madison: State Historical Society of Wisconsin, 1971); James Geary, *We Need Men: The Union Draft in the Civil War* (DeKalb: Northern Illinois University Press, 1991).

41. Herman Belz, *A New Birth of Freedom: The Republican Party and Freedmen's Rights, 1861–1866* (Westport, Conn.: Greenwood, 1976), ix, 11, 116, and *passim*.

42. Herman Belz, *Emancipation and Equal Rights: Politics and Constitutionalism in the Civil War Era* (New York: W. W. Norton, 1978), xi, xv.

43. Harold Hyman, *A More Perfect Union: The Impact of the Civil War and Reconstruction on the Constitution* (Boston: Houghton Mifflin, 1975); Morton Keller, *Affairs of State: Public Life in Late Nineteenth Century America* (Cambridge, Mass.: Harvard University Press, 1977); and Richard Franklin Bensel, *Yankee Leviathan: The Origins of Central State Authority in America, 1859–1877* (Cambridge: Cambridge University Press, 1990).

44. Theda Skocpol, *Protecting Soldiers and Mothers: The Political Origins of Social Policy in the United States* (Cambridge, Mass.: Harvard University Press, 1992).

## BEYOND STATE RIGHTS

1. The author thanks Gary W. Gallagher for his helpful suggestions on this essay.

2. "Address Delivered by Governor Z. B. Vance, of North Carolina, Before the Southern Historical Society, at White Sulphur Springs, West Virginia, August 18th, 1875," *Southern Historical Society Papers* 14 (1886): 517.

3. For assessments of earlier scholarship on Confederate politics (and other topics), see Mary Elizabeth Massey, "The Confederate States of America: The Homefront," in *Writing Southern History: Essays in Historiography in Honor of Fletcher M. Green,* ed. Arthur S. Link and Rembert W. Patrick (Baton Rouge: Louisiana State University Press, 1965), 249–72; Joe Gray Taylor, "The White South from Secession to Redemption," in *Interpreting Southern History: Histo-*

*riographical Essays in Honor of Sanford W. Higginbotham,* ed. John B. Boles and Evelyn Thomas Nolen (Baton Rouge: Louisiana State University Press, 1987), 162–198.

4. Jefferson Davis, *The Rise and Fall of the Confederate Government,* 2 vols. (New York: Appleton, 1881), 1:518.

5. Few scholars have confined their interest to only one of these topics, and the distinctions between the categories are admittedly somewhat arbitrary.

6. For a defense of the latter approach, see George C. Rable, *The Confederate Republic: A Revolution against Politics* (Chapel Hill: University of North Carolina Press, 1994), 1–5.

7. Frank Lawrence Owsley, *State Rights in the Confederacy* (Chicago: University of Chicago Press, 1925).

8. Paul D. Escott, *After Secession: Jefferson Davis and the Failure of Confederate Nationalism* (Baton Rouge: Louisiana State University Press, 1978), 74–93. For evidence that a belief in state sovereignty influenced congressional voting behavior even among strongly secessionist members, see Kenneth C. Martis, *The Historical Atlas of the Congresses of the Confederate States of America, 1861–1865* (New York: Simon & Schuster, 1994), 94.

9. Richard E. Beringer, Herman Hattaway, Archer Jones, and William N. Still, Jr., *Why the South Lost the Civil War* (Athens: University of Georgia Press, 1986), 203–26, 443–57. Studies of individual states tend to describe conflicts with the Confederate government without necessarily engaging the historiographical issues. Michael B. Dougan, *Confederate Arkansas: The People and Policies of a Frontier State in Wartime* (University, Ala.: University of Alabama Press, 1976), 75–80; Malcolm C. McMillan, *The Disintegration of a Confederate State: Three Governors and Alabama's Wartime Home Front, 1861–1865* (Macon, Ga.: Mercer University Press, 1986), 36–42. For an exception, see the excellent analysis in David D. Scarboro, "North Carolina and the Confederacy: The Weakness of States' Rights during the Civil War," *North Carolina Historical Review* 56 (April 1979): 133–49.

10. Escott, *After Secession,* 38–53, 168–95. Confederate patriotism was also weakened by the failure to protect particular economic interests. Lawrence N. Powell and Michael S. Wayne, "Self-Interest and the Decline of Confederate Nationalism," in *The Old South in the Crucible of War,* ed. Harry P. Owens and James J. Cooke (Jackson: University Press of Mississippi, 1983), 29–45.

11. Kenneth M. Stampp, "The Southern Road to Appomattox," in Stampp, *The Imperiled Union: Essays on the Background of the Civil War* (New York: Oxford University Press, 1980), 246–69; Beringer et al., *Why the South Lost,* 22–30, 66–81, 276–93, 357–67. Beringer and his colleagues based this last point on Robert Kerby's earlier description of the Confederates as reluctant revolutionaries who failed to create a genuinely "revolutionary army." Kerby believed that guerrilla tactics would have been successful against large, northern armies. Robert L. Kerby, "Why the Confederacy Lost," *Review of Politics* 35 (July 1973): 326–45.

12. Escott, *After Secession,* 35–38, 227–50; Drew Gilpin Faust, *The Creation of Confederate Nationalism: Ideology and Identity in the Civil War South*

(Baton Rouge: Louisiana State University Press, 1988), 73–81; Clarence L. Mohr, *On the Threshold of Freedom: Masters and Slaves in Civil War Georgia* (Athens: University of Georgia Press, 1986), 235–93; J. William Harris, *Plain Folk and Gentry in a Slave Society: White Liberty and Black Slavery in Augusta's Hinterlands* (Middletown, Conn.: Wesleyan University Press, 1985), 182–87. On the guilt question, see the critical but judicious summary in Gaines Foster, "Guilt over Slavery: A Historiographical Analysis," *Journal of Southern History* 56 (November 1990): 665–94.

13. Faust, *Creation of Confederate Nationalism*; Rable, *Confederate Republic*. On Confederate civil religion, see the still useful James W. Silver, *Confederate Morale and Church Propaganda* (Tuscaloosa, Ala.: Confederate Publishing Co., 1957).

14. Emory M. Thomas, *The Confederacy as a Revolutionary Experience* (Englewood Cliffs, N.J.: Prentice-Hall, 1971; rpt. Columbia: University of South Carolina Press, 1991), 1–2, 133–34; Emory M. Thomas, *The Confederate Nation, 1861–1865* (New York: Harper & Row, 1979), 46–47, 221–23, 245; Rable, *Confederate Republic*, 44–49, 63, 65, 76–78, 120–23, 134–35, 176. For additional comments on the conservatism of the Confederate revolution, see Frank E. Vandiver, *Their Tattered Flags: The Epic of the Confederacy* (New York: Harper's Magazine Press, 1970), 19; James M. McPherson, *Battle Cry of Freedom: The Civil War Era* (New York: Oxford University Press, 1988), 245. Eric H. Walther has questioned the common belief that more conservative leaders displaced the "fire-eaters" during the formation of the Confederate States of America. See Walther's *The Fire-Eaters* (Baton Rouge: Louisiana State University Press, 1992).

15. William C. Davis, *"A Government of Our Own": The Making of the Confederacy* (New York: Free Press, 1994).

16. Charles R. Lee, Jr., *The Confederate Constitutions* (Chapel Hill: University of North Carolina Press, 1963).

17. Marshall L. DeRosa, *The Confederate Constitution of 1861: An Inquiry into American Constitutionalism* (Columbia: University of Missouri Press, 1991). For a good summary of similarities to the United States Constitution that also takes into account differences in the Confederate Constitution, see Curtis Arthur Amlund, *Federalism in the Southern Confederacy* (Washington, D.C.: Public Affairs Press, 1966), 17–27. For examples of the conventional interpretation of the Confederate Constitution, see Thomas, *Confederate Nation*, 58–66; Beringer et al., *Why the South Lost*, 75–81; Richard Franklin Bensel, *Yankee Leviathan: The Origins of Central State Authority in America, 1859–1877* (Cambridge: Cambridge University Press, 1990), 99–103.

18. Don E. Fehrenbacher, *Constitutions and Constitutionalism in the Slaveholding South* (Athens: University of Georgia Press, 1989), 59–81; Donald Nieman, "Republicanism, the Confederate Constitution, and the American Constitutional Tradition," in *An Uncertain Tradition: Constitutionalism and the History of the South*, ed. Kermit L. Hall and James W. Ely, Jr. (Athens: University of Georgia Press, 1989), 201–19; Rable, *Confederate Republic*, 39–63. For an interesting Marxist analysis of how the Confederate Constitution embodied the philosophy

of a "seigniorial civilization," see Raimondo Luraghi, *The Rise and Fall of the Plantation South* (New York: Franklin Watts, 1978), 85.

19. Davis, "*A Government of Our Own*," 98–118.

20. Bell Irvin Wiley, *The Road to Appomattox* (Memphis: Memphis State College Press, 1956), 14–42; David M. Potter, "Jefferson Davis and the Political Factors in Confederate Defeat," in *Why the North Won the Civil War*, ed. David Herbert Donald (Baton Rouge: Louisiana State University Press, 1960), 91–109; Allan Nevins, *The Statesmanship of the Civil War* (New York: Macmillan, 1962), 67–95; Clement Eaton, *Jefferson Davis* (New York: Free Press, 1977), 242–50. Davis's handling of the politics of military strategy also came under critical scrutiny in Thomas Lawrence Connelly and Archer Jones, *The Politics of Command: Factions and Ideas in Confederate Strategy* (Baton Rouge: Louisiana State University Press, 1973). Escott, *After Secession*, 1–18, 62–67, 256–74; Rable, *Confederate Republic*, 64–74, 78–87, 134–77, 206–13, 248–75, 282–99.

21. Frank E. Vandiver, *Jefferson Davis and the Confederate State* (New York: Oxford University Press, 1964); Frank E. Vandiver, "Jefferson Davis—Leader without Legend," *Journal of Southern History* 43 (February 1977): 3–18; Vandiver, *Their Tattered Flags*, 35–36, 156–61, 283; Ludwell Johnson, "Jefferson Davis and Abraham Lincoln as War Presidents: Nothing Succeeds Like Success," *Civil War History* 27 (March 1981): 49–63. Grady McWhiney has pointed out that Davis was sickly throughout the war as were many of his advisers and adversaries. McWhiney, "Jefferson Davis and His Generals," in McWhiney's *Southerners and Other Americans* (New York: Basic Books, 1973), 83–90.

22. William C. Davis, *Jefferson Davis: The Man and His Hour* (New York: HarperCollins, 1991), esp. 689–705. Beringer has recently interpreted Davis's indecisiveness as a case study of "cognitive dissonance." Richard E. Beringer, "Jefferson Davis's Pursuit of Ambition: The Attractive Features of Alternative Decisions," *Civil War History* 38 (March 1992): 5–38. For a readable account of the last days of Davis's presidency, see Michael B. Ballard, *A Long Shadow: Jefferson Davis and the Final Days of the Confederacy* (Jackson: University Press of Mississippi, 1986). Rembert W. Patrick's *Jefferson Davis and His Cabinet* (Baton Rouge: Louisiana State University Press, 1944) remains the standard work on that subject. Biographies of cabinet members that contain useful information on administration politics include: William C. Harris, *Leroy Pope Walker: Confederate Secretary of War* (Tuscaloosa, Ala.: Confederate Publishing Co., 1962); Ben H. Proctor, *Not Without Honor: The Life of John H. Reagan* (Austin: University of Texas Press, 1962); William C. Davis, *Breckinridge: Statesman, Soldier, Symbol* (Baton Rouge: Louisiana State University Press, 1974); Eli N. Evans, *Judah P. Benjamin: The Jewish Confederate* (New York: Free Press, 1988); George Green Shackelford, *George Wythe Randolph and the Confederate Elite* (Athens: University of Georgia Press, 1988).

23. Lynda Lasswell Crist and Mary Seaton Dix, eds., *The Papers of Jefferson Davis*, 9 vols. to date (Baton Rouge: Louisiana State University Press, 1971– ).

24. For typical assessments, see Vandiver, *Their Tattered Flags*, 175; Peter Parish, *The American Civil War* (New York: Holmes and Meier, 1975), 218–20.

25. Wilfred Buck Yearns, *The Confederate Congress* (Athens: University of Georgia Press, 1960); Thomas B. Alexander and Richard E. Beringer, *The Anatomy of the Confederate Congress* (Nashville: Vanderbilt University Press, 1972); Martis, *Historical Atlas of Congresses of Confederate States*, 8–9, 117–18.

26. Ezra J. Warner and W. Buck Yearns, *Biographical Register of the Confederate Congress* (Baton Rouge: Louisiana State University Press, 1975); Ruth Ketring Nuermberger, *The Clays of Alabama: A Planter-Lawyer-Politician Family* (Lexington: University of Kentucky Press, 1958); William Y. Thompson, *Robert Toombs of Georgia* (Baton Rouge: Louisiana State University Press, 1966); Alvy L. King, *Louis T. Wigfall, Southern Fire-Eater* (Baton Rouge: Louisiana State University Press, 1970); Randy Reid, "Howell Cobb of Georgia: A Biography" (Ph.D. diss., Louisiana State University, 1995 [UMI #9609121]).

27. Thomas, *Confederacy as a Revolutionary Experience*, 58–78; Amlund, *Federalism in the Southern Confederacy*, 131; Escott, *After Secession*, xi–xii, 212–18; Beringer et al., *Why the South Lost*, 212–18.

28. Bensel, *Yankee Leviathan*, 35–39, 103, 116–35, 183–86, 192–209, 221–25, 233–34.

29. Charles Edward Cauthen, *South Carolina Goes to War, 1860–1865* (Chapel Hill: University of North Carolina Press, 1950), 139–63; May Spencer Ringold, *The Role of the State Legislatures in the Confederacy* (Athens: University of Georgia Press, 1966).

30. A helpful collection of essays covering all the wartime chief executives is W. Buck Yearns, ed., *The Confederate Governors* (Athens: University of Georgia Press, 1985). For additional information, consult the following works: Vincent H. Cassidy and Amos E. Simpson, *Henry Watkins Allen of Louisiana* (Baton Rouge: Louisiana State University Press, 1964); F. N. Boney, *John Letcher of Virginia: The Story of Virginia's Civil War Governor* (University, Ala.: University of Alabama Press, 1966); Robert W. Dubay, *John Jones Pettus, Mississippi Fire-Eater: His Life and Times, 1813–1867* (Jackson: University Press of Mississippi, 1975); McMillan, *Disintegration of a Confederate State*; John B. Edmunds, Jr., *Francis W. Pickens and the Politics of Destruction* (Chapel Hill: University of North Carolina Press, 1986); Alvin A. Fahrner, "William 'Extra Billy' Smith, Governor of Virginia, 1864–1865," *Virginia Magazine of History and Biography* 74 (January 1966): 68–87. See also the discussion of Zebulon Vance and Joseph E. Brown below.

31. Alexander and Beringer, *Anatomy of the Confederate Congress*, 106–38; Martis, *Historical Atlas of Congresses of Confederate States*, 96–97; Memory F. Mitchell, *Legal Aspects of Conscription and Exemption in North Carolina* (Chapel Hill: University of North Carolina Press, 1965); Rable, *Confederate Republic*, 138–43, 154–65, 199–201, 248–49, 287–96. Serious students of conscription still have to consult Albert Burton Moore, *Conscription and Conflict in the Confederacy* (New York: Macmillan, 1924; rpt. Columbia: University of South Carolina Press, 1996).

32. Owsley, *State Rights in the Confederacy*, 150–202; John B. Robbins, "The Confederacy and the Writ of Habeas Corpus," *Georgia Historical Quarterly* 55 (Summer 1971): 83–101; David Herbert Donald, "Died of Democracy," in *Why*

*the North Won,* 79–90; Rable, *Confederate Republic,* 143–44, 158–60, 188–89, 25–52, 257–63, 282–83; Robert Neil Mathis, "Freedom of the Press in the Confederacy: A Reality," *Historian* 37 (August 1975): 633–48. Again, for the votes in Congress, see Alexander and Beringer, *Anatomy of the Confederate Congress,* 173–200; Martis, *Historical Atlas of Congresses of Confederate States,* 96.

33. Thomas, *Confederacy as a Revolutionary Experience,* 79–99; Escott, *After Secession,* pp. 58–61, 67–70; Bensel, *Yankee Leviathan,* 146–67, 181–92, 209–10; James L. Roark, *Masters without Slaves: Southern Planters in the Civil War and Reconstruction* (New York: Norton, 1977), 52–54, 79–80; Peter Wallenstein, *From Slave South to New South: Public Policy in Nineteenth-Century Georgia* (Chapel Hill: University of North Carolina Press, 1987), 110–20; Mary A. DeCredico, *Patriotism for Profit: Georgia's Urban Entrepreneurs and the Confederate War Effort* (Chapel Hill: University of North Carolina Press, 1990), 21–118.

34. Richard Cecil Todd, *Confederate Finance* (Athens: University of Georgia Press, 1954); Potter, "Jefferson Davis and the Political Factors in Confederate Defeat," 91–98; Stanley Lebergott, "Why the South Lost: Commercial Purpose in the Confederacy," *Journal of American History* 70 (June 1983): 58–74; Douglas B. Ball, *Financial Failure and Confederate Defeat* (Urbana: University of Illinois Press, 1991).

35. Robert F. Durden, ed., *The Gray and the Black: The Confederate Debate on Emancipation* (Baton Rouge: Louisiana State University Press, 1972).

36. Ballard, *A Long Shadow,* 9–13; Luraghi, *Rise and Fall of the Plantation South,* 141–43; Bensel, *Yankee Leviathan,* 153–55; Beringer et al., *Why the South Lost,* 368–88; Escott, *After Secession,* 252–55; Paul D. Escott, *Many Excellent People: Power and Privilege in North Carolina, 1850–1900* (Chapel Hill: University of North Carolina Press, 1985), 50–51; Roark, *Masters without Slaves,* 101–3; Laurence Shore, *Southern Capitalists: The Ideological Leadership of an Elite, 1832–1885* (Chapel Hill: University of North Carolina Press, 1986), 92–95; Rable, *Confederate Republic,* 287–96. See also the account of the debate in Virginia: Thomas M. Preisser, "The Virginia Decision to Use Negro Soldiers in the Civil War," *Virginia Magazine of History and Biography* 83 (January 1975): 98–113; Ervin L. Jordan, *Black Confederates and Afro-Yankees in Civil War Virginia* (Charlottesville: University Press of Virginia, 1995).

37. Potter, "Davis and Political Factors in Confederate Defeat," 110–12; Eric L. McKitrick, "Politics and the Union and Confederate War Efforts," in *The American Party Systems: Stages of Political Development,* ed. William Nisbet Chambers and Walter Dean Burnham (New York: Oxford University Press, 1967), 120–51.

38. See, for example, Thomas, *Confederate Nation,* 140; Parish, *American Civil War,* 199; McPherson, *Battle Cry of Freedom,* 689–91.

39. Alexander and Beringer, *Anatomy of the Confederate Congress,* 35–43; Richard E. Beringer, "The Unconscious 'Spirit of Party' in the Confederate Congress," *Civil War History* 18 (December 1972): 312–33. Historians have also disagreed over whether a sense of Whig party identification persisted in the South during the war and after. Cf. Thomas B. Alexander, "Persistent Whiggery in the

Confederate South, 1860–1877," *Journal of Southern History* 27 (August 1961): 305–29, and John V. Mering, "Persistent Whiggery in the Confederate South: A Reconsideration," *South Atlantic Quarterly* 69 (Winter 1970): 123–43.

40. Alexander and Beringer, *Anatomy of the Confederate Congress*, 56–58, 330–45; Martis, *Historical Atlas of Congresses of Confederate States*, 56–57, 93–94, 118; Marc W. Kruman, *Parties and Politics in North Carolina, 1836–1865* (Baton Rouge: Louisiana State University Press, 1983), 222–67.

41. Bensel, *Yankee Leviathan*, 228–33; Rable, *Confederate Republic*, 2–5, 10–22, 210–13.

42. Rable, *Confederate Republic*, 88.

43. Yearns, *Confederate Congress*, 42–49; Kruman, *Parties and Politics in North Carolina*, 226–30; Dougan, *Confederate Arkansas*, 81–82. For useful accounts of state elections, see John K. Bettersworth, *Confederate Mississippi: The People and Policies of a Cotton State in Wartime* (Baton Rouge: Louisiana State University Press, 1943), 30–36; McMillan, *Disintegration of a Confederate State*, 30–33.

44. Alexander and Beringer, *Anatomy of the Confederate Congress*, 43–46; Martis, *Historical Atlas of Congresses of Confederate States*, 60–66; Rable, *Confederate Republic*, 88–110.

45. Escott, *After Secession*, 155; Martis, *Historical Atlas of Congresses of Confederate States*, 66–74; Alexander and Beringer, *Anatomy of the Confederate Congress*, 44–46; Yearns, *Confederate Congress*, 49–58; Kruman, *Parties and Politics in North Carolina*, 253–59; Rable, *Confederate Republic*, 214–35. See also, William Alexander Percy, "Localizing the Context of Confederate Politics: The Congressional Election of 1863 in Georgia's First District," *Georgia Historical Quarterly* 79 (Spring 1995): 192–209. For good accounts of state elections, consult McMillan, *Disintegration of a Confederate State*, 67–83; Bettersworth, *Confederate Mississippi*, 48–59; Dougan, *Confederate Arkansas*, 94–96.

46. Alexander and Beringer, *Anatomy of the Confederate Congress*, 66–68, 94–97, 114–15; Martis, *Historical Atlas of Congresses of Confederate States*, 29, 42–53, 92–93.

47. Wiley, *Road to Appomattox*, 99–113; Davis, *Jefferson Davis*, 435–55, 580–603; Cauthen, *South Carolina Goes to War*, 202–16. On Hammond, see Drew Gilpin Faust, *James Henry Hammond and the Old South: A Design for Mastery* (Baton Rouge: Louisiana State University Press, 1988).

48. Kruman, *Parties and Politics in North Carolina*, 242–45; Harris, *Plain Folk and Gentry in a Slave Society*, 148, 163–66; Rable, *Confederate Republic*, 174–94.

49. Thomas E. Schott, *Alexander H. Stephens of Georgia: A Biography* (Baton Rouge: Louisiana State University Press, 1988). In a provocative article, John Brumgardt denied that Stephens was a lukewarm Confederate and even defended him as a practical politician. John R. Brumgardt, "The Confederate Career of Alexander H. Stephens: The Case Reopened," *Civil War History* 27 (March 1981): 64–81.

50. Joseph H. Parks, *Joseph E. Brown of Georgia* (Baton Rouge: Louisiana

State University Press, 1977). An older but still useful study of Brown as war governor is Louise Biles Hill, *Joseph E. Brown and the Confederacy* (Chapel Hill: University of North Carolina Press, 1939).

51. Amlund, *Federalism in the Southern Confederacy,* 96, 113–14; Escott, *After Secession,* 79–85, 159–65; Paul D. Escott, "Joseph E. Brown, Jefferson Davis, and the Problem of Poverty in the Confederacy," *Georgia Historical Quarterly* 61 (Spring 1977): 59–71. For more information on Brown, see the solid study of wartime Georgia, T. Conn Bryan, *Confederate Georgia* (Athens: University of Georgia Press, 1953).

52. Glenn Tucker, *Zeb Vance: Champion of Personal Freedom* (Indianapolis: Bobbs-Merrill, 1965); Richard S. Yates, *The Confederacy and Zeb Vance* (Tuscaloosa, Ala.: Confederate Publishing Co., 1958).

53. Beringer et al., *Why the South Lost,* 277–80; Scarboro, "North Carolina and the Confederacy," 133–49.

54. Kruman, *Parties and Politics in North Carolina,* 233–70; Rable, *Confederate Republic,* 151–53, 163–65, 190–91, 200–205, 233–34, 245–47, 265–71. Students of the Confederacy will welcome the recently resumed letterpress publication of Vance's papers and especially the more complete microfilm edition. Frontis W. Johnston, *The Papers of Zebulon Baird Vance, 1843–1862* (Raleigh, N.C.: State Department of Archives and History, 1963); Joe A. Mobley, ed., *The Papers of Zebulon Baird Vance, 1863* (Raleigh, N.C.: Division of Archives and History, 1995); Gordon McKinney and Richard McMurry, eds., *Guide to the Microfilm Edition of the Papers of Zebulon Vance* (Frederick, Md.: University Publications of America, 1987).

55. Roark, *Masters without Slaves,* 21–24, 27–29, 62–67; Escott, *After Secession,* 94–166; Paul D. Escott, "'The Cry of the Sufferers': The Problem of Welfare in the Confederacy," *Civil War History* 23 (September 1977): 228–40; Escott, "The Failure of Confederate Nationalism: The Old South's Class System in the Crucible of War," in *Old South in the Crucible,* 16–28. See also Shore, *Southern Capitalists,* 79–92.

56. Elizabeth Fox-Genovese and Eugene D. Genovese, "Yeomen Farmers in a Slaveholders' Democracy," in Fox-Genovese and Genovese, *Fruits of Merchant Capital: Slavery and Bourgeois Property in the Rise and Expansion of Capitalism* (New York: Oxford University Press, 1983), 255–56; Steven Hahn, *The Roots of Southern Populism: Yeomen Farmers and the Transformation of the Georgia Upcountry, 1850–1890* (New York: Oxford University Press, 1983), 86–105.

57. Fred Arthur Bailey, *Class and Tennessee's Confederate Generation* (Chapel Hill: University of North Carolina Press, 1987).

58. Escott, *Many Excellent People,* 36–47, 59–84; Robin E. Baker, "Class Conflict and Political Upheaval: The Transformation of North Carolina Politics during the Civil War," *North Carolina Historical Review* 69 (April 1992): 148–78; William T. Auman, "Neighbor against Neighbor: The Inner Civil War in the Randolph County Area of Confederate North Carolina," *North Carolina Historical Review* 61 (January 1984): 59–92; Wayne K. Durrill, *War of Another Kind: A Southern Community in the Great Rebellion* (New York: Oxford University

Press, 1990); James Marten, *Texas Divided: Loyalty and Dissent in the Lone Star State, 1856–1874* (Lexington: University Press of Kentucky, 1990); Phillip Shaw Paludan, *Victims: A True Story of the Civil War* (Knoxville: University of Tennessee Press, 1981); Richard B. McCaslin, *Tainted Breeze: The Great Hanging at Gainesville, Texas, 1862* (Baton Rouge: Louisiana State University Press, 1994).

59. Ted R. Worley, "The Arkansas Peace Society of 1861: A Study in Mountain Unionism," *Journal of Southern History* 24 (November 1958): 445–56; William T. Auman and David D. Scarboro, "The Heroes of America in Civil War North Carolina," *North Carolina Historical Review* 58 (October 1981): 327–63; Richard Bardolph, "Inconstant Rebels: Desertion of North Carolina Troops in the Civil War," *North Carolina Historical Review* 41 (April 1964): 163–89; Richard Reid, "A Test Case of the 'Crying Evil': Desertion among North Carolina Troops during the Civil War," *North Carolina Historical Review* 58 (Summer 1981): 234–62; McMillan, *Disintegration of a Confederate State*, 105; Marten, *Texas Divided*, 36–37.

60. Escott, *After Secession*, 196–225; Alexander and Beringer, *Anatomy of the Confederate Congress*, 293–99; William L. Barney, *Flawed Victory: A New Perspective on the Civil War* (New York: Praeger, 1975), 90; John R. Brumgardt, "Alexander H. Stephens and the State Convention Movement in Georgia: A Reappraisal," *Georgia Historical Quarterly* 59 (Spring 1975): 38–49; Rable, *Confederate Republic*, 265–74; 278–81, 292–94; Larry E. Nelson, *Bullets, Ballots, and Rhetoric: Confederate Policy for the United States Presidential Contest of 1864* (University, Ala.: University of Alabama Press, 1980). See also John Hammond Moore, "The Rives Peace Resolution—March 1865," *West Virginia History* 26 (April 1965): 153–60.

61. Horace W. Raper, *William W. Holden: North Carolina's Political Enigma* (Chapel Hill: University of North Carolina Press, 1985); William C. Harris, *William Woods Holden: Firebrand of North Carolina Politics* (Baton Rouge: Louisiana State University Press, 1987); Kruman, *Parties and Politics in North Carolina*, 250–51. For a brief account of another peace advocate, see Robert D. Miller, "Samuel Field Phillips: The Odyssey of a Southern Dissenter," *North Carolina Historical Review* 58 (July 1981): 263–80.

62. John Paris, *A Sermon: Preached before Brig. Gen. Hoke's Brigade, at Kinston, N.C. on the 28th of February 1864* (Greensboro, N.C.: A. W. Ingold and Co., 1864).

## A CONSTITUTIONAL CRISIS

1. Arthur E. Bestor, Jr., "The Civil War as a Constitutional Crisis," *American Historical Review* 68 (January 1964): 327–52.

2. Ibid., 328.

3. Morton J. Keller, "Power and Rights: Two Centuries of American Constitutionalism," *Journal of American History* 74 (December 1987): 676.

4. The representative Whig historian of the United States was the great George Bancroft, who placed his *History of the Formation of the Constitution* squarely within this context. "History carries forward the study of ethics," he affirmed in

the first pages of his work. It demonstrates "that tyranny and wrong lead inevitably to decay; that freedom and right, however hard may be the struggle, always prove resistless." Then he turned to the particulars of the framing of the Constitution, "the most cheering act in the political history of mankind." George Bancroft, *History of the Formation of the Constitution of the United States of America*, 2 vols. (New York: Appleton, 1882), 1:3, 5–6.

5. Alexander H. Stephens, *A Constitutional View of the Late War Between the States*, 2 vols. (Philadelphia: National Publishing Co., 1868); quotations from 1:10; Edward A. Pollard, *The Lost Cause: A New Southern History of the War of the Confederates* (New York: E. B. Treat, 1867); Jefferson Davis, *The Rise and Fall of the Confederate Government*, 2 vols. (New York: Appleton, 1881).

6. Horace Greeley, *The American Conflict: A History of the Great Rebellion in the United States of America, 1860–65*, 2 vols. (Hartford, Conn.: O. D. Case Co., 1864–1866; rpt. New York: Negro Universities Press, 1969); Henry Wilson, *History of the Rise and Fall of the Slave Power in America*, 2 vols. (Boston: James R. Osgood, 1872–1877).

7. Greeley, *The American Conflict*, 1:122–47. Wilson's *Rise and Fall of the Slave Power* likewise stresses the rise of antislavery and civil liberties issues rather than federalism issues.

8. George Ticknor Curtis, *Constitutional History of the United States from Their Declaration of Independence to the Close of the Civil War*, vol. 2 (New York: Harper, 1896).

9. Ibid., 301–2.

10. Ibid., 247–48.

11. Ibid., 268–72.

12. Ibid., 309–10.

13. Ibid., 242–43.

14. John W. Burgess, *The Civil War and the Constitution, 1859–1865*, 2 vols. (New York: Charles Scribner's Sons, 1901); Burgess, *Reconstruction and the Constitution* (New York: Charles Scribner's Sons, 1902). James Schouler entitled his work *History of the United States of America, under the Constitution*, 7 vols. (Washington, D.C.: W. Morrison, 1880–1913). James Ford Rhodes also attended closely to constitutional issues in his *History of the United States from the Compromise of 1850 to the Restoration of Home Rule at the South in 1877*, 7 vols. (New York: Macmillan, 1893–1902), as did Edward Channing's *History of the United States*, 6 vols. (New York: Macmillan, 1905–1925).

15. For examples of classic constitutional histories of this kind, see Francis Newton Thorpe, *Constitutional History of the United States to 1850* (Chicago: Callahan, 1901); Charles Warren, *The Supreme Court in American History*, 3 vols. (Boston: Little, Brown, 1922); Andrew C. McLaughlin, *The Foundations of American Constitutionalism* (New York: New York University Press, 1932); Andrew C. McLaughlin, *A Constitutional History of the United States* (New York: Appleton-Century, 1936); James G. Randall, *Constitutional Problems under Lincoln* (New York: Appleton, 1926); Homer C. Hockett, *The Constitutional History of the United States, 1776–1876*, 2 vols. (New York: Macmillan, 1939).

16. William Archibald Dunning, "The Constitution of the United States in Civil War," in Dunning, *Essays on the Civil War and Reconstruction* (1897; rev. ed., New York: Macmillan, 1904), 1–62; Dunning, "The Constitution of the United States During Reconstruction," in *Essays,* 63–135.

17. Milo M. Quaife, *The Doctrine of Non-Intervention with Slavery in the Territories* (Chicago: Chamberlain, 1910); Edward S. Corwin, "The Dred Scott Decision in Light of Contemporary Legal Doctrines," *American Historical Review* 17 (October 1911): 52–69; Helen T. Catterall, "Some Antecedents of the Dred Scott Case," *American Historical Review* 30 (October 1924): 56–71; Charles H. McCarthy, *Lincoln's Plan of Reconstruction* (New York: McClure, Phillips, 1901); David Miller Dewitt, *The Impeachment and Trial of Andrew Johnson* (New York: Macmillan, 1903).

18. Rhodes was an exception. In his opinion, slavery and slavery alone was the cause of the conflict. "Nothing in all history is plainer than that the ferment of which I have been speaking was due solely to the existence of slavery" (*History of the United States from the Compromise of 1850,* 3:122).

19. John W. Burgess, *Political Science and Comparative Constitutional Law,* 2 vols. (Boston: Gin, 1890), 1:67. For Burgess's political philosophy, see Bernard Edward Brown, *American Conservatives: The Political Thought of Francis Lieber and John W. Burgess* (New York: Columbia University Press, 1951).

20. Burgess, *Civil War and the Constitution,* 1:76, 78, 135.

21. See Rhodes, *History of the United States from the Compromise of 1850,* 1:95, where he describes as "wondrous pitiful" Calhoun's obsession with constitutional defenses of slavery.

22. Channing, *History of the United States,* 1:v–vi.

23. Burgess, *Civil War and the Constitution,* 2:117.

24. Dunning, "Constitution of the United States in the Civil War," 24, 32–35.

25. Ibid., 114.

26. Ibid., 40–43; quotations from p. 40.

27. Rhodes, *History of the United States from the Compromise of 1850,* 4:229.

28. Ibid., 234–35.

29. Burgess, *Civil War and the Constitution,* 2:117.

30. Ibid., 218.

31. 71 U.S. (4 Wallace) 2 (1866).

32. Burgess, *Civil War and the Constitution,* 2:218.

33. Burgess, *Reconstruction and the Constitution,* 133.

34. Ibid., 2.

35. Ibid., 5–7; Burgess, *Civil War and the Constitution,* 2:81.

36. Burgess, *Reconstruction and the Constitution,* 113.

37. Ibid., 114.

38. Ibid., 244–98; Dunning, "The Undoing of Reconstruction," in Dunning, *Essays,* 353–63; Rhodes, *History of the United States from the Compromise of 1850,* 7:74–173 passim, 290–91.

39. Thomas L. Haskell, *The Emergence of Professional Social Science: The American Social Science Association and the Nineteenth-Century Crisis of Authority* (Urbana: University of Illinois Press, 1977), 241.

40. G. Edward White, "From Sociological Jurisprudence to Realism: Jurisprudence and Social Change in Early Twentieth-Century America," in White, *Patterns of American Legal Thought* (Indianapolis: Bobbs-Merrill, 1978), 99–135; Morton J. Horwitz, *The Transformation of American Law, 1870–1960: The Crisis of Legal Orthodoxy* (New York: Oxford University Press, 1992), 169–246.

41. Arthur M. Schlesinger, Sr., *New Viewpoints in American History* (New York: Macmillan, 1922), 223.

42. Ibid., 184–99, 220–44.

43. Andrew C. McLaughlin, *A Constitutional History of the United States* (New York: Appleton-Century, 1935).

44. Hockett, *Constitutional History of the United States*; James G. Randall, *Constitutional Problems under Lincoln*.

45. Paul W. Murphy, "Time to Reclaim: The Current Challenge of American Constitutional History," *American Historical Review* 69 (October 1963): 64–79.

46. David Thelen, "Introduction," *Journal of American History* 74 (December 1987): 661.

47. McLaughlin, *Constitutional History of the United States*, 426–53; Hockett, *Constitutional History of the United States*, 2:20–35.

48. See, for example, McLaughlin's discussion of the Fugitive Slave Act. McLaughlin, *Constitutional History of the United States*, 536–37.

49. Randall, *Constitutional Problems under Lincoln*, 2, 4.

50. "It would be safe to sum up the prevailing views of our judges by saying that the war powers are entirely consistent with the Constitution, and that these war powers included all that is essential to the nation's preservation" (ibid., 33).

51. Ibid., 513–19.

52. Ibid., 519–20.

53. James G. Randall, "Lincoln in the Role of Dictator," *South Atlantic Quarterly* 28 (July 1929): 236–52; Randall, *Lincoln the Liberal Statesman* (New York: Dodd, Mead, 1947); Randall, *The Civil War and Reconstruction;* Randall and David Herbert Donald, *The Civil War and Reconstruction* (rev. ed., Boston: D. C. Heath, 1961).

54. Curtis Arthur Amlund, *Federalism in the Southern Confederacy* (Washington, D.C.: Public Affairs Press, 1966).

55. Albert Burton Moore, *Conscription and Conflict in the Confederacy* (New York: Macmillan, 1924; rpt. New York: Hillary House, 1963; rpt. again, Columbia: University of South Carolina Press, 1996), viii.

56. Frank Lawrence Owsley, *State Rights in the Confederacy* (Chicago: University of Chicago Press, 1925), 1.

57. Amlund, *Federalism in the Southern Confederacy*, v.

58. William M. Robinson, Jr., "A New Deal in Constitutions," *Journal of Southern History* 4 (November 1938): 449–61; Albert N. Fitts, "The Confederate Constitution: 1. The Provisional Constitution," *Alabama Review* 2 (April 1949):

83–101; Fitts, "The Confederate Constitution: The Constitutional Debate," *Alabama Review* 2 (April 1949): 189–210.

59. Robinson, "A New Deal in Constitutions," 461.

60. Ibid., 459.

61. Charles Robert Lee, Jr., *The Confederate Constitutions* (Chapel Hill: University of North Carolina Press, 1963).

62. William M. Robinson, Jr., *Justice in Grey: A History of the Judicial System of the Confederate States of America* (Cambridge, Mass.: Harvard University Press, 1941).

63. Ibid., 448–55.

64. J. G. deRoulhac Hamilton, "The State Constitutions and the Confederate Constitution," *Journal of Southern History* 4 (November 1938): 425–48.

65. Don E. Fehrenbacher, "The Confederacy as a Constitutional System," in Fehrenbacher, *Constitutions and Constitutionalism in the Slaveholding South* (Athens: University of Georgia Press, 1989), 57–81.

66. George C. Rable, *The Confederate Republic: A Revolution against Politics* (Chapel Hill: University of North Carolina Press, 1994).

67. Donald G. Nieman, "Republicanism, the Confederate Constitution, and the American Constitutional Tradition," in *An Uncertain Tradition: Constitutionalism and the History of the South,* ed. Kermit L. Hall and James W. Ely (Athens: University of Georgia Press, 1989), 201–24; quotations from p. 219.

68. Fehrenbacher, "The Confederacy as a Constitutional System," 63.

69. Marshall L. DeRosa, *The Confederate Constitution of 1861: An Inquiry into American Constitutionalism* (Columbia: University of Missouri Press, 1991). Less analytical, but more entertaining, is William C. Davis's narrative of the framing of the Constitution and the establishment of "a government of our own" in *"A Government of Our Own": The Making of the Confederacy* (New York: Free Press, 1994).

70. Randall, *Civil War and Reconstruction,* 853–54.

71. Ibid., 729–30, 726.

72. McLaughlin, *Constitutional History of the United States,* 684.

73. The identification of Johnson's Reconstruction program with Lincoln's had begun at the turn of the century with McCarthy, *Lincoln's Plan of Reconstruction.* While the nationalist historians and Dunning had blamed the enactment of what they saw as a wrong-headed Republican Reconstruction program on his failure of leadership, a series of books in the 1920s and 1930s restored Johnson's reputation, portraying him as a courageous defender of popular rights and constitutional limitations against an aggressive, tyrannical Congress. Robert W. Winston, *Andrew Johnson, Plebeian and Patriot* (New York: Holt, 1928); Claude G. Bowers, *The Tragic Era* (Cambridge, Mass.: Houghton Mifflin, 1929); George Fort Milton, *The Age of Hate: Andrew Johnson and the Radicals* (New York: Coward, McCann, 1930); Howard K. Beale, *The Critical Year: A Study of Andrew Johnson and Reconstruction* (New York: Frederick Ungar, 1930).

74. DeWitt, *Impeachment and Trial of Andrew Johnson;* Milton, *Age of*

*Hate,* 486–612; Bowers, *Tragic Era,* 171–97; Milton H. Lomask, *Andrew Johnson: President on Trial* (New York: Farrar Straus, 1960); Irving Brant, *Impeachment: Trials and Errors* (New York: Knopf, 1972), 133–54.

75. McLaughlin, *Constitutional History of the United States,* 662.

76. Beale, *The Critical Year: A Study of Andrew Johnson and Reconstruction,* 8–9. See also William B. Hesseltine, "Economic Factors in the Abandonment of Reconstruction," *Mississippi Valley Historical Review* 22 (September 1935): 191–210; Charles A. Beard and Mary R. Beard, *The Rise of American Civilization,* 2 vols. (New York: Macmillan, 1930), 2:3–121; C. Vann Woodward, *Reunion and Reaction: The Compromise of 1877 and the End of Reconstruction* (Boston: Little, Brown, 1951).

77. Avery O. Craven, *The Repressible Conflict, 1830–1861* (Baton Rouge: Louisiana State University Press, 1939); Craven, "The Coming of the War Between the States," *Journal of Southern History* 2 (August 1936): 305.

78. Randall, "The Blundering Generation," *Mississippi Valley Historical Review* 27 (June 1940): 3–28.

79. Roy Franklin Nichols, in *The Disruption of American Democracy* (New York: Macmillan, 1948), described the fatal disintegration of the Democratic party in political terms, all but ignoring constitutional issues. Most studies of southern sectionalism continued to stress southern commitment to state rights—for example, John T. Carpenter, *The South as a Conscious Minority* (New York: New York University Press, 1930; rpt. Columbia: University of South Carolina Press, 1990), and Charles S. Sydnor, *The Development of Southern Sectionalism, 1819–1848* (Baton Rouge: Louisiana State University Press, 1948)—but Wilbur J. Cash's highly influential *The Mind of the South* (New York: Knopf, 1941) never mentioned southern constitutional commitments at all. Wartime relations between Congress and the Executive were reduced to political conflict between Lincoln and vindictive Radical Republicans. T. Harry Williams, *Lincoln and the Radicals* (Madison: University of Wisconsin Press, 1941); William Frank Zornow, *Lincoln & the Party Divided* (Norman: University of Oklahoma Press, 1954).

80. Randall and Donald, *The Civil War and Reconstruction,* 293–309.

81. Gilbert Hobbs Barnes, *The Antislavery Impulse, 1830–1844* (New York: Appleton-Century, 1933).

82. Dwight L. Dumond, *The Antislavery Origins of the Civil War in the United States* (Ann Arbor: University of Michigan Press, 1939).

83. Alfred H. Kelly and Winfred A. Harbison, *The American Constitution* (New York: Norton, 1948; rev. ed. New York: Norton, 1955; 3rd ed. New York: Norton, 1963).

84. Bernard DeVoto, "The Easy Chair," *Harper's Magazine* (February 1946): 123–26; quotations are from p. 125.

85. Arthur M. Schlesinger, Jr., "The Causes of the Civil War: A Note on Historical Sentimentalism," *Partisan Review* 16 (October 1949): 969–81.

86. Harold M. Hyman, *The Era of the Oath: Northern Loyalty Oaths during the Civil War and Reconstruction* (Philadelphia: University of Pennsylvania Press, 1954).

87. James M. McPherson, *Battle Cry of Freedom: The Civil War Era* (New York: Oxford University Press, 1988).

88. Of particular importance were the seminal works that recovered the philosophy of republicanism that played such a crucial role in the Revolution and the framing of the Constitution, Bernard Bailyn's *Ideological Origins of the American Revolution* (Cambridge, Mass.: Harvard University Press, 1967) and his student Gordon Wood's *The Creation of the American Republic, 1776–1787* (Chapel Hill: University of North Carolina Press, 1969).

89. One the central elements of so-called postmodern thought is the conviction that language is the medium through which all meanings are constructed, which corrodes the idea that truth or meaning are "out there" waiting to be "discovered." See John E. Toews, "Intellectual History after the Linguistic Turn: The Autonomy of Meaning and the Irreducibility of the Human Experience," *American Historical Review* 92 (October 1987): 879–907. Saul Cornell describes "poststructural" thought largely in terms of the "linguistic turn," although does not use the phrase itself, in "Early American History in a Postmodern Age," *William and Mary Quarterly,* 3d ser., 50 (April 1993): 329–41, which is more accessible than many accounts and provides a good entry to the literature on the subject.

90. See, for example, Bailyn, *Ideological Origins of the American Revolution;* Morton J. Keller, *Affairs of State: Public Life in Late Nineteenth Century America* (Cambridge, Mass.: Harvard University Press, 1977); Kenneth M. Stampp, "The Concept of a Perpetual Union," *Journal of American History* 65 (June 1978): 5–33; Don E. Fehrenbacher, *The Dred Scott Case: Its Significance in American Law and Politics* (New York: Oxford University Press, 1981); Michael Kammen, *A Machine that Would Go of Itself: The Constitution in American Culture* (New York: Knopf, 1986); Eric Foner, "Rights and the Constitution in Black Life during the Civil War and Reconstruction," *Journal of American History* 74 (December 1987): 863–83.

91. *Journal of American History* 74 (December 1987); also published as *The Constitution and American Life,* ed. David Thelen (Ithaca, N.Y.: Cornell University Press, 1988).

92. Among the most important have been John Phillip Reid, William E. Nelson, Mark Tushnet, Morton J. Horwitz, and G. Edward White.

93. Howard Jay Graham, "The Early Antislavery Background of the Fourteenth Amendment," in Graham, *Everyman's Constitution* (Madison: State Historical Society of Wisconsin, 1968), 152–241; Jacobus TenBroek, *Antislavery Origins of the Fourteenth Amendment* (Berkeley: University of California Press, 1951).

94. William M. Wiecek, *Sources of Antislavery Constitutionalism in America, 1760–1848* (Ithaca, N.Y.: Cornell University Press, 1977); Eric Foner, "Salmon P. Chase: The Constitution and the Slave Power," chapter 3 of Foner, *Free Soil, Free Labor, Free Men: The Ideology of the Republican Party Before the Civil War* (New York: Oxford University Press, 1970), 73–102.

95. Russel B. Nye, *Fettered Freedom: Civil Liberties and the Slavery Controversy, 1830–1860* (East Lansing: Michigan State University Press, 1949).

96. Leonard L. Richards, *Gentlemen of Property and Standing: Anti-Abolition Mobs in Jacksonian America* (New York: Oxford University Press, 1970); Michael Kent Curtis, "The Curious History of Attempts to Suppress Antislavery Speech, Press, and Petition in 1835–1837," *Northwestern University Law Review* 89 (Spring 1995): 785–870.

97. Leon F. Litwack, *North of Slavery: The Negro in the Free States, 1790–1860* (Chicago: University of Chicago Press, 1961); V. Jacque Voegeli, *Free but Not Equal: The Midwest and the Negro during the Civil War* (Chicago: University of Chicago Press, 1967); Paul Finkelman, "*Prigg v. Pennsylvania* and Northern State Courts: Antislavery Use of a Pro-Slavery Decision," *Civil War History* 25 (March 1979): 5–35; Stanley W. Campbell, *The Slave Catchers: Enforcement of the Fugitive Slave Law, 1850–1860* (Chapel Hill: University of North Carolina Press, 1968); Thomas D. Morris, *Free Men All: The Personal Liberty Laws of the North, 1780–1861* (Baltimore: Johns Hopkins University Press, 1974); Carol Wilson, *Freedom at Risk: The Kidnapping of Free Blacks in America, 1780–1865* (Lexington: University Press of Kentucky, 1994).

98. Arthur E. Bestor, "State Sovereignty and Slavery," *Journal of the Illinois State Historical Society* 54 (Summer 1961): 117–79; Robert R. Russel, "Constitutional Doctrines with Regard to Slavery in the Territories," *Journal of Southern History* 32 (November 1966): 466–86; Fehrenbacher, *Dred Scott Case.*

99. Paul W. Finkelman, *An Imperfect Union: Slavery, Federalism, and Comity* (Chapel Hill: University of North Carolina Press, 1981).

100. William M. Wiecek, "'Old Times Are Not Forgotten': The Distinctiveness of the Southern Constitutional Experience," in *An Uncertain Tradition,* 159–97.

101. Don E. Fehrenbacher, "The South and the Federal Constitution," in Fehrenbacher, *Constitutions and Constitutionalism in the Slaveholding South,* 55.

102. Paul W. Finkelman, "Slavery and the Constitutional Convention: Making a Covenant with Death," in *Beyond Confederation: Origins of the Constitution and American National Identity,* Richard Beeman et al., eds. (Chapel Hill: University of North Carolina Press, 1987), 188–225; James Oakes, "'The Compromising Expedient': Justifying a Proslavery Constitution," *Cardozo Law Review* 17 (May 1996): 2023–56.

103. Phillip Shaw Paludan, "Hercules Unbound: Lincoln, Slavery, and the Intention of the Framers," in *The Constitution, Law, and American Life: Critical Aspects of the Nineteenth-Century Experience,* ed. Donald G. Nieman (Athens: University of Georgia Press, 1992), 1–22; quotation from p. 11. For Paludan's full discussion of Lincoln and the Constitution, see his *The Presidency of Abraham Lincoln* (Lawrence: University Press of Kansas, 1994). Paludan distills the essence of his understanding of Lincoln's constitutionalism in "Emancipating the Republic: Lincoln and the Means and Ends of Antislavery," in *"We Cannot Escape History": Lincoln and the Last Best Hope of Earth,* ed. James M. McPherson (Urbana: University of Illinois Press, 1995), 45–60.

104. Garry Wills, *Lincoln at Gettysburg: The Words That Remade America* (New York: Simon & Schuster, 1992).

105. David Herbert Donald, "Abraham Lincoln: Whig in the White House," in Donald, *Lincoln Reconsidered: Essays on the Civil War Era* (New York: Vintage Books, 1961), 187–208; Herman Belz, *Lincoln and the Constitution: The Dictatorship Question Reconsidered* (Fort Wayne, Ind.: Louis A. Warren Lincoln Library and Museum, 1984); Don E. Fehrenbacher, "Lincoln and the Constitution" and "The Paradoxes of Freedom" in Fehrenbacher, *Lincoln in Text and Context: Collected Essays* (Stanford, Calif.: Stanford University Press, 1984), 113–42; Michael Les Benedict, "The Constitution of the Lincoln Presidency and the Republican Era," in *The Constitution and the American Presidency,* ed. Martin L. Fausold and Alan Shank (Albany: SUNY Press, 1991), 45–61.

Enamored of strong presidential power after the Franklin Roosevelt presidency, political scientists had admired Lincoln's ability to overcome government inertia in the Civil War. See Clinton L. Rossiter, *Constitutional Dictatorship: Crisis Government in the Modern Democracies* (Princeton: Princeton University Press, 1948). Edward S. Corwin referred to "Lincoln's 'Dictatorship'" in his classic *The President: Office and Powers, 1787–1957* (4th rev. ed., New York: New York University Press, 1957), 20. He described Lincoln as scorning Congress and claiming unlimited executive powers to cope with military emergencies and to pursue war aims (21–22, 229–33). James McGregor Burns noted Lincoln's "constitutional usurpations" in his *Presidential Government: The Crucible of Leadership* (Boston: Houghton Mifflin, 1965), 36, while Richard M. Pious referred to Lincoln's "constitutional dictatorship" in his standard text, *The American Presidency* (New York: Basic Books, 1979), 57.

106. Neely, *The Fate of Liberty: Abraham Lincoln and Civil Liberties* (New York: Oxford University Press, 1991).

107. Benjamin P. Thomas and Harold M. Hyman, *Stanton: The Life and Times of Lincoln's Secretary of War* (New York: Knopf, 1962).

108. Harold M. Hyman, *A More Perfect Union: The Impact of the Civil War and Reconstruction on the Constitution* (New York: Knopf, 1973).

109. Leonard P. Curry, *Blueprint for Modern America: Nonmilitary Legislation of the First Civil War Congress* (Nashville: Vanderbilt University Press, 1968); Richard Franklin Bensel, *Yankee Leviathan: The Origins of Central State Authority in America, 1859–1877* (Cambridge: Cambridge University Press, 1990).

110. See especially Herman J. Belz, *A New Birth of Freedom: The Republican Party and Freedmen's Rights, 1861–1866* (Westport, Conn.: Greenwood, 1976), and Belz, *Emancipation and Civil Rights* (New York: Norton, 1978); Donald J. Nieman, *Promises to Keep: African Americans and the Constitutional Order* (New York: Oxford University Press, 1991).

111. Mary F. Berry, *Military Necessity and Civil Rights Policy: Black Citizenship and the Constitution, 1861–1868* (Port Washington, N.Y.: Kennikat Press, 1977).

112. Foner, "Rights and the Constitution in Black Life during the Civil War and Reconstruction"; Donald G. Nieman, "From Slaves to Citizens: African-Ameri-

cans, Rights Consciousness, and Reconstruction," *Cardozo Law Review* 17 (May 1966): 2115–39.

113. Hans L. Trefousse, *The Radical Republicans: Lincoln's Vanguard for Racial Justice* (New York: Knopf, 1968).

114. Eric Foner, *Reconstruction: America's Unfinished Revolution* (New York: Harper & Row, 1988).

115. Hyman, *A More Perfect Union*, 438–41; Phillip Shaw Paludan, *A Covenant with Death: The Constitution, Law, and Equality in the Civil War Era* (Urbana: University of Illinois Press, 1975); Michael Les Benedict, "Preserving the Constitution: The Conservative Basis of Radical Reconstruction," *Journal of American History* 61 (June 1974): 65–90; Benedict, *A Compromise of Principle: Congressional Republicans and Reconstruction, 1863–1869* (New York: Norton, 1974).

116. Robert J. Kaczorowski, "To Begin the Nation Anew: Congress, Citizenship, and Civil Rights after the Civil War," *American Historical Review* 92 (February 1987): 45–68; Kaczorowski, *The Politics of Judicial Interpretation: The Federal Courts, Department of Justice and Civil Rights, 1866–1876* (New York: Oceana Publications, 1985).

117. Raoul Berger, *Government By Judiciary: The Transformation of the Fourteenth Amendment* (Cambridge, Mass.: Harvard University Press, 1977); William E. Nelson, *The Roots of American Bureaucracy, 1830–1900* (Cambridge, Mass.: Harvard University Press, 1982); Michael Kent Curtis, *No State Shall Abridge: The Fourteenth Amendment and the Bill of Rights* (Durham, N.C.: Duke University Press, 1986); Robert J. Kaczorowski, "Searching for the Intent of the Framers of the Fourteenth Amendment," *Connecticut Law Review,* 5 (Winter 1973): 368–98; Kaczorowski, "Revolutionary Constitutionalism in the Era of the Civil War and Reconstruction," *New York University Law Review,* 61 (November 1986): 863–940; Earl M. Maltz, *Civil Rights, the Constitution, and Congress, 1863–1869* (Lawrence: University Press of Kansas, 1990); Richard L. Aynes, "On Misreading John Bingham and the Fourteenth Amendment," *Yale Law Journal,* 103 (October 1993): 57–104.

118. William M. Wiecek, "The Reconstruction of Judicial Power, 1863–1875," *American Journal of Legal History,* 13 (October 1969): 333–59; Stanley I. Kutler, *Judicial Power and Reconstruction Politics* (Chicago: University of Chicago Press, 1968).

119. Michael Les Benedict, *The Impeachment and Trial of Andrew Johnson* (New York: Norton, 1973), 180; Benedict, "The Constitution of the Lincoln Presidency and the Republican Era," in *The Constitution and the American Presidency,* ed. Fausold and Shank, 45–61; Eric L. McKitrick, *Andrew Johnson and Reconstruction* (Chicago: University of Chicago Press, 1960); Hans L. Trefousse, *Impeachment of a President: Andrew Johnson, the Blacks, and Reconstruction* (Knoxville: University of Tennessee Press, 1975).

120. Harold M. Hyman and William M. Wiecek, *Equal Justice under Law: Constitutional Development, 1835–1875* (New York: Harper & Row, 1982).

## WHAT DID THE WINNERS WIN?

1. I wish to thank Randall Miller and Philip Scranton for their thoughtful suggestions about this essay. They are not responsible for what I have committed or omitted here.

2. Charles A. and Mary R. Beard, *The Rise of American Civilization*, 2 vols. (New York: Macmillan, 1927), 52–54; Louis M. Hacker, *The Triumph of American Capitalism* (New York: Columbia University Press, 1940), 373.

3. Albert Castel, "Andrew Johnson: His Historiographical Rise and Fall," *Mid-America* 45 (July 1963); Stanley Coben, "Northeastern Business and Radical Reconstruction," *Mississippi Valley Historical Review* 46 (June 1959); Peter Novick, *That Noble Dream: The "Objectivity Question" and the American Historical Profession* (Cambridge: Cambridge University Press, 1988), 235–38; and Thomas J. Pressly, *Americans Interpret Their Civil War* (Princeton: Princeton University Press, 1954); Harold M. Hyman, ed. *The Radical Republicans and Reconstruction* (Indianapolis: Bobbs-Merrill, 1967) xl-li.

4. On interconnection between economic and egalitarian motives in Reconstruction, see Michael Les Benedict, *A Compromise of Principle: Congressional Republicans and Reconstruction* (New York: Norton, 1974); Howard K. Beale, *The Critical Year: A Study of Andrew Johnson and Reconstruction* (New York: Ungar, 1930); Robert Sharkey, *Money, Class and Party* (Baltimore: Johns Hopkins University Press, 1959). Eric Foner, *Reconstruction: America's Unfinished Revolution, 1863–1877* (New York: Harper & Row, 1988), says that Republican divisions over the economy "heightened the importance of the Civil War and Reconstruction as touchstones that transcended local differences and served as a continuing definition of the party's identity" (487).

5. Arthur Cole had predicted Moore's argument in an excellent study of the Civil War era, *The Irrepressible Conflict, 1850–1865* (New York: Macmillan, 1934). He adopted the Beard view of a revolution but, unlike the Beards, emphasized the importance of the slavery issue. The war was the result, Cole argued, of a growing division between an increasingly industrialized North and an abidingly agrarian South. Northern victory secured the ultimate triumph of the new over the older America. Major professional reviews of the book practically ignored its contributions to social and economic history. Cole was criticized by scholars for his attitude toward the South and his condemnation of slavery. See the reviews in *American Historical Review* (40 [January 1935], 354–36) and *Mississippi Valley Historical Review* (21 [March 1935], 279–81).

6. Barrington Moore, *Social Origins of Dictatorship and Democracy: Lord and Peasant in the Making of the Modern World* (Boston: Beacon Press, 1966) 111–59; Beard and Beard, *Rise of American Civilization*, 2:40. Moore relied fully on secondary sources. Like the Beards, he did not use statistical evidence to determine the actual extent of the economic changes that the war brought. Neither Moore nor the Beards actually measured the speed of the changes in the economy. Moore was sensitive to the limitations on emancipation that followed the promises of the war era. He also recognized that the "propertied interests" of both North and South worked together to limit the extent of black freedom.

7. James M. McPherson, *The Struggle for Equality: Abolitionists and the Negro in Civil War and Reconstruction* (Princeton: Princeton University Press, 1964); McPherson, *The Abolitionist Legacy: From Reconstruction to the NAACP* (Princeton: Princeton University Press, 1975).

8. James M. McPherson, "The Second American Revolution," in McPherson's *Abraham Lincoln and the Second American Revolution* (New York: Oxford University Press, 1991), 3–22. For a parallel argument also emphasizing black gains see, Phillip Shaw Paludan, "Triumph Through Tragedy: The Benefits of the Civil War," *Civil War History* 20 (September 1974): 239–50. Roger Ransom and Richard Sutch, *One Kind of Freedom: The Economic Consequences of Emancipation* (Cambridge: Cambridge University Press, 1977); Foner, *Reconstruction*. Perhaps this is the place to note that Phillip Shaw Paludan, *"A People's Contest": The Union and Civil War, 1861–1865* (New York: Harper and Row, 1988), paid little direct attention to the Beard-Hacker thesis.

9. Beard and Beard, *Rise of American Civilization*, 53–54, 62, 105, 121.

10. Thomas Cochran, "Did the Civil War Retard Industrialization?," *Mississippi Valley Historical Review* 48 (September 1961): 197–210.

11. Jeremy Atack and Peter Passell, *A New Economic View of American History from Colonial Times to 1940* (2d ed., New York: Norton, 1994), 364.

12. Stanley Engerman, "The Economic Impact of the Civil War," *Explorations in Entrepreneurial History*, 3 (1966): 176–99; David Gilchrist and W. David Lewis, eds., *Economic Change in the Civil War Era* (Greenville, Del.: Eleutherian Mills-Hagley Foundation, 1965); Ralph Andreano, ed., *The Economic Impact of the American Civil War* (Cambridge, Mass.: Schenkman, 1967); Saul Engerbourg, "The Economic Impact of the Civil War on Manufacturing Enterprise," *Business History* 21 (1979): 148–62.

13. Three essays in the 1960s challenged Cochran directly: Stephen Salisbury, "The Effects of the Civil War on American Economic Development," in *Economic Impact,* ed. Andreano, 161–68; Pershing Vartanian, "The Cochran Thesis: A Critique in Historical Analysis," *Journal of American History* 51 (June 1964), 77–89, and Harry Scheiber, "Economic Change in the Civil War Era," *Civil War History* 11 (December 1965), 396–411. In *"A People's Contest,"* chapter 6, I was persuaded by this latter evidence to emphasize the extent of the changes. McPherson continued to argue that the war brought revolutionary changes to the economy as well. He challenged the claim by Cochran that the war had retarded economic growth by suggesting that destruction of the southern economy accounted for most of the retardation. "If we consider the northern states alone," McPherson wrote, "the stimulus of war production probably caused a spurt in the economic growth rate" ("Second American Revolution," 11). But this view was challenged by both Stanley Engerman and Jeffrey Williamson who insisted, in Williamson's words, that the "poor performance of the economy" was not "attributable to southern defeat and subsequent economic chaos below the Mason-Dixon line. . . . The annual rate of growth of per capita commodity output in the victorious North was only one percent during the war decade, . . . the lowest rate in the nineteenth century." Jeffrey Williamson, "Watersheds and Turning Points: Conjectures on

the Long Term Impact of Civil War Financing," *Journal of Economic History* 34 (September 1974): 637. Williamson relies on Stanley Engerman, "The Economic Impact of the Civil War," 178–83. Both essays and most studies of the war-era economy rely on Robert Gallman, "Commodity Output, 1839–1899," *Conference on Research in Income and Wealth: Trends in the American Economy in the Nineteenth Century* (Princeton: Princeton University Press, 1960).

14. Stanley Engerman and Robert Gallman, "U.S. Economic Growth, 1783–1860," *Research in Economic History* 8 (1983): 1–46; Douglas North, *The Economic Growth of the United States 1790–1860* (New York: Norton, 1966); Stanley Engerman, "The Economic Impact of the Civil War," 176–78; Stuart Bruchey, *Growth of the Modern American Economy* (New York: Dodd, Mead, 1975), chapter 2; Beard and Beard, *Rise of American Civilization,* 2:115. The Beards recognized that the foundations for the industrial age were laid in the 1820s. See their vol. 1, chapter 15, "The Sweep of Economic Forces." *American Economic Growth and Standards of Living before the Civil War,* ed. Robert Gallman and John J. Wallis (Chicago: University of Chicago Press, 1992). Thomas Weiss and Donald Schaeffer, in their *American Economic Development in Historical Perspective* (Stanford, Calif.: Stanford University Press, 1994), provide the latest evidence for a steady and long-range economic growth that began at least as far back as the Revolution.

15. Richard Franklin Bensel, *Yankee Leviathan: The Origins of Central State Authority in America, 1859–1877* (Cambridge: Cambridge University Press, 1990), 78–85.

16. Claudia Golden and Frank Lewis, "The Economic Cost of the American Civil War: Estimates and Implications," *Journal of Economic History* 35 (1975): 294–326.

17. *The Collected Works of Abraham Lincoln,* 9 vols., ed. Roy P. Basler (New Brunswick, N.J.: Rutgers University Press, 1953–1955), 5:518–37. William Freehling, *Road to Disunion: Volume I: Secessionists at Bay, 1776–1854* (New York: Oxford University Press, 1990), describes Deep South fears that Kentucky and other northern southern states were being drawn into the free-labor vortex.

18. While some economic historians have wrestled with the question of the impact of the war, it seems to have become a minor problem for them in recent years. In 1995 Robert Whaples asked economists and economic historians forty questions about the past, ranging from the nature of the colonial economy and the economic consequences of the American Revolution to the productivity of slaves and did not include a single question about the economic impact of the Civil War. See "Is There Consensus among American Economic Historians?," *Journal of Economic History* 55 (March 1995), 139–52.

19. Roger Ransom, *Conflict and Compromise: The Political Economy of Slavery, Emancipation and the American Civil War* (Cambridge: Cambridge University Press, 1989), 245–53.

20. See McPherson, "Second American Revolution," 3–7; Paludan, "*A People's Contest,*" 143–45.

21. Ransom, *Conflict and Compromise,* 258. For an argument that the unprecedented wartime increase in agricultural productivity was the result of more women and children working, see Lee Craig and Thomas Weiss, "Agricultural Productivity Growth During the Decade of the Civil War," *Journal of Economic History,* 53 (1993): 527–48.

22. Patrick O'Brien, *The Economic Effects of the American Civil War* (Atlantic Highlands, N.J.: Humanities Press International, 1988), 65.

23. Ransom, *Conflict and Compromise,* 279–84. See also Engerman, "Economic Impact of the Civil War," 189–90; Jonathan Hughes, *American Economic History* (Glenview, Ill.: Scott Foresman, 1990), 254.

24. Ransom, 283–84.

25. Bensel, *Yankee Leviathan,* 416–21. Bensel does say that the Beards' and Hacker's accounts are "colorful but theoretically unsatisfying." But he essentially supports their conclusions.

26. See Eugene Lerner, "Investment Uncertainty during the Civil War—A Note on the McCormick Brothers," *Journal of Economic History* 16 (March 1965): 34–40, and more recently on economic health of the city on the brink of war, see David Galenson, "Economic Opportunity on the Urban Frontier: Nativity, Work and Wealth in Early Chicago," *Journal of Economic History* 51 (September 1991), 581–604.

27. Stuart Sprague, "The Economic Impact of the Civil War: The Case of Cincinnati," *Essays in Business and Economic History* 10 (1992).

28. Howard Mumford Jones, "The Wounds of War: A Tale of Two Cities," *Harvard Library Bulletin* 20 (1972): 117–57; Alan Lessof, *The Nation and Its City: Politics, "Corruption" and Progress in Washington, D.C., 1861–1902* (Baltimore: Johns Hopkins University Press, 1994); Alan Dawley, *Class and Community: The Industrial Revolution in Lynn* (Cambridge, Mass.: Harvard University Press, 1976).

29. Matthew Gallman, *Mastering Wartime: A Social History of Philadelphia during the Civil War* (Cambridge: Cambridge University Press, 1990); Philip Scranton, *Proprietary Capitalism: The Textile Manufacture at Philadelphia, 1800–1885* (Cambridge: Cambridge University Press, 1983).

30. Atack and Passell, *A New Economic View of American History,* 373. See also recent textbooks in economic history—James F. Willis and Martin C. Primack, *An Economic History of the United States* (Englewood Cliffs, N.J.: Prentice-Hall, 1989), 196–208; Jonathan Hughes, *American Economic History* (Glenview, Ill.: Scott Foresman, 1990), 245–64—for the consensus of economic historians.

31. The most recent interpretation of workers' history, David Montgomery, *Citizen Worker: The Experience of Workers in the United States with Democracy and the Free Market during the Nineteenth Century* (Cambridge: Cambridge University Press, 1993), contains little discussion of the Civil War, other than a few pages on the 1863 draft riots. Given the fact that Montgomery's *Beyond Equality: Labor and the Radical Republicans, 1862–1872* (New York: Random House, 1967) explored the impact of the war ably, this omission is notable. My *"A People's Contest,"* chapter 8, does provide an overview of labor in the North during the war.

32. Moore, *Social Origins,* 152

33. Lee Soltow, *Men and Wealth in the United States, 1850–1870* (New Haven: Yale University Press, 1975), 98–105, 123.

34. Bensel, *Yankee Leviathan,* 433–34. Frank Klement, *Copperheads in the Middle West* (Chicago: University of Chicago Press, 1960).

35. Grace Palladino, *Another Civil War: Labor, Capital, and the State in the Anthracite Regions of Pennsylvania* (Urbana: University of Illinois Press, 1990).

36. Iver Bernstein, *The New York City Draft Riots: Their Significance for American Society and Politics in the Age of the Civil War* (New York: Oxford University Press, 1990); quotation from page 41; Paludan, *"A People's Contest,"* chapter 8.

37. Moore, *Social Origins,* 131; Beard and Beard, *Rise of American Civilization,* 1:751–52.

38. See Peter Stearns, "Social History," in Stearns, *Encyclopedia of Social History* (New York and London: Garland, 1994), 683; Lynn Hunt, "Introduction," in her *The New Cultural History* (Berkeley: University of California Press, 1989), 1.

39. Emerson Fite, *Social and Industrial Conditions in the North During the Civil War* (1910; rpt. New York: Frederick Ungar, 1963).

40. I follow Peter Novick, *That Noble Dream: The "Objectivity Question" and the American Historical Profession* (Cambridge: Cambridge University Press, 1988), chapter 4.

41. Novick, *Noble Dream,* 178–80, argues that the books lacked impact because they lacked clear, coherent narratives. However, Allan Nevins's volume in the series, *The Emergence of Modern America, 1865–1878* (New York: Macmillan, 1927), was sensitive to the large economic transitions of the postwar world and to their impact on urban workers and on farm life. Arthur Cole's volume, discussed in note 4 above, focused on describing economic transition.

42. I discuss this literature and the dearth of social history writing on the North at war in *"A People's Contest."*

43. Zunz, ed., *Reliving the Past: The Worlds of Social History* (Chapel Hill: University of North Carolina Press, 1985), 77. Zunz's contribution to this book, "The Synthesis of Social Change: Reflections on American Social History," 53–114, is the best survey of the state of the field as of 1985, and it offers useful suggestions for future inquiry. Maris A. Vinovskis, "Have Social Historians Lost the Civil War? Some Preliminary Demographic Speculations," *Journal of American History* 76 (June 1989): 34–58.

44. Here I must insert a personal note. In 1988, I published *"A People's Contest,"* an effort to synthesize work on the war era by the "new" social and economic historians and to integrate that work into more traditional types of study of the war. This was the first single-volume work since 1910 to describe northern society at war. But not one journal of social history, nor of economic history, reviewed the book.

45. I mean no insult to Timothy Haggerty, but more experienced authors on the topic clearly were available, as Vernon Burton showed in his essay for *The Encyclopedia of American Social History,* ed. Mary Kupiec Cayton, Elliott J.

Gorn, and Peter W. Williams (New York: Scribner, 1993). Seven authors contributed to Vinovskis's collection, Maris Vinovskis, *Toward a Social History of the American Civil War* (New York: Cambridge University, 1990). Grace Palladino and Iver Bernstein had also published their books by this time, and the collection of essays on gender and the war, *Divided Houses: Gender and the Civil War* (New York: Oxford University Press, 1992), edited by Catherine Clinton and Nina Silber, containing work by nineteen authors, had appeared. These volumes might have suggested other choices. The most recent study of northern society at war is *"A People's Contest."* Haggerty also omitted Reid Mitchell's *The Vacant Chair,* but that might have been due to the publisher's timetable; Mitchell's work appeared the year before the encyclopedia.

46. Maris A. Vinovskis, "Have Social Historians Lost the Civil War?"; Gerald F. Linderman, *Embattled Courage: The Experience of Combat in the Civil War* (New York: Free Press, 1987); Reid Mitchell, *Civil War Soldiers* (New York: Viking, 1988); Earl J. Hess, *Liberty, Virtue, Progress: Northerners and Their War for the Union* (New York: New York University Press, 1988); James I. Robertson, Jr., *Soldiers Blue and Gray* (Columbia: University of South Carolina Press, 1988); Randall C. Jimerson, *The Private Civil War: Popular Thought during the Sectional Conflict* (Baton Rouge: Louisiana State University Press, 1988); James M. McPherson, *What They Fought For* (Baton Rouge: Louisiana State University Press, 1994).

47. William J. Rohrbaugh, "Who Fought for the North in the Civil War? Concord, Massachusetts, Enlistments," *Journal of American History* 73 (December 1986): 695–701; McPherson, *Battle Cry of Freedom: The Civil War Era* (New York: Oxford University Press, 1988), 602–6. But see William Marvel, "A Poor Man's Fight: Civil War Enlistment Patterns in Conway, New Hampshire," *Historical New Hampshire* 43 (1988): 21–40, for evidence that Conway's poor farm areas provided 53 percent of the town's troops although those areas represented only 27 percent of the town's population.

48. Larry Logue, *To Appomattox and Beyond: The Civil War Soldier in War and Peace* (Chicago: I. R. Dee, 1996).

49. Stuart McConnell, *Glorious Contentment: The Grand Army of the Republic, 1865–1900* (Chapel Hill: University of North Carolina Press, 1992). See discussion of soldier conservatism in *"A People's Contest,"* 326–27, and the thoughtful essay by David Blight, "No Desperate Hero: Manhood and Freedom in a Union Soldier's Experience," in *Divided Houses,* 55–75.

50. Mary Ann Clawson, *Constructing Brotherhood: Class, Gender and Fraternalism* (Princeton: Princeton University Press, 1989), 11.

51. Mark C. Carnes, *Secret Ritual and Manhood in Victorian America* (New Haven: Yale University Press, 1989), 142–43.

52. For the best guide to literature on children, see Joseph Hawes and N. Ray Hiner, eds., *American Childhood: A Research Guide and Historical Handbook* (Westport, Conn.: Greenwood, 1985).

53. Tamara Haraven, "The History of the Family and the Complexity of Social Change," 96 *American Historical Review* (February 1991): 95–124.

54. See *"A People's Contest,"* 331–32; Reid Mitchell, *Vacant Chair,* has in-

teresting things to say about images of soldiers and "boys" and parental authority but says little about parenting itself. Stephen Frank, "'Rendering Aid and Comfort': Images of Fatherhood in the Letters of Civil War Soldiers from Massachusetts and Michigan," 26 *Journal of Social History* (Fall 1992): 5–32, suggests some imaginative ways of thinking about the war from the viewpoint of relationships between fathers and sons. The war seems both to have intensified father-son feelings and made them more problematic. Fathers often went seeking dead or wounded sons. Sons left the authority of their parents and met new authority figures, then returned home as "men" and challenged the father's authority.

55. In World War I the British and Irish lost slightly less men per 10,000 of the population than did both North and South together. France however lost twice the number of men per 10,000 as did the United States as a whole. But when the South is considered alone, the ratio of deaths to the population was greater in Dixie than it was in France. See Maris A. Vinovskis, "Have Social Historians Lost the Civil War?," in *Toward a Social History of the American Civil War*, ed. Vinovskis, 7n. 9.

56. William Tuttle, *Daddy's Gone to War: The Second World War in the Lives of America's Children* (New York: Oxford University Press, 1993); Robert Bremner, *The Public Good: Philanthropy and Welfare in the Civil War Era* (New York: Knopf, 1980).

57. James Marten, "For the Good, the True, and the Beautiful: Northern Children's Magazines and the Civil War," *Civil War History* 41 (March 1995): 57–75. Peter Stearns and Timothy Haggarty, "The Role of Fear: Transitions in American Emotional Standards for Children, 1850–1950," *American Historical Review* 96 (February 1991): 63–94. Peter W. Bardaglio, "The Children of Jubilee: African American Children in Wartime," in *Divided Houses*, 213–29. Harvey Graff's interpretive volume on children in U.S. history is cursory on the impact of the Civil War (*Conflicting Paths: Growing Up in America* [New York: Cambridge University Press, 1995], 68–69).

58. See Theda Skocpol, *Protecting Soldiers and Mothers: The Political Origins of Social Policy in the United States* (Cambridge, Mass.: Harvard University Press, 1992); Amy Holmes, "'Such is the Price We Pay': American Widows and the Civil War Pension System," in *Toward a Social History of the American Civil War*, ed. Maris A. Vinovskis; Megan McClintock, "Civil War Pensions and the Reconstruction of Union Families," *Journal of American History* 83 (September 1996): 456–80.

59. Lori D. Ginzberg, *Women and the Work of Benevolence: Morality, Politics and Class in the Nineteenth Century United States* (New Haven: Yale University Press, 1990), esp. chapter 5. Reid Mitchell, *The Vacant Chair: The Northern Soldier Leaves Home* (New York: Oxford University Press, 1993).

60. Eric J. Hobsbawm, "From Social History to the History of Society," *Daedalus* (Winter 1971): 20–45.

61. Herbert Gutman, *Work, Culture and Society in Industrializing America* (New York: Vintage, 1976), xii; see the warning against the same tendency in recent writings by Ardis Cameron—for example, in Cameron's review of Thomas Dublin, *Transforming Women's Work: New England Lives in the Industrial Revo-*

*lution* (Ithaca, N.Y.: Cornell University Press, 1994), in *Labor History* 37 (1996): 302–4.

62. McPherson, *Battle Cry of Freedom*, 858, describes his approach.

63. William H. Sewell, Jr., "Narratives and Social Identities" *Social Science History* 16 (Fall 1992).

64. Philip Ethington, *The Public City: The Political Construction of Urban Life in San Francisco, 1850–1900* (New York: Cambridge University Press, 1994), 170–207.

65. Terrence McDonald, "The Problem of the Political in Recent American Urban History: Liberal Pluralism and the Rise of Functionalism," *Social History* 10 (October 1985): 323–45; Peter Evans, Dietrich Rueschemeyer, and Theda Skocpol, eds., *Bringing the State Back In* (New York: Cambridge University Press, 1985); Skocpol, *Protecting Soldiers and Mothers*.

## BEHIND THE LINES

1. Gaines M. Foster, *Ghosts of the Confederacy: Defeat, the Lost Cause, and the Emergence of the New South, 1865–1913* (New York: Oxford University Press, 1987); Charles Reagan Wilson, *Baptized in Blood: The Religion of the Lost Cause, 1865–1920* (Athens: University of Georgia Press, 1980).

2. Charles Ramsdell, *Behind the Lines in the Southern Confederacy* (Baton Rouge: Louisiana State University Press, 1944).

3. Allan Nevins, "Introduction," in Paul W. Gates, *Agriculture and the Civil War* (New York: Knopf, 1965), v. In the same year, Mary Elizabeth Massey echoed Nevins, arguing that historians still wrote more about "the battles and campaigns than about life within Confederate lines, and what has been said of the home front too often spotlights the leaders and upper classes." "The Confederate States of America: The Homefront," in *Writing Southern History: Essays in Historiography in Honor of Fletcher M. Green,* ed. Arthur S. Link and Rembert W. Patrick (Baton Rouge: Louisiana State University Press, 1965), 250. Massey, of course, was an exception to the rule that historians ignored social explanations of Confederate defeat. Another exception was Bell Irvin Wiley. See Massey, *Ersatz in the Confederacy* (Columbia: University of South Carolina Press, 1952); and Wiley, *The Plain People of the Confederacy* (Baton Rouge: Louisiana State University Press, 1943).

4. For recent surveys of new Civil War literature, see David Osher and Peter Wallenstein, "Why the Confederacy Lost: An Essay Review," *Maryland Historical Magazine* 91 (1996): 95–108; Joseph T. Glatthaar, "The 'New' Civil War History: An Overview," *Pennsylvania Magazine of History and Biography* 115 (July 1991): 339–69; Richard Slotkin, "'What Shall Men Remember?': Recent Work on the Civil War," *American Literary History* 3 (Spring 1991): 120–35.

5. Steven Hahn, *The Roots of Southern Populism: Yeoman Farmers and the Transformation of the Georgia Upcountry, 1850–1890* (New York: Oxford University Press, 1983), 116.

6. For a recent overview of this important literature, see Peter A. Coclanis, "The American Civil War in Economic Perspective: Basic Questions and Some Answers," *Southern Cultures* 2 (Winter 1996): 163–75.

7. For a survey of literature on the nineteenth-century southern economy by economists, see Gavin Wright, "The Strange Career of the New Southern Economic History," *Reviews in American History* 10 (December 1982): 164–80; for a survey of work by historians, see Dan T. Carter, "From the Old South to the New: Another Look at the Theme of Change and Continuity," in *From the Old South to the New: Essays in the Transitional South*, ed. Walter J. Fraser, Jr., and Winfred B. Moore, Jr. (Westport, Conn.: Greenwood Press, 1981), 23–32.

8. Robert Tracy McKenzie, *One South or Many? Plantation Belt and Upcountry in Civil War-Era Tennessee* (Cambridge: Cambridge University Press, 1994).

9. Examples of this vast literature include Thavolia Glymph and John H. Kushma, eds., *Essays on the Postbellum Southern Economy* (College Station: Texas A&M University Press, 1985); Roger L. Ransom and Richard Sutch, *One Kind of Freedom: The Economic Consequences of Emancipation* (Cambridge: Cambridge University Press, 1977); Julie Saville, *The Work of Reconstruction: From Slave to Wage Laborer in South Carolina, 1860–1870* (Cambridge: Cambridge University Press, 1994); Gavin Wright, *Old South, New South: Revolutions in the Southern Economy since the Civil War* (New York: Basic Books, 1986); Harold D. Woodman, "Sequel to Slavery: The New History Views the Postbellum South," *Journal of Southern History* 43 (November 1977): 523–54.

10. Emory M. Thomas, "Reckoning With Rebels," in *The Old South in the Crucible of War*, ed. Harry P. Owens and James J. Cooke (Jackson: University Press of Mississippi, 1983), 13. Also see two influential books by Thomas, *The Confederacy as a Revolutionary Experience* (Englewood Cliffs, N.J.: Prentice Hall, 1971) and *The Confederate Nation, 1861–1865* (New York: Harper & Row, 1979).

11. Richard Franklin Bensel, *Yankee Leviathan: The Origins of Central State Authority in America, 1859–1877* (Cambridge: Cambridge University Press, 1990); Heather Cox Richardson, *The Greatest Nation of the Earth: Republican Economic Policies during the Civil War* (Cambridge, Mass.: Harvard University Press, 1997).

12. Harold Woodman, "How New Was the New South?" *Agricultural History* 58 (October 1984): 529–45.

13. John C. Schwab, *The Confederate States of America: A Financial and Industrial History of the South During the Civil War* (New York: Charles Scribner's Sons, 1901); Robert Cecil Todd, *Confederate Finance* (Athens: University of Georgia Press, 1954); Paul W. Gates, *Agriculture and the Civil War.*

14. Thomas, "Reckoning with Rebels," 14; see also Thomas, *The Confederacy as a Revolutionary Experience* and Raimondo Luraghi, *The Rise and Fall of the Plantation South* (New York: New Viewpoints, 1978).

15. William W. Freehling, "The Divided South, the Causes of Confederate Defeat, and the Reintegration of Narrative History," in Freehling, *The Reintegration of American History: Slavery and the Civil War* (New York: Oxford University Press, 1994). For similar arguments, see Stanley Lebergott, "Why the South Lost: Commercial Purpose in the Confederacy, 1861–1865," *Journal of American History* 70 (June 1983): 58–74; and Roger L. Ransom, *Conflict and Compromise:*

*The Political Economy of Slavery, Emancipation, and the American Civil War* (Cambridge: Cambridge University Press, 1984). Ransom concludes: "The slave system that had been so instrumental in bringing on the war, proved to be equally instrumental in determining the outcome of the fight" (175).

16. Gates, *Agriculture and the Civil War.* According to George Rable, the *Encyclopedia of Southern Culture,* edited by Charles Reagan Wilson and William Ferris, almost entirely neglects the impact of the war on southern agriculture. In fact, he claims that it slights the Civil War in general. George C. Rable, "Is the Civil War Still Central to the Study of Southern Civilization? Reflections on the *Encyclopedia of Southern Culture,*" *Civil War History* 4 (December 1990): 334–42.

17. John Solomon Otto, *Southern Agriculture during the Civil War Era, 1860–1880* (Westport, Conn.: Greenwood Press, 1994).

18. Charles P. Roland, *Louisiana Sugar Plantations during the American Civil War* (Leiden: E. J. Brill, 1957), 137; John Alfred Heitmann, *The Modernization of the Louisiana Sugar Industry, 1830–1910* (Baton Rouge: Louisiana University Press, 1987), 148.

19. John C. Rodrigue, "Raising Cane: From Slavery to Free Labor in Louisiana's Sugar Parishes, 1862–1880" (Ph.D. diss., Emory University, 1993).

20. Crandall A. Shifflett, *Patronage and Poverty in the Tobacco South: Louisa County, Virginia, 1860–1890* (Knoxville: University of Tennessee Press, 1982); Lynda Morgan, *Emancipation in Virginia's Tobacco Belt, 1850-1870* (Athens: University of Georgia Press, 1992); and Frederick F. Siegel, *The Roots of Southern Distinctiveness: Tobacco and Society in Danville, Virginia, 1780–1865* (Chapel Hill: University of North Carolina Press, 1987).

21. Peter A. Coclanis, *The Shadow of a Dream: Economic Life and Death in the South Carolina Low Country, 1670–1920* (New York: Oxford University Press, 1989).

22. Ransom and Sutch, *One Kind of Freedom,* 190–91; Michael B. Dougan, *Confederate Arkansas: The People and Policies of a Frontier State in Wartime* (University: University of Alabama Press, 1976).

23. Lebergott, "Why the South Lost," 58–74. For other studies that emphasize planter greed and selfishness, see Carl H. Moneyhon, *The Impact of the Civil War and Reconstruction on Arkansas: Persistence in the Midst of Ruin* (Baton Rouge: Louisiana State University Press, 1994); Lawrence N. Powell and Michael S. Wayne, "Self-Interest and the Decline of Confederate Nationalism," in *Old South in the Crucible,* 29–45; and James L. Roark, *Masters without Slaves: Southern Planters in the Civil War and Reconstruction* (New York: W. W. Norton, 1977).

24. McKenzie, *One South or Many?*

25. Moneyhon, *The Impact of the Civil War and Reconstruction on Arkansas.*

26. Paul D. Escott, *Many Excellent People: Power and Privilege in North Carolina, 1850–1900* (Chapel Hill: University of North Carolina Press, 1985).

27. B. Byron Price, "Don't Fence Me In: The Range Cattle Industry in the

Confederate Southwest, 1861–1865," in *Southwestern Agriculture: Pre-Columbian to Modern*, ed. Henry C. Detloff and Irvin M. May, Jr. (College Station: Texas A&M University Press, 1982): 59–72.

28. Robert A. Taylor, *Rebel Storehouse: Florida in the Confederate Economy* (Tuscaloosa: University of Alabama Press, 1995).

29. Michael Wayne, *The Reshaping of Plantation Society: The Natchez District, 1860–1880* (Baton Rouge: Louisiana State University Press, 1983).

30. Stephen V. Ash, *Middle Tennessee Society Transformed, 1860–1870: War and Peace in the Upper South* (Baton Rouge: Louisiana State University Press, 1988). See also Jonathan M. Bryant, *How Curious a Land: Conflict and Change in Greene County, Georgia, 1850–1885* (Chapel Hill: University of North Carolina Press, 1996). For a study that focuses on the mountain regions of several states, see Kenneth W. Noe and Shannon H. Wilson, ed., *The Civil War in Appalachia: Collected Essays* (Knoxville: University of Tennessee Press, 1997).

31. Stephen V. Ash, *When the Yankees Came: Conflict and Chaos in the Occupied South, 1861–1865* (Chapel Hill: University of North Carolina Press, 1995). Also see Robert H. McKenzie, "The Economic Impact of Federal Operations in Alabama During the Civil War," *Alabama Historical Quarterly* (January 1976): 51–63.

32. John Inscoe, "Mountain Masters as Confederate Opportunists: The Profitability of Slavery in Western North Carolina, 1861–65," *Slavery and Abolition* 16 (April 1995): 84–100.

33. For the most thorough documentation of the African American emancipation experience, see Ira Berlin, Barbara J. Fields, Thavolia Glymph, Joseph P. Reidy, and Leslie S. Rowland, eds., *Freedom: A Documentary History of Emancipation, 1861–1867,* 4 vols. to date (Cambridge: Cambridge University Press, 1982– ).

34. Inscoe, "Mountain Masters," 84–100.

35. Powell and Wayne, "Self-Interest and the Decline of Confederate Nationalism," 29–45.

36. Charles Ramsdell identified deteriorating railroads as a major cause of the declining economic welfare of the home front, but scholars have generally shown more interest in the railroad's role in military operations and supply. Important studies include Robert C. Black III, *The Railroads of the Confederacy* (Chapel Hill: University of North Carolina Press, 1952); George Edgar Turner, *Victory Rode the Rails: The Strategic Place of the Railroads in the Civil War* (Indianapolis: Bobbs-Merrill, 1953); James F. Doster, "Were the Southern Railroads Destroyed by the Civil War?" *Civil War History* 7 (September 1961): 310–20.

37. Otto, *Southern Agriculture,* 21; Fred Bateman and Thomas Weiss, *A Deplorable Scarcity: The Failure of Industrialization in the Slave Economy* (Chapel Hill: University of North Carolina Press, 1981), 20; Ramsdell, *Behind the Lines,* 98; Black, *The Railroads of the Confederacy,* 22–23.

38. Richard E. Beringer, Herman Hattaway, Archer Jones, and William N. Still, Jr., *Why the South Lost the Civil War* (Athens: University of Georgia Press, 1986), 59.

39. Ransom, *Conflict and Compromise,* 200.

40. Raimondo Luraghi, "The Civil War and the Modernization of American Society: Social Structure and Industrial Revolution in the Old South before and during the War," *Civil War History* 18 (September 1972): 244.

41. George C. Rable, *The Confederate Republic: A Revolution Against Politics* (Chapel Hill: University of North Carolina Press, 1994), 56; Beringer et al., *Why the South Lost,* 212–18; Maurice Kaye Melton, "Major Military Industries of the Confederate Government" (Ph. D. diss., Emory University, 1978); Thomas, *The Confederate Nation,* 134–35, 213–16.

42. Frank Vandiver, *Ploughshares into Swords: Josiah Gorgas and Confederate Ordnance* (Austin: University of Texas Press, 1952).

43. William N. Still, Jr., *Confederate Shipbuilding* (Athens: University of Georgia Press, 1969; rpt. Columbia: University of South Carolina Press, 1987).

44. Charles B. Dew, *Ironmaker to the Confederacy: Joseph R. Anderson and the Tredegar Iron Works* (New Haven: Yale University Press, 1966).

45. Mary A. DeCredico, *Patriotism for Profit: Georgia's Urban Entrepreneurs and the Confederate War Effort* (Chapel Hill: University of North Carolina Press, 1990).

46. Clarence L. Mohr, *On the Threshold of Freedom: Masters and Slaves in Civil War Georgia* (Athens: University of Georgia Press, 1986). Virginia's "crash course in industrialization" meant using slave labor in a wide variety of industries and businesses, Lynda J. Morgan declares. "Confederates rated their labor, including that of women and children, as an indispensable economic resource," she found. But Virginia slaveowners resisted renting out their slaves. To mollify the masters, the state government first exploited the labor power of free people of color, then forced masters to release their slaves for war work. Morgan, *Emancipation,* 99. See also Ervin L. Jordan, Jr., *Black Confederates and Afro-Yankees in Civil War Virginia* (Charlottesville: University Press of Virginia, 1995).

47. Charles B. Dew, *Bond of Iron: Master and Slave at Buffalo Forge* (New York: W. W. Norton, 1994).

48. Ransom, *Conflict and Compromise,* 200.

49. Schwab, *Confederate States of America,* and Todd, *Confederate Finance.*

50. Peter Wallenstein, *From Slave South to New South: Public Policy in Nineteenth-Century Georgia* (Chapel Hill: University of North Carolina Press, 1987).

51. Douglas B. Ball, *Financial Failure and Confederate Defeat* (Urbana: University of Illinois Press, 1991).

52. Todd, *Confederate Finance.*

53. Lebergott, "Why the South Lost," 67–68.

54. Ransom, *Conflict and Compromise,* 201–2.

55. The list of Richmond's financial sins is lengthy. Larry Schweikart argues that southern banks were sound at secession but that by enacting debilitating regulations and taxes, state and Confederate governments placed them "on the road to financial ruin." *Banking in the American South from the Age of Jackson to Reconstruction* (Baton Rouge: Louisiana State University Press, 1987); and Schweikart, "Secession and Southern Banks," *Civil War History* 31 (June 1985):

111–25. In *Graybacks and Gold: Confederate Monetary Policy* (Pensacola, Fla.: Perdido Bay Press, 1985), James Morgan skewers the Confederate government's failure to meet the South's currency needs, but a solid study of Confederate monetary policy is needed.

56. Disagreement is not new. Nearly seventy years ago, Frank L. Owsley said that the blockade was so porous that it was nothing more than "old Abe's . . . practical joke on the world." *King Cotton Diplomacy: Foreign Relations of the Confederate States of America* (2d rev. ed., Chicago: University of Chicago Press, 1959): 229–30. (Owsley first published this study in 1931.) But Paul Gates countered, "In no modern war save World War I has a country been so successfully blockaded by sea and surrounded by land as the South in the Civil War." *Agriculture during the Civil War,* 73.

57. Stephen R. Wise, *Lifeline of the Confederacy: Blockade Running during the Civil War* (Columbia: University of South Carolina Press, 1988).

58. Beringer et al., *Why the South Lost,* 53–63.

59. James M. McPherson, *Battle Cry of Freedom: The Civil War Era* (New York: Oxford University Press, 1988), 381. Robert B. Ekelund, Jr., and Mark Thorton argue that the blockade contributed to the demise of the Confederacy by encouraging blockade-runners to carry luxury items, elite cargoes that depressed the morale of the common folk. "The Union Blockade and Demoralization of the South: Relative Prices in the Confederacy," *Social Science Quarterly* 73 (December 1992): 890–902. For additional works on Confederate supply, see Richard D. Goff, *Confederate Supply* (Durham: Duke University Press, 1969); Jerrold Northrop Moore, *Confederate Commissary General: Lucius Bellinger Northrop and the Subsistence Bureau of the Southern Army* (Shippensburg, Penn.: White Mane Publishers, 1996), and Richard I. Lester, *Confederate Finance and Purchasing in Great Britain* (Charlottesville: University Press of Virginia, 1975).

60. Powell and Wayne, "Self-Interest and the Decline of Confederate Nationalism"; Drew Gilpin Faust, "Altars of Sacrifice: Confederate Women and the Narratives of War," *Journal of American History* 76 (March 1990): 1200–1228; Rable, *The Confederate Republic;* Roark, *Masters without Slaves.*

61. Wallenstein, *From Slave South to New South,* 120. Also see Paul D. Escott, "Joseph E. Brown, Jefferson Davis, and the Problem of Poverty in the Confederacy," *Georgia Historical Quarterly* 61 (Spring 1977): 59–71.

62. William A. Blair, "Virginia's Private War: The Contours of Dissent and Loyalty in the Confederacy, 1861–1865" (Ph.D. diss., Pennsylvania State University, 1995).

63. Paul D. Escott, "Poverty and Governmental Aid for the Poor in Confederate North Carolina," *North Carolina Historical Review* 61 (October 1984): 462–80.

64. The Arkansas legislature appropriated money for relief, but the Arkansas economy could not make war and feed civilians at the same time. "No amount of money . . . could buy food and supplies that simply were unavailable." Moneyhon, *The Impact of the Civil War and Reconstruction on Arkansas,* 118–19.

65. Paul D. Escott, *After Secession: Jefferson Davis and the Failure of Con-*

*federate Nationalism* (Baton Rouge: Louisiana State University Press, 1978), 159; and Escott, "The Cry of the Sufferers: The Problem of Welfare in the Confederacy," *Civil War History* 23 (September 1977): 228–40; Blair, "Virginia's Private War"; and Wallenstein, *From Slave South to New South.*

66. Abraham Lincoln, *The Collected Works of Abraham Lincoln,* 9 vols., ed. Roy P. Basler (New Brunswick, N.J.: Rutgers University Press, 1953–1955), 8:151.

67. Mark Grimsley, *The Hard Hand of War: Union Military Policy toward Southern Civilians, 1861–1865* (Cambridge: Cambridge University Press, 1995). Charles Royster emphasizes the war's devastation with his title: *The Destructive War: William Tecumseh Sherman, Stonewall Jackson, and the Americans* (New York: Knopf, 1991).

68. Richard N. Current, "God and the Strongest Battalions," in *Why the North Won the Civil War,* ed. David Herbert Donald (Baton Rouge: Louisiana State University, 1960), 22.

69. Beringer et al., *Why the South Lost,* 59.

70. In 1967, David M. Potter observed that southern historians are "far from agreeing about so basic a question as the nature of ante-bellum society." "Depletion and Renewal in Southern History," in *Perspectives on the South: Agenda for Research,* ed. Edgar T. Thompson (Durham: Duke University Press, 1967), 84–85. Two decades later, Randolph B. Campbell concluded his historiographical survey of southern white society on the eve of secession with a wry observation: "In short, interpretations of the antebellum South have tended to outpace knowledge of the region's social structure." "Planters and Plain Folks: The Social Structure of the Antebellum South," in *Interpreting Southern History: Historiographical Essays in Honor of Sanford W. Higginbotham,* ed. John B. Boles and Evelyn Thomas Nolen (Baton Rouge: Louisiana State University Press, 1987), 77.

71. Recent years have witnessed a revolution in our understanding of the Civil War histories of African Americans and white women. Their complex stories deserve and receive separate treatment in this volume. For a comprehensive overview of Confederate society, see Orville Vernon Burton, "Society," in *Encyclopedia of the Confederacy,* ed. Richard N. Current (New York: Simon and Schuster, 1993), 4:1483–93. For an overview of social class in southern history, see J. Wayne Flynt, "Social Class," in *Encyclopedia of Southern Culture,* ed. Charles Reagan Wilson and William Ferris (Chapel Hill: University of North Carolina Press, 1989), 1383–89.

72. Carl N. Degler, *The Other South: Southern Dissenters in the Nineteenth Century* (New York: Harper and Row, 1974).

73. Daniel Crofts, *Reluctant Confederates: Upper South Unionists in the Secession Crisis* (Chapel Hill: University of North Carolina Press, 1989).

74. Margaret Storey's dissertation, in progress at Emory University, will break new ground when it follows "consistent Unionists" in Alabama from the secession crisis through Reconstruction.

75. Georgia Lee Tatum managed to advance our understanding of southern unionism simply by recognizing that unionists were numerous and that not all of them were slack-jawed imbeciles or cowards. *Disloyalty in the Confederacy* (Chapel

Hill: University of North Carolina Press, 1934).

76. Escott, *After Secession;* Escott, *Many Excellent People.*

77. Marc W. Kruman, "Dissent in the Confederacy: The North Carolina Experience," *Civil War History* 27 (December 1981): 293–313.

78. Richard N. Current, *Lincoln's Loyalists: Union Soldiers from the Confederacy* (Boston: Northeastern University Press, 1992).

79. Phillip Shaw Paludan, *Victims: A True Story of the Civil War* (Knoxville: University of Tennessee Press, 1981); William T. Auman, "Neighbor against Neighbor: The Inner Civil War in the Randolph Country Area of Confederate North Carolina," *North Carolina Historical Review* 61 (January 1984): 59–92; William T. Auman and David D. Scarboro, "The Heroes of America in Civil War North Carolina," *North Carolina Historical Review* 58 (October 1981): 327–63; Richard B. McCaslin, *Tainted Breeze: The Great Hanging at Gainesville, Texas, 1862* (Baton Rouge: Louisiana State University Press, 1994).

80. Wayne K. Durrill, *War of Another Kind: A Southern Community in the Great Rebellion* (New York: Oxford University Press, 1990). Other studies that attributed defeat to internal conflicts include: Escott, *After Secession;* Hahn, *Roots of Southern Populism;* Owens and Cooke, eds., *Old South in the Crucible of War;* Harris, *Plain Folk and Gentry in a Slave Society,* Beringer et al., *Why the South Lost;* Drew Gilpin Faust, *The Creation of Confederate Nationalism: Ideology and Identity in the Civil War South* (Baton Rouge: Louisiana State University Press, 1988); Faust, "Altars of Sacrifice"; James Marten, *Texas Divided: Loyalty and Dissent in the Lone Star State, 1856–1874* (Lexington: University Press of Kentucky, 1990); Tatum, *Disloyalty in the Confederacy;* Malcolm C. McMillan, *The Disintegration of a Confederate State: Three Governors and Alabama's Wartime Home Front, 1861–1865* (Macon, Ga.: Mercer University Press, 1986); David Williams, "'Rich Man's War': Class, Caste, and Confederate Defeat in Southwest Georgia," *Journal of Southwest Georgia History* 11 (Fall 1996): 1–42.

81. Blair, "Virginia's Private War." Blair admits that the boundary between battlefield and home front blurred more in Virginia than in most other states, but he nevertheless finds Virginia's experience useful in understanding how the Confederacy managed to hold together for four years. Other studies that contend that the Confederacy lost less because of internal conflicts than a combination of factors, especially the impact of the Union army, include: Ash, *Middle Tennessee Transformed;* Gabor S. Boritt, ed., *Why the Confederacy Lost* (New York: Oxford University Press, 1992); McPherson, *Battle Cry of Freedom;* Thomas, *The Confederate Nation;* Roark, *Masters without Slaves.*

82. William W. Freehling, "The Divided South, the Causes of Confederate Defeat, and the Reintegration of Narrative History," in Freehling, *The Reintegration of American History,* 252.

83. Ash, *Middle Tennessee Society,* 172.

84. Thomas, *The Confederate Nation,* 234.

85. Christine Leigh Heyrman, *Southern Cross: The Beginnings of the Bible Belt* (New York: Knopf, 1997).

86. Donald G. Mathews, *Religion in the Old South* (Chicago: University of

Chicago Press, 1977); Anne C. Loveland, *Southern Evangelicals and the Social Order, 1800–1860* (Baton Rouge: Louisiana State University Press, 1980); Eugene D. Genovese and Elizabeth Fox-Genovese, "The Religious Ideals of a Slave Society," *Georgia Historical Quarterly* 70 (Spring 1986): 1–16; Eugene D. Genovese and Elizabeth Fox-Genovese, "The Divine Sanction of Social Order: Religious Foundations of the Southern Slaveholders' World View," *Journal of the American Academy of Religion* 55 (1987): 211–33; Michael Snay, "American Thought and Southern Distinctiveness: The Southern Clergy and the Sanctification of Slavery," *Civil War History* 35 (December 1989): 311–28.

87. Stephanie McCurry, *Masters of Small Worlds: Yeoman Households, Gender Relations, and the Political Culture of the Antebellum South Carolina Low Country* (New York: Oxford University Press, 1995).

88. Drew Gilpin Faust, *Mothers of Invention: Women of the Slaveholding South in the American Civil War* (Chapel Hill: University of North Carolina Press, 1996), 180. Also see R. Drew Smith, "Slavery, Secession, and Southern Protestant Shifts on the Authority of the State," *Journal of Church and State* 36 (Spring 1994): 261–76. For examples of clergy who opposed slavery, secession, and the Confederacy, see David B. Chesebrough, *Clergy Dissent in the Old South, 1830–1865* (Carbondale: Southern Illinois University Press, 1996).

89. But not one of the more than a dozen books that Boles evaluates concentrates on religion in the Confederacy. Boles, "The Discovery of Southern Religious History," in *Interpreting Southern History,* 510–48.

90. Faust, *Mothers of Invention;* Faust, "Altars of Sacrifice"; Faust, *Creation of Confederate Nationalism;* LeeAnn Whites, *The Civil War as a Crisis in Gender: Augusta, Georgia, 1860–1890* (Athens: University of Georgia Press, 1995); James Silver, *Confederate Morale and Church Propaganda* (New York: Norton, 1957); Beringer et al., *Why the South Lost,* 82–107; George C. Rable, *Civil Wars: Women and the Crisis of Southern Nationalism* (Urbana: University of Illinois Press, 1989), 123–25.

91. Bell Irvin Wiley, "The Movement to Humanize the Institution of Slavery during the Confederacy," *Emory University Quarterly* 5 (December 1949): 207–20.

92. Beringer et al., *Why the South Lost,* 291–93.

93. Wilson, *Baptized in Blood;* Rable, *Civil Wars,* 202–20.

94. The obvious utility of such studies led Reid Mitchell to predict recently that the community study would remain the "leading edge" of Civil War history for some time. "Sitting on the Front Porch Watching the War," *Reviews in American History* 24 (December 1996): 614. Robert C. Kenzer identifies rural kin-based neighborhoods as a basic unit of southern culture. *Kinship and Neighborhood in a Southern Community: Orange County, North Carolina, 1849–1881* (Knoxville: University of Tennessee Press, 1987).

95. Orville Vernon Burton, *In My Father's House Are Many Mansions: Family and Community in Edgefield, South Carolina* (Chapel Hill: University of North Carolina Press, 1985), 222–23. Jonathan M. Bryant makes the similar point when he observes that people "experience events within the cultural, social, and economic context of their community." *How Curious a Land,* 12.

96. McCurry, *Masters of Small Worlds.*

97. Rable, *Civil Wars,* 50–72. Rable describes the war as "a family crisis."

98. Anne Firor Scott, *The Southern Lady: From Pedestal to Politics, 1830–1930* (Chicago: University of Chicago Press, 1970); LeeAnn Whites, *The Civil War as a Crisis in Gender;* Victoria E. Bynum, *Unruly Women: The Politics of Social and Sexual Control in the Old South* (Chapel Hill: University of North Carolina Press, 1992); Donna Rebecca D. Krug, "The Folks Back Home: The Confederate Homefront during the Civil War" (Ph.D. diss., University of California, Irvine, 1990).

99. Mary Margaret Johnston-Miller, "Heirs to Paternalism: Elite Women and Their Servants in Alabama and Georgia, 1861–1874" (Ph.D., diss., Emory University, 1994); Krug, "The Folks Back Home"; Rable, *Civil Wars;* Whites, *The Civil War as a Crisis in Gender;* Faust, *Mothers of Invention;* Catherine Clinton and Nina Silber, eds., *Divided Houses: Gender and the Civil War* (New York: Oxford University Press, 1992).

100. Rable, *Civil Wars,* 135; and Whites, "The Civil War as a Crisis in Gender," in *Divided Houses,* 19.

101. Maris A. Vinovskis, "Have Social Historians Lost the Civil War?: Some Preliminary Demographic Speculations," in *Toward a Social History of the American Civil War: Exploratory Essays,* ed. Vinovskis (Cambridge: Cambridge University Press, 1990), 1–30.

102. Scott, *The Southern Lady;* Carol Bleser and Frederick M. Heath, "The Clays of Alabama: The Impact of the Civil War on a Southern Marriage," in *In Joy and in Sorrow: Women, Family, and Marriage in the Victorian South, 1830–1900,* ed. Carol Bleser (New York: Oxford University Press, 1991), 135–53; Joan Cashin, "'Since the War Broke Out': The Marriage of Kate and William McLure," in *Divided Houses,* 200–212; Kenzer, *Kinship and Neighborhood in a Southern Community,* 97–98.

103. Peter W. Bardaglio, *Reconstructing the Household: Families, Sex, and the Law in the Nineteenth-Century South* (Chapel Hill: University of North Carolina Press, 1995).

104. Johnston-Miller, "Heirs to Paternalism." See also Laura Edward, *Gendered Strife & Confusion: The Political Culture of Reconstruction* (Urbana: University of Illinois Press, 1997); and Victoria Bynum, "Reshaping the Bonds of Womanhood: Divorce in Reconstruction North Carolina," in *Divided Houses,* 320–33.

105. Armstead L. Robinson, "In the Shadow of Old John Brown: Insurrection, Anxiety and Confederate Mobilization, 1861–1863," *Journal of Negro History* 65 (Fall 1980): 279–97.

106. Ash, *Middle Tennessee.*

107. Escott, *Many Excellent People,* 83. Daniel W. Crofts, *Old Southampton: Politics and Society in a Virginia County, 1834–1869* (Charlottesville: University Press of Virginia, 1994), emphasizes divisions along the lines of antebellum politics.

108. Durrill, *War of Another Kind.* In his analysis of Missouri and the border states, Michael Fellman found that guerrilla war "erased the line between combatant and civilian." *Inside War: The Guerrilla Conflict in Missouri during the*

*American Civil War* (New York: Oxford University Press, 1989). Also see Suzanne Marshall, *Violence in the Black Patch of Kentucky and Tennessee* (Columbia, Mo.: University of Missouri Press, 1994).

109. Harris, *Plain Folks and Gentry in a Slave Society,* 7.

110. Daniel E. Sutherland, *Seasons of War: The Ordeal of a Confederate Community, 1861–1865* (New York: Free Press, 1995).

111. Kenzer, *Kinship and Neighborhood.*

112. For other community studies that argue limited class consciousness and conflict, see Blair, "Virginia's Private War"; Burton, *In My Father's House;* Bryant, *How Curious a Land;* Wayne, *The Reshaping of Plantation Society;* and Randolph B. Campbell, *A Southern Community in Crisis: Harrison County, Texas, 1850–1880* (Austin: Texas State Historical Association, 1983).

113. Brief general accounts of the urban Confederacy can be found in Thomas, *The Confederate Nation,* McPherson, *Battle Cry of Freedom,* and E. Merton Coulter, *The Confederate States of America, 1861–1865* (Baton Rouge: Louisiana State University Press, 1950).

114. For two examples, see Don H. Doyle, *New Men, New Cities, New South: Atlanta, Nashville, Charleston, Mobile, 1860–1910* (Chapel Hill: University of North Carolina Press, 1990), and James M. Russell, *Atlanta, 1847–1890: City Building in the Old South and the New* (Baton Rouge: Louisiana State University Press, 1988). For the best interpretive survey of the urban South, see David Goldfield, *Cotton Fields and Skyscrapers: Southern City and Region, 1607–1980* (Baton Rouge: Louisiana State University Press, 1982). For a discussion of a central issue, see Howard Rabinowitz, "Continuity and Change: Southern Urban Development, 1860–1900," in *The City in Southern History: The Growth of Urban Civilization in the South,* ed. Blaine Brownell and David Goldfield (Port Washington, N.Y.: Kennikat Press, 1977).

115. Chester G. Hearn, *Six Years of Hell: Harpers Ferry during the Civil War* (Baton Rouge: Louisiana State University Press, 1996); Ernest B. Furgurson, *Ashes of Glory: Richmond at War* (New York: Knopf, 1996).

116. Michael Shirley, *From Congregation Town to Industrial City: Culture and Social Change in a Southern Community* (New York: New York University Press, 1994); Harriet Amos, *Cotton City: Urban Development in Antebellum Mobile* (Tuscaloosa: University of Alabama Press, 1985); Arthur W. Bergeron, *Confederate Mobile* (Jackson: University Press of Mississippi, 1991); Kenneth Coleman, *Confederate Athens, 1861–1865* (Athens: University of Georgia Press, 1967); DeCredico, *Patriotism for Profit.* Also see Emory M. Thomas, *The Confederate State of Richmond: A Biography of the Capital* (Austin: University of Texas Press, 1971); Robert N. Rosen, *Confederate Charleston: An Illustrated History of the City and the People during the Civil War* (Columbia: University of South Carolina Press, 1994); and John H. Napier III, "Montgomery during the Civil War," *Alabama Review* 41 (1988): 103–31.

117. Gerald M. Capers, *Occupied City: New Orleans under the Federals, 1862–1865* (Lexington: University of Kentucky Press, 1965); Walter T. Durham, *Nashville, the Occupied City: The First Seventeen Months—February 16, 1862, to June 30, 1963* (Nashville: Tennessee Historical Society, 1985); Walter T. Durham,

*Reluctant Partners: Nashville and the Union, July 1, 1863, to June 30, 1865* (Nashville: Tennessee Historical Society, 1987); Peter Maslowski, *Treason Must be Made Odious: Military Occupation and Wartime Reconstruction in Nashville, Tennessee, 1862–1865* (Millwood, N.Y.: KTO Press, 1978); Ash, *When the Yankees Came.*

118. John W. Blassingame, *Black New Orleans, 1860–1880* (Chicago: University of Chicago Press, 1973); Robert Francis Engs, *Freedom's First Generation: Black Hampton, Virginia, 1861–1890* (Philadelphia: University of Pennsylvania Press, 1979); Bernard E. Powers, Jr., *Black Charlestonians: A Social History, 1822–1885* (Fayetteville: University of Arkansas Press, 1994); Whittington B. Johnson, *Black Savannah, 1788–1864* (Fayetteville: University of Arkansas Press, 1996).

119. Steven Elliott Tripp, *Yankee Town, Southern City: Race and Class Relations in Civil War Lynchburg* (New York: New York University Press, 1997); quotation is taken from page 2.

120. Avery O. Craven, *The Growth of Southern Nationalism, 1848–1861* (Baton Rouge: Louisiana State University Press, 1953).

121. John McCardell, *The Idea of a Southern Nation: Southern Nationalists and Southern Nationalism, 1830–1860* (New York: W. W. Norton, 1979).

122. Faust, *The Creation of Confederate Nationalism.* The starting point for any investigation of nationalism remains David M. Potter's enduring essay, "The Historian's Use of Nationalism and Vice Versa," in Potter, *The South and the Sectional Conflict* (Baton Rouge: Louisiana State University Press, 1968), 34–83.

123. Freehling, "The Divided South, the Causes of Confederate Defeat, and the Reintegration of Narrative History," 242.

124. Kenneth M. Stampp, "The Southern Road to Appomattox," in Stampp, *The Imperiled Union: Essays on the Background of the Civil War* (New York: Oxford University Press, 1980), 246–69.

125. Mohr, *On the Threshold of Freedom,* 235–93.

126. Quoted in Roark, *Masters without Slaves,* 101. See also Wilson, *Baptized in Blood;* Leon F. Litwack, *Been in the Storm So Long: The Aftermath of Slavery* (New York: Knopf, 1979); Gaines Foster, "Guilt over Slavery: A Historiographical Analysis," *Journal of Southern History* 56 (November 1990): 665–94. James M. McPherson found the letters of Confederate soldiers filled with references to slavery and liberty as the goals for which they fought. McPherson, *For Cause & Comrades: Why Men Fought in the Civil War* (New York: Oxford University Press, 1997), 20.

127. Quoted in James M. McPherson, "Why Did the Confederacy Lose?" in McPherson, *Drawn with the Sword: Reflections on the American Civil War* (New York: Oxford University Press, 1996), 115.

128. Sutherland, *Seasons of War,* vii.

129. Carl N. Degler, "Thesis, Antithesis, Synthesis: The South, the North, and the Nation," *Journal of Southern History* 53 (February 1987): 9.

130. George M. Fredrickson, "Why the Confederacy Did Not Fight a Guerrilla War after the Fall of Richmond: A Comparative View," Robert Fortenbaugh Memorial Lecture, Gettysburg College (1996).

131. In the mid-1960s, Mary Elizabeth Massey regretted that "Many of the unexplored areas he [Ramsdell] mentioned in the thirties have not yet been subject to thorough investigation." Massey, "The Confederate States of America: The Homefront," 272.

132. Ramsdell, *Behind the Lines in the Southern Confederacy,* 121.

133. Rable, *The Confederate Republic,* 300. Others who share Rable's perspective and develop their arguments persuasively, include James M. McPherson, *Drawn with the Sword* and Gary W. Gallagher, *The Confederate War* (Cambridge, Mass.: Harvard University Press, 1997).

## "OURS AS WELL AS THAT OF THE MEN"

1. Kate Cumming, *Kate: The Journal of a Confederate Nurse,* ed. Richard Barksdale Harwell (Baton Rouge: Louisiana State University Press, 1959), 39. The present essay focuses on historians' accounts of women and the war and does not attempt to provide a comprehensive overview of the many published writings—memoirs, letters, diaries—of Civil War women themselves. A useful bibliography of these published primary sources appears at the end of Marilyn Mayer Culpepper's *Trials and Triumphs: Women of the American Civil War* (East Lansing: Michigan State University Press, 1991); a bibliography on southern women is included in *A Woman's War: Southern Women, Civil War, and the Confederate Legacy,* ed. Edward D. C. Campbell and Kym S. Rice (Charlottesville: University Press of Virginia, 1997).

2. Henry Timrod, "The Two Armies," in *The Collected Poems of Henry Timrod,* ed. Edd Winfield Parks and Aileen Wells Parks (Athens: University of Georgia Press, 1965), 125. See a similar remark by a northerner: "Iowa had two armies serving the nation" (S. H. M. Byers, *Iowa in War Times* [Des Moines: W. D. Condit, 1888]), 47.

3. L. P. Brockett and Mary C. Vaughan, *Women's Work in the Civil War: A Record of Heroism, Patriotism, and Patience* (Philadelphia: Zeigler, McCurdy, 1867), 39; Elizabeth Leonard, *Yankee Women: Gender Battles in the Civil War* (New York: Norton, 1994), 277.

4. Leonard, 162; Frank Moore, *Women of the War: Their Heroism and Self-Sacrifice* (Hartford: S. S. Scranton, 1866).

5. Elizabeth Cady Stanton, Susan B. Anthony, and Matilda Joslyn Gage, *History of Woman Suffrage,* 2 vols. (New York: Fowler and Wells, 1882), 2:23. Volume two contains an extremely useful account of northern women's wartime activities.

6. Chapters of the United Daughters of the Confederacy collected and published women's wartime reminiscences in volumes that have something of the character of printed scrapbooks but contain valuable historical material. See, for example, Mrs. A. T. Smythe, Miss M. B. Poppenheim, and Mrs. Thomas Taylor, *South Carolina Women in the Confederacy,* 2 vols. (Columbia: The State Co., 1903–1907); *Confederate Women of Arkansas in the Civil War* (Little Rock: H. G. Pugh, 1907); and *War Reminiscences of Columbus, Mississippi* (West Point, Miss.: Sullivan's, 1961).

7. For early-twentieth-century celebrations, see John Levi Underwood, *The Women of the Confederacy, in Which Is Presented the Heroism of the Women of the Confederacy with Accounts of Their Trials during the War and the Period of Reconstruction, with Their Ultimate Triumph over Adversity* (New York: Neale, 1906), and Matthew Page Andrews, *The Women of the South in Wartime* (Baltimore: Norman Remington, 1920), which is largely a compilation of primary documents. Sylvia Dannett's *Noble Women of the North* (New York: Thomas Yoseloff, 1959) appeared later but exhibits the same celebratory tone and the framework of lengthy quotations from primary sources interspersed with brief commentary. Francis Butler Simkins and James Welch Patton, *Women of the Confederacy* (Richmond: Garrett and Massie, 1936).

8. Mary Elizabeth Massey, *Bonnet Brigades: American Women and the Civil War* (New York: Knopf, 1966); reprinted as *Women in the Civil War* (Lincoln: University of Nebraska Press, 1994); quotation from p. x; Agatha B. Young, *The Women and the Crisis: Women of the North in the Civil War* (New York: McDowell, Obolensky, 1959), 3. Massey's book emerged from earlier work she had done on the war that dealt extensively with women's experiences although she never acknowledged women as an explicit topic of investigation. See Massey, *Refugee Life in the Confederacy* (Baton Rouge: Louisiana State University Press, 1964) and *Ersatz in the Confederacy* (1952; rpt. Columbia: University of South Carolina Press, 1993).

9. Race and class are discussed at length below. For an example of an intriguing study of the impact of women's ages on their reactions to war, see Jane Turner Censer, "A Changing World of Work: North Carolina Elite Women, 1865–1895," *North Carolina Historical Review* 73 (January 1996): 28–55. For attention to a neglected subregion of the South, see John C. Inscoe, "The Civil War's Empowerment of an Appalachian Woman: The 1864 Slave Purchases of Mary Bell," in *Discovering the Women in Slavery,* ed. Patricia Morton (Athens: University of Georgia, 1996), 61–81; Inscoe, "Coping in Confederate Appalachia: A Portrait of a Mountain Woman and her Community at War," *North Carolina Historical Review* 69 (October 1992): 388–413; and Gordon B. McKinney, "Women's Role in Civil War Western North Carolina," *North Carolina Historical Review* 69 (January 1992): 37–56.

10. Anne Firor Scott, *The Southern Lady: From Pedestal to Politics, 1830–1930* (Chicago: University of Chicago Press, 1970). In the same year H. E. Sterkx published *Partners in Rebellion: Alabama Women in the Civil War* (Rutherford, N.J.: Farleigh Dickinson University Press, 1970), a volume that carried out on a state level much of the agenda set by Simkins and Patton more than three decades earlier. Sterkx tried to avoid any interpretive stance, insisting "It has been difficult to reach general conclusions of the impact of war on a cast of thousands" (11).

11. Bell Irvin Wiley, *Confederate Women* (Westport, Conn.: Greenwood, 1975). 163, 177; Wiley, *The Plain People of the Confederacy* (Baton Rouge: Louisiana State University Press, 1944); Wiley, *Southern Negroes 1861–1865* (New Haven: Yale University Press, 1938); Victoria Bynum, "'War within a War': Women's Participation in the Revolt of the North Carolina Piedmont," *Frontiers*

9, no. 3 (1987): 43–49; Bynum, *Unruly Women: The Politics of Social and Sexual Control in the Old South* (Chapel Hill: University of North Carolina Press, 1992); on bread riots see Michael Chesson, "Harlots or Heroines? A New Look at the Richmond Bread Riot," *Virginia Magazine of History and Biography* 92 (1984):131–75; William J. Kimball, "The Bread Riot in Richmond," *Civil War History* 7 (1961): 149–54; Emory M. Thomas, "The Richmond Bread Riot of 1863," *Virginia Cavalcade* 18 (Summer 1968): 41–47; Douglas O. Tice, "Bread or Blood: The Richmond Bread Riot," *Civil War Times Illustrated* 12 (February 1974): 12–19. John Inscoe's studies of a small slaveholder, cited in note 9 above, and Philip Racine's treatment of a Piedmont farmer are valuable additions to the literature on non-plantation women. See Philip N. Racine, "Emily Lyles Harris: A Piedmont Farmer during the Civil War," *South Atlantic Quarterly* 79 (Fall 1980): 386–97. See also Drew Gilpin Faust, "Trying to Do a Man's Business: Gender, Violence and Slave Management in Civil War Texas," in Faust, *Southern Stories: Slaveholders in Peace and War* (Columbia: University of Missouri Press, 1992), 174–92.

12. Jacqueline Jones, *Labor of Love, Labor of Sorrow: Black Women, Work, and the Family from Slavery to the Present* (New York: Basic Books, 1985), 49. See also Jones, *Soldiers of Light and Love: Northern Teachers and Georgia Blacks, 1865–1873* (Chapel Hill: University of North Carolina Press, 1980).

13. Ira Berlin, Barbara J. Fields, Thavolia Glymph, Joseph P. Reidy, and Leslie S. Rowland, eds., *Freedom: A Documentary History of Emancipation, 1861–1867, Series 1, Volume 1: The Destruction of Slavery* (Cambridge: Cambridge University Press, 1985), and Ira Berlin, Joseph P. Reidy and Leslie S. Rowland, eds., *Freedom: A Documentary History of Emancipation, 1861–1867, Series 2: The Black Military Experience* (Cambridge: Cambridge University Press, 1982).

14. Catherine Clinton, *Tara Revisited: Women, War and the Plantation Legend* (New York: Abbeville Press, 1995) 103; see also Clinton's chapter on the Civil War in her *The Other Civil War: American Women in the Nineteenth Century* (New York: Hill and Wang, 1984); Noralee Frankel, "The Southern Side of 'Glory': Mississippi African American Women During the Civil War," in *"We Specialize in the Wholly Impossible:" A Reader in Black Women's History,* ed. Darlene Clark Hine, Wilma King, and Linda Reed (New York: Carlson Publishing, 1995), 335–41; Frankel, "Freedom's Women: African American Women in Mississippi, 1860–1870," forthcoming; Nancy Dunlap Bercaw, "Politics of Household during the Transition from Slavery to Freedom in the Yazoo-Mississippi Delta, 1861–1876" (Ph.D. diss., University of Pennsylvania, 1996); Marli Frances Weiner, "Plantation Mistress and Female Slaves: Gender, Race and South Carolina Women, 1830–1880" (Ph.D. diss., University of Rochester, 1985); Leslie Schwalm, "The Meaning of Freedom: African American Women and Their Transition from Slavery to Freedom in Low Country South Carolina" (Ph.D. diss., University of Wisconsin, 1991); Tera W. Hunter, "Household Workers in the Making: Afro American Women in Atlanta and the New South, 1861–1920" (Ph.D. diss., Yale University, 1990); Thavolia Glymph, "This Species of Property: Female Slave Contrabandists in the Civil War," in *A Woman's War*, 55–71. See also Wilma

King, "The Mistress and Her Maids: White and Black Women in a Louisiana Household, 1858–1868," in *Discovering the Women in Slavery,* 82–106. Nell Irvin Painter provides insight into the life of one exceptional woman in *Sojourner Truth: A Life, A Symbol* (New York: Norton, 1996). Curiously there has been no comparable scholarly modern treatment of Harriet Tubman, but see Earl Conrad, *Harriet Tubman* (Washington, D.C.: Associated Publishers, 1943). Lives of African American women during the war are included in more general studies by W. E.B. DuBois, *Black Reconstruction in America* (New York: Harcourt, Brace, 1935); Leon F. Litwack, *Been in the Storm So Long* (New York: Knopf, 1979); James M. McPherson, *The Negro's Civil War: How American Negroes Felt and Acted during the War for the Union* (New York: Pantheon, 1965); Joseph P. Reidy, *From Slavery to Agrarian Capitalism in the Cotton South: Central Georgia, 1800–1880* (Chapel Hill: University of North Carolina Press, 1992); Clarence L. Mohr, *On the Threshold of Freedom: Masters and Slaves in Civil War Georgia* (Athens: University of Georgia Press, 1986); Barbara J. Fields, *Slavery and Freedom on the Middle Ground: Maryland during the Nineteenth Century* (New Haven: Yale University Press, 1985).

15. Jane E. Schultz, "The Inhospitable Hospital: Gender and Professionalism in Civil War Medicine," *Signs* 17 (Winter 1992): 363–92. See also her "Women at the Front: Gender and Genre in Literature of the American Civil War" (Ph.D. diss., University of Michigan, 1988), and Jane E. Schultz, "Race, Gender, and Bureaucracy: Civil War Army Nurses and the Pension Bureau," *Journal of Women's History* 6 (Summer 1994); Clarence Mohr, *On the Threshold of Freedom;* Drew Gilpin Faust, *Mothers of Invention: Women of the Slaveholding South in the American Civil War* (Chapel Hill: University of North Carolina Press, 1996). See also on nursing Kristie Ross, "Arranging a Doll's House: Refined Women as Union Nurses," in *Divided Houses: Gender and the Civil War,* ed. Catherine Clinton and Nina Silber (New York: Oxford University Press, 1992); Ann Douglas Wood, "The War within a War: Women Nurses in the Union Army," *Civil War History* 18 (September 1972): 197–212; Nina Bennett Smith, "The Women Who Went to War: The Union Army Nurse in the Civil War" (Ph.D. diss., Northwestern University, 1981); Sister Mary Denis Maher, *To Bind Up the Wounds: Catholic Sister Nurses in the U.S. Civil War* (Westport, Conn.: Greenwood, 1989); Anne L. Austin, *The Woolsey Sisters of New York: A Family's Involvement in the Civil War and a New Profession* (Philadelphia: American Philosophical Society, 1971); Charles McCool Snyder, *Dr. Mary Walker: The Little Lady in Pants* (New York: Vantage, 1962); Leroy Fischer, "Cairo's Civil War Angel: Mary Jane Safford," *Illinois State Historical Society Journal* 54 (Fall 1961): 229–45; Wynell Burroughs, "Surgeon General's Office, Dorothea Dix and Organized Nurses during the Civil War," *Social Education* 52 (January 1988), 66; Elizabeth Leonard, "Civil War Nurse, Civil War Nursing: Rebecca Usher of Maine," *Civil War History* 41(September 1995): 190–208; Lucille Griffith, "Mrs. Juliet Opie Hopkins and Alabama Military Hospitals," *Alabama Review* 6 (April 1953): 99–120; David Sabine, "Captain Sally Tompkins," *Civil War Times Illustrated* 4 (November 1965): 36–38; Peggy Braise Siegel, "She Went to War: Indiana Women Nurses in the Civil War," *Indi-*

*ana Magazine of History* 86 (March 1990): 1–27; Francis B. Simkins and James W. Patton, "The Work of Southern Women among the Sick and Wounded of the Confederate Armies," *Journal of Southern History* 1 (Fall 1935): 475–96; Quincealea Brunk, "Caring Without Politics: Lessons for the First Nurses of the North and South," *Nursing History Review* 2 (1994): 119–36; Bonnie Bullough and Vern Bullough, "The Origins of Modern American Nursing: The Civil War Era," *Nursing Forum* 11 (1963): 12–27; Philip A. Kalish and Beatrice J. Kalish, "Untrained but Undaunted: The Women Nurses of the Blue and the Gray," *Nursing Forum* 15 (1976): 4–33; Myrtle P. Matejski, "Ladies' Aid Societies and the Nurses of Lincoln's Army," *Journal of Nursing History* 1 (April 1986): 3–51; Isabel Quattlebaum, "Twelve Women in the First Days of the Confederacy," *Civil War History* 7 (December 1961): 370–87; Ruth W. Davis, "Behind the Battle of Gettysburg: American Nursing is Born," *Pennsylvania Heritage* 13 (Fall 1987): 10–15; Dolores Liptak, "To Bind Up the Wounds: Catholic Sister Nurses in the U.S. Civil War," *Catholic Historical Review* 77 (January 1991): 137–38; Norah Smaridge, *Hands of Mercy: The Story of Sister-Nurses during the Civil War* (New York: Benziger Brothers, 1960); Nina Brown Baker, *Cyclone in Calico: The Story of Mary Ann Bickerdyke* (Boston: Little, Brown, 1952). Older works on nursing are numerous and include Mary Holland, *Our Army Nurses* (Boston: B. Wilkins, 1895); George Barton, *Angels of the Battlefield* (Philadelphia: Catholic Art Publishing, 1897); Ellen Jolly, *Nuns of the Battlefield* (Providence: Providence Visitor Press, 1927); Marjorie Greenbie, *Lincoln's Daughters of Mercy* (New York: G. P. Putnam, 1944). I have not included participants' own memoirs, diaries, or letters here. A useful sampling of such published sources is cited in the notes of Jane Schultz's "Inhospitable Hospital" and may serve as a guide to further reading. Treatment of other wartime women's work is much sketchier. See on government workers Janet E. Kaufman, "Treasury Girls," *Civil War Times Illustrated* 25 (May 1986): 32–38; Charles Cooney, "The State of the Treasury, 1864: 'Nothing More . . . Than a Whorehouse,'" *Civil War Times Illustrated* 21 (August 1982): 40–43. There is no specific study of teaching, but see Rachel Bryan Stillman, "Education in the Confederate States of America, 1861–1865" (Ph.D. diss., University of Illinois at Champaign-Urbana, 1972).

16. There are excellent recent biographies of both Barton and Dix. See David Gollaher, *Voice for the Mad: The Life of Dorothea Dix* (New York: Free Press, 1995); Elizabeth Brown Pryor, *Clara Barton: Professional Angel* (Philadelphia: University of Pennsylvania Press, 1987); Stephen Oates, *A Woman of Valor: Clara Barton and the Civil War* (New York: Free Press, 1994). See also David Burton, *Clara Barton: In the Service of Humanity* (Westport, Conn.: Greenwood, 1995); Ishbel Ross, *Angel of the Battlefield* (New York: Harper, 1956); Helen Marshall, *Dorothea Dix: Forgotten Samaritan* (Chapel Hill: University of North Carolina Press, 1937); Francis Tiffany, *The Life of Dorothea Lynde Dix* (Boston: Houghton Mifflin, 1890).

17. On the comparison of reform North and South see Elizabeth Fox-Genovese, *Within the Plantation Household: Black and White Women of the Old South* (Chapel Hill: University of North Carolina Press, 1988). On political ac-

tions by white southern women see Elizabeth Varon, "Tippecanoe and the Ladies, Too: White Women and Party Politics in Antebellum Virginia," *Journal of American History* 82 (1995): 494–521; George C. Rable, "'Missing in Action,' Women of the Confederacy," in *Divided Houses,* 134–46; Michael Fellman, "Women and Guerrilla Warfare," in *Divided Houses,* 147–65; Mary P. Ryan, *Women in Public: Between Banners and Ballots, 1825–1880* (Baltimore: Johns Hopkins University Press, 1990), has a suggestive chapter on Confederate women's public actions against Union General Butler in New Orleans. On northern women and wartime activism, see Wendy Hamand Venet, *Neither Ballots nor Bullets: Women Abolitionists and the Civil War* (Charlottesville: University Press of Virginia, 1991), 161, and her article "The Woman's National Loyal League: Feminist Abolitionists and the Civil War," *Civil War History* 35 (1989): 39–58; Lori D. Ginzberg, *Women and the Work of Benevolence: Morality, Politics and Class in the Nineteenth-Century United States* (New Haven: Yale University Press, 1990), 162. The life of abolitionist and political orator Anna Dickinson is best described in James Harvey Young, "Anna Elizabeth Dickinson and the Civil War" (Ph.D. diss., University of Illinois at Champaign-Urbana, 1941), and his article "Anna Elizabeth Dickinson and the Civil War: For and Against Lincoln," *Mississippi Valley Historical Review* 31 (June 1944): 59–80. James M. McPherson's *The Struggle For Equality: Abolitionists and the Negro in the Civil War and Reconstruction* (Princeton: Princeton University Press, 1964) describes the actions of female abolitionists, as does Jean Fagin Yellin, *Women and Sisters: The Antislavery Feminists in American Culture* (New Haven: Yale University Press, 1989). On women's activism in the political sphere, see also Benjamin Abramowitz, "Anna Ella Carroll: Invisible Member of Lincoln's Cabinet," *Minerva* 8 (Winter 1990): 30–40; Janet L. Coryell, *Neither Heroine nor Fool: Anna Ella Carroll of Maryland* (Kent, Ohio: Kent State University Press, 1990); Deborah Pickman Clifford, *Mine Eyes Have Seen the Glory: A Biography of Julia Ward Howe* (Boston: Little, Brown, 1979); Deborah Pickman Clifford, *Crusader for Freedom: A Life of Lydia Maria Child* (Boston: Beacon, 1992); Carolyn L. Karcher, *The First Woman in the Republic: A Cultural Biography of Lydia Maria Child* (Durham: Duke University Press, 1994); Kathleen Endres, "The Women's Press in the Civil War: A Portrait of Patriotism, Propaganda and Prodding," *Civil War History* 30 (1984): 31–53; Linda Selleck, *Gentle Invaders: Quaker Women Educators and Racial Issues during the Civil War and Reconstruction* (Richmond: Friends United Press, 1995).

18. Jeanie Attie, "Warwork and the Crisis of Domesticity in the North," in *Divided Houses,* 259. See also Rejean Attie, "'A Swindling Concern': The United States Sanitary Commission and the Northern Female Public, 1861–1865" (Ph.D. diss., Columbia University, 1987). The standard work on the Sanitary Commission is William Quentin Maxwell, *Lincoln's Fifth Wheel: A Political History of the United States Sanitary Commission* (New York: Longmans, Green, 1956), but it comes close to ignoring women's role. See also Robert W. Schoeberlein, "A Fair to Remember: Maryland Women in Aid of the Union," *Maryland Historical Magazine* 90 (Winter 1995): 467–88 and J. Matthew Gallman's consideration of women and the Philadelphia Sanitary Fair in *Mastering Wartime: A Social History of Philadelphia during the Civil War* (Cambridge: Cambridge University Press, 1990).

See also Tom Sillanpa, *Annie Wittenmyer: God's Angel* (Evanston, Ill.: Signal Press, 1972).

19. Leonard, *Yankee Women*, 201.

20. Suzanne Lebsock, *The Free Women of Petersburg: Status and Culture in a Southern Town, 1784–1860* (New York: Norton, 1984); Jean E. Friedman, *The Enclosed Garden: Women and Community in the Evangelical South, 1830–1900* (Chapel Hill: University of North Carolina Press, 1985); George C. Rable, *Civil Wars: Women and the Crisis of Southern Nationalism* (Urbana: University of Illinois Press, 1989), 265, 288.

21. Faust, *Mothers of Invention.* See also my "Altars of Sacrifice: Confederate Women and the Narratives of War," *Journal of American History* 76 (March 1990): 1200–1228. For another recent consideration of elite women, see Cita Cook, "Growing Up White, Genteel and Female in a Changing South, 1845–1917" (Ph.D. diss., University of California at Berkeley, 1993).

22. Mitchell, in *Divided Houses*, 43–54; Mitchell, *The Vacant Chair: The Northern Soldier Leaves Home* (New York: Oxford University Press, 1993) 14. On African American soldiers and gender issues, see Jim Cullen, "I's a Man Now: Gender and African American Men," in *Divided Houses*, 76–96. The study of marriage provides a neat window into male-female interactions. See Carol Bleser and Frederick M. Heath, "The Clays of Alabama: The Impact of the Civil War on a Southern Marriage," in *In Joy and in Sorrow: Women, Family, and Marriage in the Victorian South, 1830–1900*, ed. Bleser (New York: Oxford University Press, 1991), 135–53, and Joan Cashin, "'Since the War Broke Out:' The Marriage of Kate and William McClure," in *Divided Houses*, 200–212.

23. LeeAnn Whites, *The Civil War as a Crisis in Gender: Augusta, Georgia, 1860–1890* (Athens: University of Georgia Press, 1995), 11, 18, 136, 224. See also her "The Charitable and the Poor: The Emergence of Domestic Politics in Augusta, Georgia, 1860–1880," *Journal of Social History* 17 (1984): 606–16.

24. Nina Silber, *The Romance of Reunion: Northerners and the South, 1865–1900* (Chapel Hill: University of North Carolina Press, 1993), and Silber, "Intemperate Men, Spiteful Women, and Jefferson Davis," in *Divided Houses*, 283–305. For an important part of this process see Megan McClintock, "Binding Up the Nation's Wounds: Civil War Pensions and American Families, 1861–1890" (Ph.D. diss., Rutgers University, 1993), and McClintock, "Civil War Pensions and the Reconstruction of Union Families," *Journal of American History* 83 (September 1996): 456–80.

25. Joan Hedrick, *Harriet Beecher Stowe: A Life* (New York: Oxford University Press, 1994); Patricia R. Hill, "Writing Out the War: Harriet Beecher Stowe's Averted Gaze," in *Divided Houses*, 260–82; Jane Tompkins, *Sensational Designs: The Cultural Work of American Fiction* (New York: Oxford University Press, 1985); Sarah Elbert, *A Hunger for Home: Louisa May Alcott and Little Women* (Philadelphia: Temple University Press, 1984); Carolyn L. Karcher, *The First Woman in the Republic: A Cultural Biography of Lydia Maria Child* (Durham: Duke University Press, 1994); Mary Kelley, *Private Woman, Public Stage: Literary Domesticity in Nineteenth-Century America* (New York: Oxford University Press, 1984); William Perry Fidler, *Augusta Evans Wilson, 1835–1909* (Tuscaloosa:

University of Alabama Press, 1951); Drew Gilpin Faust, "A War Story for Confederate Women: Augusta Jane Evans' *Macaria*," in Faust, *Southern Stories: Slaveholders in Peace and War* (Columbia: University of Missouri Press, 1992); Carol T. Williams, "'The Power of a True Woman's Heart': Augusta Jane Evans and Feminine Civil War Values," *Journal of Southwest Georgia History* 8 (1993): 39–46. See also Clara Juncker, "Behind Confederate Lines: Sarah Morgan Dawson," *Southern Quarterly* 30 (Fall 1991): 7–18; Lydia Cullen Sizer, "Between the Lines: Gender, Race and Politics in Women's Writing on the American Civil War" (Ph.D. diss., Brown University, 1993); Elisabeth Muhlenfeld, *Mary Boykin Chesnut: A Biography* (Baton Rouge: Louisiana State University Press, 1981); Melissa Mentzer, "Rewriting Herself: Mary Chesnut's Narrative Strategies," *Connecticut Review* 14 (1992): 49–56; C. Vann Woodward, *Mary Chesnut's Civil War* (New Haven: Yale University Press, 1981); C. Vann Woodward and Elisabeth Muhlenfeld, *The Private Mary Chesnut* (New York: Oxford University Press, 1984); Drew Gilpin Faust, "Introduction: Writing the War," in *Brokenburn: The Journal of Kate Stone, 1861–1868,* ed. John Q. Anderson (Baton Rouge: Louisiana State University Press, 1995), xxix-xl; Jane E. Schultz, "Mute Fury: Southern Women's Diaries of Sherman's March to the Sea," in *Arms and the Woman: War, Gender and Literary Representation,* ed. Helen Cooper et al. (Chapel Hill: University of North Carolina Press, 1989), 59–79; and Schultz's "Women at the Front"; Camille Kunkle, "'It is What It Does To The Souls': Women's Views on the Civil War," *Atlanta History* 33 (1989): 56–70; Faust, *Mothers of Invention,* chapter 7; Monroe C. Gwin, "Introduction," in Cornelia Peake McDonald, *A Woman's Civil War* (Madison: University of Wisconsin Press, 1992), 3–18; Nell Irvin Painter, "Introduction: The Journal of Ella Gertrude Clanton Thomas: An Educated White Woman in the Eras of Slavery, War, and Reconstruction," in *The Secret Eye: The Journal of Ella Gertrude Clanton Thomas, 1848–1889,* ed. Virginia Ingraham Burr (Chapel Hill: University of North Carolina Press, 1990); Terrell Armistead Crow, "'As Thy Days, So Shall Thy Strength Be': North Carolina Planter Women in War and Peace," in *Women and War: History of Women in the United States,* ed. Nancy F. Cott (Munich: K. G. Sauer, 1993), 45–52. On gender and Civil War literature, see Timothy Morris, "'A Glorious Solution': Gender, Families, Relationships and the Civil War Story," *Arizona Quarterly* 51 (Spring 1995): 61–79; Kathleen Diffley, *Where My Heart Is Turning Ever: Civil War Stories and Constitutional Reform, 1861–1876* (Athens: University of Georgia, 1992).

26. For Mary Livermore's estimate, see Livermore, *My Story of the War* (Hartford: A. D. Worthington, 1888), 119–20. For community studies that include the experience of women, see Wayne K. Durrill, *War of Another Kind: A Southern Community in the Great Rebellion* (New York: Oxford University Press, 1990); Daniel Sutherland, *Seasons of War: The Ordeal of a Confederate Community, 1861–1865* (New York: Free Press, 1995); Robert C. Kenzer, *Kinship and Neighborhood in a Southern Community: Orange County, North Carolina, 1849–1881* (Knoxville: University of Tennessee Press, 1987); O. Vernon Burton, *In My Father's House Are Many Mansions: Family and Community in Edgefield, South Carolina* (Chapel Hill: University of North Carolina Press, 1985); Stephen Ash, *Middle*

*Tennessee Society Transformed, 1860–1870: War and Peace in the Upper South* (Baton Rouge: Louisiana State University Press, 1988). Margaretta Barton Colt's *Defend the Valley: A Shenandoah Family in the Civil War* (New York: Orion Books, 1994) tells a community story through family letters; Stephen V. Ash's *When the Yankees Came: Conflict and Chaos in the Occupied South* (Chapel Hill: University of North Carolina Press, 1995) is a useful portrait of the southern home front under pressure. See also Donna R. D. Krug, "The Folks Back Home: The Confederate Home Front during the Civil War" (Ph.D. diss., University of California at Irvine, 1990). For a pathbreaking new approach to the study of community in the Civil War, see the website created by Edward Ayers to explore the experience of war in two communities, one southern, one northern, in the Shenandoah Valley: http://jefferson.village.virginia.edu/vshadow 2/.

Iver Bernstein's *The New York City Draft Riots* (New York: Oxford University Press, 1990) is essentially a community study; see also Alessandra Lorini, "Class, Race, Gender and Public Rituals: The New York African American Community in the Civil War," *Storia Nordamericana* 7, no. 2 (1990): 117–37; Gallman, *Mastering Wartime*. For general treatments of the northern home front and women within it, see Phillip Shaw Paludan, *"A People's Contest": The Union and the Civil War* (1988; rpt. Lawrence: University Press of Kansas, 1996), and J. Matthew Gallman, *The North Fights the Civil War: The Homefront* (Chicago: I. R. Dee, 1994); Louise Stevenson, *The Victorian Homefront: American Thought and Culture, 1860–1880* (New York: Twayne, 1991); Anne C. Rose, *Victorian America and the Civil War* (Cambridge: Cambridge University Press, 1992).

27. On women as soldiers, see Lauren Cook Burgess, ed., *An Uncommon Soldier: The Civil War Letters of Sarah Rosetta Wakeman* (New York: Oxford University Press, 1994); DeAnne Blanton, "Women Soldiers of the Civil War," *Prologue: The Journal of the National Archives* 25 (Spring 1993): 27–35; Janet Kaufmann, "Under the Petticoat Flag: Women Soldiers in the Confederate Army," *Southern Studies* 23 (Winter 1984): 363–75; Pat Lammers and Amy Boyce, "Alias Franklin Thompson: A Female in the Ranks," *Civil War Times Illustrated* 22 (September 1984): 24–31; Kay C. Larson, "Bonnie Yank and Ginnie Reb, " *Minerva* 8 (Spring, 1990): 33–48; Rodney O. Davis, "Private Albert Cashier as Regarded by His/Her Comrades," *Illinois Historical Journal* 13 (Winter 1989): 108–12; Richard Hall, *Patriots in Disguise: Women Warriors of the Civil War* (New York: Paragon House, 1993); Richard Hall, "They All Fought at Bull Run," *Minerva* 9 (Fall 1991): 48–54; Richard Hall, "Women in Battle in the Civil War," *Social Education* 58 (February 1994): 80–82; Linda Grant DePauw, "Roles of Women in the American Revolution and the Civil War," *Social Education* 58 (February 1994): 77–79. Sylvia G. L. Dannett, *She Rode with the Generals: The True and Incredible Story of Sara Emma Seelye, alias Franklin Thompson* (New York: Thomas Nelson, 1960). On women spies, a subject that cries out for further scholarly treatment—and a reassessment of the meaning and significance of the identity "spy"—see Penny Colman, *Spies! Women in the Civil War* (Cincinnati: Shoe Tree Press, 1992); Nancy Samuelson, "Employment of Female Spies in the American Civil War," *Minerva* 7 (1989): 57–66; Oscar Kinchen, *Women Who Spied for the*

*Blue and Gray* (Philadelphia: Dorrance, 1972); Ishbel Ross, *Rebel Rose: Life of Rose O'Neal Greenhow, Confederate Spy* (New York: Harper, 1954); Ruth Scarborough, *Belle Boyd: Siren of the South* (Macon, Ga.: Mercer University Press, 1983); Louis Sigaud, *Belle Boyd: Confederate Spy* (Richmond: Dietz Press, 1944); Lyde Cullen Sizer, "Acting Her Part: Narratives of Union Spies," in *Divided Houses,* 114–33. Darla Brock considers female spies of Memphis in "Our Hands Are at Your Service: The Story of Confederate Women in Memphis," *Western Tennessee Historical Papers* 45 (1991): 19–34.

28. Hodes, in *Divided Houses,* 230–46; see also Martha Elizabeth Hodes, *White Women, Black Men: Illicit Sex in the Nineteenth-Century South* (New Haven: Yale University Press, 1997); Hodes, "The Sexualization of Reconstruction Politics: White Women and Black Men in the South after the Civil War," *Journal of the History of Sexuality* 3 (January 1993): 402–17; Thomas Lowry, *The Story the Soldiers Wouldn't Tell: Sex in the Civil War* (Mechanicsburg, Pa.: Stackpole, 1994); the "low-rape war" designation is Susan Brownmiller's, quoted in Mitchell, *Vacant Chair,* 105; see also Catherine Clinton, "Bloody Terrain: Freedwomen, Sexuality, and Violence During Reconstruction," *Georgia Historical Quarterly* 76 (1992): 313–32, and Michael Fellman, *Inside War: The Guerilla Conflict in Missouri during the American Civil War* (New York: Oxford University Press, 1989) on sexual violence against women in the context of Missouri's guerilla warfare. See Ervin L. Jordan, "Sleeping with the Enemy: Sex, Black Women and the Civil War," *Western Journal of Black Studies* 2 (Summer 1994): 55–63; James Boyd Jones, Jr., "A Tale of Two Cities: The Hidden Battle against Venereal Disease in Civil War Nashville and Memphis," *Civil War History* 31 (Summer 1985): 270–76. For a unique story of an intense and physical relationship between two black women, see Farah Jasmine Griffin, ed., *Beloved Sisters and Loving Friends: The Addie Brown-Rebecca Primus Correspondence* (New York: Knopf, forthcoming).

29. Some recent renditions of women's hardships in the Civil War South include William Harris, "East Tennessee's Civil War Refugees and the Impact of War on Civilians," *Journal of East Tennessee History* 64 (1992): 3–19; Daniel Sutherland, "Introduction to War: The Civilians of Culpeper County, Virginia," *Civil War History* 37 (1991): 120–37; Sutherland, "Looking for a Home: Louisiana Emigrants During the Civil War and Reconstruction," *Louisiana History* 21 (1980): 341–59; Joan E. Cashin, "Into the Trackless Wilderness: The Refugee Experience in the Civil War," in *A Woman's War,* 29–53; Suzy Clarke Holstein, "'Offering Up Her Life:' Confederate Women on the Altars of Sacrifice," *Southern Studies* 2 (1991): 113–30; Nancy T. Kondert, "The Romance and Reality of Defeat: Southern Women in 1865," in *Women and War,* 81–93. For a fascinating study of a northern community deeply affected by the war, see Nancy Grey Osterud, "Rural Women during the Civil War: New York's Nanticoke Valley," *New York History* 62 (October 1990): 357–85.

Biography has been one means of providing a definable focus. See Jean H. Baker, *Mary Todd Lincoln: A Biography* (New York: Norton, 1987) for an excellent example. Joan E. Cashin is at work on a study of the Confederacy's first lady.

See Cashin, "Varina Howell Davis," in *Portraits of American Women,* ed. G .J. Barker-Benfield and Catherine Clinton (New York: St. Martin's, 1991), 259–77.

30. For two recent considerations of the literature on Civil War women, see Lee Chambers-Schiller, "Gender, Equality and the Civil War," *Reviews in American History* 23 (December 1995), 612–17, and Joan E. Cashin, "Women at War," *Reviews in American History* 18 (September 1990): 343–48. Burgeoning recent interest in women and the war has yielded efforts to reach out to a general public. Marilyn Culpepper's *Trials and Triumphs* is largely a compilation of northern and southern women's words within a dated celebratory framework suggested by its title. Walter Sullivan's *The War Women Lived: Confederate Voices* (Nashville: J. S. Sanders, 1996) is also aimed at the popular reader. Far more successful as an effort to combine sound scholarship with public outreach is the lavishly illustrated book published by the Museum of the Confederacy to accompany its exhibit, *A Woman's War: Southern Women, Civil War, and the Confederate Legacy,* ed. Edward D. C. Campbell and Kym S. Rice. Other treatments of women's wartime material culture, a promising and largely neglected area for study, include Joan Severa, *Dressed for the Photographer: Ordinary Americans and Fashion, 1840–1900* (Kent, Ohio: Kent State University Press, 1995); Juanita Leisch, *Who Wore What? Women's Wear, 1861–1865* (Gettysburg: Thomas Publications, 1995); and Lauren Taylor, "A Common Thread: A Review of Civil War Fashions," *Civil War Times Illustrated* 24 (1985): 32–41; Drew Gilpin Faust, "Race, Gender and Confederate Nationalism: William D. Washington's *The Burial of Latane,*" *Southern Review* 25 (1989): 297–307.

## SLAVERY AND FREEDOM IN THE CIVIL WAR SOUTH

1. See, e.g, Charles W. Ramsdell, "The Natural Limits of Slavery Expansion," *Mississippi Valley Historical Review,* 16 (September 1929), 151–71; Avery O. Craven, *The Repressible Conflict, 1830–1861* (Baton Rouge: Louisiana State University Press, 1939); James G. Randall, "The Blundering Generation," *Mississippi Valley Historical Review* 27 (June 1940): 3–28.

2. The best enunciation of this widely held thesis is to be found in the work of Howard K. Beale; see "The Tariff and Reconstruction," *American Historical Review* 35 (January 1930): 276–94, and *The Critical Year: A Study of Andrew Johnson and Reconstruction* (New York: Harcourt, Brace and Company, 1930). The view of Radical Republicans as self-seeking scoundrels who used southern blacks in order to pursue policies favorable to northeastern business is more pronounced in the work of Charles Beard's followers than in that of Beard himself (either alone or in collaboration with his wife Mary); although he devoted little attention to blacks, he held relatively enlightened racial views for his era and expressed real ambivalence toward the radicals. On Beard as progressive historian, see Richard Hofstadter, *The Progressive Historians: Turner, Beard, Parrington* (Chicago: University of Chicago Press, 1968), 167–317; for the "Second American Revolution," see Charles A. and Mary R. Beard, *The Rise of American Civilization,* 2 vols. (New York: The Macmillan Company, 1928), chapter 18, 2:52–121.

3. For two important—and generally ignored—studies, see W. E. B. DuBois, *Black Reconstruction in America,* (New York: Harcourt, Brace and Company, 1935), and James S. Allen, *Reconstruction: The Battle for Democracy, 1865–1877* (New York: International Publishers, 1937). DuBois's volume, now widely regarded as a classic, was not reviewed by the *American Historical Review.* See also Herbert Aptheker, *The Negro in the Civil War* (New York: International Publishers, 1938), and Harvey Wish, "Slave Disloyalty under the Confederacy," *Journal of Negro History* 23 (October 1938): 435–50. For Marx and Engels's view of the Civil War as a struggle over slavery, see their newspaper articles and letters reprinted in Karl Marx and Frederick Engels, *The Civil War in the United States* (New York: International Publishers, 1937); but for a critique of Marx and Engels's "unMarxist" enthusiasm for the northern cause, see Eugene D. Genovese, "Marxian Interpretations of the Slave South," in his *In Red and Black: Marxian Explorations in Southern and Afro-American History* (New York: Pantheon Books, 1971), esp. 325–37.

4. For a general survey of how historians from the 1860s to the 1950s dealt with the Civil War (especially Civil War causation), see Thomas J. Pressly, *Americans Interpret Their Civil War* (rev. ed., New York: Collier Books, 1962).

5. For a useful presentation of this contrast in the way World Wars I and II shaped historical interpretation of the Civil War, see John S. Rosenberg, "Toward a New Civil War Revisionism," *American Scholar* 38 (Spring 1969): 251–59.

6. See David Herbert Donald, "The Radicals and Lincoln," in his *Lincoln Reconsidered: Essays on the Civil War Era* (New York: Knopf, 1956), 103–27; Stanley Coben, "Northeastern Business and Radical Reconstruction: A Re-examination," *Mississippi Valley Historical Review* 46 (June 1959): 67–90; Robert P. Sharkey, *Money, Class, and Party: An Economic Study of Civil War and Reconstruction* (Baltimore: Johns Hopkins Press, 1959); Glenn M. Linden, "Congressmen, 'Radicalism' and Economic Issues, 1861–1873" ( Ph.D. diss., University of Washington, 1963); Irwin Unger, *The Greenback Era: A Social and Political History of American Finance, 1865–1879* (Princeton, 1964); Peter Kolchin, "The Business Press and Reconstruction, 1865–1868," *Journal of Southern History,* 33 (May 1967):183–96; and David Montgomery, *Beyond Equality: Labor and the Radical Republicans, 1862–1872* (New York: Knopf, 1967).

7. Declaring Jeffersonian egalitarianism "fundamentally wrong," Confederate vice president Alexander H. Stephens at the outset of the war proclaimed as the "cornerstone" of the Confederacy "the great truth that the negro is not equal to the white man; that slavery . . . is his natural and moral condition." Michael Perman, ed., *Major Problems in the Civil War and Reconstruction* (Lexington, Mass.: D. C. Heath and Company, 1991), 280. Although political considerations at first led him to insist that the war had nothing to do with slavery, President Lincoln expressed much the same judgment as Stephens concerning slavery's centrality to the war (albeit from a very different perspective) in his second inaugural address; asserting that "all knew" that slavery was "somehow, the cause of the war," he now pronounced the war God's way of ending slavery — and punishing Americans *for* slavery. Andrew Delbanco, ed., *The Portable Abraham Lincoln*

(New York: Penguin Books, 1992), 320–21. For evidence that both slaveowners and Confederate leaders saw the war as one for slavery, see James L. Roark, *Masters Without Slaves: Southern Planters in the Civil War and Reconstruction* (New York: Norton, 1977), 1–32, 68–108; and Drew Gilpin Faust, *The Creation of Confederate Nationalism: Ideology and Identity in the Civil War South* (Baton Rouge: Louisiana State University Press, 1988), 59–60. And for evidence that both Union and Confederate soldiers took ideology seriously, see James M. McPherson, *What They Fought For, 1861–1865* (Baton Rouge: Louisiana State University Press, 1994).

8. Bell Irvin Wiley, *Southern Negroes, 1861–1865* (New Haven: Yale University Press, 1938), 69, 77, 259, 43, 84. The description of this book as the "first full-scale study . . ." is from C. Vann Woodward's foreword to the volume's 1965 printing (New Haven: Yale University Press, 1965).

9. Benjamin Quarles, *The Negro in the Civil War* (Boston: Little, Brown and Company, 1953), xi. Quarles was cautious in his assertion of black agency, and in some ways he continued to adhere to traditional assumptions that would soon be challenged; he argued that house servants were especially loyal to their owners, for example, and suggested that "on the whole the field hands on the plantations in the interior behaved much the same as though the masters were not away" (262, 263).

10. Dudley Taylor Cornish, *The Sable Arm: Negro Troops in the Union Army, 1861–1865* (1956; New York: W. W. Norton & Company, 1966), 291.

11. James M. McPherson, *The Negro's Civil War: How American Negroes Felt and Acted during the War for the Union* (New York: Pantheon Books, 1965), xi.

12. James Brewer, *The Confederate Negro: Virginia's Craftsmen and Military Laborers, 1861–1865* (Durham: Duke University Press, 1969), xvi; Ervin L. Jordan, Jr., *Black Confederates and Afro-Yankees in Civil War Virginia* (Charlottesville: University Press of Virginia, 1995), 216, 309. For an unusual group of free blacks in Louisiana who volunteered for Confederate service but quickly switched sides when New Orleans fell to Federal forces, see Mary F. Berry, "Negro Troops in Blue and Gray: The Louisiana Native Guards, 1861–1863," *Louisiana History* 8 (Spring 1967): 165–90; and James G. Hollandsworth, Jr., *The Louisiana Native Guards: The Black Military Experience during the Civil War* (Baton Rouge: Louisiana State University Press, 1995), which focuses on the Native Guards' longer, pro-Unionist phase. For the pro-Confederate activities of a wealthy, free family of color in Charleston, see Michael P. Johnson and James L. Roark, *Black Masters: A Free Family of Color in the Old South* (New York: W. W. Norton & Company, 1984), 288–312.

13. Statistics on black military service are from Ira Berlin, Barbara J. Fields, Steven F. Miller, Joseph P. Reidy, and Leslie S. Rowland, *Slaves No More: Three Essays on Emancipation and the Civil War* (Cambridge: Cambridge University Press, 1992), 203; the quotation is from Joseph T. Glatthaar, *Forged in Battle: The Civil War Alliance of Black Soldiers and White Officers* (New York: The Free Press, 1990), 137. See also John W. Blassingame, "The Recruitment of Colored

Troops in Kentucky, Maryland and Missouri, 1863–1865," *Historian* 29 (August 1967): 533–45; and Joseph T. Glatthaar, "Black Glory: The African-American Role in Union Victory," in *Why the Confederacy Lost,* ed. Gabor S. Boritt (New York: Oxford University Press, 1992), 133–62, 176–78. For the notion that self-assertion, both in and out of the military, gave blacks a "sense of manhood," see John W. Blassingame, *Black New Orleans, 1860–1880* (Chicago: University of Chicago Press, 1973), 46; and Joel Williamson, *After Slavery: The Negro in South Carolina during Reconstruction, 1861–1877* (Chapel Hill: University of North Carolina Press, 1965), 25–31. Discussion of the "black man" and interest in black "manhood" reached a peak in the 1960s and 1970s, as scholars sought to rebut Stanley Elkins's model of the (implicitly male) slave who was infantilized and emasculated and Daniel Patrick Moynihan's thesis that, in part as a legacy of slavery, current black families were frequently pathological because they lacked strong men; see Stanley M. Elkins, *Slavery: A Problem in American Institutional and Intellectual Life* (Chicago: University of Chicago Press, 1959), and, for the "Moynihan Report," U.S. Department of Labor, Office of Policy Planning and Research, *The Negro Family: The Case for National Action* (Washington, D.C.: GPO, 1965). For recent reiteration of "a widely shared sense" among blacks "that the Civil War did indeed mark a watershed for black manhood," see Jim Cullen, "'I's a Man Now': Gender and African American Men," in *Divided Houses: Gender and the Civil War,* ed. Catherine Clinton and Nina Silber (New York, 1992), 77.

14. The great majority of slaves, of course, never served, and indeed never had a chance to serve. Only a small minority of slaves were males of military age, and most of them lacked access to Federal positions. Still, in areas where enlistment was feasible, a very high proportion served. In Tennessee, for example, 39 percent of black men between 18 and 45 years old served in the Union army; in Louisiana, 31 percent did. See Berlin et al., *Slaves No More,* 203. Although most black soldiers volunteered, some were impressed and served against their will.

15. For some of the many works exploring these topics, see Willie Lee Rose, *Rehearsal for Reconstruction: The Port Royal Experiment* (New York: Vintage Books, 1967); Blassingame, *Black New Orleans;* C. Peter Ripley, *Slaves and Freedmen in Civil War Louisiana* (Baton Rouge: Louisiana State University Press, 1976); Leon F. Litwack, *Been in the Storm So Long: The Aftermath of Slavery* (New York: Alfred A. Knopf, 1979); Victor B. Howard, *Black Liberation in Kentucky: Emancipation and Freedom, 1862–1864* (Lexington: The University Press of Kentucky, 1983); Clarence L. Mohr, *On the Threshold of Freedom: Masters and Slaves in Civil War Georgia* (Athens: The University of Georgia Press, 1986); Berlin et al., *Slaves No More;* and Julie Saville, *The Work of Reconstruction: From Slave to Wage Laborer in South Carolina, 1860–1870* (New York: Cambridge University Press, 1994).

16. Roark, *Masters without Slaves,* 35–108; quotation from p. 35. See also Emory M. Thomas, *The Confederacy as a Revolutionary Experience* (Englewood Cliffs, N.J.: Prentice Hall, Inc., 1971), 119–32; Litwack, *Been in the Storm So Long,* 3–166; Berlin et al., *Slaves No More,* 1–76; Ripley, *Slaves and Freedmen in*

*Civil War Louisiana,* 5–24; Mohr, *On the Threshold of Freedom,* esp. 210–35; Howard, *Black Liberation in Kentucky,* 12–90, 108–21; Armstead L. Robinson, "'Worser dan Jeff Davis': The Coming of Free Labor during the Civil War, 1861–1865," in *Essays on the Postbellum Southern Economy,* ed. Thavolia Glymph and John J. Kushma (College Station, Tex.: Texas A&M University Press, 1985), 11–47; Barbara Jeanne Fields, *Slavery and Freedom on the Middle Ground: Maryland during the Nineteenth Century* (New Haven: Yale University Press, 1985), 100–130; Wayne K. Durrill, *War of Another Kind: A Southern Community in the Great Rebellion* (New York: Oxford University Press, 1990), esp. 6, 68–90; Joseph P. Reidy, *From Slavery to Agrarian Capitalism in the Cotton South: Central Georgia, 1800–1880* (Chapel Hill: University of North Carolina Press, 1992), 108–35; Carl H. Moneyhon, *The Impact of the Civil War and Reconstruction on Arkansas: Persistence in the Midst of Ruin* (Baton Rouge: Louisiana State University Press, 1994), esp. 114–16, 122–23, 135–41; and Steven V. Ash, *When the Yankees Came: Conflict and Chaos in the Occupied South, 1861–1865* (Chapel Hill: University of North Carolina Press, 1995), esp. 149–56.

17. Almost every facet of the unraveling of slavery has been subject to divergent interpretation. To take one small example: whereas Edmund L. Drago stressed the sheer joy with which Georgia blacks met General William T. Sherman's army in 1864 —"Most blacks welcomed Sherman and his army with hardly any reservations"— Paul D. Escott argued that "Southern bondsmen greeted the northern troops with a mixture of fear, suspicion, hope and watchful waiting. In many cases this initial posture of cautious observation turned to dislike by the time the men in blue uniforms left." See Edmund L. Drago, "How Sherman's March Through Georgia Affected the Slaves," *Georgia Historical Quarterly* 57 (Fall 1973): 78; and Paul D. Escott, "The Context of Freedom: Georgia's Slaves during the Civil War," *Georgia Historical Quarterly,* 58 (Spring 1974), 102. It is worth noting that Escott based his conclusion on the *subsequent* recollections of blacks interviewed in the Federal Writers' Project, recollections that he took essentially at face value: "A large majority of those slaves in the Georgia narratives who had come into contact with Sherman's men during the war revealed that they had reacted coolly or negatively to the invaders" (102).

18. Drew Gilpin Faust, "'Trying to Do a Man's Business': Slavery, Violence and Gender in the American Civil War," *Gender and History* 4 (Summer 1992): 197–214, and *Mothers of Invention: Women of the Slaveholding South in the American Civil War* (Chapel Hill: University of North Carolina Press, 1996), esp. 53–79; quotation from p. 70. In "Altars of Sacrifice: Confederate Women and the Narratives of War," *Journal of American History* 76 (March 1990): 200–228, Faust discussed white women's increasing disillusionment with the war (although not with slavery), a disillusionment that she suggested contributed significantly to Confederate defeat; see also George C. Rable, *Civil Wars: Women and the Crisis of Southern Nationalism* (Urbana: University of Illinois Press, 1989), 113–21. For two interesting accounts of white women's new experiences handling slaves while their husbands were away in military service, see John C. Inscoe, "The Civil War's Empowerment of an Appalachian Woman: The 1864 Slave Purchases of Mary

Bell," in *Discovering the Women in Slavery: Emancipating Perspectives on the American Past*, ed. Patricia Morton (Athens: University of Georgia Press, 1996), 61–81; and Joan Cashin, "'Since the War Broke Out': The Marriage of Kate and William McLure," in *Divided Houses*, 200–212.

19. Jacqueline Jones, *Labor of Love, Labor of Sorrow: Black Women, Work, and the Family from Slavery to the Present* (New York: Basic Books, Inc., 1985), esp. 46–51; Peter Bardaglio, "The Children of Jubilee: African American Childhood in Wartime," in *Divided Houses*, ed. Clinton and Silber, 213–29; and Wilma King, *Stolen Childhood: Slave Youth in Nineteenth-Century America* (Bloomington: Indiana University Press, 1995), 129–39. Although historians have paid relatively little attention to slave children, many of the Federal Writers' Project interviews with slaves reflect a child's perspective on slavery, for the simple reason that almost two-thirds of those interviewed had been under ten years old when the war began; see Paul D. Escott, *Slavery Remembered: A Record of Twentieth-Century Slave Narratives* (Chapel Hill: University of North Carolina Press, 1979), 16–17.

20. Thomas, *The Confederacy as a Revolutionary Experience*, 127–28; Mohr, *On the Threshold of Freedom*, 236–71; Mohr, "Slaves and White Churches in Confederate Georgia," in *Masters and Slaves in the House of the Lord: Race and Religion in the American South, 1740–1870*, ed. John B. Boles (Lexington: University Press of Kentucky, 1988), 153–72. For an early expression of the view that had the Confederacy won, "it is not altogether unlikely that ultimately [slavery] would have been 'reformed to death' by its friends," see Wiley, *Southern Negroes*, 166–72; quotation from p. 172.

21. Faust, *The Creation of Confederate Nationalism*, 74–81; quotation from p. 80. For a similar view, see Eugene D. Genovese, *Roll, Jordan, Roll: The World the Slaves Made* (New York: Pantheon Books, 1974), 69–70. But for the suggestion that even *antebellum* reform efforts "might have subverted the system" had the war not occurred, see Thomas D. Morris, *Southern Slavery and the Law, 1619–1860* (Chapel Hill: University of North Carolina Press, 1996), 439.

22. Robert F. Durden, *The Gray and the Black: The Confederate Debate on Emancipation* (Baton Rouge: Louisiana State University Press, 1972); Thomas, *The Confederacy as a Revolutionary Experience*, 130–32; quotation from p. 131; Mohr, *On the Threshold of Freedom*, 272–95; George C. Rable, *The Confederate Republic: A Revolution Against Politics* (Chapel Hill: University of North Carolina Press, 1994), 284–96; Richard E. Beringer, Herman Hattaway, Archer Jones, and William N. Still, Jr., *Why the South Lost the Civil War* (Athens: University of Georgia Press, 1986), 368–98.

23. The multiplicity of black and white reactions to the end of slavery is sensitively portrayed in Litwack, *Been in the Storm So Long*, 104–66. See also Williamson, *After Slavery*, esp. 32–39; Genovese, *Roll, Jordan, Roll*, 97–112 ("moment of truth," 97); Berlin et al., *Slaves No More*, 1–76, passim; and Roark, *Masters without Slaves*, esp. 83–85. On lowcountry violence, see Saville, *The Work of Reconstruction*; quotation from p. 34; and William Dusinberre, *Them Dark Days: Slavery in the American Rice Swamps* (New York: Oxford University Press, 1996), 376–84; "For a few weeks," Dusinberre noted of the Allstons' Chicora

Woods plantation, "the scene bore a certain resemblance to an outburst of the peasantry during the Russian Revolution" (377). For similar violence on the sea islands, including both very purposeful destruction of cotton gins and "looting of houses" for "plunder" and "satisfaction," see Rose, *Rehearsal for Reconstruction*, 16, 106. On "Juneteenth," see Randolph B. Campbell, *An Empire for Slavery: The Peculiar Institution in Texas, 1821–1865* (Baton Rouge: Louisiana State University Press, 1989), 249–51.

24. To date, four volumes of this documentary collection have appeared: Ira Berlin et al., eds., *Freedom: A Documentary History of Emancipation, 1861– 1867* (Cambridge: Cambridge University Press): Series 1, Volume 1, *The Destruction of Slavery* (1985); Series 1, Volume 2, *The Wartime Genesis of Free Labor: The Upper South* (1993); Series 1, Volume 3, *The Wartime Genesis of Free Labor: The Lower South* (1990); and Series 2, *The Black Military Experience* (1982). For selections from these volumes, see Ira Berlin, Barbara J. Fields, Steven F. Miller, Joseph P. Reidy, and Leslie S. Rowland, *Free at Last: A Documentary History of Slavery, Freedom, and the Civil War* (New York: New Press, 1992).

25. Berlin et al., *Slaves No More*, 5–6; Barbara J. Fields, "Who Freed the Slaves?" in Geoffrey C. Ward, *The Civil War: An Illustrated History* (New York: Knopf, 1990), 178–81; quotations from pp. 180, 181. For a similar interpretation, see Michael Fellman, "Emancipation in Missouri," *Missouri Historical Review* 83 (October 1988): 36–56. Noting that "military action and self-emancipation undermined the institution of slavery" (40), Fellman wrote that "in Missouri, blacks gained more freedom by seizing opportunities during the war than Republican politicians later granted them" (36).

26. James M. McPherson, "Who Freed the Slaves?" *Reconstruction* 2, no. 3 (1994): 35–40, and reprinted in his *Drawn With the Sword: Reflections on the American Civil War* (New York: Oxford University Press, 1996), 192–207; quotations from pp. 198, 206, 196, 207. For McPherson's defense of Lincoln as a "conservative revolutionary," see *Abraham Lincoln and the Second American Revolution* (New York: Oxford University Press, 1991), esp. 23–42; quotation from p. 41.

27. Ira Berlin, "Emancipation and Its Meaning in American Life," *Reconstruction* 2, no. 3 (1994): 41–44; quotations from pp. 42, 42, 43, 44, 43.

28. Vincent Harding, *There Is a River: The Black Struggle for Freedom in America* (New York: Harcourt Brace Jovanovich, 1981), 225; Litwack, *Been in the Storm So Long*, 162. For a similar evaluation, see Genovese, *Roll, Jordan, Roll*, 149–58. For a recent study of an insurrection scare, see Winthrop D. Jordan, *Tumult and Silence at Second Creek: An Inquiry into a Civil War Slave Conspiracy* (Baton Rouge: Louisiana State University Press, 1993). On the Saint Domingue revolution, see C. L. R. James, *The Black Jacobins: Toussaint L'Ouverture and the San Domingo Revolution* (1938; New York: Vintage Books, 1963); and Carolyn E. Fick, *The Making of Haiti: The Saint Domingue Revolution from Below* (Knoxville: University of Tennessee Press, 1990).

29. Delbanco, ed., *The Portable Abraham Lincoln*, 240. For powerful defenses of Lincoln's antislavery credentials, see LaWanda Cox, *Lincoln and Black*

*Freedom: A Study in Presidential Leadership* (Columbia: University of South Carolina Press, 1981), esp. 3–43; and McPherson, *Abraham Lincoln and the Second American Revolution,* 23–64. The best and most recent biography of Lincoln is David Herbert Donald, *Lincoln* (New York: Simon & Schuster, 1995).

30. Many of the works cited above portray the wartime erosion of slavery as a consequence of the interaction of decisions taken by both slaves and the Federal government. See, e.g., Roark, *Masters without Slaves,* 68–120; Durrill, *War of Another Kind,* 68–90; and Ash, *When the Yankees Came,* 149–56. So, too, do the documents in the *Freedom* volumes, which—in contrast to some of the editors' comments—focus heavily on the actions of Federal officials. The classic study of the Emancipation Proclamation remains John Hope Franklin, *The Emancipation Proclamation* (Garden City, N.Y.: Doubleday, 1963). On the Proclamation as symbolic turning point, see Eric Foner, *Reconstruction: America's Unfinished Revolution, 1863–1877* (New York: Harper & Row, 1988), 1–3, 7.

31. See Rose, *Rehearsal for Reconstruction;* Louis S. Gerteis, *From Contraband to Freedman: Federal Policy towards Southern Blacks, 1861–1865* (Westport, Conn.: Greenwood Press, 1973); William F. Messner, *Freedmen and the Ideology of Free Labor: Louisiana, 1862–1865* (Lafayette, La.: Center for Louisiana Studies, University of Southwestern Louisiana, 1978); James T. Currie, *Enclave: Vicksburg and her Plantations, 1863–1870* (Jackson: University Press of Mississippi, 1980); Lawrence N. Powell, *New Masters: Northern Planters during the Civil War and Reconstruction* (New Haven: Yale University Press, 1980); Michael Wayne, *The Reshaping of Plantation Society: The Natchez District, 1860–1880* (Baton Rouge: Louisiana State University Press, 1983); Robinson, "'Worser dan Jeff Davis,'"; Ira Berlin et al., "The Wartime Genesis of Free Labor, 1861–1865," in their *Slaves No More,* 77–186.

32. Rose, *Rehearsal for Reconstruction,* 51, 67, 85, 79, 228.

33. Messner, *Freedmen and the Ideology of Free Labor,* 88, xii, 187. See also William F. Messner, "Black Violence and White Response: Louisiana, 1862," *Journal of Southern History* 41 (February 1975): 19–38; Thomas J. May, "Continuity and Change in the Labor Program of the Union Army and Freedmen's Bureau," *Civil War History* 17 (September 1971): 245–54; Gerteis, *From Contraband to Freedman;* Ripley, *Slaves and Freedmen in Civil War Louisiana,* 40–68; Moneyhon, *The Impact of the Civil War and Reconstruction on Arkansas,* 142–55, 207–21; William S. McFeely, *Yankee Stepfather: General O. O. Howard and the Freedmen* (New Haven: Yale University Press, 1968). For a less judgmental, if still critical, study of Federal policy in Louisiana, see Peyton McCrary, *Abraham Lincoln and Reconstruction: The Louisiana Experiment* (Princeton: Princeton University Press, 1978); terming the labor system established by General Nathaniel P. Banks "a halfway house between slavery and freedom" (138), McCrary argued that Banks's caution (as well as Lincoln's) was politically motivated and concluded that "in all his voluminous correspondence there is no evidence of overt racism in the general's personal attitude toward black people" (158).

34. See, e.g., Joe M. Richardson, *Christian Reconstruction: The American Missionary Association and Southern Blacks, 1861–1890* (Athens: University of

Georgia Press, 1986). "It is at last their unbounded faith in education that alone removes the stigma of cynicism from the projects of the planter-missionaries," wrote Willie Lee Rose in *Rehearsal for Reconstruction,* 229; similarly, Lawrence N. Powell suggested that "possibly the interest of the newcomers in educating the freedmen redeems somewhat the greedier aspects of their enterprises" (*New Masters,* 93).

35. Robert Francis Engs, *Freedom's First Generation: Black Hampton, Virginia, 1861–1890* (Philadelphia: University of Pennsylvania Press, 1979), 65; Jacqueline Jones, *Soldiers of Light and Love: Northern Teachers and Georgia Blacks, 1865–1873* (Chapel Hill: University of North Carolina Press, 1980), 138–39, 4.

36. Williamson, *After Slavery,* 67; Herman Belz, *Emancipation and Equal Rights: Politics and Constitutionalism in the Civil War Era* (New York: Norton, 1978), passim; quotation from p. 149; Barry A. Crouch, *The Freedmen's Bureau and Black Texans* (Austin: University of Texas Press, 1992), 128, ix; James M. McPherson, *The Struggle for Equality: Abolitionists and the Negro in the Civil War and Reconstruction* (Princeton: Princeton University Press, 1964); McPherson, *The Abolitionist Legacy: From Reconstruction to the NAACP* (Princeton: Princeton University Press, 1975). For a successful free-labor experiment on Joseph Davis's plantations at Davis Bend, Mississippi, see Janet Sharp Hermann, *The Pursuit of a Dream* (New York: Oxford University Press, 1981); for an early defense of the Freedmen's Bureau, see John H. Cox and LaWanda Cox, "General O. O. Howard and the 'Misrepresented Bureau,'" *Journal of Southern History* 19 (November 1953): 427–56.

37. See Foner, *Reconstruction,* 35–76; Saville, *The Work of Reconstruction;* Roark, *Masters without Slaves,* esp. 115; Lynda J. Morgan, *Emancipation in Virginia's Tobacco Belt, 1850–1870* (Athens: University of Georgia Press, 1992); Mohr, *On the Threshold of Freedom.* Much of the new work on Reconstruction accepts this concept of a triangular struggle over the status of the freedpeople; for a recent account of how such a struggle led to the widespread adoption of sharecropping, see Edward Royce, *The Origins of Southern Sharecropping* (Philadelphia: Temple University Press, 1993).

38. Morgan, *Emancipation in Virginia's Tobacco Belt,* 173, 134; Roark, *Masters without Slaves,* 115; Eric Foner, "Reconstruction and the Crisis of Free Labor," in his *Politics and Ideology in the Age of the Civil War* (New York: Oxford University Press, 1980), 101.

39. For an early delineation of these themes, see Peter Kolchin, *First Freedom: The Responses of Alabama's Blacks to Emancipation and Reconstruction* (Westport, Conn.: Greenwood Press, 1972).

40. Edward Magdol, *A Right to the Land: Essays on the Freedmen's Community* (Westport, Conn.: Greenwood Press, 1976); Eric Foner, *Nothing but Freedom: Emancipation and Its Legacy* (Baton Rouge: Louisiana State University Press, 1983), 74–110; Mohr, *On the Threshold of Freedom,* 96; Saville, *The Work of Reconstruction,* passim, esp. 42–70.

41. Note how the subtitle of Eric Foner's book *Reconstruction: America's*

*Unfinished Revolution* manages to imply both substantial change (revolution) and—because it is unfinished—failure. For a discussion of the failure theme in Reconstruction historiography, see Peter Kolchin, "The Tragic Era? Interpreting Reconstruction in Comparative Perspective," in *The Meaning of Freedom: Economics, Politics, and Culture after Slavery*, ed. Frank McGlynn and Seymour Drescher (Pittsburgh: University of Pittsburgh Press, 1992), 291–314.

42. Roger L. Ransom and Richard Sutch, *One Kind of Freedom: The Economic Consequences of Emancipation* (Cambridge: Cambridge University Press, 1977), 13; Jonathan M. Wiener, *Social Origins of the New South: Alabama, 1860–1885* (Baton Rouge: Louisiana State University Press, 1978), 6; Jay R. Mandle, *The Roots of Black Poverty: The Southern Plantation Economy after the Civil War* (Durham: Duke University Press, 1978), 16–17, recently republished with slight revisions as *Not Slave, Not Free: The African American Economic Experience since the Civil War* (Durham: Duke University Press, 1992), 14.

43. C. Vann Woodward, "Equality: The Deferred Commitment," in his *The Burden of Southern History* (1960; New York: Vintage, 1961), 69–87; V. Jacque Voegeli, *Free but not Equal: The Midwest and the Negro during the Civil War* (Chicago: University of Chicago Press, 1967); Forrest G. Wood, *Black Scare: The Racist Response to Emancipation and Reconstruction* (Berkeley: University of California Press, 1968); George M. Fredrickson, *The Black Image in the White Mind: The Debate on Afro-American Character and Destiny, 1817–1914* (New York, Harper & Row, 1971), 97–320; Joel Williamson, *The Crucible of Race: Black-White Relations in the American South since Emancipation* (New York: Oxford University Press, 1984).

44. Roger L. Ransom and Richard Sutch saw the usurious credit system as being at the heart of the "flawed economic institutions" that held the postwar South back; Gavin Wright, by contrast, pointed to the South's "separate regional labor market"; and Jonathan M. Wiener faulted the "Prussian Road" to capitalism, "with its dominant planter class and its labor-repressive system of agricultural production." Ransom and Sutch, *One Kind of Freedom;* 2; Gavin Wright, *Old South, New South: Revolutions in the Southern Economy since the Civil War* (New York: Basic Books, 1986); Wiener, *Social Origins of the New South*, 72–73.

45. Crandall A. Shifflett, *Patronage and Poverty in the Tobacco South: Louisa County, Virginia, 1860–1900* (Knoxville: University of Tennessee Press, 1982), 64, 65, 103. Some scholars have gone further, arguing not just for continuity but for declension after the war. According to Robert William Fogel and Stanley L. Engerman, who emphasized the relatively good material treatment of antebellum slaves, "it appears that the life expectations of blacks declined by 10 percent between the last quarter of the antebellum era and the last two decades of the nineteenth century. The diet of blacks deteriorated." *Time on the Cross: The Economics of American Negro Slavery* (Boston: Little, Brown & Co., 1974), 261. See also Edward Meekar, "Mortality Trends of Southern Blacks, 1850–1910: Some Preliminary Findings," *Explorations in Economic History* 13 (January 1976): 23–37.

46. Rosenberg, "Toward a New Civil War Revisionism," 259–72; quotations from 261, 272; Phillip Shaw Paludan, "The American Civil War: Triumph through Tragedy," *Civil War History* 20 (September 1974): 239–51; quotations from pp. 241, 250; John S. Rosenberg, "The American Civil War and the Problem of 'Presentism': A Reply to Phillip S. Paludan," *Civil War History,* 21 (September 1975): 242–53; Phillip Shaw Paludan, "Taking the Benefits of the Civil War Seriously: A Rejoinder to John S. Rosenberg," ibid., 254–60.

47. Harold D. Woodman, "The Reconstruction of the Cotton Plantation in the New South," in *Essays on the Postbellum Southern Economy,* ed. Glymph and Kushma, 99; Roark, *Masters without Slaves,* 156, 196; Foner, *Reconstruction,* 11. Some of many other works that specifically refer to "revolution" or "transformation" in discussing Civil War–era changes are Thavolia Glymph's introduction to *Essays on the Postbellum Southern Economy,* ed. Glymph and Kushma, 3; Barbara J. Fields, "The Advent of Capitalist Agriculture: The New South in a Bourgeois World," in ibid., 81; Robinson, "'Worser dan Jeff Davis,'" 12; Saville, *The Work of Reconstruction,* 1–2; Berlin et al., *Slaves no More,* ix, xi, 76; McPherson, *Abraham Lincoln and the Second American Revolution,* 3–42, passim; Wright, *Old South, New South,* 18; Reidy, *From Slavery to Agrarian Capitalism,* 138.

48. Foner, *Reconstruction,* xxiv. The theme of revolution or transformation appears even in the works of some scholars who stress continuity. Roger L. Ransom and Richard Sutch, for example, while emphasizing the "flawed economic institutions" that kept the postbellum South from modernizing, noted that "emancipation had destroyed the foundations of the southern economy and southern society. Freedom meant that the immediate postwar years had to be literally years of reconstruction, and freedom meant that the new economy and the new society that were to be constructed on the site of the old could not be patterned on the old design" (*One Kind of Freedom,*1). Similarly, in stressing the persistence of planter hegemony in the New South, Jonathan M. Wiener opened his book with an assertion of a "bourgeois revolution" and went on to explain that "the postwar planters were a new class because they were in new social relations of production" (Wiener, *Social Origins of the New South,* 3, 35).

49. Ransom and Sutch, *One Kind of Freedom,* 1.

50. "Whether measured by the dreams inspired by emancipation or the more limited goals of securing blacks' rights as citizens and as free laborers, and establishing an enduring Republican presence in the South," wrote Foner, "Reconstruction can only be judged a failure" (*Reconstruction,* 603). For examples of similar suggestions, see Thavolia Glymph, "Freedpeople and Ex-Masters: Shaping a New Order in the Postbellum South, 1865–1868," in *Essays on the Postbellum Southern Economy,* ed. Glymph and Kushma, 60–66; and Fields, "The Advent of Capitalist Agriculture," 84–89.

51. Claude F. Oubre, *Forty Acres and a Mule: The Freedmen's Bureau and Black Landownership* (Baton Rouge: Louisiana State University Press, 1978); Loren Schweninger, *Black Property Owners in the South, 1790–1915* (Urbana: University of Illinois Press, 1990), 146–226; statistics from p. 174; William Cohen, "Negro

Involuntary Servitude in the South, 1865–1940: A Preliminary Analysis," *Journal of Southern History* 42 (February 1976): 31–60; William Cohen, *At Freedom's Edge: Black Mobility and the Southern White Quest for Racial Control, 1861–1917* (Baton Rouge: Louisiana State University Press, 1991), xii, xvi. See also Williamson, *After Slavery,* who argued that "the gains won during these early years enabled the Negro community to continue to move forward in vital areas of human endeavor in the post-Reconstruction period" (63).

52. "In the regulation of domestic and sexual relations," Peter W. Bardaglio has recently argued, "the South entered the mainstream of American legal development by the end of the nineteenth century." Nevertheless, he found considerable inertia in "customs and conventions regarding race, blood, and gender." As a result, "continuity and discontinuity . . . existed in tension with each other, creating a distinctive dynamic—profound economic and political alterations with a strong undertow of cultural continuity"; *Reconstructing the Household: Families, Sex, and the Law in the Nineteenth-Century South* (Chapel Hill: University of North Carolina Press, 1995), 227, 176.

53. As Howard N. Rabinowitz astutely pointed out, the segregated schools (and other institutions) of the Civil War–era South seemed regressive to most historians of the 1960s and 1970s, but from the perspective of the 1860s, when the alternative to segregated education had been no education at all, the situation looked very different; one's judgment of segregation depends in part on whether one's point of reference is integration or exclusion. See Rabinowitz, "From Exclusion to Segregation: Southern Race Relations, 1865–1890," *Journal of American History* 63 (September 1976): 325–50. Joel Williamson made a similar point: "measured by the admittedly minimal standards of his existence in slavery, Reconstruction was, for the Negro, a tremendous success"(*After Slavery,* 179); see also Belz, *Emancipation and Equal Rights,* 144–50.

54. For more extensive development of these points, see Kolchin, "The Tragic Era?"

55. The database, the first stage of the Civil War Soldiers and Sailors System (CWSS) that will eventually include *all* soldiers who served in the Civil War, is available at http://www.itd.nps.gov/cwss/usct.html. For the suggestion that "military service . . . provided a steppingstone to leadership in the black community" in the postwar era, see Berlin et al., *Slaves No More,* 230, and Foner, *Reconstruction,* 9–10. Of 1,465 black officeholders during Reconstruction identified by Eric Foner, at least 129 had served in the Union military; see Foner, *Freedom's Lawmakers: A Directory of Black Officeholders during Reconstruction* (New York: Oxford University Press, 1993), xxv. Of 201 Reconstruction black politicians in New Orleans identified by David C. Rankin, 59 had seen military service during the war; see Rankin, "The Origins of Black Leadership in New Orleans during Reconstruction," *Journal of Southern History* 40 (August 1974): 434.

56. See, for example, Foner, *Nothing But Freedom,* 39–73; Thomas J. Pressly, "Reconstruction in the Southern United States: A Comparative Perspective," *OAH Magazine of History* 4 (Winter 1989): 14–34; Kolchin, "The Tragic Era?"; Kolchin, "Some Controversial Questions Concerning Nineteenth-Century Emancipation

from Slavery and Serfdom," in *Serfdom and Slavery: Studies in Legal Bondage,* ed. M. L. Bush (London, 1996), esp. 52–58.

57. C. Vann Woodward, "The Price of Freedom," in *What Was Freedom's Price?* ed. David G. Sansing (Jackson: University Press of Mississippi, 1978), 97. On southern slaveowners' unusually strong commitment to slavery, see Eugene D. Genovese, *The World the Slaveholders Made: Two Essays in Interpretation* (New York: Pantheon Books, 1969); and Peter Kolchin, *Unfree Labor: American Slavery and Russian Serfdom* (Cambridge, Mass.: Harbard University Press, 1987), pt. 1.

58. For an interesting effort to place the American Civil War in comparative perspective, see Carl N. Degler's Fortenbaugh Memorial Lecture, *One Among Many: The Civil War in Comparative Perspective* (Gettysburg: Gettysburg College, 1990).

59. Litwack, *Been in the Storm So Long,* passim; Berlin et al., *Slaves No More,* passim; quotation from p. 74.

60. Campbell, *An Empire for Liberty,* 247, 248. On the preference for cooperative landholding and disinclination to production for market among lowcountry freedpeople, see the sources cited in note 40, above. On distinctive patterns of work and life among lowcountry blacks, see especially Philip D. Morgan, "Work and Culture: The Task System and the World of Lowcountry Blacks, 1770 to 1880," *William and Mary Quarterly* 39 (October 1982): 563–99; for a very different portrait of lowcountry slavery, which stresses the savagery of slave treatment and the degradation of slave life, see Dusinberre, *Them Dark Days.*

61. James M. McPherson, "The War that Never Goes Away," in his *Drawn with the Sword,* 59.

# CONTRIBUTORS

*Michael Les Benedict*—professor of history, Ohio State University. He has written *The Impeachment and Trial of Andrew Johnson* and *A Compromise of Principle: Congressional Republicans and Reconstruction, 1863–1869.*

*William J. Cooper, Jr.*—Boyd Professor of history, Louisiana State University. His books include *The South and the Politics of Slavery, 1826–1856; Liberty and Slavery: Southern Politics to 1860;* and *The American South: A History* (co-author).

*Drew Gilpin Faust*—Annenberg Professor of History, University of Pennsylvania. Among her books are *James Henry Hammond and the Old South: A Design for Mastery; The Creation of Confederate Nationalism: Ideology and Identity in the Civil War South;* and *Mothers of Invention: Women of the Slaveholding South in the American Civil War.*

*Gary W. Gallagher*—professor of history, University of Virginia. His books are *Stephen Dodson Ramseur: Lee's Gallant General; The Confederate War;* and *Lee and His Generals in War and Memory.*

*Joseph T. Glatthaar*—professor of history, University of Houston. His books are *The March to the Sea and Beyond: Sherman's Troops in the Savannah and Carolinas Campaign; Forged in Battle: The Civil War Alliance of Black Soldiers and White Officers;* and *Partners in Command: Relationships between Civil War Leaders.*

*Michael F. Holt*—Langbourne M. Williams Professor of American History, University of Virginia. He has written *Forging a Majority: The Formation of the Republican Party in Pittsburgh, 1848–1860; The Political Crisis of the 1850s;* and *Political Parties and American Political Development from the Age of Jackson to the Age of Lincoln.*

*Peter Kolchin*—Henry Clay Reed Professor of History, University of Delaware. His books are *First Freedom: The Responses of Alabama's Blacks to Emancipation and Reconstruction; Unfree Labor: American Slavery and Russian Serfdom;* and *American Slavery, 1619–1877.*

*James M. McPherson*—George Henry Davis Professor of American History, Princeton University. His books include *Battle Cry of Freedom: The Civil War Era; Abraham Lincoln and the Second American Revolution;* and *For Cause and Comrades: Why Men Fought in the Civil War.*

*Reid Mitchell*—professor of history, University of Maryland, Baltimore County. He has written *Civil War Soldiers: Their Expectations and Experiences; The Vacant Chair: The Northern Soldier Leaves Home;* and *A Man under Authority.*

*Mark E. Neely, Jr.*—McCabe Greer Professor in the American Civil War Era, Pennsylvania State University. His books include *The Abraham Lincoln Encyclopedia; The Fate of Liberty: Abraham Lincoln and Civil Liberties;* and *The Last Best Hope of Earth: Abraham Lincoln and The Promise of America.*

*Phillip Shaw Paludan*—professor of history, University of Kansas. Among his books are *Victims: A True Story of the Civil War; A People's Contest: The Union and the Civil War, 1861–1865;* and *The Presidency of Abraham Lincoln.*

*George C. Rable*—Charles G. Summersell Professor of Southern History, University of Alabama. He has written *But There Was No Peace: The Role of Violence in the Politics of Reconstruction; Civil Wars: Women and the Crisis of Southern Nationalism;* and *Confederate Republic: A Revolution against Politics.*

*James L. Roark*—Samuel Candler Dobbs Professor of American History, Emory University. His books are *Masters without Slaves: Southern Planters in the Civil War and Reconstruction* and *Black Masters: A Free Family of Color in the Old South* (co-author).

*Emory M. Thomas*—Regents Professor of History, University of Georgia. His books include *Confederate Nation, 1861–1865; Bold Dragoon: The Life of J. E. B. Stuart;* and *Robert E. Lee: A Biography.*

# INDEX